The New NDP

Communication, Strategy, and Politics
THIERRY GIASSON AND ALEX MARLAND, SERIES EDITORS

Communication, Strategy, and Politics is a groundbreaking new series from UBC Press that examines elite decision making and political communication in today's hyper-mediated and highly competitive environment. Publications in this series look at the intricate relations among marketing strategy, the media, and political actors and explain how they affect Canadian democracy. They also investigate such interconnected themes as strategic communication, mediatization, opinion research, electioneering, political management, public policy, and e-politics in a Canadian context and in comparison to other countries. Designed as a coherent and consolidated space for diffusion of research about Canadian political communication, the series promotes an interdisciplinary, multi-method, and theoretically pluralistic approach.

Other volumes in the series are

Political Marketing in Canada, edited by Alex Marland, Thierry Giasson, and Jennifer Lees-Marshment
Political Communication in Canada: Meet the Press and Tweet the Rest, edited by Alex Marland, Thierry Giasson, and Tamara A. Small
Framed: Media and the Coverage of Race in Canadian Politics, by Erin Tolley
Brand Command: Canadian Politics and Democracy in the Age of Message Control, by Alex Marland
Permanent Campaigning in Canada, edited by Alex Marland, Thierry Giasson, and Anna Lennox Esselment
Breaking News? Politics, Journalism, and Infotainment on Quebec Television, by Frédérick Bastien
Political Elites in Canada: Power and Influence in Instantaneous Times, edited by Alex Marland, Thierry Giasson, and Andrea Lawlor
Opening the Government of Canada: The Federal Bureaucracy in the Digital Age, by Amanda Clarke

See also:

Canadian Election Analysis 2015: Communication, Strategy, and Democracy, edited by Alex Marland and Thierry Giasson. Open access compilation available at http://www.ubcpress.ca/canadianelectionanalysis2015.

The New NDP

Moderation, Modernization, and Political Marketing

...... David McGrane

UBCPress · Vancouver · Toronto

© UBC Press 2019

All rights reserved. No part of this publication may be reproduced, stored in a retrieval system, or transmitted, in any form or by any means, without prior written permission of the publisher, or, in Canada, in the case of photocopying or other reprographic copying, a licence from Access Copyright, www.accesscopyright.ca.

28 27 26 25 24 23 22 21 20 19   5 4 3 2 1

Printed in Canada on FSC-certified ancient-forest-free paper (100% post-consumer recycled) that is processed chlorine- and acid-free.

Library and Archives Canada Cataloguing in Publication

McGrane, David, author
  The new NDP : moderation, modernization, and political marketing / by David McGrane.

Includes bibliographical references and index.
Issued in print and electronic formats.
ISBN 978-0-7748-6045-1 (hardcover). – ISBN 978-0-7748-6046-8 (softcover). – ISBN 978-0-7748-6047-5 (PDF). – ISBN 978-0-7748-6048-2 (EPUB). – ISBN 978-0-7748-6049-9 (Kindle)

  1. New Democratic Party. 2. Marketing – Political aspects – Canada. 3. Political campaigns – Canada. 4. Political parties – Canada. I. Title.

JL197.N4M34 2019   324.27107   C2018-906458-7
                                                      SC2018-906459-5

Canadä

UBC Press gratefully acknowledges the financial support for our publishing program of the Government of Canada (through the Canada Book Fund), the Canada Council for the Arts, and the British Columbia Arts Council.

This book has been published with the help of a grant from the Canadian Federation for the Humanities and Social Sciences, through the Awards to Scholarly Publications Program, using funds provided by the Social Sciences and Humanities Research Council of Canada.

Printed and bound in Canada by Friesens
Set in Scala and Minion by Artegraphica Design Co. Ltd.
Copy editor: Dallas Harrison
Proofreader: Alison Strobel
Cover designer: Will Brown

UBC Press
The University of British Columbia
2029 West Mall
Vancouver, BC V6T 1Z2
www.ubcpress.ca

This book is dedicated to my son, Gabriel,
the best little sports buddy that a guy could ever wish for!

Contents

List of Figures and Tables	ix
Acknowledgments	xiii
List of Abbreviations	xv
Introduction	3
1 Ferment in the Party: The Federal NDP, 2000–03	24
2 The Rise of Party Headquarters: Internal Party Organization	40
3 Imposing Discipline and Order: The NDP inside the House of Commons	89
4 Dare to Dream: Campaign Strategies, 2000–15	123
5 Continuity and Change: The Ideology and Policies of the NDP	177
6 Stealing Market Share: Electoral Market Segmentation and the NDP, 2000–11	212
7 Heartbreak: NDP Voter Behaviour and the 2015 Federal Election	275
8 Which Way Now?	319
Appendix A: List of Semi-Structured Interviews	338
Appendix B: Canadian Election Studies, 2000–11; and Ipsos-Reid Exit Polls, 2006–11	343
Appendix C: 2015 Canadian Federal Election Panel Survey on Social Democracy	355
Notes	365
References	371
Index	384

Figures and Tables

FIGURES

2.1	Revenue of the federal NDP, 2001–12	57
2.2	Federal NDP members' views on member and external political market orientations, 2015	81
2.3	Federal NDP members' views on voter and competitor political market orientations, 2015	82
5.1	Percentage of NDP platform made up of commitments similar to those in LPC platform, 2000–15	190
6.1a	Parties NDP voters supported in the 2000–11 federal elections, ROC	215
6.1b	Parties LPC voters supported in the 2000–11 federal elections, ROC	216
6.1c	Parties CPC voters supported in the 2000–11 federal elections, ROC	216
6.2a	Parties NDP voters supported in the 2006–11 federal elections, QC	239
6.2b	Parties BQ voters supported in the 2006–11 federal elections, QC	240
6.2c	Parties LPC voters supported in the 2006–11 federal elections, QC	240
6.2d	Parties CPC voters supported in the 2006–11 federal elections, QC	241
6.3a	Vote choice of hard sovereignists, 2006–11 federal elections, QC	248

6.3b	Vote choice of soft nationalists, 2006–11 federal elections, QC	248
6.3c	Vote choice of hard federalists, 2006–11 federal elections, QC	249
6.4a	Leadership traits, 2008 federal election, QC	260
6.4b	Leadership traits, 2011 federal election, QC	260
7.1	Certainty to vote for major parties in the ROC, August 10–20, 2015	278
7.2	Certainty to vote for major parties in francophone Quebec, August 10–20, 2015	279
7.3	Conversion rates of the NDP in English Canada, 2015 federal election	281
7.4	Conversion rates of the NDP in francophone Quebec, 2015 federal election	282
7.5	Significant average marginal effects on the probability of being a solid NDPer in the ROC, 2015 federal election	289
7.6	Significant average marginal effects on the probability of being a solid NDPer in francophone Quebec, 2015 federal election	292
7.7	Significant average marginal effects on the probability of being a converted NDPer in the ROC, 2015 federal election	295
7.8	Significant average marginal effects on the probability of being a converted NDPer in francophone Quebec, 2015 federal election	297
7.9	Significant average marginal effects on the probability of being an anti-NDPer in the ROC, 2015 federal election	300
7.10	Significant average marginal effects on the probability of being an anti-NDPer in francophone Quebec, 2015 federal election	302
7.11	Significant average marginal effects on the probability of being a lost NDPer in the ROC, 2015 federal election	304
7.12	Significant average marginal effects on the probability of being a lost NDPer in francophone Quebec, 2015 federal election	308

TABLES

1.1	Robert Ormrod's concept of political market orientation	7
1.2	Premodern, modern, and postmodern campaigning	10
2.1	OLS regression of political market orientation of federal NDP members, 2015	84
3.1	Topics of NDP questions in Question Period, Thirty-Seventh to Forty-First Parliaments	106
3.2	Parliamentary activity of NDP MPs, 2014	116
4.1	Coverage of themes in 2000 NDP news releases and English television/radio commercials	130
4.2	Coverage of themes in 2004 NDP news releases and English television commercials	135
4.3	Coverage of themes in 2006 NDP news releases and English and French television commercials	141
4.4	Coverage of themes in 2008 NDP news releases and English and French television commercials	149
4.5	Coverage of themes in 2011 NDP news releases and English and French television commercials	156
4.6	Coverage of themes in 2015 NDP news releases and English and French television commercials	167
5.1	NDP members' values of collectivism/individualism (conflicting statements) in 1997 and 2015	179
5.2	NDP members' values measured with reference to public policies in 1997 and 2015	180
5.3	Policy commitments by category, 2000–15 NDP platforms	183
5.4	Commitments in NDP platforms similar to those in LPC platforms by category, 2000–15	189
5.5	Statements measuring NDP's internal left–right spectrum	198
5.6	Means of statements of NDP's internal left–right political spectrum with standard deviation in parentheses	200
5.7	Open coding of NDP MPs' textual responses to internal left–right spectrum questions, 2015	204
6.1	NDP voting in the ROC, 2000–11	214
6.2	Sociodemographic variables, 2000–11 federal elections, ROC	221

6.3	Underlying values variables, 2000–11 federal elections, ROC	225
6.4	Party identification variables, 2000–11 federal elections, ROC	228
6.5	Economic perspective variables, 2000–11 federal elections, ROC	228
6.6	Issue position variables, 2000–11 federal elections, ROC	232
6.7	Leadership evaluation variables, 2000–11 federal elections, ROC	232
6.8	NDP voting in Quebec, 2000–11 federal elections	237
6.9	Sociodemographic variables, 2006–11 federal elections, QC	244
6.10	General orientation variables, 2006–11 federal elections, QC	246
6.11	Economic perception variables, 2006–11 federal elections, QC	252
6.12	Most important issue variables, 2006–11 federal elections, QC	252
6.13	Leader evaluation variables, 2006–11 federal elections, QC	256
6.14	Strategic consideration variables, 2006–11 federal elections, QC	263
6.15	Examples of stealing market share related to the NDP in the ROC, 2000–11	268
6.16	Examples of stealing market share related to the NDP in Quebec, 2006–11	270

Acknowledgments

Any book is the result of the efforts of many people besides the author, and this book is no different. I would like to thank all of my very capable research assistants who worked so hard to gather data for this project – Charles Plante, Alexander Steffen, Erica Lee, Kent Peterson, David DesBaillets, Aidan Murphy, and David Blocker. My colleagues Steve White and Jason Roy provided invaluable advice on the statistical procedures in Chapters 6 and 7. My friend and colleague Alex Marland graciously volunteered to keep me on track to submit the manuscript on time. I want to thank the two anonymous reviewers for their insightful comments, which strengthened the book, and the editorial staff at UBC Press for their work on this book, especially Randy Schmidt and Emily Andrew. I was also aided along the way by colleagues who had written on the federal NDP. In particular, I would like to thank Alan Whitehorn for granting me access to his impressive archives of historical material on the CCF-NDP, David Laycock and Lynda Erickson for permitting me to use data from their 1997 survey of NDP members, and Graham Truelove for sending me his research on Svend Robinson's political activities in the early 2000s. The staff at SOM Research and Surveys in Quebec City and the University of Saskatchewan's Social Sciences Research Laboratories provided excellent advice and assistance throughout the administration of the panel survey during the 2015 federal election.

This book owes a great intellectual debt to the fifty-eight NDP MPs and over sixty NDP operatives who took time out of their busy schedules to share their recollections and experiences. I also want to thank the staff at NDP Headquarters, particularly Michael Roy and Anne McGrath, for arranging for the administration of an online survey of NDP members in 2014. I am especially grateful to the 2,400 NDP members who filled out the survey. The willingness and enthusiasm of NDP members, staff, and politicians to participate in my project reflect the openness of the party to academic research and the eagerness of New Democrats to learn about themselves. The NDP is truly the best party in Canada to study.

I would like to thank the Social Sciences and Humanities Research Council for the Insight Development Grant awarded in 2013 that funded the research for this project and the subsidy from the Awards to Scholarly Publications Program that funded the publication of this book. I am also grateful to St. Thomas More College and the University of Saskatchewan for providing me with the resources needed to complete this book, and I appreciate the support of my colleagues in the Department of Political Studies. I cannot imagine a better place to work. Finally, I want to thank my family – Caroline, Anne, and Gabriel – for their patience with me as I was away researching this book or in the basement writing it. I love all three of you dearly.

Abbreviations

BQ	Bloc Québécois
CAW	Canadian Auto Workers
CBC	Canadian Broadcasting Corporation
CCF	Cooperative Commonwealth Federation
CEP	Communications, Energy, and Paperworkers
CES	Canadian Election Study
CLC	Canadian Labour Congress
CPC	Conservative Party of Canada
CPP	Canada Pension Plan
CUPE	Canadian Union of Public Employees
EDA	electoral district association
EPC	Election Planning Committee
FTQ	Fédération des travailleurs et travailleuses du Québec
GST	Goods and Services Tax
HST	Harmonized Sales Tax
LPC	Liberal Party of Canada
MP	Member of Parliament
NAFTA	North American Free Trade Agreement
NGO	nongovernmental organization
NDP	New Democratic Party
NPI	New Politics Initiative
OLO	Office of the Leader of the Official Opposition
OLS	ordinary least-squares regression
OMOV	one-member-one-vote
RCMP	Royal Canadian Mounted Police
TPP	Trans-Pacific Partnership
UFCW	United Food and Commercial Workers
WTO	World Trade Organization

The New NDP..........

Introduction

This book traces the activity of the New Democratic Party of Canada (NDP) from the night of the 2000 federal election to the night of the 2015 federal election. It is about a political roller coaster, about a party that went from near extinction to the cusp of forming the federal government only to be bitterly disappointed on an election night when it was supposed to make history.

On November 27, 2000, the federal NDP experienced one of the worst electoral defeats in its history. It received only 8.5 percent of the popular vote and barely clung to official party status in the House of Commons by winning thirteen seats. This disappointing outcome reversed the minor comeback that the party had experienced in the 1997 federal election after its unexpected electoral disaster in 1993. The glory days of the party seemed to be a distant memory, its morale was exceedingly low, and it was soon plunged into the instability of a leadership race.

Under the new leadership of Jack Layton, the party started to see incremental improvements in its electoral fortunes. In each of the 2004, 2006, and 2008 elections, its percentage of the popular vote and its number of seats crept upward. The NDP subsequently made a dramatic breakthrough in the 2011 federal election, forming the official opposition for the first time in its history and winning a large majority of seats in Quebec. When Layton's untimely death shortly after the election shocked the party and all Canadians, the NDP was forced into a leadership race that chose Thomas (Tom) Mulcair as the new leader. Entering the 2015 federal election, the party was a serious contender to form the next federal government for the first time in its history. Instead of fulfilling its long-held dream of attaining power, on October 19, 2015, the NDP lost half of its seats as its popular vote fell from 31 percent to 20 percent, and it was relegated to its traditional status as the third party in the House of Commons.

This book describes how this roller-coaster ride from being an afterthought in Canadian politics to being at centre stage as a potential governing party and then plummeting back to third-party status transformed the federal NDP. Through an analysis of the NDP's political marketing from 2000 to 2015, I make three interrelated arguments: 1) the NDP went through a process of moderation and modernization; 2) this process was driven by the agency of political operatives gathered around the leader of the party and changes to party financing rules; and 3) the moderation and modernization of the NDP positioned the party well to steal electoral market share from its left-of-centre opponents (the Liberal Party of Canada [LPC] and the Bloc Québécois [BQ]) as the popularity of these parties faltered during the 2000s. In short, a new set of agents came to control the party after Layton became leader, and these new actors played by new party financing rules, the most important being the creation of a per-vote subsidy that provided higher as well as more stable and predictable funding. Armed with innovative ideas and the financial resources to act on them, these agents changed how the NDP organized itself both inside and outside the House of Commons and how the party fought elections. The party revitalized itself and the "New NDP," one that was more modern and more moderate, was born.

However, the book ends with a paradox. The process of moderation and modernization brought the NDP closer to power than it had ever been, but this transformation of the party did not take it all the way. The culmination of this process was the highly professionalized and sophisticated 2015 campaign that NDP operatives had built around experienced leadership, safe change, and a two-way race between the NDP and the Conservative Party. Ultimately, large segments of electoral market share that the NDP had stolen from its competitors in previous elections returned to them. The NDP campaign was simply unable to generate the excitement and momentum needed to prevent its potential supporters from migrating to the Liberal Party or, to a lesser extent, the Bloc Québécois, as unexpected events arose during the campaign. The book ends by summarizing seven lessons emanating from this study for NDPers and political marketing scholars and by asking a difficult question: was the moderation and modernization of the NDP the way to go after all?

Defining Moderation and Modernization: A Political Marketing Approach

To construct a definition of the process of moderation and modernization that created the "New NDP," I turn to the field of political marketing. It is a common misconception that political marketing is simply the study of advertising done by political parties during elections. Political marketing refers to a much broader swath of activities in which parties engage.

For the purposes of this book, I define political marketing as the study of how political parties win elections. It is a "constant process involving [the] gathering of market intelligence through informal and formal means, developing party policies and a party brand, mobilizing party members, building relationships with stakeholders, positioning in relation to competing parties, targeting certain segments of voters, allocating scarce resources, and communicating a party's policy offerings through paid advertising and the management of news media" (McGrane 2011, 77–78). My definition of political marketing sees political parties as institutions made up of people, assets, and rules primarily dedicated to winning elections. As institutions engaged in running candidates in elections, all political parties do political marketing. Contesting an election requires a political party to perform all of the actions contained in the definition above, even if it does some of these actions unconsciously. Branding is a good example. Even if a political party does not engage in formal branding, it still has a brand that it presents to voters.

The struggles within political parties in the early twenty-first century are often disagreements over the type of political marketing that the party should adopt. Which types of voters should be targeted? What is the role of polling in determining the ideas contained in the election platform? Where should resources be allocated? How a party markets itself, in the largest sense of the term, is continually contested. Agents within political parties do not always agree on the type of political marketing to adopt. As the example of Layton and the NDP will illustrate, a tumultuous time within a party when it questions its identity and raison d'être often provides opportunities to transform that party's political marketing. Such opportunities are enlarged when there are significant changes in the rules under which the party operates, such as changes to campaign financing rules. Under such conditions, a veritable revolution in a party's political marketing can take place.

I refer to the "revolution" in the federal NDP's political marketing from 2000 to 2015 as the process of moderation and modernization of the party. I conceptualize this process as encompassing two primary changes in its political marketing: tilting its political market orientation more toward voters and competitors and adopting postmodern campaign techniques, including branding exercises and sophisticated electoral market segmentation. These two changes constituted the process of moderation and modernization of the federal NDP. They were funded by changes to campaign financing rules, specifically the advent of the per-vote subsidy, and their implementation was driven by the agency of Layton and his team of political operatives.

There are several theories of political market orientation, but the flexible model developed by Robert Ormrod is most suitable to the case of the federal NDP.[1] All contemporary political parties have a political market orientation that Ormrod defines as the manner in which "members of the party are sensitive to internal and external stakeholders' attitudes, needs and wants, and synthesize these within a framework of constraints imposed by all stakeholders to develop policies and programmes with which to reach the party's objectives" (2005, 51). According to Ormrod, all parties must simultaneously orient their organization, policy offerings, and strategies toward four distinct groups: voters, other political parties, powerful stakeholders in society, and party members. As can be seen in Table 1.1, Ormrod refers to these orientations, respectively, as voter, competitor, external, and member. Depending on their unique circumstances, parties emphasize certain orientations and de-emphasize others. Over time, they can become more oriented in one way and therefore less oriented in another way.

Formal market intelligence, defined as internal party polling or focus group data, often plays an important part in determining a party's political market orientation (Ormrod 2006, 112–13; Ormrod 2007, 81). The extent to which a party uses market intelligence is the key component of Lees-Marshment's (2001) popular concept of product/sales/market-oriented parties. A product-oriented party does not use market intelligence, preferring to base its policy offerings solely on its ideological principles; a sales-oriented party bases its policy offerings on its ideological principles but then tries to find the best ways to communicate those policies to targeted voters using market intelligence; and a market-oriented party uses market intelligence to discover the needs and desires of targeted voters and then crafts policy offerings that fit with its ideology to meet those needs and desires. In Ormrod's framework, a market-oriented party can be said to have a voter orientation because its activities are largely determined by the wants and needs of its voters as opposed to the strategies of its opponents or the wants and needs of its members and external stakeholders. I use the work of Ormrod here because it encompasses Lees-Marshment's point about the

TABLE 1.1

Robert Ormrod's concept of political market orientation

Orientation	Description of orientation
Voter	Discovering and satisfying the needs and wants of a party's targeted voters as determined primarily through market intelligence such as polling and focus groups.
Competitor	Campaign strategy and policy offerings shaped in light of political competition and the possibilities for future cooperation or conflict with other parties.
External	Engaging with powerful stakeholders in society such as churches, businesses, unions, and social movements by using their research to develop policy offerings, adopting policy positions that would garner their public approval, and entering into formal or informal alliances.
Member	Marshalling the financial and volunteer support of party members, involving members in policy development to ensure that party policies meet their approval, using members as sources of information to discern what targeted voters desire, and decentralizing campaign structures to increase members' ability to shape local and national campaign strategies.

SOURCES: Adapted from Ormrod (2005, 2006, 2007).

importance of market intelligence in political market orientation and provides analytical tools to understand how a political party is constantly pulled in different directions and must simultaneously act and react in relation to the actions and reactions of its members, stakeholders, and competitors.

At the beginning of the 2000s, the NDP's political market orientation was excessively geared toward party members and key external stakeholders – unions – and only superficially toward voters or competitors. During the Layton years, an important part of the party's moderation and modernization was becoming more voter and competitor oriented and less stakeholder and member oriented. Before Layton, the party's principles and the policies that an NDP government would enact to fulfill those principles were the foundation of any campaign. With the policies considered sacrosanct, the discussion revolved around how best to "sell" them to voters, believed to be open to changing their minds given good and rational arguments. Under Layton, the NDP had greater financial resources that resulted from changes to party financing, such as the per-vote subsidy, to increase its use of polling and focus groups. Using this formal market intelligence, Layton and his team sought first to find out what targeted voters wanted and then to search for ideas congruent with party ideology to appeal to those voters. The NDP, under Layton, became more oriented toward voters, to use Ormrod's concepts, or moved from being a sales-oriented party to a market-oriented party, to use Lees-Marshment's terms.

This new orientation toward voters was an important part of the moderation and modernization of the party. In reaction to what its market intelligence was telling it about the needs and desires of voters, the party altered certain policy positions, emphasized its ideas on certain issues while downplaying its ideas on other issues, and framed platforms in terms of practical solutions to concrete problems as opposed to wide-ranging social changes. Whereas the previous approach was "preference shaping," the new approach was "preference accommodating" (Farrell and Webb 2000, 130). The NDP's aim became to accommodate what voters preferred using policies that fit with the party's social democratic ideology and not to try to change the minds of voters. The primary means of communicating to voters how the party was accommodating their preferences was paid media (i.e., advertisements) and earned media (i.e., televised and printed news stories). Hence, media relations and paid advertising became paramount functions of the party under the leadership of Layton.

During his time as leader, the NDP also became more competitor-oriented by aiming at soft Liberal Party voters and soft BQ voters, another important part of its moderation and modernization. In contrast to past campaigns, the NDP under Layton clearly stated the party's intention to form the government as opposed to being the "conscience" of Parliament. As such, it shifted its "market position" (Butler and Collins 1996) within the Canadian electoral market away from being a niche marketer and toward becoming the market leader. Instead of focusing on winning a handful of seats across the country using the appeal of being the defender of social justice and the voice of unions, the NDP explicitly attempted to replace the Liberal Party as the broad-based and pan-Canadian "progressive" alternative to the governing Conservative Party.[2]

As it increased its voter and competitor orientation, the NDP became less oriented toward external stakeholders and internal members. Gradually, the party reduced its reliance on the labour movement as its key external stakeholder and quietly dropped its ambitious plans to become more integrated with Canada's social movements that arose from the 2002–03 leadership race. The term "social movements" as it was used during this phase of the NDP's history referred to a wide range of groups, from formal nongovernmental organizations such as the Council of Canadians, Greenpeace, and Amnesty International, to think tanks such as the Canadian Centre for Policy Alternatives, to the transitory "antiglobalization" groups that sprouted up in opposition to the Free Trade Agreements of the Americas and protested at meetings of the World Trade Organization in Seattle and the International Monetary Fund/World Bank in Washington (Van Aelst and Walgrave 2002). By the time it took over as the official opposition following the 2011 election, the NDP came to focus on what the Leader's Office called "stakeholder relations" with all types of groups in civil society, including business, as opposed to trying to be the so-called party of social movements or political arm of labour. At the same time, the party's member orientation was reduced. The roles of NDP members and volunteers in providing informal market intelligence and in determining the party's platform and election strategies diminished. Also, the roles of local campaign managers and staff from provincial parties close to grassroots members spread across the country were overturned in favour of greater control of local campaigns by party headquarters in Ottawa.

The NDP's choice to adopt political market orientation more voter oriented and competitor oriented was accompanied by the adoption of what the literature on political marketing calls "postmodern campaigning." According to recent research, there was a modernization of campaigning during the twentieth century as it passed from a "premodern" phase to a "modern" phase and then to a "postmodern" phase. Table 1.2 is adapted from the works of several political scientists and illustrates the different elements of each phase.

This book illustrates that NDP campaigning was a mixture of premodern and modern characteristics in 2000. Its campaigns were premodern in their low budgets, short-term and ad hoc nature, dependence on local campaign managers and provincial party staff, and reliance on regional and cleavage-based voting behaviour. However, at the turn of the century, NDP campaigns did tend to be more modern in the sense that they were television centred, based on sound bites broadcast by national media, extensively used commercial phone banks, and engaged in mass direct mailings. By the 2015 federal election, the NDP had adopted postmodern campaigning techniques such as the permanent campaign, multimedia communication, micro-targeted canvassing, email and social media campaigns, upward-spiralling spending, and campaign units that used specialized consultants. As seen

TABLE 1.2

Premodern, modern, and postmodern campaigning

	Premodern	Modern	Postmodern
Means of communication	Party members and travelling politicians	Television dominated	Multimedia (television, radio, internet, robocalls)
Style of communication	Messages along party lines transmitted by party members	Sound bites on television	Narrow-casted and targeted micromessages through multiple media of communication
Dominant advertising media	Newspaper advertisements, posters, pamphlets, and mass rallies	Nationwide television advertisements, local radio advertising, mass direct mailing	Targeted direct mailing, email campaigns, social media campaigns, internet advertising to supplement radio and television
Voter identification	Local "party men" responsible for residents of their ridings	Foot canvass and phone banks aiming at all voters with data collection at local level	Foot canvass and phone banks targeting specific voters based on individual-level data with all data feeding into country-wide databases
Campaign coordination	Local campaign managers; decentralization	Leader and small group of advisers around leader; centralization of many campaign functions	Special campaign units in party bureaucracy working with specialized political consultants; growth of the leader's office; decentralization with central scrutiny
Sources of feedback	Impressionistic or "feel"-based reports by foot canvassers and local volunteers	Occasional large-scale telephone polls, focus groups	Regular polling using a greater range of techniques (live telephone, online, Interactive Voice Response) and focus groups supplemented by assessments of social media activity

Focus	Centred on the local candidate as the representative of the party and part of the leader's team; elected MPs choose the leader	Party image and leader image are equally important; the focus on local candidates diminishes; leaders are chosen at delegated conventions	Presidentialization – the party moulds itself to the leader's brand after a "one-member-one-vote" leadership selection process; the party has a single overarching brand
Election preparation	Short-term, ad hoc	Long-term campaign with a specialist committee struck one–two years before an election	Permanent campaign
Campaign expenditure	Low budget	Moderate budget	High costs with spending spiralling up to election day
Vision of the electorate	Divided by enduring socio-demographic cleavages, stable voting behaviour, high partisan attachments	Catch-all, trying to mobilize voters across all categories	Segmented, issue based, leader-centric, highly volatile voting behaviour coupled with weak partisan attachments

SOURCES: Adapted from Farrell and Webb (2000); Marland (2012); Norris (2000); Plasser and Plasser (2002); and Strömbäck (2007).

following the elections of Layton and Mulcair as leaders, the party moulded itself to the leader's image following a one-member-one-vote selection process. The presidentialization of the federal NDP entailed market research and subsequent branding exercises to promote a singular leader/party brand – "Jack Layton's New Democrats" or "Tom Mulcair's NDP." Simply put, the moderation and modernization of the NDP entailed fully embracing what political marketing scholars call postmodern campaign techniques by the time of the 2015 election campaign.

A transition to postmodern campaigning requires the growing professionalization of a party (Marland 2012; Strömbäck 2009). Several scholars have noted the professionalization of political parties that has taken place since the late 1980s (Gibson and Römmele 2001, 2009; Katz and Mair 1995, 2009; Panebianco 1988). This research has documented a change in the ethos and practice of political parties whereby they have come to rely almost exclusively on professionals for nearly all of their key functions, from communication and contact with voters to policy development to searching for candidates and mobilizing volunteers. This professionalization has led to the rise of political operatives who have come to play an increasing important role in party life.

In the early 2000s, the NDP was more reflective of premodern and modern campaigning by relying on local volunteers, labour unions, and part-time party employees who would gather together at election time to organize fundraising, identify supporters, and distribute campaign literature in the areas where they lived. NDP headquarters in Ottawa dealt with national advertising (e.g., television commercials) and organized leader's tours but generally let local volunteers, labour leaders, sitting MPs, nominated candidates, and part-time employees run local campaigns how they saw fit. In particular, staff and activists from provincial wings of the party had firm control of local campaigns. Volunteer activists also had a hand in constructing the party's platform through the Federal Council and Election Planning Committee (EPC).

With the changes in party financing rules such as the advent of the per-vote subsidy, the NDP had more money to hire professionals to take on the functions previously performed by volunteers. In its move to postmodern campaigning, the NDP became increasingly organized by professionals, and power became centralized in NDP headquarters. From fundraising to policy development to campaign strategy to vetting potential candidates, these professionals took over tasks traditionally performed by volunteers, local party activists, and labour union leaders. Because of changes in campaign financing laws, staff from provincial wings began to play reduced roles in federal election campaigns. Rather, regional organizers who reported directly to Ottawa played influential roles in mobilizing local volunteers and setting up local campaigns.

In short, postmodern campaigning restructured how the NDP operated and changed the relationship between party activists and the central party apparatus in Ottawa. Professional political operatives working out of party headquarters became the dominant players influencing the NDP's political strategy and the way in which the party operated. For the time frame in this book, I define political operatives as permanent staff working at NDP headquarters on Laurier Street in Ottawa (now called the Jack Layton Building); permanent regional organizers employed by the federal NDP working in various cities across the country; and permanent staff working on Parliament Hill in the Leader's Office. Volunteers remained important in local campaigns, but they took direction from political operatives and no longer played large roles in the development of party policy. In the story of moderation and modernization that unfolds in this book, the political operatives are like the stars of the movie, whereas the volunteers, and even to a certain extent the elected MPs, are more like the extras.

The final element of the NDP's process of moderation and modernization is alluded to in the last row of Table 1.2: more sophisticated electoral market segmentation. In the first half of the twentieth century, political parties conceived of the electorate as being based on stable voting behaviour and high partisan attachments. Any divisions within the electorate were related to long-term and unchanging cleavages of race and religion. Starting in the 1960s, parties became more "catch-all" and tried to mobilize voters of all types. The principal idea was to develop policies to appeal to the largest number of voters possible, and get-out-the-vote tactics such as phone banks were used to reach the largest number of voters as possible. It has been well documented how, beginning in the late 1990s and early 2000s, political parties began to define subcategories of voters to allow for more efficient targeting of their communications and get-out-the-vote efforts (Baines 1999; Kavanagh 1995; Smith and Hirst 2001; Wring 2005). This type of electoral market segmentation encapsulates a different vision of the electorate. Voters are characterized by highly volatile voting behaviour and very weak partisan attachments. They are motivated by short-term factors such as the appearance of a controversial issue or the emergence of a charismatic leader. The electorate is seen as being divided not just along sociodemographic lines. New categories of voters are envisioned, such as economy voters (citizens who believe that the economy is the most important issue in the election) or strategic voters (citizens who vote to get a certain party out of power). At its most sophisticated and creative level, electoral market segmentation combines several characteristics of a voter into a profile of the typical supporter of the party (Flanagan 2009, 220–25; Turcotte 2012, 84–86). For example, a federalist living in Quebec concerned about crime and high levels of immigration could be considered a core Conservative Party supporter. Parts of the party's platform are then crafted to appeal to such key voters, and voter identification efforts are made to find them.

Indeed, the division of electoral markets into distinct segments by NDP operatives during the Layton years becomes important in understanding how the party modernized itself. Segmentation became part of the party's lexicon during the Layton and Mulcair years in a way that it was not during the reigns of previous leaders. Professionalization was a necessary prerequisite for the NDP to embrace electoral market segmentation. With the flow of money into party headquarters from the per-vote subsidy, professional party operatives gradually gained the power to shape the party's communications using formal market intelligence and an assessment of the party's position within the electoral market. Electoral market segmentation required surgical precision to choose the issues that appealed to soft Liberal Party and BQ voters and to frame these issues within the complex context of multi-party competition, minority Parliaments, and strategic voting. By the end of the time period examined here, the party had both the financial resources and the professional expertise to perform the type of electoral market segmentation required of a political party using postmodern campaigning techniques.

Why Political Marketing? Canadian Political Science and the NDP

Unlike most previous research on the federal NDP (formerly the Cooperative Commonwealth Federation or CCF), in this book I apply a political marketing theoretical framework. This approach allows me to take advantage of theoretical and conceptual advances within the field of political marketing that did not exist at the time of publication of seminal works on the NDP, such as Walter Young's *The Anatomy of a Party: The National CCF, 1932–1961* (1969) and Alan Whitehorn's *Canadian Socialism: Essays on the*

CCF-NDP (1992). For instance, there is now a large international literature on the political marketing of left-wing parties, especially work that examines the rise of "the third way," Blairism, and New Labour in Great Britain (Scammell 2007; White and De Chernatony 2002; Wring 2005). There are parallels in the stories of the NDP and New Labour. Like Tony Blair's Labour Party, the NDP adopted a voter political market orientation by shaping its policies through the use of market intelligence and reducing the roles played by rank-and-file activists in determining campaign strategies.

With a political marketing approach to examining the federal NDP, this book becomes part of the emerging literature on political marketing in Canada. This subfield has installed new concepts such as branding, the permanent campaign, microtargeting, and market intelligence into the lexicon of Canadian political scientists, and these new concepts are needed to understand the activities and contexts of Canadian political parties in the early twenty-first century (see Marland, Giasson, and Esselment 2017; Marland, Giasson, and Lees-Marshment 2012; and Marland, Giasson, and Small 2014). However, outside my previous work in this area (McGrane 2011, 2016, 2017), the NDP has generally escaped the attention of political marketing scholars in Canada, with the exception of two book chapters in which the party was analyzed among other cases. In *Political Marketing in Canada* (2012), Alex Marland examines the campaigns of political parties in the 1993 and 2006 federal elections and contends that the NDP's campaign was more "amateur" or "semi-professional" than those of the other major political parties. In *Political Communication in Canada: Meet the Press and Tweet the Rest* (2014), Jared Wesley and Mike Moyes analyze the election platforms of the Manitoba NDP, Nova Scotia NDP, and federal NDP during the 1990s and 2000s to argue that these parties adopted a common formula for "selling social democracy" that encompassed inoculation (shifting the focus away from negative brand traits), moderation (toning down bold left-wing policies), and simplification (reducing the number of commitments in their platforms). Here I build on and expand these two book chapters as well as my previous work in this area to provide the first comprehensive account of the federal NDP's political marketing in the twenty-first century.

Although the federal NDP has never formed government, it and its predecessor, the CCF, have been popular topics in Canadian political science. The older literature on the party provides a useful starting point, yet the explanation of the party's current situation is enhanced when one uses the conceptual and theoretical advances of recent Canadian and international literature on political marketing discussed above. One can illustrate this point by breaking down the literature on the federal party into three interrelated debates that focus, respectively, on ideology, internal party organization, and affiliation with the labour movement.

First, using sources such as internal party debates, campaign platforms, leaders' speeches, and surveys of party members, researchers have thoroughly discussed the ideology of the NDP. Two schools of thought have emerged. One school stresses that party ideology has gradually become less socialist and more liberal (Campbell and Christian 1996; Carroll 2005; Cross 1974; Evans 2012; Young 1969; Zakuta 1964). The other school focuses on how, despite changes in specific policies, party ideology remains true to social democratic principles (Archer and Whitehorn 1997; Erickson and Laycock 2002; Laycock 2015; Pétry 2015; Whitehorn 1992; Wiseman and Isitt 2007). The tone of this literature mirrors those of recent European debates on whether the third way of Tony Blair and Gerhard Schröder was a betrayal of social democratic principles (Panitch and Leys 2003) or a necessary update of social democracy for the twenty-first century that stayed true to the original ideology (Giddens 1998, 2007).

The evidence in this book illustrates that, from 2000 to 2015, the federal NDP increasingly adopted an ideology that represented a moderate version of social democracy. However, this version did not entail an overhaul of its basic values or the adoption of policies representative of a reform liberal ideology similar to that of the Liberal Party. Important differences in the values and policy prescriptions of the two parties remain. More importantly, a political marketing lens can illustrate that moderation means more than changing a party's ideas. The NDP became more moderate in how it presented its ideas to Canadians, which ideas it emphasized, and even how it thought of itself. As such, moderation is a larger concept than just moving to the centre in terms of envisioning the policies that an eventual NDP federal government would enact. It involves deeper changes in the overall political marketing of the party, including its political market orientation, its campaign tactics, and how it sees its relationship with the electorate. Simply put, using political marketing to look at the NDP's branding, advertising, and electoral market segmentation can deepen our understanding of the moderation of its ideology. Indeed, how the NDP markets itself intertwines with its ideology. Members on the right of the party's ideological spectrum are much more comfortable with a shift toward voter and competitor political market orientations than members on the left. Indeed, older literature on the party was fixated on describing its "right" and "left." In Chapter 2, I use a political marketing approach to illustrate that a right/left division still exists, but it is more appropriate now to talk about "left-wing marketing skeptics" and "right-wing marketing enthusiasts."

The second debate in the academic literature on the NDP revolves around internal party structures and arguments about the extent to which the party has shifted from being a "mass party" to a "cadre party" (Duverger 1963, 63–79). A mass party issues from and is affiliated with extraparliamentary movements such as churches or trade unions; encourages a large and active membership; ensures that party policy is determined by party members; possesses a rigid, doctrinaire ideology; and runs its election campaigns with local volunteers. A "cadre party" has the opposite characteristics: parliamentary origins; a small and inactive membership; party policy made by leaders; a flexible, catch-all ideology; campaigns run by a centralized group of professionals; and no formal affiliations with extraparliamentary groups. Again two schools of thought have emerged. One school has argued that the NDP is a "protest movement becalmed" (Zakuta 1964) as it incrementally shed its mass party characteristics as power became concentrated in the hands of leaders and party bureaucrats willing to water down the party's socialist ideology in the name of electoral expediency (Avakumovic 1978; Brodie 1985; Camfield 2011; Palmer 2016; Penner 1992; Young 1969). The other school has argued that the NDP is the prototypical mass party of Canadian politics because of its enduring affiliation with unions and the important role played by party activists in ensuring that the party does not stray too far from its social democratic roots (Engelmann 1956; Morton 1986; Sayers 1999; Whitehorn 1992).

The NDP did increasingly adopt characteristics that Duverger (1963) would identify as being representative of a cadre party during its process of moderation and modernization from 2000 to 2015. The central party office came to determine party platforms, the leader obtained a considerable amount of power, and campaigns were primarily run by a group of professionals in Ottawa. However, the party continued to make efforts to mobilize its membership to be active in local campaigns and riding associations. In fact, one of the main tasks of the professionals in party headquarters was to mobilize local volunteers and increase the participation of rank-and-file members in party activities. The ideology of the party might have moved to the centre, but it is not completely flexible and catch-all. Certain values continue to underpin NDP ideology, and many policy positions have undergone very little change. Most importantly, the conceptual framework of the postmodern campaign is broader than what the mass party/cadre party dichotomy allows. Professionalization and centralization of party operations are only two aspects of postmodern campaigning, which also entails new ways of communicating and engaging with the electorate, the permanent campaign, and branding exercises. These aspects of postmodern campaigning are not present in the mass party/cadre party dichotomy that emerged in the 1960s, and by using the conceptual framework of postmodern campaigning I can analyze a wider range of activities undertaken by the federal NDP in the early twenty-first century than if I were to stick to a mass party/cadre party conceptual framework.

The third debate in the academic literature on the federal NDP involves the affiliation of the party with organized labour. Scholars have examined both the tensions inherent in the relationship and how the labour movement influences the party's strategies and policies. The discussion in this literature centres on whether the NDP genuinely represents workers' concerns (Evans 2012; Horowitz 1968; Panitch 1961; Savage 2012) and on the extent to which the affiliation of the NDP with the labour movement might hurt its electoral chances (Archer 1985, 1987, 1990). Researchers have also looked at how a closer connection between the NDP and social movements could either supplement or replace the relationship that the party has developed with the labour movement (Cameron 2005; Erickson and Zakharova 2015; McLeod 1994). Recently, there has been an examination of how new party financing laws banning union donations to the NDP have affected its relationship with labour and whether the party should still be considered a "labour party." Whereas Jansen and Young (2009, 658) argue that "shared ideological commitment and overlapping personnel" are responsible for maintaining a labour influence in the NDP, Pilon, Ross, and Savage (2011, 33) contend that much deeper historical forces are at work and that the labour unions' continued support for the NDP is the product of "lessons learnt in the attempts to cope [with], respond to and resist changes in political economic structures."

The concept of "political market orientation" is effective in analyzing the complex relationship among the labour movement, social movements, and the federal NDP in the twenty-first century. On the one hand, the NDP is still a labour party in the sense that it remains officially affiliated with the Canadian Labour Congress (CLC), and both local and national labour leaders continue to be integrated into the party's structures. On the other hand, the NDP has gradually become less oriented toward the labour movement as it key external stakeholder. Indeed, both the party and the labour movement have sought more independence from one another than in the past. Similarly, the NDP began to develop relationships with social movements on an informal level when it courted groups such as third-party validators for policy announcements during the 2015 federal election campaign even if a formal affiliation between the NDP and the social movement did not materialize. The concept of political market orientation allows us to think more deeply about how the labour movement, social movements, and the NDP interact with each other. It allows us to see how the NDP remains oriented to some degree toward the labour movement and social movements but how that orientation has been reduced in favour of a greater emphasis on building relationships with voters and engaging with competing political parties.

Overall, the evidence presented in this book indicates that the moderation and modernization of the NDP has moved its ideology to the centre, made the party more of a cadre party in Duverger's (1963) sense of the term, and made it less of a labour party. However, the new theoretical tools provided by political marketing allow for more nuance. We can look at old debates in new ways. We can see that the rigid dichotomies in previous academic literature on the NDP concerning its status as a mass party/cadre party, liberal party/socialist party, and labour party/nonlabour party do not adequately capture the recent transformation of the party. Thus, though distinctions in older academic literature on the NDP are useful starting points, the political marketing approach that I have outlined above takes a broader view of the transformation of the party in the early twenty-first century.

Research Design and Outline of the Book

In this book, I adopt a "mixed methods research" design. Over the past two decades, mixed methods research has become more prevalent in the social sciences, and a number of methodologists have explored its potential and outlined its use (Creswell 2003; Greene and Caracelli 1997; Miles and Huberman 1994; Newman and Benz 1998; Tashakkori and Teddlie 1998, 2003). Indeed, the *Journal of Mixed Methods Research* was launched in 2007. A broad definition of mixed methods research is "research in which the investigator collects and analyzes data, integrates the findings, and draws inferences using both qualitative and quantitative approaches or methods in a single study or a program of inquiry" (Tashakkori and Creswell 2007, 3). A key consideration for mixed methods research is the extent to which it *integrates* qualitative and quantitative findings so that the end product is more than just the sum of the individual quantitative and qualitative parts (Bryman 2007).

In this book, I have used mixed methods research in seeking to integrate the analysis of numerical data with the analysis of textual data. I have analyzed two main sources of numerical data using Stata, a statistical software package. First, from January 13 to 26, 2015, I administered an online survey of 2,440 NDP members. I compared this survey with an NDP member survey administered by Erickson and Laycock in 1997 generously provided to me for use in this book. Second, a custom survey of over 4,000 voters commissioned for this book and entitled the 2015 Canadian Federal Election Panel Survey on Social Democracy was administered during the first week of the 2015 federal election campaign and two weeks immediately following the 2015 federal election (the same voters were surveyed in both waves). I compared this survey with publicly available data from voter surveys in English Canada from the 2000 to the 2011 Canadian Election Studies and voter surveys done by Ipsos-Reid in Quebec on the days of the federal elections of 2006, 2008, and 2011.

The most important source of textual data that I use in this book is a set of semi-structured interviews with open-ended questions (Kvale and Brinkmann 2009) that I completed with over sixty NDP operatives, party activists, and politicians concerning their experiences from 2000 to 2015. Access to these party insiders was facilitated by my lifelong involvement in the NDP at federal and provincial levels, including elected positions with the youth wing, work with various riding associations, and being a member of the Saskatchewan NDP Provincial Council and Saskatchewan NDP Provincial Executive. About one year after finishing the interviews, I was elected president of the Saskatchewan NDP. Some of these interviews were conducted in person, and others took place by telephone. Each interview lasted approximately one hour, and some of the interviewees were spoken to more than once. I used a funnel interview protocol (Harrell and Bradley 2009, 50–55) that moved from broad to specific questions. As opposed to making recordings, I took handwritten notes during the interviews that were later typed. A list of the interviewees and short descriptions of their involvement in the federal NDP are contained in Appendix A.

Certainly, handwritten notes lack the exactitude of recorded interview data. However, several interviewees indicated that they would not participate in the project if discussions were recorded. Also, the absence of a recorder undoubtedly made the interviewees more comfortable and open. I judged the imperatives of guaranteeing an appropriate level of participation of research subjects to carry out the project and ensuring that interviews remained candid to be more important than improving the precision of my data collection by recording the interviews. Since I decided not to record the interviews, it was important to add additonal steps to the research design to ensure accuracy of the data from these semi-structured interviews. I subsequently sent a typed version of my handwritten notes to each interviewee to verify their accuracy; I also sent to the interviewees the sentences from the book in which they are cited as sources. These extra steps of verifying the accuracy of my notes from the interviews and ensuring that the interviewees validated their cited statements provide increased confidence in what I heard and wrote down during the interviews.

In addition to data from the sixty interviews featured throughout the book, there are three sources of textual data that I gathered and analyzed. Despite significant challenges in scheduling, my research assistants and I were able to administer anonymous, structured, and recorded interviews to fifty-eight sitting NDP MPs representing 60 percent of the federal NDP caucus from April to December 2014. If the 2015 federal election had gone differently, then these MPs would have formed the basis of the first federal NDP cabinet and government caucus. These interviews, composed primarily of open-ended questions, were subsequently transcribed and coded using NVivo 10. Also, using Stata, I constructed and analyzed a data set containing all of the 18,701 questions asked in Question Period by NDP MPs during the Thirty-Seventh to Forty-First Parliaments (2001–15). Finally, from internet archives (https://archive.org/web) and Alan Whitehorn's personal archives, I collected all of the platforms, news releases, and television commercials of the federal NDP from the 2000 to the 2015 elections. I also gathered the radio advertising for the NDP for the 2000 election when the party relied heavily on that medium. These platforms, news releases, and commercials were subsequently transcribed into a digital format and analyzed using NVivo 10. The analysis of these three additional textual sources helps to validate or invalidate the recollections of the interviewees related to me during the semi-structured interviews.

All of the Stata files for member surveys and the 2015 Canadian Federal Election Panel Survey on Social Democracy, as well as the Stata and Excel files for the Question Period data, have been placed in the University of Saskatchewan Archives. Transcripts of my notes from the semi-structured interviews with NDP operatives, party activists, and politicians are also available at the University of Saskatchewan Archives, along with the platforms, news releases, and television commercials of the federal NDP from the 2000 to the 2015 elections. All of these documents are in PDF format. As per an agreement with the sitting NDP MPs interviewed, the transcripts of their fifty-eight recorded interviews will be made available to the public in 2024 in the University of Saskatchewan Archives. Since these MPs were assured anonymity, parts of the transcripts that could be used to identify them have been redacted. I hope that future researchers will be able to use these data to test and expand my findings in this book or to launch scholarly inquiries of their own.

This book is structured thematically to allow the reader to understand how agents within the NDP (primarily political operatives) used newfound financial resources from party financing reform to drive the process of moderation and modernization of the party and how this process contributed to its electoral success. In Chapter 1, I use the semi-structured interviews with NDP operatives and politicians as well as campaign materials from the 2002–03 leadership race to describe the dire situation of the party following the 2000 election, particularly its finances. In Chapter 2, using the semi-structured interviews with NDP operatives and Elections Canada data on NDP finances, I look closely at the adoption of postmodern campaigning in terms of the transformation of the organization of the party. Using interviews with NDP MPs and the Question Period data set, in Chapter 3 I explore how changes in the federal party's political marketing affected the functioning of the NDP caucus in the House of Commons. With a combination of semi-structured interviews with NDP operatives and content analysis of NDP advertising and news releases, in Chapter 4 I then look at the political marketing of the party by closely examining strategies followed by the party in the six federal election campaigns from 2000 to 2015. In Chapter 5, I analyze election platforms and surveys of NDP members, MPs, and potential voters to investigate how new approaches to political marketing of the party affected its ideology from 2000 to 2015. For readers interested in my explanation of the party's historic breakthrough in the 2011 federal election, particularly the surprising "orange wave" in Quebec, Chapter 6 is the best place to look. In it, I use publicly available voter surveys to explore the attitudes and behaviours of NDP voters from 2000 to 2011 through the lens of electoral market segmentation – a key part of the party's new political marketing – and relate these findings back to the analyses of previous chapters. Following up on the analysis in the previous chapter, in Chapter 7 I examine the party's heartbreaking defeat in the 2015 federal election using the 2015 Canadian Federal Election Panel Survey on Social Democracy, a custom voter survey commissioned for this book. In the conclusion, I try to understand the implications of the NDP's disheartening 2015 campaign for the future of the party and literature on political marketing.

It is hard to deny that the NDP's political roller-coaster ride from 2000 to 2015 is simply a great story. Popular books (Chow 2014; Gidluck 2012; Lavigne 2013; Turk and Wahl 2012) and even a CBC movie on Layton's life have told the tale of a scrappy group of underdogs who believed so strongly in their cause that they succeeded against all odds. Subsequently, tragedy struck when Layton died, and his dedicated followers had to pick up the pieces to contest another election in which their Hollywood ending of realizing the dream of their fallen leader did not come true.

Here I intend to supplement the intriguing human elements of the story of the federal NDP with thorough academic analysis of its political marketing. Although moderation and modernization of the party did not propel it to power, the revolutionizing of its political marketing did allow it to reassert itself as an important player in Canadian politics and as a party whose activities can affect Canadian political discourse. As such, the transformation of the party's political marketing rearranged Canada's party system, and how the "new NDP" functions and where its internal politics are headed remain important for the future of Canada and continue to merit serious academic attention.

1
Ferment in the Party:
The Federal NDP, 2000–03

Like the other opposition political parties, the New Democratic Party was caught off guard when the Liberal Party government decided to call a snap election in late October 2000 (Greenspon 2001, 172–75; Lavigne 2013, 6–8). After running what even NDP operatives considered to be an incoherent and disorganized campaign (Fraser interview, 2014) the party registered a discouraging result, losing eight of its twenty-one seats and receiving only 8.5 percent of the popular vote.[1] The shock of this electoral setback created the realization that major change was needed to revitalize the party, thereby setting off a period of considerable ferment within the party.

This chapter traces this tumultuous time in the party's history began on November 28, 2000, the day following the federal election. The NDP found itself in a grim situation after the 2000 election, and the difficulties of the party eventually led to the resignation of Alexa McDonough as leader on June 5, 2002. The ensuing leadership race ended with the election of Jack Layton as leader on January 25, 2003. Holding a leadership race within the context of considerable ferment within the party created an opportunity for Layton and his campaign team to propose new goals and strategies for the political marketing of the NDP that would increase its voter, competitor, and external stakeholder orientations. As it turned out, this brief time period was a catalyst for revolutionary changes in the party's political marketing and the embronyic period of the "new NDP."

The Morning After: The NDP Following the 2000 Election
The results of the 1997 federal election allowed the NDP to have a cautious sense of optimism. It made a historic breakthrough in Atlantic Canada and more than doubled its seat count after the disastrous 1993 campaign. However, the disappointing results of the 2000 election created a general sense

of pessimism and negativity. Elections are a game of numbers, and the numbers from the 2000 election were overwhelmingly discouraging. The party lost eight of the seats that it had won in 1997 and did not win any nonincumbent seats. Four of the eight seats that it lost had been won in the so-called Atlantic Wave of NDP support in the previous election. The party came second in only twenty-six seats, and its candidates received the required 15 percent of the vote to attain their financial rebates in only 57 of 301 ridings (Whitehorn 2001, 130–31). The party's share of the popular vote dropped below 15 percent in seven provinces (Nova Scotia, Manitoba, and Saskatchewan being the exceptions). The NDP's challenges in Canada's two largest provinces were particularly disturbing. The party won one seat and 8.3 percent of the popular vote in Ontario and dropped into electoral oblivion with only 1.8 percent of the popular vote in Quebec and no seats.

Although McDonough stated that she would continue to be leader on election night, there were several questions about her leadership. The party's decision to stress the experience of its local incumbents in the 2000 election and not to feature her prominently in television advertisements left the impression that she was not a strong leader. McDonough had a limited national profile, and her struggles with French hurt her appeal in Quebec (Nystrom interview, 2015). She was also perceived as one-dimensional during the 2000 campaign because of her exclusive focus on health care (Bill Blaikie interview, 2015). Indicative of her difficulties, a poll taken immediately after the 2000 English-language leaders' debate showed that only 5 percent of English Canadian respondents believed that McDonough had won the debate; this was last place, behind Gilles Duceppe at 9 percent, a Quebec sovereignist (Pammett 2001, 308).

Soon after the election, rumours began to circulate of caucus members wishing to replace McDonough, and the *Globe and Mail* reported that there was an "unofficial leadership race" under way, with Svend Robinson, Lorne Nystrom, and Bill Blaikie said to be interested in becoming leader (MacKinnon 2001b, A4). Her gender and the fact that she had succeeded a female leader also seemed to undermine her (Smallman interview, 2014). As Whitehorn (2001, 132) put it in his chapter in *The Canadian General Election of 2000*, "questions still emerge about a third straight disappointing election outcome with a female leader from a less populous region." There was also a sense that McDonough was not fully in control of her caucus, with NDP MPs routinely making statements or taking positions without consulting her (Godin interview, 2014; Martin interview, 2014). Her support among party members appeared to be dissipating as well. At the 2001 NDP convention, McDonough faced the unusual and awkward situation of having her leadership formally challenged by Marcel Hatch, an activist from the party's socialist caucus, and having 16 percent of the delegates vote against her.

Organizationally, the NDP had virtually no presence in many regions of Canada, meaning that it could not run a truly "national campaign." The most glaring example of the party's regional weaknesses was in Quebec. The executive of the small Quebec wing of the party had resigned en masse because of the decision by McDonough and her caucus in 2000 to vote in favour of the Clarity Bill, even though the NDP's Federal Council had passed a resolution urging the caucus to oppose it (Ducasse interview, 2014; Moran interview, 2014). The result was that the NDP ran only "paper candidates" in Quebec in 2000 for whom it could not even provide phone or fax numbers (Whitehorn 2001, 136). Further, in 2000, no television advertisements were produced in French or ran in Quebec. The party ran a similarly skeletal campaign in Alberta and Newfoundland, where it also did not air any television advertisements.

By the end of the 1990s, the finances of the party had become extremely tight. It spent only $2 million on advertising in the 2000 election, not only much less than other parties but also much less than what it had spent in 1988 ($3 million) and 1993 ($3.28 million), especially when inflation is taken into account. There were not enough resources for adequate national polling, and no NDP advertisements ran on national television networks during the 2000 campaign (see Whitehorn 2001, 118–25). Coming out of that election, caucus had to lay off a number of staff because of the reduced number of NDP MPs (Bélanger interview, 2014). Similarly, party headquarters had to reduce its staff because of the debt accumulated during the campaign, and many local NDP riding associations were in difficult financial positions because they did not receive their financial rebates after failing to attain 15 percent of the popular vote (Giambrone interview, 2014).

On top of these leadership and organizational challenges, there had been ideological tension within the NDP leading up to the 2000 election. In late 1998, McDonough suggested that Tony Blair's Labour Party could serve as "the NDP's model for a new pro-business party with a social conscience" and that she wanted to create a "pragmatic and fiscally responsible party [that] can appeal to middle-class voters, not just big labour" (Fife 1998, A1). There was an immediate backlash (Blakeney interview, 2015; Davies interview,

2014). Buzz Hargrove, president of the Canadian Auto Workers (CAW) union, stated that the NDP should move itself left as opposed to adopting Blairism, and he even threatened to withdraw his union's funding of the party and form a "new leftist political force." Bob White, president of the Canadian Labour Congress, also stated his disagreement with McDonough (Gatehouse 1998, A1). She was forced publicly to retreat by claiming that her initial comments had been misconstrued (McDonough 1998), and later she clarified that "while it is important for us to look at what Britain is doing ... you can't simply impose holus bolus a social democratic model from somewhere else" (quoted in Alberts 1999, A7).

The 1999 NDP convention became the site of considerable debate on the party's ideological direction, with delegates and leaders sending mixed signals about ideological identity. The convention gave almost unanimous support for a resolution ruling out a move to Blair's "third way," and it rejected a policy paper on stimulating the economy because it did not envision a large enough role for state intervention and touted partnerships between the government and the private sector (Adams 1999, A1). At the same time, roughly two-thirds of the delegates endorsed a policy paper that promised balanced budgets "over the business cycle" and tax relief for the middle class, such as a reduction of the GST after a debate in which opponents of the paper called it a betrayal of social democratic principles (Bellavance and Alberts 1999, A7). Delegates also approved the creation of a task force on small business to improve the party's relationship with that sector of the economy. NDP MPs and union leaders came down on different sides of these issues.[2] McDonough herself closed the convention by agreeing with delegates that the NDP should not follow the third way while touting the party's embrace of centrist ideas such as fiscal responsibility and tax relief for the middle class (Williamson 1999, A19).

In many ways, the ferment in the NDP around the time of the 2000 election created an opportunity for a change in its political marketing. The party reflected on the deep challenges that it faced in terms of its ideology, finances, organization, and leadership. The strong feeling in the party following the 2000 election was that all options should be put on the table and that the party should question long-held traditions and ways of doing things (McDonough interview, 2015). The comfort of following the same models of organization and ideology that the NDP had always followed now seemed to be outweighed by the cost to the party of becoming totally irrelevant to Canadian politics.

Ferment in the Party: Agents React

Tumultuous times in political parties can allow for significant changes to be made to a party's political marketing. Various agents in the NDP adopted different strategies in reaction to the disappointing results of the 2000 election. These strategies, successful to varying degrees, are important in understanding the changes in the NDP's political marketing that gradually emerged in the 2000s. Indeed, different political marketing options were available to the party during this period, and there was much debate on and conflict over which direction to follow.

The two most formal and organized reactions to the difficult situation in which the party found itself following the 2000 election were the New Politics Initiative (NPI) and NDProgress. In many ways, they represented the two poles of the debate on the party's future. The NPI began in June 2001 as the initiative of a group in Toronto consisting of long-time activists such as Judy Rebick, Jim Stanford, and Naomi Klein, soon joined by MPs Libby Davies and Svend Robinson and several other left-wing activists around Canada. The impetus for the initiative came from the surge of youth activism related to the emergence of the antiglobalization movement in the early 2000s. It was thought that the energy of these young activists could be channelled to reform the NDP to become a more radical left-wing force (Rebick interview, 2015; Stanford interview, 2015).

The NPI proposed a complete transformation of the political marketing of the NDP to orient it much more toward members and external stakeholders. Moreover, its emphases on member control of the party and on nonhierarchical decision-making structures were throwbacks to premodern campaigning as opposed to postmodern campaigning. The basic premise of the NPI was that the NDP should disband and reconstitute itself as a new party open to forming alliances with social movements, labour unions, and citizens' groups. The new party would recognize the importance of new forms of political action (including civil disobedience) and ensure that discussions within the party were based on models of deliberative democracy and consensus building that empowered local riding associations (Stanford interview, 2015). The NPI did not want to stifle debate by coming out with a full set of policies contained within a manifesto (Rebick interview, 2015; Stanford interview, 2015). Nonetheless, its initial open letter signalled its stridently left-wing ideological orientation by calling for a fight against the "increased power for corporations and free markets" by abolishing the North American Free Trade Agreement (NAFTA) and the World Trade

Organization (WTO), forgiving the debts of Third World countries, undertaking aggressive measures to meet Canada's Kyoto Protocol commitments, and ensuring citizen control of the economy through public input on investment decisions (New Politics Initiative 2001a). The NPI also resisted the professionalization of the NDP – a key part of postmodern campaigning. The group was concerned that the party establishment was going to push Blairism and follow a centrist ideological direction similar to that of the Liberal Party in the wake of the disappointing 2000 election results (Merran Proctor interview, 2015; Stanford interview, 2015). Greater internal party democracy and member control of party policy were intended as bulwarks against creeping Blairism and the growing power of professionals hired as party staff (Ibid.).

As a network with little hierarchy and a loose sense of organization, the NPI immediately began holding meetings across Canada to garner support for its vision of renewal of the NDP. Within four months, over 1,000 Canadians, some NDP members and other activists outside the party, had publicly endorsed the group's call for a new party. More importantly, the NPI organized to have a resolution put to the NDP convention in November 2001 in Winnipeg for the party to initiate a process leading to a "bold, visionary, activist, progressive new federal political party" (New Politics Initiative 2001b). The NPI organizers released the outline of a process that would invite unions and left-wing social movements to participate formally in the founding of the new party. After a series of regional conferences and the establishment of local "new party committees," the creation of a new party would have to be ratified by a national NDP convention, a referendum of NDP members, and internal processes of unions and social movements that desired affiliation. The resolution was jointly submitted by over thirty riding associations, union locals, and provincial youth wings.

Despite a well-attended NPI event on the Friday night of the Winnipeg convention and an inspiring speech by Robinson from the convention floor on Saturday, the NPI's resolution was defeated, with 37 percent (401 votes) in favour and 63 percent (684 votes) against (Rebick interview, 2015; Stanford interview, 2015). Labour delegates split over the resolution, with CAW, CUPE, Canadian Union of Postal Workers, and Public Service Alliance of Canada delegates being supportive and delegates representing the Steelworkers, United Food and Commercial Workers (UFCW), and Communications, Energy, and Paperworkers (CEP) being hostile (Stanford interview, 2015). Although the NPI dropped the idea of creating a new party following the convention, it did vow to carry on its "efforts among both NDP members and non-members to build a new way of doing politics on Canada's left" (New Politics Initiative 2001c).

However, the momentum of the group began to fade (Merran Proctor interview, 2015; Stanford interview, 2015). In the year following the Winnipeg convention, the NPI continued to distribute a national newsletter and hold meetings of the National Coordinating Committee, and local chapters held periodic events (Merran Proctor interview, 2015). As the NDP leadership campaign started, NPI activists who were party members became involved with the various leadership campaigns (particularly the Layton and Comartin campaigns), and NPI activists who were not party members moved on to other endeavours (Rebick interview, 2015). The NPI ended up playing a minor role in the leadership campaign. It did not formally endorse any candidate, and its main activity was to distribute the results of a questionnaire of the candidates to its members. The NPI was officially disbanded approximately a year after the leadership race, ending with Layton, now the leader of the party, speaking at its final event.

NDProgress was a group of New Democrats, several of whom were party staff or former party staff, formed to support the proposal for party renewal put forth by MP Peter Stoffer in an open letter shortly after the 2000 election. Contrary to the NPI, NDProgress proposed a political market orientation toward voters and away from external stakeholders. It also embraced postmodern campaigning. In particular, the group was interested in how Blairism could be adapted to the Canadian context (Cardy interview, 2015), and Stoffer publicly stated that the NDP "has a lot to learn" from Blair's Labour Party (quoted in MacKinnon 2001b, A4). However, the group made a strategic decision not to mention Blairism because of its obvious unpopularity within the party (Cardy interview, 2015).

Instead, NDProgress decided that ideas for structural reform of the NDP to create a "modern social democratic party" (MacKinnon 2001a, A4) and make it more electable would gain more traction (Cardy interview, 2015; Stoffer interview, 2014). In particular, NDProgress argued that the party's link to the labour movement hurt the party because it appears to voters that it privileges one part of society over another. So the group called for unions to be disaffiliated with the party and for the party to stop taking donations from both unions and corporations. Since the federal NDP was often unfairly blamed by voters for actions taken by provincial counterparts, NDProgress argued that the federal party should be reconstituted as an entity fully separate from its provincial wings. NDProgress thought that this reform would give the federal NDP a national vision and more control over its own resources (NDProgress 2001). To empower existing members and recruit new ones, as well as to reduce the power of labour delegates at leadership conventions, NDProgress argued that the party should adopt a one-member-one-vote (OMOV) system to select its leaders (Stoffer 2001). In a nod to postmodern campaigning, the NDP would adopt a new name as a rebranding exercise to signal to the public that it had transformed itself and become more independent of the labour movement and its provincial counterparts (Ibid.). NDProgress insisted that these structural reforms needed to occur prior to larger discussions on renewing party policies and ideas (Ibid.). However, the group believed that moderate policy ideas would inevitably flow from structural reforms: decreasing the power of the labour movement could reduce internal resistance to Blairism, and the OMOV process was more likely to elect a moderate leader not beholden to the left-wing faction of the NDP overrepresented at party conventions (Cardy interview, 2015). In this way, OMOV would lead to the postmodern campaign practice of having the party mould itself to the image of its leader.

The most substantial success of NDProgress was getting McDonough to endorse the principle of OMOV for leadership races when she spoke to a NDProgress meeting in April 2001. At the Winnipeg convention, NDProgress organizers quietly opposed the NPI resolution and worked to get NPI delegates to support their plan for OMOV (Cardy interview, 2015). Subsequently, the convention adopted OMOV for the next leadership race, albeit with 25 percent of the vote being allotted to union representatives, an amendment that NDProgress disagreed with but accepted in order to secure union support for its idea (Ibid.). With the adoption of OMOV and the defeat of the NPI resolution, NDProgress decided to disband after the 2001 convention, and its activists migrated into different leadership campaigns (Cardy interview, 2015; Stoffer interview, 2014).

Prominent members of the NDP caucus had to react to the NDProgress/NPI debate. Both Davies and Robinson championed the NPI. Although he never officially endorsed the NPI on its website, Joe Comartin positioned himself on the left of the caucus and did vote for the NPI resolution in Winnipeg (Comartin interview, 2014). For their parts, Blaikie and Nystrom were interested in the NDProgress ideas about structural reform but never endorsed the group (Stoffer interview, 2014). Nystrom was suspicious of its Blairist tendencies (Nystrom interview, 2015), and Blaikie disagreed with its plans to reduce the power of the labour movement (Bill Blaikie interview, 2015). Both were explicit, however, in their opposition to the NPI. In what proved to be the most memorable moment of the 2001 NDP convention, Blaikie made an impassioned speech against the NPI resolution as the crowd chanted "NDP! NDP!" In particular, he argued that the party did not represent the "mushy middle" or Blairism, as evident from its brave opposition to antiterrorism legislation in the post-9/11 era, its continuing opposition to free-trade agreements, and its defence of public ownership at the provincial level (Blaikie 2011, 101). When the NPI was formed, Nystrom stated that he was against it because it involved setting up a process parallel to the party's sanctioned renewal efforts and threatened to divide the left in Canada (Lawton 2001a, A6; Nystrom interview, 2015).

Beyond the NPI/NDProgress dichotomy, other agents within the party were also strategizing in reaction to the disappointing 2000 election results. For example, Adam Giambrone, a young NDP activist from Toronto, won the race for party president at the 2001 convention, beating Elizabeth Weir, former leader of the New Brunswick NDP. Although Giambrone had the tacit support of the NPI, he attempted to steer clear of the NPI/NDProgress debate, preferring to stress his plans to professionalize the party and to improve its organization (Giambrone interview, 2014). His ideas about professionalization foreshadowed a move by the NDP in the coming decade to postmodern campaigning.

There was general agreement among the interviewees that McDonough was an embattled leader following the 2000 election who saw both the NPI and NDProgress as threats to her leadership (Bélanger interview, 2014; Davies interview, 2014; Stoffer interview, 2014). She also struggled to keep her caucus united since there were MPs on opposing sides of the NPI-NDProgress debate as well as MPs who positioned themselves for a potential leadership race. Her principal strategy in reaction to the ferment within the party was to be "an honest broker" between the competing NPI and NDProgress factions to prevent the NDP and the broader Canadian left from tearing itself apart (Bélanger interview, 2014; McDonough interview, 2015).

This honest broker strategy consisted of four elements. First, McDonough admitted that the 2000 election results were bitterly disappointing and agreed that every option should be put on the table in terms of renewing the party (Blakeney interview, 2015; McDonough interview, 2015). Second, she supported a resolution by the NDP Federal Council to create a Federal Steering Committee on the Future of the New Democratic Party as a way to determine which changes were needed without throwing out the party's history and existing internal structures (McDonough interview, 2015). Although the committee's work was largely overshadowed by the activities of NDProgress and the NPI (Bill Blaikie interview, 2015; Cardy interview, 2015; Dick Proctor interview, 2015; Rebick interview, 2015), the committee did offer a formal process by which members could submit their ideas for party renewal. Its final report, passed by the Winnipeg convention, agreed with the NPI that the party should not shy away from extraparliamentary activism and left-wing stances on the environment, free trade, and globalization. Following the ideas of NDProgress, the committee urged the party to rethink its relationship with the labour movement even though it did not specify how. Third, McDonough opposed both NDProgress and the NPI while displaying openness to their ideas. She agreed that OMOV was important in recruiting new members, yet she also agreed with the NPI that moving ideologically toward Blairism would be counterproductive since that space was already occupied by the Liberals (McDonough interview, 2015). She opposed the NPI's resolution because she thought that it was unworkable for a political party to merge with social movements (Ibid.), and her office organized lobbying efforts prior to the Winnipeg convention to ensure that the resolution would fail (Blakeney interview, 2015). Nonetheless, at the close of the convention, she made a nod to the NPI's ideas by suggesting that the party should follow what she characterized as the "go green and go loud" plan laid out by the Steering Committee (Lawton 2001b, A30). And fourth, McDonough strove to keep the caucus and the party focused on providing left-wing opposition to the Chrétien government as opposed to infighting over leadership questions and different visions of party renewal. In particular, the NDP caucus concentrated on protecting civil liberties in the aftermath of the 9/11 terrorist attacks and raising the profile of the case of Maher Arar (Blakeney interview, 2015; McDonough interview, 2015; Dick Proctor interview, 2015).

By straddling the NPI/NDProgress divide, McDonough was successful in preventing the NDP from tearing itself apart. Her efforts in this regard were buoyed by an unexpected win in a by-election in Windsor West, a riding previously held by the Liberals. The win provided a significant boost to the morale of caucus, party staff, and grassroots activists and had a calming effect on members, who began to think that perhaps things were not as bad as they had seemed on election night in 2000 (Bélanger interview, 2014; Giambrone interview, 2014). Ironically, it was the night of the Windsor West by-election that McDonough decided to step down as leader. She picked that moment because she wanted to leave when the party's support was on an "upswing," the internal tension had subsided, and the rebuilding process was well under way (McDonough interview, 2015).

Although McDonough was unable to resuscitate her leadership, many interviewees stressed that she should be credited with ensuring that the party survived a very divisive period in its history (Bélanger interview, 2014; Blakeney interview, 2015; Comartin interview, 2014; Dick Proctor interview, 2015; Smallman interview, 2014). When she resigned, the debate over whether or not to create a new party and adopt a new name had been settled. Also, the decision to move to the OMOV leadership selection method with a designated labour vote had been made. The party had a young president dedicated to modernization, and an additional seat in the House of Commons from Ontario gave it a sense of momentum. Most importantly, the party had time to generate and debate new ideas about its ideology and political marketing without the frenzy of a leadership race. In many ways, these positive outcomes from McDonough's final year and a half as NDP leader ensured a leadership race that ultimately proved to be productive for the party's future.

A Vote for Change: The 2002–03 Leadership Race

It is important to examine the leadership campaigns in the leadership race of 2002–03 because they represent different recipes for changes to the ideological outlook and political marketing of the federal NDP. The outcome of the race ended up shaping the political marketing of the party in the future.

The goal of Bev Meslo, the Socialist Caucus candidate, was to raise awareness that party elites were not respecting the will of the convention and that the NDP had embarked on a failed experiment during the 2000 campaign by "standing in the mushy middle ground while looking for a Third Way" and by "trying to be all things to all people." So she proposed political marketing whereby the NDP would take uncompromising left-wing positions such as "social ownership under workers' control," a shorter work week without loss of pay, abrogation of NAFTA, and free postsecondary education. She advocated for a "more democratic, more open" party by devoting more convention time to resolutions and by subjecting NDP MPs and the leader to a recall process if they did not respect convention resolutions (Meslo 2002a, 2002b).

Pierre Ducasse, who broke new ground by being the first Québécois to seek the leadership of the federal NDP, knew that he was unlikely to win (Ducasse interview, 2014). He ran in order to create discussion on new and innovative policy ideas. His primary issue was that the NDP should focus on "economic democracy," by which he meant that "economic institutions should not only be controlled either by big business or by the state, but should also be controlled by civil society in a way that is participatory, decentralized, and democratic" (Ducasse 2003). One of his ideas that eventually became an important part of the NDP's political marketing was targeting more resources for Quebec. Ducasse pushed hard for the party to be aggressive in building capacity in Quebec and to endorse asymmetrical federalism, which would allow for the Quebec government to opt out of federal programs with full financial compensation. Echoing some of the ideas of NDProgress, he also proposed doing away with integrated provincial-federal membership, increasing the independence of the party from unions, and changing the party's name to the Social Democratic Party.

For his part, Joe Comartin attempted to make the leadership campaign about taking the party to the left by repudiating Blairism and focusing on issues such as a noninterventionist/nonmilitary foreign policy, fighting racism, proportional representation, and greater environmental protection (Comartin 2002; Comartin interview, 2014). Indeed, he garnered the endorsement of Buzz Hargrove and ensured that the socialist caucus pledged their support to him as their second preference (Comartin interview, 2014). His campaign also tried to focus members' attention on which leadership candidate was the best "on the ground" organizer and highlighted how Comartin had created a grassroots coalition of citizens' groups that achieved the NDP's first federal electoral victory in Ontario in over a decade during the 2000 election. His ideas on political marketing were focused on alliances with citizens' groups and a sophisticated ground game that could be considered part of postmodern campaigning.

Similar to postmodern campaigning's emphasis on branding, Lorne Nystrom focused on the perception of the NDP as being weak when it came to the economy. He focused his leadership campaign on the need to increase the party's credibility on economic issues and the necessity of having a leader with extensive experience (Nystrom interview, 2015). Nystrom argued that the NDP's lack of success in recent years had resulted from mistrust among Canadians of the party on economic issues. He reiterated that

"Tommy Douglas once told me: If you're successful at the till, then they'll trust you at the ballot box" (Nystrom 2002). To this end, he stressed the need for fiscally responsible government and a focus on "bread and butter issues" such as job creation (Nystrom 2003, A19). His campaign argued that he could effectively convince voters of the NDP's credibility on economic issues because of his thirty years of experience as a MP and in the private sector.

For his part, Bill Blaikie wanted a political market orientation toward competitors. He centred his leadership campaign on the need to provide effective opposition to the Chrétien government in the House of Commons and asked which candidate had the best record as a parliamentarian (Bill Blaikie interview, 2015; Dick Proctor interview, 2015). His campaign materials stressed his accomplishments in each session of Parliament stretching back to 1979, and the bases of his policies were speeches that he had given in the House of Commons. He argued that "change means adopting a more aggressive and tactical strategy in Parliament so Canadians are made aware of the NDP and what it stands for on a day-to-day basis" (Blaikie 2003, A18). Although he did not want to focus on policy, he did defend the record of the federal NDP caucus by bringing up issues on which he and the caucus had been decidedly not Blairist: opposition to trade liberalization, defence of public health care, advocacy of democratic reform, and stronger environmental protection (Bill Blaikie interview, 2015).

Jack Layton's leadership campaign argued that the NDP's political marketing needed a greater political market orientation toward voters. The campaign strategy was encapsulated in a pamphlet produced shortly before the convention that asked "before you vote, ask yourself: WHO CAN RE-ENERGIZE OUR PARTY AND ELECT MORE NDP MPS?" (Layton 2003a). His campaign wanted Layton to be seen as an outsider who would bring change to the party so that it could be a more relevant force in Canadian politics (Penner interview 2015; Smith interview, 2014). Similar to Barack Obama's "yes, we can" approach, exactly what such change would entail was intentionally left vague so that NDP members could project their own concerns and desires onto Layton (Ibid.). To this end, the campaign stressed various types of change that Layton would bring to the party. Because he was media savvy, there was the suggestion that he could get the party in the news on a more regular basis to get the attention of voters. His bilingualism and the fact that Layton grew up in Quebec were used to illustrate that he could take on the Bloc Québécois, which appeared to have a lock on the support of left-wing voters in that province. He had governing experience at the municipal level in Toronto, and his presidency of the Federation of Canadian Municipalities meant a new focus on urban affairs and the problems of cities, where most Canadian voters lived. Although policy was a secondary focus of his campaign, Layton did stress that his policies were pragmatic and focused on finding solutions to pressing problems that voters faced every day (Ibid.). His campaign released fifteen detailed policy papers covering several activities of the federal government to illustrate that "Jack has the knowledge and energy to present the practical solutions Canadians want" (Layton 2003b). For the most part, his policies were in line with what Blaikie was proposing and agreeable to most NDPers. However, Layton did pick out three positions to place him slightly to the left of Blaikie: decreasing military spending, taking a pro-Palestinian stance on the Middle East, and favouring the long gun registry (Bill Blaikie interview, 2015).

Layton also stressed that the NDP should have a greater political market orientation toward external stakeholders – especially in terms of reaching out to social movements to partner with the party. His positioning slightly to the left of Blaikie on the three issues mentioned above, and his emphasis on how he would concentrate on coalition building between the party and social movements, helped him to court NPI supporters (Penner interview, 2015). However, Layton was strategic in relation to the NPI. Since Robinson and Davies were supporting him, he was seen to be sympathetic to the NPI even though he never formally endorsed it on its website (Davies interview, 2014; Rebick interview, 2015; Stanford interview, 2015). Ultimately, Layton was able to harness much of the energy of the NPI and attracted several of its supporters to work on his campaign without formally coming out in favour of the group and its principles. Though, it should be noted that Layton did vote in favour of the NPI resolution at the Winnipeg convention held a year prior to the leadership race (Davies interview, 2014).

Layton won a convincing victory on the first ballot at the leadership convention in Toronto with 53.5 percent of the vote.[3] The overwhelming consensus of the interview sample was that Layton won because he represented a credible agent for change. Coming out of the disappointing 2000 election and the divisive internal debates of the 2001 Winnipeg convention, there was a sense in the party that the status quo was no longer working and that something new, fresh, and different in the political marketing of the NDP was needed. In this context, strategies based on emphasizing parliamentarianism or experience within the party worked poorly. Strategies that centred on producing detailed policy, rehashing ideological left/right internal debates, or proposing structural reform of the party were similarly ineffective. Rather, the successful strategy adopted by Layton focused on the need for broad change, even if the definition of such change was left slightly vague.

Conclusion

The results of the 2000 federal election were a shock to the NDP, sending it into a period of intense self-reflection and internal conflict. It was not only McDonough's leadership that was questioned. The organization of the party, its ideological identity, and even what it ultimately wanted to contribute to Canadian politics were hotly debated. The ferment in the party eventually led to a leadership race. Holding a leadership race in the context of a sentiment within the party that major changes were needed for it to remain politically relevant ended up being an opportunity for agents to propose substantial changes to the political marketing of the party.

Layton and his campaign team took advantage of this opportunity. The change that he was proposing was essentially outward looking and oriented toward voters. Layton did not want the NDP to be the conscience of the House of Commons and focus exclusively on providing effective opposition to the government (Penner interview, 2015; Smith interview, 2014). His campaign was relatively uninterested in engaging in debates among party members about ideology and internal governance structures preferring to focus on getting members excited about the party's prospects for future electoral success (Ibid.). Rather, the focus of his campaign was to re-energize the NDP so that average Canadians became aware of how the party proposed to solve the country's problems. The way to achieve this goal was outlined in general terms and connected to the personal traits of Layton. It meant having a leader known to be aggressive in getting media attention, and he would frame NDP policies as practical solutions as opposed to moral imperatives. Since most voters lived in cities, the NDP needed to stress urban issues, and through his experience at the Federation of Canadian Municipalities Layton was well positioned to do this. Similarly, being relevant compared with political competitors necessitated a larger presence for the party in Quebec, and a bilingual leader with roots in that province could only help to bring that about. The NDP also needed a leader with experience in governing and building coalitions with social movements in Canada's largest city.

In many ways, Layton was subtly proposing change in the party's political market orientation. He thought that the party was skewed toward debates about internal governance and ideology. Rather, he was attempting to orient the party toward the needs and desires of voters, understanding the competitive realities of the Canadian political marketplace, and building coalitions with organizations not then associated with the party. To use Ormrod's terms, Layton saw that the party needed more voter, external, and competitor orientation and less member orientation. The disappointing 2000 election results and the internal division that followed primed the NDP to hear and embrace his message. In short, Layton had the right strategy at the right time.

Analyzing the time period 2000–03 in the history of the federal NDP is an important starting point for understanding the broader transformation of the party's political marketing. Coming out of the 2002–03 leadership race, the political marketing of the party that had been built up over several decades meant that the party was still oriented toward members and external stakeholders, and its campaigns were a mix of premodern and modern techniques. Many of the themes of Layton's leadership campaign and even some of the themes of other leadership campaigns and NDProgress became the foundation on which the NDP gradually redefined its political marketing during the rest of the 2000s, leading to moderation and modernization of the party and the "new NDP."

2
The Rise of Party Headquarters: Internal Party Organization

The internal organization of the federal NDP – how the party generated financial resources, governed itself, and organized for elections from 2000 to 2015 – can be broken into three different eras: the era immediately preceding Jack Layton (2000–02), the Layton era (2003–11), and the Tom Mulcair era (2012–15). Within each era, the various internal functions of the party can be examined, such as fundraising, member relations, policy development, building organization in traditionally weak regions, supporting constituency associations, liaising with affiliated unions, maintaining relations between federal and provincial NDP parties, preparing for elections, nominating candidates, and undertaking outreach to extraparliamentary groups.

This chapter argues that, in creating the "new NDP," Layton and his staff took advantage of new party financing rules to alter important aspects of the internal organization of the NDP. The role played by volunteers working in "member-controlled" bodies, staff of provincial parties, and union representatives gradually diminished as increased financial resources from the per-vote subsidy allowed their functions to be taken over by permanent employees at party headquarters in Ottawa. The result was a gradual increase of the power of party headquarters as these professionals led the moderation and modernization of the party by adopting postmodern campaign techniques and an increasing political market orientation toward voters and competitors as opposed to external stakeholders and party members.

Electoral success was key for two reasons in the ability of Layton's political operatives to accomplish the moderation and modernization of the NDP. First, increasing the party's share of the popular vote and the number of seats confirmed the wisdom of moderating and modernizing the party. There was no impetus to reverse the change because operatives could point out that it was working, and the process therefore met with little internal opposition. Second, greater electoral success meant a higher per-vote subsidy.

Increased levels of funding were necessary to pay for the expansion of expensive postmodern campaign techniques such as databases and market intelligence from polls and focus groups. Moreover, higher funding allowed the agents to reproduce themselves – they could hire more professionals at party headquarters dedicated to pushing forward the process of moderation and modernization of the party. In a virtuous circle, electoral success and moderation and modernization reinforced each other.

Therefore, by 2015, the internal organization of the NDP had been thoroughly modernized, and it had become a more moderate party. Because of its electoral success, this transformation took place with a minimal amount of public controversy and complaint by rank-and-file NDP members. However, as a survey of NDP members administered in January 2015 illustrates, there was not complete consensus among members on these changes to the party's political marketing, with some members opposing the diminished power of local activists and other members supporting the greater role of professionals at party headquarters. In particular, members on the right of the NDP ideological spectrum were more likely than members on the left to support the transformation of the political market orientation of the NDP.

The Pre-Layton Era, 2000–02

By 2000, the federal NDP had an entrenched model of internal organization that had been built up since its creation in 1961 (Blakeney interview, 2015; Kerwin interview, 2015). The foundation of its organizational model comprised its federalized structure, its dependence on volunteers and staff on short-term contracts, and its role as "the political arm of labour." These three characteristics formed the key elements of the internal organization of the party immediately preceding Layton's election as leader.

The federalized structure of the NDP went back to the founding in 1932 of the Cooperative Commonwealth Federation as a "federation" of nine different provincial sections. The creation of the federal NDP in 1961 kept this structure– every member of the federal party had to sign up with the relevant provincial party and then automatically became a member of the federal party. The exception was Quebec, where a provincial party at times had not been operative or estranged from the federal NDP. By 2000, members signed up with the New Democratic Party of Canada–Quebec section (NDP-Q) but were officially allowed to adhere to any party at the provincial level.

The result was that the federal NDP in 2000 was organized like a federation of sovereign provincial entities. Indeed, it was almost a feudal system of governance. Each provincial party was responsible for relations with members in its jurisdiction, and the federal party was not even given access to membership lists (Fraser interview, 2014). Often federal electoral district associations (EDAs) were not permanent standing entities. They would form from the executives of provincial riding associations close to a federal election and then disband after the election was over (Ibid.). There was a very distant relationship between the federal party and its members, and federal party activists really came together only for elections and biannual national conventions.

There was a strict rule that any communication by the federal party with its members had to be administered through the provincial parties. Fundraising from NDP members generally took place through direct mailings, events, or phone calls organized by provincial party offices or local provincial riding associations. A certain portion of these fundraising dollars would flow upward to the federal NDP through a complex revenue-sharing formula between the provincial parties and the federal party. The formula was often the subject of intense negotiation between federal party headquarters and provincial party offices. The Federal Council, primarily made up of representatives elected by each provincial section, ultimately had to decide on the final form of revenue sharing. By 2000, as part of revenue-sharing negotiations, the federal party was able to negotiate limited access to provincial membership lists for occasional direct mailings.

Election preparedness was built on this federalized structure. As the election approached, parts of provincial party offices would temporarily become federal election headquarters for their jurisdictions. Provincial party staff would work with federal party staff in Ottawa to organize local advertising and set the strategy for the province (including visits by the federal leader). Subsequently, provincial party staff would work with local activists to ensure that federal EDAs were formed, campaign schools started, candidate searches performed, and short-term campaign staff hired. The role of the federal party in kick-starting election preparedness was limited to phone calls to provincial party staff and local activists to check up on their progress (Fraser interview, 2014). There was no vetting of local candidates by party headquarters, and the nomination process was completely controlled at the local level, with logistical support provided by provincial party staff. Candidates were nominated and election preparation began very close to the start of the federal election campaign.

An important consequence of the federalized structure of the NDP was that the party was organizationally strong where the provincial parties were strong and organizationally weak where the provincial parties were weak. In general, there was a high level of organizational development in provinces where the NDP was a perennial contender for the provincial government (British Columbia, Saskatchewan, and Manitoba), and there was underdevelopment and a lack of resources in provinces where the NDP was uncompetitive in provincial elections (Newfoundland and Labrador, Quebec, and Alberta). Moreover, there was little that party headquarters could do to change this situation since control of fundraising and election preparedness lay in the hands of provincial party offices. It was difficult to shift resources into a region of the country where strong electoral results had yet to occur. In fact, a vicious circle formed where stronger provincial sections demanded and received more resources because of their strength and weaker provincial sections were never given the resources to enhance their organization. Quebec was a perfect example of this dilemma. In 2000, with only 200 members and very weak polling numbers, it received support from party headquarters that amounted to finding enough "paper candidates" to ensure one in each riding (Ducasse interview, 2014; Fraser interview, 2014). Even in this it did not succeed, for the NDP failed to field candidates in two Quebec ridings.

The second element of the NDP's internal organization was its reliance on volunteers and staff on short-term contracts (Fraser interview, 2014). The party relied on volunteers out of necessity – it simply lacked the funding to hire full-time professionals to perform many of the crucial tasks involved in preparing for an election against well-funded opponents (Ibid.). Party headquarters in 2000 had only ten staff stuffed into a small office in Ottawa. Their functions were mostly administrative: keeping financial records, supporting the party's internal governance committees, and preparing for conventions, Federal Council, and federal executive meetings. There was little capacity for research on specific issues, and the party mostly relied on research from the Canadian Labour Congress and other large unions. Polling and holding focus groups were not done regularly, only when elections were imminent. Party headquarters also provided little support to the NDP's parliamentary caucus, and interaction between party headquarters and NDP staff on Parliament Hill was minimal (Ibid.). Indeed, party headquarters played no role in media relations or outreach to stakeholders since these functions were considered to be the responsibilities of MPs, the Leader's Office, and the caucus staff.

Given the limited capacity of party headquarters, many important functions were performed by volunteers or employees working on short-term contracts. At the local level, volunteers in a riding's Election Planning Committee had to accomplish all of the tasks associated with election preparation: searching for a candidate, holding a nomination, fundraising, reaching out to important local stakeholders, mobilizing volunteers to undertake foot and phone canvasses, ordering signs, finding office space, devising a campaign budget, and hiring short-term campaign staff. After the election, further outreach to stakeholders, communication with local NDP members, or storage of voter contact data from the election fell to local volunteers willing to take on these tasks. In the few ridings that the NDP held, the work of local EPCs could persist between elections and be supported by local constituency assistants outside their work hours and MPs themselves. However, in the vast majority of ridings, there was simply no activity by the federal NDP between elections.

Even on the national level, there was a similar dependence on volunteer labour and short-term contracts when it came to election preparations. The primary body for election preparation was the Election Planning Committee, populated by volunteer members of the federal executive, union representatives, short-term campaign staff, the federal secretary, and the assistant federal secretary (Whitehorn 2001, 116). In 2000, the national EPC met once every two weeks in the six months leading up to the election to set overall strategic goals and ensure the hiring of campaign staff to carry out the campaign at the national level. The EPC was subsequently disbanded after the election was over. The only permanent staff of the party closely involved in the high-level preparations of the 2000 campaign were the federal secretary and assistant federal secretary (Hébert-Daly interview, 2014). The rest of the preparations depended on volunteers, representatives employed by unions, and those hired on short-term contracts.

Volunteers and short-term employees of the party similarly drove the crucial task of policy development. In 2000, resolutions passed at the biannual convention were considered the ultimate authority on party policy. Between conventions, a Policy Committee made up of volunteers from the Federal Council refined policy-making processes and suggested new areas for policy development (Moran interview, 2014; Smallman interview, 2014).

Any special policy development initiative, such as the Social Democratic Forum on Canada's Future in 1998–99, was administered by short-term hires. In 2000, the platform was generated by a subcommittee of the national EPC made up of volunteers and staff on short-term contracts. The Federal Council, made up of grassroots activists, subsequently approved the platform just before the election began.

The third element of the federal NDP's internal organization was its affiliation with trade unions. The relationship between the NDP and the labour movement in 2000 can be summed up in the phrase, often used in party circles, that the party was the political arm of labour. The idea was that the NDP was not an independent entity in Canadian politics but an extension of the labour movement within the federal electoral arena. This idea became ingrained in the financial practices of the party. Besides revenue sharing with the provincial sections and rebates for election expenses from Elections Canada in ridings where the party managed to garner 15 percent of the vote, the party relied on direct donations from unions. In fact, the NDP refused to take donations from corporations with over fifty employees since these corporations were essentially the "enemy" of the labour movement and represented interests fundamentally opposed to unions' interests. For their part, unions appeared to view the party as an entity to be mobilized at election time and then demobilized between elections as unions were busy with other matters, such as collective bargaining or pushing governments for the extension of workers' rights. Consequently, unions would ramp up their contributions to the NDP during election years and give it little between elections. The result was that party financing was not stable but punctuated by periodic highs and lows depending on the timing of elections (Jansen and Young 2009, 664).

As the political arm of labour, the NDP was required to have representatives of the labour movement integrated into its internal governance structures. Besides each union having delegates present at the biannual national convention, there were designated places for labour representatives in the party's structures – the Federal Council, the federal executive, and any commission or committee formed between elections to deal with specific tasks or problems. Through its representatives at all levels of the NDP, the labour movement wielded direct control over the internal governance of the party and was always a formidable voting bloc. In fact, labour retained a fair amount of veto power over decisions on the ideology of the party. Indeed,

Alexa McDonough was forced to backtrack on comments that she had made about the desirability of adopting third way social democracy in the lead-up to the 1999 convention because of comments by union leaders.

Beyond ideological guidance, the labour movement was a driving force behind the NDP's election preparations (Fraser interview, 2014). Much of the planning had to wait until the party had an indication of how much money unions would donate for the upcoming campaign. In many ways, election preparedness was a two-step process: unions had to approve their election budgets and strategies, and then the party could begin its preparations. Unions had considerable control over campaigns through the representatives on the EPC and the staff that they seconded to both the national campaign and local campaigns. In addition, union representatives and research from union offices were crucial in the development of election platforms.

Overall, the federal NDP in 2000–02 had a political market orientation primarily toward party members and the labour movement as its key external stakeholder. Party headquarters was essentially constituted to support internal governance by party members. The biannual convention was the ultimate source of party policy, and further policy development was largely driven by volunteer members. Importantly, the election platform had to be approved by the Federal Council immediately preceding the election. At the local level and even the national level, volunteer party members played crucial roles in developing and implementing campaign strategies. Members therefore became closely involved in discerning what targeted voters desired and in framing strategies to meet those desires. The labour movement played a similarly important role. It was not a "hands-off" funder of the NDP. Along with providing financial support, labour representatives exercised direct control over small-scale governance decisions on the internal organization of the party, the overall goals of election campaigns, the ideological direction of the party, the research that the party received, and day-to-day preparations in the lead-up to the writ being dropped. The independence of the NDP from the labour movement was indeed limited as the moniker "the political arm of labour" implied.

Along with a political orientation toward members and the labour movement, the federal NDP's campaigning displayed mostly premodern and modern characteristics. Typical of premodern campaigning, the party's preparations were short term and ad hoc, with staff being hired and strategies being devised only months before the election. No consideration was given to running pre-election advertising or advertising between elections (Fraser interview, 2014). There was a premodern focus on NDP candidates as representatives of local ridings and members of the leader's "team." Moreover, there was a fair degree of decentralization, local volunteers and local part-time staff being primarily responsible for campaign structure at the riding level. In congruence with modern campaigning, telephone opinion polls and focus groups were used in the lead-up to the election, and data were stored between elections at the local level. In the war room in party headquarters, the focus was generally on the leader's tour and the sound bites on national and local television news that it generated.

The Layton Era, 2003–11

The beginning of the Layton era coincided with two developments that had the potential to create a revolution in the political marketing of the federal NDP: the ferment in the party after the disappointing results of the 2000 election and the creation of new party financing rules. The outcome of the 2000 election created consensus within the party that thorough change was needed for its renewal. Various strategies for renewal were suggested by different agents, from reform of the party's internal governing structures, to refounding the party to become more formally linked to social movements, to moving party ideology sharply to the left. During the leadership race, Jack Layton was able to position himself as the "candidate of change" without precisely outlining what change would entail other than that the NDP would become a relevant political force under his guidance. In other words, he was able to harness the desire for change without getting caught up in specific proposals. Rather, Layton personified the type of change that he envisioned by being media savvy, emphasizing practical solutions, having roots in Quebec, building coalitions, stressing urban issues, and having experience governing at the municipal level. In essence, he was the personification of how the political market orientation of the party needed to shift toward voters, competitors, and external stakeholders and away from members.

Although the ferment in the party following the 2000 election and Layton's winning the leadership of the party in 2003 created an expectation for change, the real opportunity for Layton and his team to enact change came with new party financing rules on January 1, 2004. The new rules had wide-ranging and immediate consequences for the NDP. However, the repercussions of the new rules were not readily apparent to political operatives, and there was much uncertainty about and debate on how best to comply with the new legislation (Cox interview, 2015). Although the operatives might not have realized it at the time, a combination of the ferment in the 2000–03 time period and the changes to party financing rules opened up the opportunity for the gradual breaking down of the three key elements of the NDP's internal organization described above. The party gradually brought itself in line with the practices of the two other major political parties during the latter 2000s. The NDP became a full participant in what Flanagan (2012, 135) suggestively calls the "political arms race," by which he means how a string of minority federal governments from 2004 to 2011 and high revenues from per-vote subsidies pushed the three major federal parties into permanent campaigning mode by engaging new innovations to their fundraising, voter contact, and paid advertising on a year-round basis. Although Flanagan correctly points out that the Conservative Party was the key innovator in this regard, the analysis below shows that the NDP followed their lead in order to compete with the major parties during federal elections.

First, the common understanding of the NDP as the political arm of labour was questioned. The new rules prohibited in-kind and monetary donations directly to the party from unions and corporations (Jansen and Young 2009). Initially, unions could give up to $1,000 annually to local candidates or local EDAs with careful coordination, but this practice was banned in 2006. The new rules also ended the seconding of union employees to local and national NDP campaigns. To be active in these campaigns, union employees would be forced to volunteer outside their working hours or to take vacation time. Union influence on local NDP nomination contests and NDP leadership races was similarly affected. The limit of $1,100 was placed on union donations to a candidate in a nomination race or to a candidate in the leadership race. Moreover, all monetary or in-kind donations over $200 made by unions to candidates in leadership or nomination races now had to be publicly disclosed, and spending limits were placed on these types of races. Unions also had to register as "third parties" in order to do any public advertising promoting or opposing a registered political party or any issue associated with a registered political party during an election campaign. The spending of unions in this regard was subject to strict limits ($183,300 nationally and $3,666 in an electoral district), and it had to be publicly disclosed. However, no spending limit was placed on communications between unions and their members, even if such communications were explicitly partisan. The elimination of corporate donations had little direct effect on the NDP since it had refused all donations from corporations with more than fifty employees and only received limited donations from small businesses. Similarly, the imposition of a cap of $5,000 (reduced to $1,000 in 2006) on individual donations did not have a drastic effect on the party since it had always relied on donations of small amounts of money from a large number of individuals. The Liberals, however, were hurt badly by the banning of corporate donations since they had not built up a base of grassroots donors giving small amounts like the Conservatives and New Democrats had (Flanagan 2012, 144).

As it turned out, the changes in party financing laws coincided with a time when the relationship between the labour movement and the party was already in considerable flux. The 2000 election had made it painfully obvious that unions were not able to deliver a large number of votes to the federal NDP (especially in Ontario). Consequently, NDProgess suggested that the labour movement's power in the party should be reduced, whereas the NPI wanted to reach out to social movements in order to supplement the work that unions were doing within the Canadian left. The move toward OMOV in the 2002–03 leadership race meant that the labour movement enjoyed less of a veto over the result than it had in the past. The NDP was gradually seeing the labour movement in a different light and seeking a larger degree of independence from unions. For its part, the labour movement was also re-evaluating its position vis-à-vis the NDP. Under Hargrove, the Canadian Auto Workers union was exasperated with what it perceived as a right-wing drift of the party under McDonough's leadership, and it considered advocating strategic voting. Other unions also questioned the results that a small federal NDP caucus could deliver, and they struggled to figure out how to convince their members to support the NDP at election time (Stanford interview, 2014). Adding to the flux within the party-labour relationship, new political actors arrived on the scene. Layton brought with him a whole new team of political operatives, many of whom were not directly connected to the union movement. In the Canadian Labour Congress, President Bob White and long-serving Political Action Director Pat Kerwin retired and were replaced by Ken Georgetti and Danny Mallett, respectively.

So, when the financial and organizational dependence of the NDP on the labour movement was eliminated by the new party financing rules, these new actors were able to reorganize the labour-party relationship. The NDP was no longer the appendage of labour in the House of Commons and during elections. Rather, the party was an independent equal of the labour movement. Its organizing and strategizing took place in consultation with labour, but labour did not exercise direct control as in the past. For its part, labour became an independent political force that intervened in elections and lobbied on Parliament Hill on its own terms. It consulted the NDP on how it should structure its political action, but it was not as integrated with that of the NDP as it had been. In short, the relationship between the party and labour became more about consultation and independence and less about integration and control. This change in the party-labour relationship, brought about by the banning of union donations, also meant that Layton's political operatives were free to pursue the moderation and modernization of the party without any interference from the labour movement. In addition, from the perspective of branding, the old charge that the party was in the "back pocket of labour" and therefore looked out only for the interests of unions no longer held (McGrane 2011, 79).

The first step in the growing independence of the NDP from labour was the official severing of financial ties symbolized by a final round of large donations to the party in late 2003. The party used the money from those donations to buy the three-storey building in downtown Ottawa in which party headquarters was located (Hébert-Daly interview, 2014; McGrath interview, 2014). The building became invaluable as a source of revenue since the party could rent out the space that it was not using and as collateral to secure loans at election time.

At the same time, the NDP was forced to hire its own election organizers as opposed to relying on staff seconded from unions. Ultimately, the party acquired more independence in hiring election staff. These workers reported only to party headquarters since their salaries were paid by the party, and there was no expectation that they would return to their union employers following the election. Since labour no longer provided donations or seconded personnel, it became more peripheral to the election preparations of the party (Fraser interview, 2014). For instance, the input of labour on platform development was solicited, but it began to exercise less control over the final version of the platform than in the past (Mallett interview, 2014). Many interviewees stressed how there continued to be much informal consultation between Layton and labour leaders as well as between union staff and party staff in Ottawa (Fraser interview, 2014; Hébert-Daly interview, 2014; Mallett interview, 2014; McGrath interview, 2014). However, the integration of union staff and the merging of labour's political action strategies into the NDP's campaign preparations and structures were greatly reduced.

Within the federal NDP's internal governance structures, two important changes related to labour's role in the party were also made. First, the changes to party financing rules were used as one of the justifications for moving to a pure OMOV leadership selection process and for eliminating the provision for 25 percent of the vote being allotted to labour delegates. It was argued that the labour movement should not receive a special bloc of votes if it was not financially supporting the party (Hébert-Daly interview, 2014). Second, the level of representation of unions in the NDP had been determined traditionally by the size of a union's membership. This tradition reflected the idea that all members of a union had collectively decided to affiliate with the party and therefore should be considered "affiliated members" (Whitehorn 1992, 105–6). Indeed, affiliated unions would forward a percentage of members' dues to the party as a monthly sum. So a union member could be an NDP member in some sense even if she or he was unaware of this fact and did not even vote for the party. This practice of monthly forwarding a percentage of members' dues to the NDP was prohibited under the new party financing rules. As of 2006, the representation of affiliated unions at NDP conventions and on its Federal Council became determined by how many members of the union actually signed NDP membership cards and paid their own membership dues. Besides these two alterations, unions remained affiliated with the party, and the positions devoted to labour representatives in the party's structures were always filled (McGrath interview, 2014).

Labour itself was eager to become more independent and alter its political strategies. Layton became leader of the NDP as the CLC re-evaluated its political strategies, resulting in a ten-year plan entitled *Capacity Building for Change* released in 2005 (Mallett interview, 2014). The document made it clear that the new party financing rules provided "an opportunity for unions to develop new tactics and strategies" and referred to "post–Bill C-24 realities" (Canadian Labour Congress 2005, 6, 7). The centrepiece of the plan was the Better Choices advertising campaign that the CLC ran in the lead-up to federal elections from 2004 to 2011. Unlike CLC campaigns in the past, the CLC did not urge its members to vote for the NDP. Rather, it urged them to vote based on issues (e.g., pensions or health care) that its polling showed would generally lead members to vote for the NDP (Mallett interview, 2014). Indeed, there was a stress on speaking to members on a continuous basis to increase their political engagement and to shape how they thought about politics (Canadian Labour Congress 2005, 6). In tandem with the Better Choices campaign, the CLC no longer let the NDP caucus be its lobbying force on Parliament Hill and decided to lobby the government and politicians from other opposition parties on its own. The CLC also began to focus on municipal politics, in which the NDP had no official presence.

In addition to the realities imposed by the new party financing rules, alterations in the CLC's political strategy were motivated by differences among the constituent unions. Some unions within the CLC wanted complete independence from the NDP. Notably, the CAW was angered that the NDP caucus decided to bring down the Liberal minority government in 2005, for it believed that immediate gains for labour could have been made if the government had been allowed to continue, and there were fears about opening the door to a Harper-led government (Stanford interview, 2015). The result was that the CAW began to advocate strategic voting for Liberal candidates in the 2006 election in ridings where the NDP did not have a chance of winning and even went as far as to have Paul Martin come to its convention during the campaign to emphasize its new stance (Savage 2012). After the Ontario NDP revoked the membership of CAW President Buzz Hargrove, the union voted to disaffiliate with the NDP in April 2006 because of the need for an "independent and flexible approach" by which the union's political interventions would be made in its own name as opposed to being mediated through a political party (Stanford 2006). Unions such as the Steelworkers and UFCW maintained a more traditional view of the party-union relationship and continued to urge their members to vote for the NDP and gave their staff vacation time to campaign for the party (Savage 2012; Stanford interview, 2015).

For Layton's team, a restructuring of the party's relationship with unions was intended to take place in concert with a new emphasis on reaching out to social movements, which would increase the external political market orientation of the NDP. Several interviewees noted that there was a genuine willingness to work more closely with social movements early in Layton's leadership inspired by the ideas of the NPI and Layton's pledge during the leadership race to build coalitions with these movements (Bélanger interview, 2014; Bill Blaikie interview, 2015; Davies interview, 2014; Giambrone interview, 2014; Hartmann interview, 2015; Dick Proctor interview, 2015). After his election as leader, Layton hired Franz Hartmann as a permanent full-time employee working out of the Leader's Office to help connect the party with social movements. Hartmann's primary innovation was so-called issues caucuses made up of NDP MPs, representatives of unions, and social movement leaders to advise the party on specific issues (Hartmann interview, 2015). Each NDP MP was assigned to one or two of these issue caucuses. The conceptual framework was that the caucus would create a proposal that could be endorsed by the social movements and the unions involved and then be introduced as NDP policy during an election campaign or as a bill in the House of Commons. The only issue caucus that actually functioned in this manner was the green transportation caucus (Ibid.). Indeed, the 2004 NDP platform touted "Canada's first green car industrial strategy," endorsed by both Greenpeace and the CAW (NDP 2004, 22). The other issue caucuses failed to produce anything concrete, and they were discontinued following the 2004 election. Hartmann left his position in the Leader's Office in 2006. Similarly, there were extensive discussions early in Layton's leadership on giving social movements seats on the Federal Council. Nothing came of these discussions since few social movements indicated their willingness to move in this direction, and there were considerable challenges in defining the amount of power that social movement representatives would hold in relation to labour and provincial party representatives (Giambrone interview, 2014).

Ultimately, formal links between the federal NDP and social movements proved to be unworkable, and the increase in external political market orientation never materialized. Interviewees pointed to a variety of reasons why these attempts during the first half of the 2000s to create formal links failed. As in a romantic relationship, there were different interpretations of the failure, whether the fault of the social movements, the fault of the party, or nobody's fault in that it was simply the result of a political situation that prevented closer ties from being formed. A common theme among interviewees was that social movements themselves were unwilling formally to affiliate with or endorse the NDP. Brad Lavigne argued that social movements were inclined to work with and support the Liberals, usually either in power or the official opposition (Lavigne interview, 2014). Similarly, Lorne Nystrom noted that social movements wanted to lobby the government on specific issues, and their lack of interest in building electoral machines dampened their enthusiasm for linking with the NDP (Nystrom interview, 2014). Several interviewees pointed out that social movements could not endorse the NDP because they are required to be nonpartisan in order to work with governments of varying political stripes after elections, respect the diverse political views of their members, and maintain their charitable status (Giambrone interview, 2014; Hébert-Daly interview, 2014; Nash interview, 2014; Stoffer interview, 2014). Hartmann argued that Layton's initiatives to move the party closer to social movements were also hampered by MPs who were unconvinced that the strategy would help their chances of re-election; by the string of minority governments that drew the attention of party staff to election preparation as opposed to outreach to social movements; by caucus staff who focused exclusively on the theatrics of Question Period and media relations; and by the lack of permanent federal EDAs in the early 2000s that could link with social movements at the local level (Hartmann interview, 2015). Hartmann attempted to argue for the long-term benefits of building alliances with social movements in a political context in which short-term considerations were viewed as much more important (Ibid.).

By the second half of the 2000s, there was a realization within the NDP that official affiliations and formalized linkages between the party and social movements were simply not going to happen (McGrath interview, 2014; Nash interview, 2014). A new model was adopted with the creation of a stakeholder relations unit at party headquarters. The unit was dedicated to building informal relationships with social movements in order to consult them on party policy and potentially have them endorse specific policy positions adopted by the NDP (Hébert-Daly interview, 2014; McGrath interview, 2014; Nash interview, 2014). Coming out of this relationship building, leaders of social movements often did help out during election campaigns as individuals as opposed to representatives of their organizations, though explicit endorsements of the NDP's positions by social movements remained elusive (Topp interview, 2015). Thus, the NDP did have some external political market orientation through these informal relationships with social movements, but the strong links envisioned by Layton, Hartmann, and the NPI never developed.

The new campaign financing rules created the need to revamp structures related to the federalized nature of the party. Layton himself, along with the new staff whom he brought into the party, was keen to decrease the interdependence of the federal party and the provincial wings, and they saw the changes to the party financing laws as an opportunity to pursue this project (Cox interview, 2015). In particular, Layton and his staff desired unfettered access to membership lists, the ability to use fundraising from the provincial parties in whatever manner they saw fit, and the capacity to run national campaigns not dependent on collaboration with the provincial offices

(Ibid.). They thought that these offices were naturally inclined to put provincial, as opposed to federal, NDP interests first (Ibid.).

As it turned out, the independence of the federal NDP from its provincial wings was a key precondition that allowed Layton's team of operatives to pursue their project of modernization through the adoption of postmodern campaigning techniques. The new party financing rules prohibited transfers of money between provincial and federal sections of the same party (Pilon, Ross, and Savage 2011). Furthermore, any organizational aid given by the provincial section of the NDP to the federal party was considered an in-kind contribution and subjected to a $1,000 annual limit. The federal NDP depended on its provincial sections to raise money from individual NDP members, which was then transferred to the federal party through complex revenue-sharing arrangements. The federal party's election campaigns were also dependent on the staff and infrastructure provided by the headquarters of provincial parties.

These decades-old practices were reconfigured in light of the new party financing rules. Since revenue-sharing arrangements between the federal and provincial parties were rendered illegal, initially they were replaced with service contracts that maintained limits on the federal party's access to membership lists and the number of times that the federal party could contact NDP members. However, Layton's staff and the president of the federal party aggressively pushed for a greater disentanglement. After a period of tension, the federal party eventually succeeded in negotiating a large degree of financial separation from its provincial wings as well as unrestricted access to NDP membership lists (McGrath interview, 2014). This access allowed the federal party to centralize its fundraising operations to take advantage of the economies of scale and greater sophistication afforded by professional fundraising firms. The party could now adopt the postmodern campaign practice of aggressive year-round fundraising that ramped up in intensity as an election approached. At the same time, the federal NDP began to hire its own organizers in each province because any organizing that provincial party staff did on behalf of the federal party would be deemed an in-kind donation under the new rules. Although there could be informal cooperation between federal and provincial staff, election preparations by federal organizers were directed solely by party headquarters in Ottawa. Indeed, party headquarters increased its score on the Campaign Professionalization Index from 6 out of 30 in 2004 to 27 out of 30 in 2008 (Rebecca Blaikie interview, 2014; Lavigne interview, 2014).[1]

The new party financing rules also forced the creation of permanent federal NDP EDAs. Before 2004, formal financial accounting was required only of the revenues and expenditures of the campaigns of federal NDP candidates during the writ period. There was no regulation of the spending and revenue of federal EDAs between elections. These rules allowed a situation in which a number of NDP provincial riding associations could unite to form temporarily a federal EDA close to an election to raise the funding necessary for the upcoming campaign. Once the writ was dropped, any funds raised would be transferred to the candidate's campaign and be administered by the candidate's official agent. After the election, the federal EDA essentially became dormant, with any remaining funds or rebates placed into a savings account for the next election watched over by a local volunteer, likely a member of a provincial riding association. The new rules required the formal and legal registration of federal EDAs for each riding in Canada where the NDP intended to present a candidate (Coletto and Eagles 2011, 108). These EDAs were then required to report regularly on their financial assets and expenditures between elections to Elections Canada.

Gradually, this new financial structure created the permanent institutionalization of federal NDP EDAs separate from provincial riding associations. Primary tasks of federal organizers hired by party headquarters were to sustain the existence of permanent federal NDP EDAs and ensure that they regularly fundraised, held meetings, and proactively recruited candidates (McGrath interview, 2014). This situation created greater levels of commitment among and continuous activity by local volunteers, ensuring that the federal NDP was better prepared for elections than in the past. Indeed, during the 2000s, when minority Parliaments meant that an election could be called at any time, it was necessary for professionals employed by the federal NDP to ensure that local EDAs were constantly ready to be thrust into an election campaign. Party headquarters in Ottawa became dedicated to building capacity at the local level. For instance, in the lead-up to the 2011 federal election, the central party ran a program that matched fifty cents of every dollar raised by EDAs (McGrane 2011, 97). The emphasis of party headquarters on ensuring that local organizations of volunteers were constantly preparing themselves for the next campaign was similar to that of the new Conservative Party of Canada (CPC), downplaying the policy-making role of members that had developed under the Reform Party and concentrating on "building grassroots teams for signage, door-knocking, and phone-banking" (Flanagan 2013, 91).

FIGURE 2.1

Revenue of the federal NDP, 2001–12

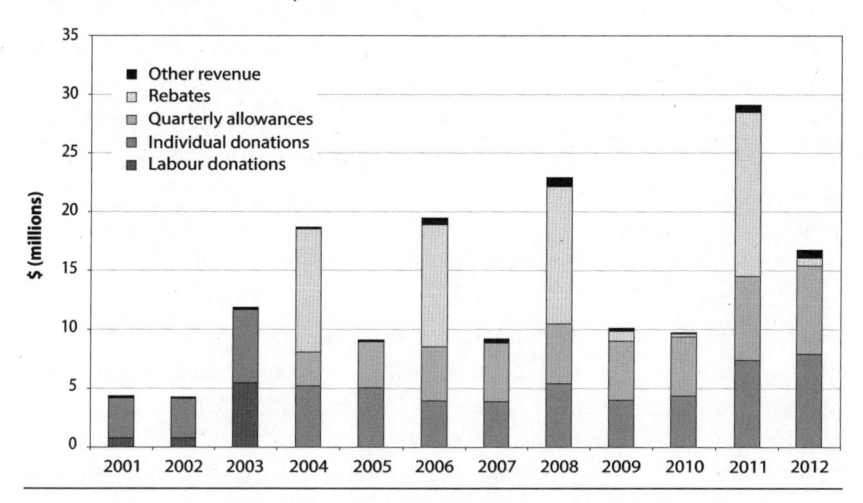

[Figure 2.1: Stacked bar chart showing revenue of the federal NDP from 2001 to 2012, in $ millions. Categories include: Other revenue, Rebates, Quarterly allowances, Individual donations, Labour donations.]

SOURCE: Audited financial reports of the federal NDP submitted to Elections Canada (2001–12).

Adam Giambrone had promised professionalization – a key element of postmodern campaigning – of the federal NDP during his campaign for party president. The money that began to flow directly to the party gave Layton, Giambrone, and new party staff the opportunity to expand the operations of party headquarters and make its permanent staff responsible for various functions of the party that had been performed by local volunteers or employees on short-term contracts. In particular, the new legislation guaranteed that a steady stream of income would flow to the national party as a quarterly allowance based on the number of votes that the NDP received in the previous federal election. On top of this allowance, more public funding came to the national party because of a much higher postelection rebate (50 percent as opposed to 22.5 percent) and since more types of expenses, such as polling, were now eligible for reimbursement. The tax credit for political contributions was also increased, which encouraged higher levels of individual donations at both local and national levels.

In Figure 2.1, we can see the effect that the new party financing rules had on NDP revenue.

Unfortunately, 2000 could not be used as a starting point for this figure since reporting requirements were changed in 2001, making comparisons with previous periods difficult (Fortin interview, 2015). Nonetheless, we can see the favourable effect of the party financing reforms using the audited reports produced by the party from 2001 to 2012. The total revenue of the party hovered around $4 million in 2001 and 2002, nonelection years. In the nonelection years after the party financing rules were implemented (i.e., 2005, 2007, 2009, and 2010), the total revenue of the party was from $9 million to $10 million. For the most part, this improved financial performance was attributable to rising quarterly allowances from 2004 to 2012. By 2012, a nonelection year, quarterly allowances brought in $7.4 million or 44 percent of NDP revenue. Interestingly, the fundraising performance of the party did not dramatically improve during most of this period. We can see that the money obtained from individual donations in 2001 and 2002 was not that different from that in the later 2000s, once inflation is taken into account. Indeed, the work of Jansen and Young (2011, 91) illustrates that, in constant dollars, the NDP was fundraising slightly less from individuals in the late 2000s compared with the late 1990s. The primary reason for this underwhelming performance was that, while money from the quarterly allowances allowed the federal NDP to improve its fundraising capabilities by hiring professional fundraising firms, it still had limited access to provincial membership lists (McGrath interview, 2014). In fact, the federal NDP's funds raised from individuals did not increase dramatically until 2011 when agreements with provincial sections ceased to limit the number of times that the federal NDP could make fundraising appeals to its members. The party's electoral success in that breakthrough election encouraged an increase in the number of donors and size of donations (Rotman interview, 2015).

Figure 2.1 shows that the elimination of union donations was more than offset by a generous public funding regime. We should recall that 2003 was an anomaly since unions were giving their final donations to the party to purchase the building in which party headquarters was located. We can see that union donations were under $1 million in 2001 and 2002, whereas quarterly allowances in later years were routinely from $3 million to $5 million. Evidently, the level of quarterly allowances rose along with the party's popular vote, so electoral success was a key factor in increasing the funding available to political operatives at party headquarters. In many ways, the reliance of the NDP on short-term contract employees had been imposed on it because unions gave large sums in election years and small sums in nonelection years. It is crucial to understand that consistent cash flow provided by higher quarterly allowances allowed the NDP to move away from short-term contracts and to hire permanent employees at party headquarters and as field organizers around the country. Also, since the party had more electoral success, its quarterly allowances increased, and it brought aboard even more full-time employees.

Professionalization of the NDP – paid partly by the new quarterly allowances – had dramatic effects on the internal organization of the party since several functions were no longer performed by volunteers and short-term contract employees. For the 2000 election, nominations were almost entirely the purview of local riding associations, and the role of party headquarters was limited to phoning local activists to implore them to move faster to get their candidates nominated (Fraser interview, 2014). The first step taken that enlarged the role of party headquarters in local nominations was the adoption of an affirmative action policy for federal NDP candidate recruitment during the 1990s (Cross 2004, 70–71). The crux of this policy was that every nomination race had to include at least one affirmative action candidate (i.e., women, visible minorities, Aboriginals, youth, persons with disabilities, and gays and lesbians) before party headquarters would sanction a nomination. EDAs could apply for an exemption to this rule if they could prove to party headquarters that they had made considerable efforts to recruit an affirmative action candidate (Peel interview, 2015).

Following this initial intrusion into local nomination processes, the professionals at party headquarters began to institute much greater control over the nomination of candidates during the 2000s. Although local volunteers continued to approach potential candidates, a full-time candidate search coordinator was hired at party headquarters who routinely called on MPs, regional organizers, and even Layton to recruit candidates. For the 2004, 2006, and 2008 elections, a process was put in place by which candidates were required to disclose potentially embarrassing facets of their personal lives in order for the party to prepare a response (Peel interview, 2015). After past digressions of certain NDP candidates made national news during the 2008 election, the party put in place a strict vetting process that could disallow candidacies that the leader, advised by staff at party headquarters, believed could be problematic during an election campaign (Lavigne interview, 2014).[2] The new system did not rely just on disclosure. Party headquarters started to do "opposition research" on potential candidates to uncover embarrassing past behaviour (Peel interview, 2015). Because of the complexity of nomination rules introduced as part of the new party financing rules in 2004, employees at party headquarters became heavily involved in ensuring rule compliance by candidates in nomination races to guard against embarrassing media stories about the NDP not correctly following the rules. The institution of a rigorous vetting process, affirmative action guidelines, and rule compliance exercises necessitated that party headquarters be given authority over the date of the nomination convention and therefore the cut-off date for new members to be eligible to vote. In short, party headquarters came to play a dominant role in the nomination process and thus created the professionalization of nominations and decreased their control by rank-and-file local members.

How federal NDP platforms were traditionally developed reflected the member political market orientation of the party. Resolutions passed by members at biannual conventions were regarded as the primary means of policy development and intended to be the basis of election platforms (Whitehorn 1992, 112–13). Resolutions that did not make it to the floor of the convention were referred to the Federal Council for passage or rejection. Following this model, the council had a developed policy capacity in the early 2000s (Bhattacharya interview, 2015; Moran interview, 2014; Smallman interview, 2014). Indeed, staff hired on short-term contracts developed the first drafts of the 2000 and 2004 election platforms, and it was the task of volunteers who were members of the national Election Planning Committee to review those platforms and make suggestions (Smallman interview, 2014). The Federal Council subsequently approved these platforms just prior to these elections being called. The volunteers and short-term staff had limited access to market intelligence when developing these platforms. During this period, market intelligence in the NDP was generally used to understand how to "sell" the platform after it had been created rather than to develop the platform.

There was a feeling among the political operatives involved in the 2004 election that this method of policy development generated an unwieldy and unhelpful platform (Penner interview, 2015; Topp interview, 2015). Poor judgment by senior campaign staff and reliance on volunteers on the EPC who supervised staff on short-term contracts resulted in numerous spending commitments and multiple revenue generation mechanisms. During the campaign, Layton was constantly thrown off message and forced to defend the details of his platform, such as the party's proposal for an inheritance tax (Ibid.).

For subsequent elections, the platform was drafted by the policy department at party headquarters using market intelligence such as polling and focus groups as well as consultations with MPs and union leaders (McGrath interview, 2014; Nash interview, 2014). The policy department also consulted with officials in the Manitoba and Nova Scotia NDP governments in search of practical policy ideas (McGrane 2011, 94). Using market intelligence as the starting point of platform development reflected a greater political market orientation toward voters. It meant that the NDP was more in tune with the needs and wants of targeted voters, that its platform was less likely to contain controversial elements, and that its platform document could be used to generate an effective frame for the entire campaign (Lavigne interview, 2014; Topp interview, 2015). The language of the platform was even tested to ensure that it attracted, rather than repelled, voters hesitating between the Liberals and the New Democrats. In particular, the term "middle class" resonated with these voters as opposed to the term "working families" (Anderson interview, 2014). Conducting opposition research also took on a higher priority. This research was saved and used at strategically opportune times to destabilize the campaigns of other parties in the 2008 and 2011 elections. There was also research on political opinion in certain ethnic communities (e.g., Chinese, Sikh, and Portuguese), leading to targeted narrowcasting within media outlets that served these communities (Ibid.). In addition, Layton's behaviour, wardrobe, and image were thoroughly researched in the lead-up to elections (Capstick interview, 2015), and a "zinger team" was created to prepare for the 2011 debates to have Layton concentrate less on reciting policies and more on generating memorable sound bites (Topp interview, 2015). Indeed, his celebrated line about Ignatieff's poor attendance in the House of Commons was planned and tested in focus groups (Anderson interview, 2014).[3]

At the same time that the developmental process of the platform was altered, the Federal Council passed a motion to make the federal executive the permanent EPC in order to respond to the reality of minority Parliaments, when elections could be called at any time (McGrane 2011, 93). The federal executive, acting as the permanent EPC, would then receive reports from staff at party headquarters on election preparations at their regularly scheduled meetings and be consulted on platform development (McGrath interview, 2014; Nash interview, 2014). Within this new structure, the national EPC took on a strategic rather than an operational role in election preparations (Topp interview, 2015). For instance, final approval of the platform, as prepared by professionals at party headquarters, came to rest with Layton himself (as opposed to the Federal Council or the national EPC), in line with the presidentialization inherent in postmodern campaigning. Giving Layton final approval of the platform illustrated the extent to which the NDP moulded itself to its leader's image following the 2002–03 OMOV leadership selection.

The resolutions process and formal policy-making function of biannual federal NDP conventions and the Federal Council remained intact during this period. However, certain changes were introduced. Before a resolution could reach the plenary of the convention floor, it had to pass through a smaller session closed to the media at which a group of delegates debated, amended, and ultimately approved or rejected it (Morin interview, 2014). Several of these breakout sessions were held at the same time, and delegates had to choose which session to attend. This new model resulted in more polished resolutions reaching the convention floor and helped to prevent controversial resolutions from reaching the plenary session, at which the media could report on divisive debates. At the 1995 federal NDP convention, a sunset clause was introduced that eliminated a resolution as party policy after eight years unless convention delegates brought it back and passed it again. Coincidentally, the convention at which Layton became leader corresponded with elimination of the entire NDP policy manual, which contained a number of older resolutions that could have been considered radically left wing (Bhattacharya interview, 2015). Prior to Layton, there was no publicly available federal policy manual since resolutions were filed at party headquarters. In response to this situation, staff in the Leader's Office used the elimination of approximately forty years of resolutions to craft a policy manual based on the resolutions passed at the most recent conventions (Ibid.). The result was a completely new policy manual broken into appropriate sections that outlined the various policies on which New Democrats agreed. The most recent version was made available for download from the internet, and the radically left-wing resolutions of the early party that could surprise voters disappeared – again evidence of greater political market orientation toward voters.

The time devoted to resolutions and policy discussions at the Federal Council and the party's biannual conventions was reduced. There was more focus on providing training opportunities for party activists present and on generating reports by senior party staff on election readiness (McGrath interview, 2014; Nash interview, 2015). Moreover, staff studied the conventions of American and British political parties (Lavigne 2013, 132). As a result, staff attempted to theme conventions with messages that they hoped would be transferred to voters through the media. Such theming involved slogans prominently displayed in the convention halls and keynote speakers who reinforced the party's messaging (Giambrone interview, 2014).

Interestingly, methods of voter contact and activist training did not alter drastically during the Layton era. The NDP continued to rely on paid and volunteer foot canvassers at the local level combined with centrally located phone banks. These canvassing methods contacted as many voters in a riding as possible to identify potential supporters to be contacted by local campaigns to come out to vote on election day. Activist training remained centred on locally run "campaign schools" just before an election at which volunteers were taught the basics of campaigning by other volunteers or the local federal organizer (Fraser interview, 2014). However, the Federal Council and conventions did become opportunities for more advanced activist training (McGrath interview, 2015). Another innovation was the introduction of a computerized database called NDPVote (Fraser interview, 2014). It was essentially a software program that allowed each constituency to build its own voter contact database. Data collection remained localized, but the templates for canvass sheets and the conventions for gathering data were standardized across the party. In this respect, the New Democrats were behind the Conservatives, who had eliminated localized databases in favour of a single national database – the Constituency Information Management System – for the 2004 election (Flanagan 2009, 189–91).

As mentioned, there was a tendency in the pre-Layton NDP to focus resources on traditionally strong regions for the party. This inclination was reinforced by control of fundraising and election preparations being in the hands of provincial party offices, and it was difficult to direct resources to aspirational regions, as suggested by Ducasse during his leadership campaign. Unions were also keen to see their contributions invested in regions where MPs could be elected. However, the new party financing rules created an opportunity to break away from traditional practices. Consistent cash flow provided by quarterly allowances replaced union funding and allowed party headquarters to make long-term investments that would not immediately yield MPs. Also, disentanglement of the federal and provincial parties in the wake of changes to party financing rules led to a pool of federally controlled paid organizers that could be deployed however headquarters saw fit.

One aspirational region in which the NDP invested money from its quarterly allowances was Quebec. The 2004 federal election in Quebec was run on the traditional model, with the Quebec section of the federal party hiring an organizer about a year prior to the election. However, Layton did spend some time in Quebec prior to the election, and there were fewer paper candidates and even a call centre in Montreal for voter contact in French (Bussières interview, 2015). Francophone NDP members who had left the party over McDonough's support for the Clarity Bill also returned to the fold and were heartened by Layton's criticism of the bill during a campaign stop in the face of public negative reaction from caucus colleagues such as Bill Blaikie (Ducasse interview, 2014). The efforts appeared to pay some dividends, for the NDP's share of the popular vote in Quebec inched upward from 1.8 percent in 2000 to 4.6 percent in 2004.

Following that election, Layton and the political operatives at party headquarters were able to convince a skeptical volunteer federal executive to approve plans to invest more resources in Quebec (Rebecca Blaikie interview, 2014). Layton and his team argued that the NDP needed a base of Quebec seats if it was ever to be seen as a serious contender to form the government (Giambrone interview, 2014; Hébert-Daly interview, 2014; McGrath interview, 2014). There was also the potential for an NDP breakthrough in Quebec because voters there held social democratic values, and the new per-vote subsidy meant that increased support in Quebec would translate into higher revenue for the NDP even if no MP was elected there (Ibid.). Rebecca Blaikie, the daughter of Manitoba MP Bill Blaikie, who had gone to university in Quebec and run against Prime Minister Paul Martin in 2004 in a Quebec riding, was hired on a permanent basis as director of the Quebec section of the party, and her staff complement was gradually ramped up to five full-time employees. Control of the budget for organizing in Quebec was transferred to party headquarters in Ottawa, and the volunteer executive of the Quebec section was given a budget only to hold meetings (Bussières interview, 2015).

Over the next six years, party headquarters gave Blaikie (replaced by Nicolas-Dominic Audet in 2008) and her team of professionals "free rein" to build a postmodern campaign infrastructure in Quebec and to create a presence for the party within the province (Rebecca Blaikie interview, 2014). A primary task of these professional political operatives was to make unsolicited phone calls to francophone opinion makers such as journalists, artists, leaders of social movements, and environmentalists to invite them to meet with Layton or NDP staff. The initial efforts focused on making a positive impression on these opinion makers to increase their awareness of the party as opposed to asking them to volunteer on NDP campaigns. The campaign infrastructure built up during this time was mostly professional and based in the Quebec section's Montreal headquarters because it was difficult to find volunteers to create functioning EDAs around the province (Ducasse interview, 2014). For the most part, professional party operatives would recruit candidates and then hope that the candidates themselves would find volunteers to create active EDA executives (Ibid.).

One important effort of the volunteer executive of the Quebec section was to oversee the drafting of the Sherbrooke Declaration, debated and passed at the Quebec NDP Council in May 2005 and then passed at the 2006 federal NDP convention to become official party policy and be inserted into subsequent election platforms. The declaration laid out the intellectual foundation of the NDP's accommodation of Québécois nationalism that encompassed asymmetrical federalism, opting out of federal social programs with financial compensation, recognizing the national character of Quebec, and a 50 percent plus one majority for a seccession referendum. It became an important part of the political market orientation of the NDP toward francophone voters in Quebec as it reflected the desire of these voters to have the nationhood of the Quebecois recognized by a major federalist party. The declaration also proved to be a valuable recruiting tool for candidates and volunteers for the party and was promoted in pamphlets during elections (Gébert interview, 2014). However, even the Sherbrooke Declaration was not solely the product of volunteers. The volunteers on the executive of the Quebec section were guided by Pierre Ducasse and other staff in the Leader's Office. Indeed, the declaration itself was primarily written by Ducasse and Layton and his staff were consulted on the final version put forth to members at the convention (Ducasse interview, 2014; McGrath interview, 2014).

Interviewees described how the work of professional political operatives generated momentum for the NDP in Quebec leading up to the party's electoral breakthrough in 2011. They cited the party's decision to have its convention in Quebec City following the 2006 election, with a speech by Thomas Mulcair (who had recently resigned from the provincial cabinet) and nearly unanimous support for the Sherbrooke Declaration, as a turning point (Bussières interview, 2015; Ducasse interview, 2014). The convention received extensive coverage in Quebec's French-language media, and eight months later Mulcair won a by-election in Outremont, a Liberal stronghold. He was named co-deputy leader of the NDP and started to tour Quebec extensively, both alone and with Layton. These tours of the province began to be reported in Quebec media, and internal polling started to show a trend toward the NDP being the second choice of Bloc Québécois and Liberal Party voters and growing name recognition and popularity for Layton (Audet interview, 2014; Bussières interview, 2015). Higher-quality candidates such as Françoise Boivin, Romeo Saganash, and Nycole Turmel validated that the NDP was a serious party in Quebec politics, and it captured 12.1 percent of the popular vote in the 2008 election and held on to Mulcair's seat. The increase in the party's vote share in 2008 resulted in a large per-vote subsidy from Quebec, and this financial gain was used to justify even more investment by party headquarters in Quebec (Bussières interview, 2015; Gébert interview, 2014). The result of the larger budget was more Quebec-specific advertisements, messages, slogans, and canvassing materials that could be market-tested using focus groups and polling (Ducasse interview, 2014). Paid organizers also ensured that at least one permanent EDA had been established in each region of the province by the time of the 2011 election, though only five or six ridings in Quebec had what could be considered a fully functioning EDA when the writ was dropped because organizers had been preoccupied with running general elections and by-elections (Audet interview, 2014; Bussières interview, 2015). During the 2011 campaign, Mulcair held press conferences by himself in Quebec for province-wide francophone media, and a star NDP candidate was identified in every region of Quebec for local media hits (Bélanger interview, 2011).

The traditional NDP model used in English Canada of a party affiliated with unions and dependent on volunteers for financing and organizing was simply not followed in Quebec during the Layton years. Indeed, the NDP did not even attempt to fundraise from Quebec residents during this period because it found that, though Quebecers were sympathetic to the party, they were very unwilling to give money to it (Audet interview, 2014). Quebec unions were hostile to the NDP and organizationally and financially supported the Bloc Québécois (Bussières interview, 2015; Ducasse interview, 2014). Rather, with funding primarily from party headquarters in Ottawa, permanent employees designed a professional, postmodern campaign infrastructure and created a presence for the NDP in the spheres of Quebec media and civil society. Although the success of the party in terms of winning new seats was less dramatic, a similar approach was used in creating regional beachheads in Alberta and Newfoundland. Using funding from quarterly subsidies, party headquarters sent permanent paid organizers to those two provinces during the early Layton years to build up the NDP's campaign infrastructure, recruit candidates, and increase the party's presence in local media (McGrath interview, 2014). The result was a gradual increase in the share of the NDP's popular vote in these two provinces during the Layton period, leading to higher per-vote subsidies for party headquarters and the election of one MP in each province in the 2008 election. In 2011, the NDP was able to maintain its Alberta seat and add another seat in Newfoundland.

It is important to emphasize the role played by electoral success in allowing Layton and his team of political operatives to perpetuate and eventually entrench the moderation and modernization of the NDP. The frustration after the electoral failure of the 2000 election had built up an appetite for change among party members and a willingness to try new tactics and strategies. When the tentative changes that Layton's team put in place in the early 2000s began to bear fruit in terms of a larger number of seats and a higher popular vote, they were able to pursue even greater changes. With each incremental electoral success, the political operatives could convince party members to trust professionals at party headquarters to craft strategies and policies that would move the NDP closer to its dream of forming the federal government. Moreover, each additional vote that the party gained amounted to $1.75 more in funding per year (indexed for inflation). As its share of the popular vote grew, its agents could hire more professionals at party headquarters who believed in the need to moderate and modernize the party – additional agents dedicated to their cause. The party became able to afford the expensive features of postmodern campaigning such as polling, focus groups, and branding. Without the accompanying electoral success, it is doubtful that Layton and his team could have pushed the moderation and modernization of the party as far as they did.

The Mulcair Era, 2012–15

In terms of internal NDP organization, the Mulcair era solidified the changes that the Layton era had put in place. To appreciate this point, it is important to recall the three key elements of internal organization that had become entrenched in the pre-Layton era: a federalized structure, a dependence on volunteers and staff on short-term contracts, and an emphasis on the party's role as the political arm of labour. By the Mulcair era, these three elements had almost ceased to exist. They had been replaced by the adoption of postmodern campaign techniques and a political market orientation toward voters and competitors as opposed to party members and external stakeholders.

It is difficult to speak of the NDP as the political arm of labour during the run-up to the 2015 federal election. Prior to 2000, helping the party was the only way for unions to be involved in federal politics. By 2015, helping the party was only one of the many ways in which unions could be involved in federal politics. A few unions, such as UFCW and CUPE, still explicitly called on their members to vote for the NDP in the 2015 election by advertising in mainstream media and through internal channels. The CLC targeted eighty-eight ridings in English Canada (double the number that it targeted in 2011) in which it ran parallel campaigns designed to help elect a new NDP candidate or defend an NDP incumbent. In these targeted ridings, union staff would organize their members to volunteer for the party, communicate directly with local unionists to outline why they should vote for the party, and set up meet-and-greet sessions between union members and NDP candidates. The data from any canvassing done by unions of their members could not be shared with the NDP because it would be considered an in-kind donation under the new party financing rules (Pratt interview, 2015).

However, alongside these traditional practices, labour had become a more independent player in federal politics. The best evidence of its independence was that it definitively moved away from having a monogamous relationship with the NDP and toward seeking to maintain relationships with both the New Democrats and the Liberals. For instance, the CLC met with the Liberals regarding their platform in the lead-up to the 2015 election (Mallett interview, 2015). Thus, as opposed to unions focusing on playing a large role in determining the NDP's platform and exercising their informal veto power given their status as donors, the CLC lobbied both parties to include labour issues in their platforms but respected the freedom of each party to determine its final platform.

Interestingly, the stated goal of the CLC in 2015 was more nuanced than just electing a majority NDP government, even though such an objective was less laughable than at any other time in Canadian history. Rather, the labour central's main goal was to defeat the Harper government and elect as many New Democrats as possible. CLC market research showed that over three-quarters of union members wanted a change in the government but were split over whether New Democrats or Liberals should be elected. So the CLC campaign pushed a broad "time for change" message different from the CLC campaign in 2011, when it urged union members to vote based on issues that would generally lead to voting for the NDP. This change in electoral strategy was reflective of an overwhelming consensus among union leaders in Canada that their most important goal in 2015 was "getting rid of Harper" (Mallett interview, 2015).

Another indication of labour's desire to maintain its independence from the NDP was the creation of Unifor with a merger of the CAW and CEP in late 2013 to create Canada's largest private sector union. Although the CEP had always been affiliated with the NDP and was one of the party's strongest supporters, the CAW had disaffiliated with the party and had started to endorse strategic voting. With relatively little public debate, the newly formed union decided against affiliating with the NDP and instead endorsing strategic voting in the 2015 election, with several Liberal candidates receiving aid from Unifor, particularly in Ontario. The Fédération des travailleurs et travailleuses du Québec (FTQ) strategy mirrored that of Unifor. In the past, it had supported the Bloc Québécois. In 2015, the FTQ announced that it would concentrate its efforts on a handful of seats held by Conservatives and support the party with the best chance of defeating them in those ridings. In practical terms, this meant that the FTQ would support the efforts of a number of NDP candidates in and around Quebec City but also help Liberal Party and BQ candidates in other areas of the province.

For its part, the NDP under Mulcair had tilted away from an external political market orientation that entailed seeing itself as the political arm of labour or pursuing formal alliances with social movements. Rather, it adopted broader stakeholder relations. Instead of focusing on traditional allies such as unions and social movements, the party began to communicate, consult, and build relationships with a wide array of groups in Canadian society. For the NDP, a stakeholder was essentially any group in Canada that could have an impact on federal politics, including the business community. Indeed, the Canadian Federation of Independent Business accepted an invitation to attend a federal NDP caucus meeting to discuss small business taxes (Watkins interview, 2015).

Importantly, the NDP's breakthrough in 2011 had greatly increased the capacity of the Leader's Office of Mulcair compared with that of the Leader's Office of Layton. Whereas the stakeholder relations unit was at party headquarters during the Layton era, Mulcair created an outreach and stakeholder relations unit in the Office of the Leader of the Official Opposition or OLO as it was commonly known. The unit undertook various activities such as setting up meetings between the leader and MPs with stakeholder groups, holding hospitality suites and setting up booths at key stakeholder events, and seeking policy advice from stakeholders. The process was generally issue driven: political operatives in the OLO sought to engage with different groups depending on the issue on which the party needed advice, support, and guidance (Watkins interview, 2015). These groups were not asked explicitly to endorse the NDP or a specific policy or to provide resources to election campaigns. Rather, the process would create a catalogue of "third-party validators" who could be called on to support the stance of the party on a particular issue by stating that they "applaud" or "welcome" the approach (Ibid.). For instance, on the day that Mulcair made a pre-election announcement that the NDP would extend the accelerated capital cost allowance, the work of the outreach and stakeholder relations unit was important in ensuring that the Canadian Manufacturers and Exporters (2015) sent out a press release stating that it "applauds the priority that NDP leader Thomas Mulcair placed on Canada's manufacturing sector in his policy announcement today in Ottawa." During the 2015 election, each policy released by the NDP had three or four quotations from third-party validators. Obtaining these endorsements necessitated sending stakeholder groups embargoed copies of NDP announcements and even making last-minute changes to secure their support (Ibid.). In many ways, the unit was in a competition for stakeholder support with the Liberals and, to a lesser extent, the Conservatives, also contacting these groups to convince them to validate their own policies. This competition for third-party validators often entailed having to follow up with stakeholders after they had talked to the other parties to ensure that the NDP's opponents were not mischaracterizing the party's position (Ibid.).

During the Mulcair era, federal and provincial NDP structures became completely independent of each other. The federal NDP remained officially integrated with its provincial wings because anyone wishing to be a member of the federal NDP had to be a member of a provincial NDP. However, the federal party was able to sign up members through its website and other means as long as it transferred a portion of the membership fee back to the appropriate provincial party (Hare interview, 2015). The federal party was no longer even obliged to inform prospective members that they were simultaneously becoming provincial party members. Coordination among the professionals employed by the federal and provincial parties was reduced to keeping each other informed of overall plans and provincial party staff occasionally being contracted to do some federal organizing (Pratt interview,

2015). Indeed, in the lead-up to the 2015 election, there was a focus on how party headquarters could help to strengthen federal EDAs to stand on their own with little assistance from provincial parties (Ibid.)

The final element of the federal NDP's internal organization no longer operational in the Mulcair era was reliance on volunteers or short-term employees to perform most of the functions of the party. Its high level of professionalization allowed the federal NDP to adopt fully the postmodern campaign tactics identified in Table 1.2. In the early 2000s, party headquarters resembled a fledgling NGO with a handful of employees, but in the lead-up to the 2015 federal election it looked more like the head office of a Fortune 500 company. The key difference between party headquarters in the run-up to the 2015 election and earlier periods was twofold. First, in the past, the national campaign manager was hired months before an election and was not a permanent employee of the party. In 2015, all of the directors of the different elements of the campaign were permanent employees, and those brought on board through short-term contracts played supporting roles only. Second, the number of employees had greatly increased. During the 2000 election, about twenty people worked at party headquarters, split equally between permanent staff and short-term hires (Fraser interview, 2014). The headquarters on Laurier Street in Ottawa that housed roughly forty-five permanent employees in 2014 swelled to 250 employees at the beginning of the 2015 campaign in nine departments: fundraising, war room, tour, administration, digital, products/research, policy/platform, organization, and targeted ridings (Fortin interview, 2015). Each department had its own director reporting to Anne McGrath, the national campaign director. The party now had so many employees because it had decided to bring as many functions of the 2015 campaign as possible "in house." Like Conservatives and Liberals (Flanagan 2012, 137–38; Patten 2017, 53–55), New Democrats now had the capacity to run their own call centre, design their own printed materials, administer their own online presence, do their own fundraising, and perform their own research and data analysis.

The Mulcair era also saw the continued professionalization of the nomination process, policy/platform development, voter contact, activist training, and development of the party's base in Quebec. Although some volunteers in local NDP EDAs found candidates for their ridings for the 2015 election, the dominant roles in the nomination process were now played by federal organizers stationed across the country and the candidate search coordinator at party headquarters. Once a person was convinced to seek nomination, he or she was vetted based on the information disclosed and the research done by professionals at the party office. The final decision on allowing the person to stand for nomination resided with the national director even if the local EDA had approved or disapproved of the candidate (Pratt interview, 2015). To protect the privacy of potential candidates who did not make it through the vetting process, party headquarters did not disclose the names of candidates not approved, or discuss the grounds on which these candidates were disqualified, either to the public or to the local EDA and federal executive. The closed nature of this process did create some tension within the party in the lead-up to the 2015 election when several potential candidates who had been "vetted out" claimed in mainstream media and social media that they had been excluded based on their stances on particular policy issues, generating complaints from rank-and-file members while party headquarters steadfastly refused to comment.[4] The national director and the party leader also reserved the right to remove candidates once they were nominated, and this happened twice during the 2015 election because controversial social media comments about the Israeli-Palestinian conflict surfaced that had been posted two to three years prior to the election (see Jonasson 2015; and Raj 2015). The Liberals and the Conservatives had implemented similar vetting practices in response to the rise of "interpretive journalism," which heavily reports scandals and process stories and focuses on covering campaigns as if they were sports events at which small strategic mistakes are amplified (Flanagan 2014, 179–85; Nadeau and Bastien 2017, 376–77). Like their opponents, the federal New Democrats were forced to adapt to this new media environment.

Under Mulcair, platform and policy development was centralized and professionalized, reflecting the emphasis on voters, as opposed to members, in the political market orientation of the NDP. After controversy at the 2011 convention over removal of the word *socialism* from the preamble of the party's constitution, the federal executive appointed a group of party elders (Brian Topp, Bill Blaikie, and Alexa McDonough) to suggest new wording. The preparation paid off as delegates at the 2013 convention passed the preamble, which referred to the party's "social democratic and democratic socialist traditions" after a vigorous but respectful debate (Rebecca Blaikie interview, 2015). This success left party staff to sell the main message of the convention to the media encapsulated in the *Toronto Star* headline "NDP Convention in Montreal about Preparing for 2015 Federal Election" (Smith 2013).

As in 2011, the federal executive was transformed into the EPC for the 2015 election, and a few meetings were held at which it was updated on election readiness, passed an election budget, and consulted on the platform (Rebecca Blaikie interview, 2015; Pratt interview, 2015). The EPC stopped meeting once the writ was dropped, and all operational decisions during the campaign were made by the senior campaign team in Ottawa in consultation with the leader's staff on the campaign plane (Bélanger interview, 2015; Lucy Watson interview, 2015). Although the party's policy book and resolutions passed at the convention were the "inspiration" for the 2015 platform, they were a small part of a much larger and professional process of platform development (Rebecca Blaikie interview, 2015; Watkins interview, 2015). Greater capacity in the Leader's Office allowed it to take the lead on platform development in a way not possible during Layton's time as leader. For the 2015 election, the two-year process leading up to the release of the final platform was directed by the "policy shop" in the OLO, and party headquarters no longer had a formal policy department. The OLO policy shop brainstormed a large number of platform items based on its consultations with MPs, stakeholders, the Federal Council, the federal executive, and party commissions such as the youth and women's commission (Watkins interview, 2015). Unions and provincial parties were not formally consulted, but union and provincial representatives were present on the Federal Council and the federal executive. Senior staff at party headquarters then decided which items suggested by the OLO policy shop would be included in the platform and where and when they would be announced based on their market research. Indeed, the senior campaign team had undertaken an ambitious market research project in the fall of 2014 involving focus groups and polling that informed all of their decisions on advertising, policy development, and party/leader branding (Lucy Watson interview, 2015).

Reflecting a tilt away from party members, all decisions regarding the inclusion or exclusion of platform items made by the senior campaign team were approved by Mulcair as opposed to a member-controlled body of the party. And, to avoid confusion over exactly what the NDP was proposing in the 2015 election, its policy manual based on resolutions passed by members at the convention was removed from the party website for the duration of the campaign. In commenting on the removal of the policy manual, an NDP spokesperson stated that "the policy document is not the platform," and "just as the Conservative and Liberal leaders aren't bound by the policy resolutions of their own members, Mulcair is not obliged to campaign on everything his grassroots put in their policy booklet" (Kennedy 2015, A8).

The flexible nature of platform development, and the fact that it was heavily controlled by the OLO and senior campaign staff as opposed to volunteers, allowed the NDP to make a number of promises at strategic times in the pre-election period and after the writ was dropped. For instance, the party decided to announce a national plan for fifteen-dollar child-care spaces and a fifteen-dollar-per-hour federal minimum wage in the fall of 2014. These policy announcements were made months before the campaign to get the media talking about something other than Justin Trudeau's rise in the polls after assuming the Liberal leadership (Moran interview, 2015; Watkins interview, 2015). Aware of the controversy during the June 2014 provincial election in Ontario, when the media picked up on a letter from some disgruntled NDP members stating that party leader Andrea Horwath had drifted to the right of Kathleen Wynne's Liberals, these two policies were also designed to cement the federal NDP as "progressive" compared with the Trudeau Liberals and to draw attention to the fact that the Liberals had made few policy announcements (CBC 2014; Moran interview, 2015; Watkins interview, 2015). During the campaign, control of the content of the party's platform by the leader's entourage and senior campaign staff meant that the final version could be changed in reaction to events of the campaign or to feedback from third-party validators. The potential for last-minute changes required that a policy person be assigned to the leader's plane to ensure that Mulcair was fully briefed and consented to any alterations to the platform (Watkins interview, 2015).

The two areas where there was the most change in the party's internal organization during the Mulcair era were voter contact and activist training/mobilization. Similar to Liberals and Conservatives (see Ellis 2016; Jeffrey 2016; Patten 2017), New Democrats constantly began to mobilize volunteers and identify voters since they were in permanent campaign mode in the four years leading up to the 2015 election. The best way to describe the model adopted by the NDP is to call it local capacity building led by the centre. Federal organizers around Canada were instructed by party headquarters to hold parties, canvass blitzes, and other events in key ridings where the EDAs were weak and there was the potential for the NDP to pick up seats (Pratt interview, 2015; Sampson interview, 2015). Party headquarters also provided a large array of services to local EDAs, such as phone banks, direct mailouts, recruitment of prospective volunteers on social media, and access to digital platforms for volunteer mobilization. The connections between party headquarters and local volunteers were strengthened by recent advances in digital technologies, and the capabilities that New Democrats were developing brought them in line with what Liberals and Conservatives were doing online (Small 2017). For instance, the party used online tools developed by Blue State Digital, an American political consulting firm, to provide local volunteer organizers with a series of predetermined recruitment emails paired with internet-based RSVP mechanisms to advertise and coordinate events in their ridings (Roy interview, 2015). Often these local events were national "days of action" called by party headquarters in the lead-up to the 2015 election held on certain issues that would excite local activists, such as fifteen-dollar-a-day child care or fighting the end of home mail delivery by Canada Post. The idea behind these days of action was to identify members and registered sympathizers who could be mobilized during the campaign period, build up the skills and confidence levels of local activists, and pinpoint leaders who could move up "the ladder of engagement" to volunteer positions with more responsibilities (Sampson interview, 2015).

Activist training was professionalized, centralized, and standardized in the lead-up to the 2015 election using techniques developed by 270 Strategies, an American consulting company that specialized in grassroots organizing. The party created a curriculum taught face to face by employees from party headquarters who travelled across Canada or virtually through video conferencing with trainers based in Ottawa (Sampson interview, 2015). This training was supported by the development of Campaign Central – a website for activists only that contained materials such as training manuals, canvassing scripts, Elections Canada forms, and recordings of training sessions. Like any adult education program, the training was structured into different levels, from beginner to advanced, and focused on the various specializations required by local campaigns, such as data entry, financial reporting, and volunteer recruitment.

In the 2011 federal election, there was still no nationwide NDP voter contact database, a necessity for postmodern campaigning. In preparations for the 2015 election, the party had as a top priority the creation of a single national voter contact database called Populus accessible through a web portal (Pratt interview, 2015). The creation of Populus was accompanied by an emphasis on foot and phone canvassing prior to the writ being dropped. In particular, data on voter intentions gathered during the pre-election days of action began to be fed into Populus. It had several advantages over NDPVote. It could track voter intention even when voters moved from one riding to another between elections. It allowed voters to be easily "tagged" with certain issues or characteristics, thus facilitating more targeted canvassing efforts. The federal NDP also ran its own call centre in Ottawa during the 2015 election that engaged in conversations with voters on hot-button issues and strategic voting in ways that commercial call centres that the party had used in the past could not (Hare interview, 2015). Local campaigns immediately benefited from the call centre's sophisticated voter contacts because data were merged nightly into Populus and available the next day. Sociodemographic data on "likely to vote NDP" scores and "likely to be able to be persuaded to vote NDP" scores were constructed by an American analytics company and merged into Populus, allowing local campaigns to target their canvassing efforts (Ibid.). Populus was even used to track donors to the party and to evaluate the numbers of volunteers and their training levels across ridings. The advent of Populus placed New Democrats on par with Liberals and Conservatives, who had also developed new databases in the lead-up to the 2015 election (Patten 2017).

Building up local capacity using resources at party headquarters led to greater central scrutiny of local campaigns. Populus allowed for real-time analysis by party headquarters of the strengths and weaknesses of NDP support and even issue salience in all ridings across Canada. Not only did such information allow for the efficient allocation of central resources, but also the call centre in Ottawa and canvassers at doorsteps became sources of market intelligence for party headquarters since the issues that voters were raising could be instantly aggregated and analyzed (Hare interview, 2015; Lucy Watson interview, 2015). In particular, Populus created the opportunity to track local progress across many different types of goals, such as doors knocked on, sign locations, volunteers engaged, and new donors recruited (Pratt interview, 2015). The central tracking of progress on these goals allowed party headquarters to instruct field organizers to intervene if they saw that a certain riding was struggling (Sampson interview, 2015). It was even possible to have friendly competitions with prizes such as new clipboards or free phone bank time for the riding with the most doors knocked on or the most new volunteers recruited during a certain time period.

The 2011 electoral breakthrough in Quebec led to the continued professionalization of the NDP's campaign infrastructure and party structures in that province as postmodern campaign tactics were adopted for the 2015 election. Party headquarters increased the number of paid organizers in Quebec from five to fifteen, and a permanent French-language phone bank for fundraising and voter identification was established in Ottawa. French-language online fundraising, direct mailing, and social media engagement were also run out of party headquarters. Outreach to local stakeholders in the Quebec City and Montreal areas was initially performed by "satellite offices" paid for through the parliamentary budgets of MPs from 2012 to 2014, when the practice was deemed to violate House of Commons rules. Also, each of Quebec's fifty-nine NDP MPs had two local staff who could do community outreach during work hours and partisan tasks outside work hours. In particular, along with the organizers hired by party headquarters, the staff of NDP MPs worked outside their formal work hours to establish active EDAs where none had existed before.

During the 2015 election, the NDP hired roughly 100 staff in its Quebec operations. In particular, a head office for the Quebec campaign was established in Montreal, and five regional offices throughout Quebec were created. Party strategists were cognizant that many of the Quebec MPs elected four years earlier had never actually run local campaigns, and the party's infrastructure in Quebec was underdeveloped (Rebecca Blaikie interview, 2015). The regional offices provided direct support to local campaigns and immediate and in-person organizational assistance to struggling campaigns (Gébert interview, 2015). Like the party's regional offices elsewhere in Canada, the Montreal office and its regional offices in Quebec had only "ground game" responsibilities such as organizing voter contact. In Quebec, "air game" responsibilities such as television and online advertising as well as media relations were run out of party headquarters in Ottawa.

Evidently, the large number of resources and professionals associated with the full adoption of postmodern campaigning both inside Quebec and throughout the rest of Canada was the result of the NDP's rosier financial picture. Although the increases in the party's quarterly allowances because of its improved electoral performances were responsible for increased revenues during the Layton era, in the Mulcair era the NDP saw its quarterly allowances gradually phased out from 2012 to 2015 because of the passage of Bill C-13 by the Harper government. Yet a report from Elections Canada

(2015, 12) illustrates that the combined net worth (assets minus liabilities) of the federal NDP and all of its EDAs doubled from approximately $5 million to just over $10 million from 2012 to 2014 after adjustment for inflation. Given its strong financial position, the party was able to increase its central spending for the 2015 campaign from a projected $24 million to approximately $30 million when it announced that the legal spending limit would be increased because of the longer campaign (Fortin interview, 2015). The central party was also able to send cash transfers to some targeted ridings whose EDAs lacked resources while relying on strong EDAs to carry themselves through the election with little help from party headquarters (Ibid.).

The federal NDP was able to increase its net worth despite the phasing out of quarterly allowances because of its greater prowess at fundraising. The professionals at party headquarters used the money coming in from the last quarterly allowances to build a sophisticated fundraising machine that could be relied on when the allowances ran out (Fortin interview, 2015). In particular, the NDP was able to lower the cost of fundraising while increasing the amount of money raised (Fortin interview, 2015; Hare interview, 2015).

The improvement to the NDP's fundraising during the Mulcair era had five parts. First, electoral success simply made it easier to fundraise since there was a feeling among donors that they were contributing to forming the first federal NDP government, and being the official opposition kept the party in the media spotlight (Rotman interview, 2015). Second, there was an emphasis on providing EDAs with the tools that they needed to fundraise effectively since some donors only wanted to give locally and since EDAs often did not spend the legal limit during campaigns (Hare interview, 2015). Third, the central party's fundraising success during the Mulcair era was not necessarily driven by greater access to provincial membership lists and the removal of limits on how many times the federal party could contact provincial members, though that might have helped. Rather, party headquarters sought to expand its donor base beyond members. The emphasis was on the recruitment of registered sympathizers – those unwilling to become party members but willing to donate money to and receive communications from the party. As the party expanded its number of registered sympathizers, it realized that members were actually unlikely to donate more than sympathizers, and the distinction between member and nonmember became increasingly meaningless for fundraising purposes (Hare interview, 2015; Roy interview, 2015). Moreover, the administrative costs of maintaining a relationship with a sympathizer were lower than those of maintaining a relationship with a member, who required yearly renewal, processing of the membership fee, and coordination with eleven provincial wings. Getting away from fundraising exclusively from members actually lowered fundraising costs. Fourth, the party's telephone and direct mail operations were modernized to include a data analytics component to differentiate among donors. The party was able to raise more money with fewer phone calls and letters by tailoring its messages to individual donors, understanding the optimal amount to ask for, and being aware of the medium through which donors liked to give money (Hare interview, 2015). The party had come a long way from the pre-Layton era when it would arrange for provincial offices to send out a standard letter on its behalf to all members living in the province. And fifth, the NDP created a digital department that maintained a large email list of donors and used social media advertising to recruit sympathizers. The party began to send out multiple fundraising emails every day, which allowed testing to hone variables such as the optimal length, message, donation button placement, and requested amount (Roy interview, 2015).

Since adoption of the newest postmodern campaign techniques is expensive, money is a key component of winning the political arms race. All of the NDP's efforts to improve fundraising capacity appeared to pay off in the run-up to the election campaign when the party had a stellar third quarter of 2015, beating the Liberals and coming just behind the Conservatives in terms of central party fundraising.[5] However, New Democrats were routinely beat by Liberals and Conservatives at both local and central levels from 2012 to 2014 (Elections Canada 2015, 18). The Liberals used this newfound wealth to catch up to the Conservatives in adopting the latest and most sophisticated campaign technology, which some observers claim was a key part of their success in 2015 (Jeffrey 2016, 63–65; Patten 2017, 53–58). Although the NDP had more money than at any other time in its history, it was still outspent in 2015 by its opponents. Data on spending in the 2015 election campaign show that the Conservatives spent approximately $50 million centrally, the Liberals $40 million, and the New Democrats $30 million (Bryden 2015).

The Views of Members

As we have seen, the internal organization of the federal NDP was transformed during the time period that I examine. Particularly, the power of party headquarters grew as postmodern campaign techniques were adopted.

There was also a moderation of the party as its political market orientation toward voters and competitors increased.

Interestingly, the semi-structured interviews did not indicate that this change in political marketing led to much public controversy – with the exception that some members were disgruntled when candidates were not approved for nominations because of what appeared to be ideological reasons. Party members appeared to accept the centralization of power at party headquarters as a trade-off for winning more seats (McGrane 2011, 98). How did party members feel about this revolution in the political marketing of the NDP? To answer that question, I use a survey of 2,440 party members administered in January 2015.[6]

First, a series of questions was designed to ascertain the level of consensus within the NDP on its political market orientation. Respondents were asked about their level of agreement with the statements outlined in Figures 2.2 and 2.3. For ease of interpretation and to set up the ordinary least-squares regression (OLS) used later in the chapter, "strongly disagree" is recoded as 0.0, "somewhat disagree" is recoded as 0.25, "somewhat agree" is recoded as 0.75, and "strongly agree" is recoded as 1.0. The closer the mean of responses is to 1.0, the higher the agreement with the statement. Similarly, the closer the mean of responses is to 0.0, the higher the disagreement with the statement. If the mean of responses hovers around 0.5, then members' opinions are split on the statement, and consensus is not present. Standard deviation is reported as an additional way to measure consensus. Standard deviation approaching 0.0 indicates little dispersion in the responses to the survey question, thus indicating a high level of consensus, whereas standard deviation closer to 1.0 indicates more dispersion and a low level of consensus.

As Figure 2.2 indicates, NDP members generally place a high value on orienting the party externally toward social movements. There is a high level of consensus on building alliances with social movements, even if the question does not identify exactly what forms those alliances would take. When it comes to being externally oriented toward labour, a slightly more nuanced picture emerges. There is a somewhat high level of consensus among members that workers benefit when their unions support the NDP. This finding can be taken as evidence that members value the party-union linkage and want their party to be oriented toward this key external stakeholder. However, with a mean of 0.68, there is skepticism, within at least part of the membership, that union support is necessary for NDP success.

Figure 2.2

Federal NDP members' views on member and external political market orientations, 2015

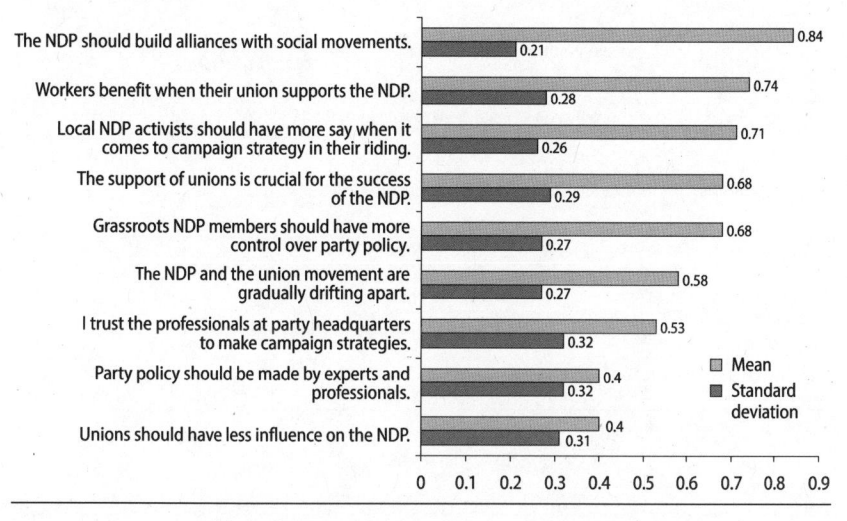

Statement	Mean	Standard deviation
The NDP should build alliances with social movements.	0.84	0.21
Workers benefit when their union supports the NDP.	0.74	0.28
Local NDP activists should have more say when it comes to campaign strategy in their riding.	0.71	0.26
The support of unions is crucial for the success of the NDP.	0.68	0.29
Grassroots NDP members should have more control over party policy.	0.68	0.27
The NDP and the union movement are gradually drifting apart.	0.58	0.27
I trust the professionals at party headquarters to make campaign strategies.	0.53	0.32
Party policy should be made by experts and professionals.	0.4	0.32
Unions should have less influence on the NDP.	0.4	0.31

SOURCE: 2015 survey of federal NDP members (all provinces and territories).

Furthermore, a mean of 0.40 illustrates that a sizable minority of NDP members actually believe that unions should have less influence on the party. The lack of consensus on this point is seen with the high standard deviation of 0.31. Finally, a mean of 0.58 illustrates that members are split on the question of whether unions and the NDP are "drifting apart."

Figure 2.2 also illustrates a preference for the NDP to have an internal political orientation toward members. There is general support for the idea that local party activists should have more control over policy and campaign strategy within their ridings. However, with the statements related to local control having means of 0.71 and 0.68, this preference is not overwhelming. Party members are split on the question of trusting "the professionals" at party headquarters to make campaign strategies, and with a mean of 0.40 there is support among some members for party policies being made by "professionals and experts." In fact, the high standard deviation on these two measures (0.32) illustrates that there is not a strong consensus on either point.

Within the federal NDP, the move toward greater voter and competitor orientations meant that the party moderated its strident left-wing image,

Figure 2.3

Federal NDP members' views on voter and competitor political market orientations, 2015

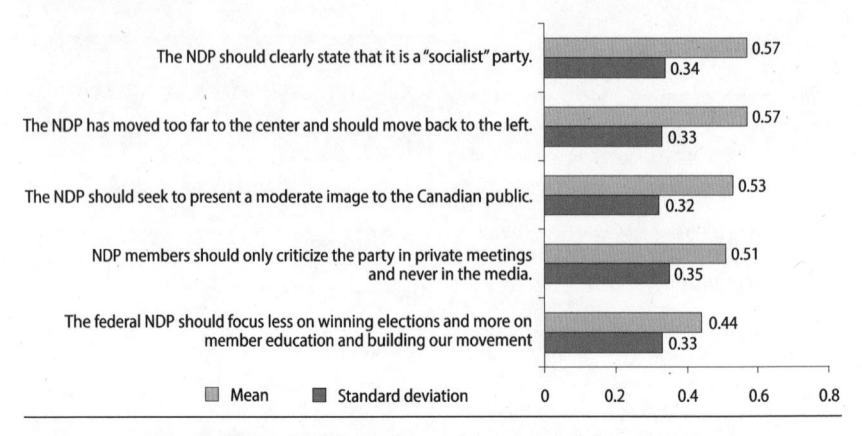

Statement	Mean	Standard deviation
The NDP should clearly state that it is a "socialist" party.	0.57	0.34
The NDP has moved too far to the center and should move back to the left.	0.57	0.33
The NDP should seek to present a moderate image to the Canadian public.	0.53	0.32
NDP members should only criticize the party in private meetings and never in the media.	0.51	0.35
The federal NDP should focus less on winning elections and more on member education and building our movement	0.44	0.33

SOURCE: 2015 survey of federal NDP members (all provinces and territories).

focused on understanding voters' desires to win elections, and limited the public's exposure to internal party disagreements. Figure 2.3 illustrates the agreement of members with statements related to voter and competitor orientations. The scale is the same as in Figure 2.2.

On all five of these measurements, the mean hovers around the 0.5 mark, and the standard deviation is over 0.30, indicating that there is a lack of consensus. Approximately half of members want the NDP to move back to the left and state that it is "socialist," and they disagree with the attempt to present a moderate image to please the public. The other half think otherwise. The members surveyed are also split on the need for the NDP to keep internal dissent private. Similarly, respondents are divided on whether the raison d'être of the NDP is to win elections or to build the "movement" and educate members.

Overall, Figures 2.2 and 2.3 illustrate a preference for a party both externally and member-oriented. However, the preference is far from universally held. There is a lack of consensus among NDP members surveyed on the party's move toward voter and competitor orientations and away from member and external orientations. Using other questions asked in the survey, it is possible to run an OLS regression to evaluate which characteristics of party members push them toward supporting greater member and external orientations or pull them toward accepting the party's voter and competitor orientations. To do this, I have constructed two indices corresponding to the two figures. The first index, labelled the member and external orientations index, encompasses all of the questions in Figure 2.2. Construction of the index necessitated that scales for three of the questions had to be reversed, resulting in higher scores for respondents on the index if they were supportive of a party both internally and externally oriented.[7] This index has a mean of 0.65 and a Cronbach's alpha of 0.70. The second index, labelled the voter and competitor orientations index, encompasses all of the questions in Figure 2.3. Again construction of the index necessitated that the scales for three of the questions had to be reversed, resulting in higher scores for respondents on the index if they were supportive of a party both voter and competitor oriented.[8] This index has a mean of 0.52 and a Cronbach's alpha of 0.69. These two indices are my dependent variables for the OLS regression presented below.

The independent variables for that regression are level of activity in the party, ideology, length of membership, and sociodemographic characteristics. Level of activity was measured using an index constructed by asking respondents if they very often, sometimes, not very often, or never engaged in a list of eleven party activities.[9] The index ranges from 1.0 if the respondent had never engaged in any of these activities to 4.0 if the respondent had engaged very often in all eleven activities (Cronbach's alpha = 0.87, mean = 2.74). Similarly, an index of the respondent's ideology was created using the seven questions concerning the NDP's internal ideological spectrum as outlined in Chapter 5. These questions asked respondents the extent to which they agreed with stridently left-wing as opposed to moderately left-wing statements on government policy pertaining to topics such as public ownership, free-trade agreements, taxation, deficits, and social conservatism. The ideology variable is a scale from 0 to 10, with 0 meaning that the respondent took the most left-wing position on each of the seven items presented, whereas 10 meant that the respondent took the most right-wing position on each of the items (Cronbach's alpha = 0.73, mean = 5.44). The length of membership variable is simply the respondent's answer to the question "for how long have you been a member of the federal NDP?" The sociodemographic characteristics are region, education, sex, union membership, religiosity, age, rural/urban, mother tongue, immigrant status, visible minority, public sector worker, and income.[10]

TABLE 2.1

OLS regression of political market orientation of federal NDP members, 2015

	Member-external orientation B	(SE)	Voter-competitor orientation B	(SE)
Length of membership	0.04	(.0015145)	-0.04	(.0024805)
Ideology index	-0.38	(.0014935)***	0.43	(.0024462)***
Activity index	0.17	(.0045016)***	0.07	(.0073732)**
Atlantic†	-0.03	(.0113647)	0.01	(.0186142)
Quebec†	-0.11	(.011159)***	0.003	(.0182773)
Prairies†	-0.06	(.0077874)**	0.04	(.012755)
British Columbia†	-0.10	(.0081586)	0.11	(.013363)***
Sex	0.02	(.005708)	-0.05	(.009349)*
Education	-0.07	(.0017816)***	0.09	(.0029181)***
Union	0.09	(.0064382)***	0.04	(.010545)
Religiosity	0.004	(.0026087)	-0.04	(.010545)*
Age	-0.14	(.0001934)***	0.03	(.0003168)
Rural	-0.01	(.0072583)	0.02	(.0118883)
Francophone	-0.03	(.0113216)	-0.01	(.0185436)
Immigrant	0.001	(.0078926)	-0.06	(.0129273)**
Visible minority	0.05	(.0100836)*	-0.03	(.0165159)
Public sector	-0.02	(.0076438)	-0.0003	(.0125198)
Income	-0.08	(.0005854)***	0.08	(.0009588)***
Constant	3.10	(.3832022)***	-0.73	(.6276443)***
R^2	0.20		0.24	
N	2161		2161	

NOTES: *** $p \leq .001$; ** $p \leq .01$; * $p \leq .05$. Reference category † = Ontario.

Although length of membership is not significant in Table 2.1, the level of a member's activity is somewhat important in determining attitudes concerning the political market orientation of the NDP. More active members were more likely to want a member-external orientation than less active members. However, more active members were also more likely to want a voter-competitor orientation, suggesting that a high level of activity can also lead to appreciation of and respect for the efforts of the professional political operatives at party headquarters. In terms of sociodemographic characteristics, income and education stand out. The results of the OLS regression indicate that higher income and higher education levels lead members to be more supportive of a voter-competitor orientation and less supportive of an internal-external orientation. The other sociodemographic variables either were not significant or illustrated inconsistent patterns: that is, female members were slightly less likely to support a voter-competitor orientation but neither more nor less likely to support a member-external orientation.

Most striking about Table 2.1 is the role that ideology plays. The strength of the beta for the ideology index clearly illustrates that the ideology of party members is the primary determinant of what they think about the political market orientation of the federal NDP. Support for an internal-external orientation increases as the member's ideology index approaches 0 (i.e., the most left-wing positions in the index). Conversely, support for a voter-competitor orientation increases as the member's ideology index approaches 10 (i.e., the most right-wing positions in the index).

Therefore, what comes out of Table 2.1 is that there are two types of New Democrats: left-wing marketing skeptics and right-wing marketing enthusiasts. In this sense, the division in the federal NDP is not just about right versus left but also about what members think regarding the very concept of political marketing.

Left-wing marketing skeptics are not only philosophically on the left of the party in terms of their positions on government policy but also suspicious of the role that marketing plays in politics, and they insist on internal party democracy. In this sense, the lack of support of left-wing NDP members for a voter-competitor orientation is connected to their antipathy toward the use of marketing in politics. Indeed, in their study on branding and the federal NDP, Wesley and Moyes (2014, 74–76) argue that political marketing sits "uneasily with many in the Canadian left, and those in the New Democratic Party," because it can lead left-wing parties to stray from their socialist roots as they compete for votes with their opponents. It also involves practices imported from the business world into the political world (e.g., branding) and implicit acceptance of the notion that citizens are reducible to consumers. Members on the left of the NDP do not like a market-based approach to anything – neither the economy nor political campaigning. Left-wing elements of the NDP, as the case of the NPI illustrated, wish to decrease the decision-making power of professional operatives and increase that of rank-and-file activists through greater respect for internal party democracy. For these activists, the NDP's policies and election platforms need to be democratically determined by party members at forums such as conventions or the Federal Council – even if the media report on disagreements within the party. Left-wing marketing skeptics within the party have a deep philosophical objection to envisioning the electorate as a market, and they oppose the suggestion that the starting point for the party's electoral platform should be discerning the wants and needs of voters through market intelligence and polling instead of the ideology and principles of party members. As opposed to being an electoral machine, the NDP is a movement that should concentrate on the education of voters to help them understand the imperative of bringing about social democratic change. That means being unafraid to state that the NDP is a socialist party and ensuring that it does not drift too far toward the centre of the Canadian political spectrum. Making alliances with social movements and ensuring that unions maintain their influence on the party are key parts of carrying out this mission.

The right-wing marketing enthusiasts are moderate in terms of their positions on public policy, and they accept the need for the federal NDP to professionalize and become a savvy political marketer to win elections. As opposed to left-wing marketing skeptics, who insist on giving grassroots activists the power to direct campaign strategies to ensure that the party stands firm on its principles, right-wing marketing enthusiasts trust professional operatives to moderate party policies to target soft voters from competing parties, and they do not support having the party state that it is a socialist party or veering away from the centre of the political spectrum and toward the left. They want the NDP to present a moderate image to the public and to ensure that the party appears to be united by keeping internal disagreements out of the media. Making alliances with social movements and ensuring that the party remains the political arm of labour are not overly important concerns. In short, they accept that there is a marketing logic to politics. The NDP is primarily a political party (not a social movement) dedicated to winning elections first by discerning what voters want and then by offering policies broadly within the Canadian tradition of social democracy to fulfill those wants. Politics requires an awareness of the electoral market as well as the policy offerings and activities of competitors. The market research and branding exercises brought into the party by professionals are key ingredients of a winning recipe for gaining power.

As we can see, the differences between left-wing marketing skeptics and right-wing marketing enthusiasts in the federal NDP are not just about the policies that an NDP government should enact. The vision of politics and the role that marketing plays in politics distinguish left-wing party members and right-wing party members. So the ideological tension within the federal NDP is not just about policies and values but also about the extent to which the party adopts marketing principles imported from the business world that have been taken on by other major Canadian political parties.

Conclusion

The internal organization of the federal NDP underwent a dramatic transformation from 2000 to 2015. The creation of the "new NDP" was driven by agents – Jack Layton and his team of professional political operatives, who took advantage of opportunities provided by new party financing rules and the need for renewal of the party. Its new model of organization and the influx of new financial resources allowed professionals to adopt postmodern campaign techniques and to tilt the political market orientation of the party toward voters and competitors. The electoral success of the party under Layton enabled this transformation as it cemented the power of his political operatives and led to higher per-vote subsidies that could be used to hire more professionals and pursue the latest campaign techniques. Indeed, by 2015, party organization was thoroughly professionalized, relatively independent from unions, and disentangled from provincial sections. The campaign technologies and techniques that New Democrats were using were nearly on par with those of Conservatives and Liberals.

With the exception of limited pushback from members on the process of vetting candidates in the lead-up to the 2015 election, party members appeared to acquiesce to this organizational transformation spearheaded by political operatives at party headquarters in Ottawa. Interviewees did not suggest that these organizational changes were in any way divisive. This lack of controversy might have been because many of the changes were low profile and the transformation of the political marketing of the party was gradual. It might also have been because members refrained from publicly criticizing the centralization of power in party headquarters because the NDP was continually increasing its share of the popular vote and winning more seats. If members complained about the reduced power of the grassroots, political operatives could always point toward the party's electoral success as justifying the changes. Indeed, the 2011 breakthrough appeared to be definitive proof that the moderation and modernization of the party was paying dividends.

Nonetheless, there was some tension below the surface. A membership survey, administered in January 2015 before the federal election later that year, suggests that members on the left of the party as well as those with lower levels of education and income were uncomfortable with the growing power of professionals at party headquarters and the party's tendency to be image conscious and centrist. Yet the survey also suggests that many party members (particularly those on the right of the party) were content with the party's shift of its political market orientation toward voters and competitors. So, though the transformation of the political marketing of the party did not generate a lot of public controversy, members were divided in their assessments of the wisdom of the changes.

Moderation and modernization of the political marketing of the federal NDP encompassed changes not only at party headquarters and in ridings across Canada but also on Parliament Hill as the caucus was reorganized to impose a much higher level of order and discipline. Once again, the agency of political operatives and the creation of per-vote subsidies drove these wide-ranging changes in political marketing.

3
Imposing Discipline and Order: The NDP inside the House of Commons

From 2000 to 2015, there were changes in how the New Democratic Party functioned on Parliament Hill, including its relationship with the media, its performance in Question Period, the operation of its caucus, the activities of its MPs, and its strategies for opposing the government of the day. The creation of the "new NDP," driven by the process of moderation and modernization, entailed the imposition of discipline and order on the party's parliamentary operations. With increased resources at party headquarters from quarterly allowances based on per-vote subsidies, there was greater coordination and information sharing between headquarters and NDP offices on Parliament Hill as the role of labour representatives within caucus operations diminished. Public subsidies also helped the NDP to win more seats during elections, and more seats meant greater resources in terms of staffing and research for parliamentary operations. With enlarged resources, the Leader's Office gradually became more involved in the daily activities of NDP MPs. Agents within the Leader's Office sought to control interactions between the caucus and the media to push certain narratives, reinforce the branding of Layton, and make the NDP relevant to voters by focusing on high-profile negotiations within the minority Parliaments of 2004 to 2011. These initiatives of political operatives in the Leader's Office, justified by the growing electoral success of the party, aligned with the broader changes made to the political marketing of the party – a political market orientation toward voters and competitors as well as the adoption of postmodern campaign techniques.

Here I outline the restructuring of the NDP caucus during the Layton and early Mulcair years through interviews with long-time MPs and caucus staff. I also examine a data set of questions asked by the NDP in the House of Commons from 2000 to 2015 and undertake a content analysis using NVivo 10 of a data set of recorded interviews with fifty-eight NDP MPs in 2014.

The statistical analysis of questions asked by the NDP during Question Period shows that the range of subjects narrowed and that the party focused more on topics that would receive heavy play in the media, such as scandals, mismanagement, and the economy, as the Leader's Office increasingly began to control preparations for Question Period. Questions began to refer to the NDP's practical solutions to problems raised in Question Period and to use more alarmist language and specific examples to capture the attention of voters. The analysis of recorded interviews with NDP MPs illustrates that they met regularly with a wide range of groups and considered a wide range of groups to be their allies, including the business community. MPs also stressed the role of the Leader's Office in crafting their communications and the importance of the "party line" in determining how they voted on bills, reflecting a caucus culture centred on both the leader and the NDP brand. One can thus argue that the independence of individual MPs was curtailed as a result of the process of moderation and modernization of the NDP.

The Views of Long-Time Participants

Part of the challenge of studying the evolution of a political party's legislative activity is that it takes place on a daily basis over many years often behind closed doors. Insights can be gained, however, from semi-structured interviews with NDP MPs and operatives who long worked on Parliament Hill.

Interviewees described how, prior to Layton's leadership, three important traditions had been established in the federal NDP caucus: MPs maintained a high degree of independence from the Leader's Office, the offices of MPs on Parliament Hill were operationally separate from party headquarters, and labour had direct oversight of caucus activity. Interviewees described how these three traditions gradually broke down during Layton's time as leader and how Mulcair solidified the changes that Layton had initiated.

Following the 2000 election, the NDP entered the House of Commons with a small caucus of thirteen, one more than needed for official party status. Alexa McDonough faced questions about whether she should continue as leader. Her situation was made more difficult by a practice that several interviewees referred to as "freelancing" within the caucus (Broadbent interview, 2014; Godin interview, 2014; Martin interview, 2014; Masse interview, 2014; McDonough interview, 2015). Freelancing essentially meant that an MP would take part in an activity that could be controversial without informing the caucus or leader. The highest-profile freelancer was

Svend Robinson, who routinely took public positions on contentious issues without consulting McDonough and the rest of the caucus. For instance, he placed McDonough in an awkward position when he presented a petition calling for removal of the reference to God in the Constitution and when he travelled to Palestine and stated that the Israeli military was guilty of murder (Truelove 2013, 229–45). Although such freelancing created tensions within the caucus, and Robinson was disciplined once by being moved to the back bench, it was generally accepted as an MP's prerogative to upstage the leader and occasionally take positions at odds with the rest of the caucus (Davies interview, 2014; Godin interview, 2014; Martin interview, 2014; McDonough interview, 2014; Dick Proctor interview, 2015; Stoffer interview, 2014).

The independence of MPs from the Leader's Office and the rest of the caucus was also reflected in practices not nearly as high profile as Robinson's freelancing. MPs were free to operate in their areas of critic they saw fit and to pursue issues of importance to them with little control or oversight by the Leader's Office or party headquarters. There was separation between the small research department in the Leader's Office and individual MPs' communications. For the most part, the research department produced factual backgrounders on major issues of the day with no suggested communications angle (Dorse interview, 2015). The MPs would interpret the backgrounders and use them in the communications strategies that they devised themselves (Davies interview, 2014; Dorse interview, 2015). Media requests were generally fielded by the MPs' offices, and individual MPs' staff devised the talking points. Members statements or petitions presented to the House of Commons did not need to be vetted by the caucus or the Leader's Office (Godin interview, 2014). Also, after the general topic was authorized by the caucus, an MP would write out the question in consultation with staff, and it did not have to go through the Leader's Office prior to being asked in Question Period (Ibid.).

An interesting by-product of the independence of NDP MPs was the need for much collaborative decision making in the caucus because their adherence to a common position could not be assumed. The caucus met almost daily when the House of Commons was sitting for meetings that sometimes lasted three hours. At these meetings, the chairs and tables were set in a rectangle, and generally every MP had a say on most decisions. In terms of Question Period, MPs would bring their suggested topics for questions to the caucus meeting, and then the caucus chair would "go around the table" for input from each MP (Davies interview, 2014; Godin interview, 2014; Kerwin interview, 2014; Dick Proctor interview, 2015). After receiving feedback from each MP on the proposed questions, the executive of the caucus (chair, whip, and leader) would deliberate in front of their caucus colleagues to make the final decision on which questions should be pursued, including those to be asked by the leader. A similar process was followed for determining which way to vote on bills in the House of Commons. After the critic for the area to which the bill pertained made an oral recommendation, the caucus chair would go around the table to get feedback from each MP, and generally a consensus would form (Dick Proctor interview, 2015). At times, a vote would be required, and it was understood that MPs should adhere to the decision of the majority, even though on occasion MPs did exercise their prerogative to vote against the rest of the caucus.

In addition to the independence of NDP MPs, an important tradition that had developed within the caucus was direct oversight by labour through two formal mechanisms. First, the MP who was the labour critic was required to go to each CLC executive and council meeting to report on the activity of the caucus and to bring the feedback of union leaders to the caucus (Kerwin interview, 2014; Martin interview, 2014). In addition, since the late 1970s, a representative of the Canadian Labour Congress had sat at the caucus table for at least one meeting every week that the House of Commons was sitting (usually Wednesdays). From 1977 to 2003, this role was filled by Pat Kerwin, the CLC political action director. He always reported to the caucus on important developments in the labour movement and reported back to the CLC on what went on in the caucus meeting without breaching caucus confidentiality (Kerwin interview, 2014). Although he did not have a formal vote, he acted almost like an MP, giving input on bills and strategies as the caucus chair went around the table (Blakeney interview, 2014; Broadbent interview, 2014; Kerwin interview, 2014). He commented on how unions would perceive the actions of the caucus, relayed the CLC executive's thoughts on certain issues, and later in his career provided historical perspectives since he had been attending caucus meetings for over two decades (Kerwin interview, 2014).

There was also some supervision of the caucus by member-controlled bodies of the federal NDP. In the early 2000s, MPs were expected to attend Federal Council meetings held three times a year to hear the concerns of party members, and the Federal Council even had a committee to provide regular advice to the caucus on international affairs (Davies interview, 2014). MPs were also expected to take a leading role in developing policies to be brought to the biannual convention. For example, MPs worked with rank-and-file party members to write four policy papers to be presented at the 1999 federal convention, one of which was rejected by convention delegates and sent back to be rewritten (Martin interview, 2014).

The third important tradition that had developed by the end of McDonough's time as leader was a separation between the operations of party headquarters and the activities of Parliament Hill staff. Party headquarters in the early 2000s stuck to the administration of the party's finances and internal governance as well as preparations for campaigns when an election appeared to be imminent. So there was limited interaction between the staff at party headquarters and the staff in MPs' offices, the caucus office, or the Leader's Office (Fraser interview, 2014). The federal secretary, essentially the CEO of party headquarters, rarely attended caucus meetings and did not report regularly to the caucus (Davies interview, 2014).

Layton and his team gradually broke down these three traditions in the caucus. By the time it exploded in size following the 2011 election and Mulcair had become leader, the caucus had already begun to operate in a much different manner than it had under McDonough. These changes in the parliamentary operations of the NDP dovetailed with a political market orientation toward voters, and caucus activities started to work in conjunction with the party's adoption of postmodern campaign techniques.

One initial move that Layton made was to reduce the freelancing and upstaging of the leader that had taken place. Interviewees pointed to how he personally consulted with members of the caucus prior to meetings to understand their positions (Bill Blaikie interview, 2014; Broadbent interview, 2014; Godin interview, 2014; Nystrom interview, 2014). During meetings, he worked to be seen as the "first among equals," similar to how a prime minister relates to the cabinet (Davies interview, 2014; Martin interview, 2014; Stoffer interview, 2014). Layton developed the habit of listening to the concerns of his colleagues and pronouncing what he saw as consensus only when the debate was finished. After he had built consensus through debate in the caucus, Layton was adamant that there be a united front in public and that he be the only spokesperson for the position of the caucus (Broadbent interview, 2014). In the early part of his leadership, he asserted control over the caucus by making Robinson apologize to his colleagues for getting angry at a meeting and removing Bev Desjarlais from her portfolio when she voted against the legalization of same-sex marriage (Broadbent interview, 2014; Godin interview, 2014).

Layton's insistence on being the exclusive spokesperson for the caucus was consistent with the postmodern campaign tactic of having the party mould itself to the image of its leader. It also reflected a new era of politics in Canada in which central control of party messaging became standard. Indeed, Layton's emphasis on message control was consistent with the tight party discipline of the Harper government described by Alex Marland (2016) and Tom Flanagan (2009). Like Harper's cabinet ministers, NDP MPs were "brand ambassadors" (Marland 2016, 165–200) expected to stay on the script given to them by the Leader's Office and to avoid comments that would create incorrect brand images. The NDP caucus accepted this discipline because the growing electoral success of the party as the 2000s progressed confirmed the effectiveness of having Layton be the party's primary spokesperson – especially when MPs saw internal polling showing his growing popularity with voters (Capstick interview, 2015).

In addition to Layton's prime ministerial leadership style, the formal mechanisms by which the caucus made decisions changed as well. One significant change was how the caucus organized itself for Question Period. The increased number of seats that the NDP won in 2004 and 2006 expanded the resources in the Leader's Office. The staff there decided to put a significant amount of the newfound resources into Question Period since the national press regularly attended it, and the performance of the NDP could create and drive media narratives to which voters could be exposed (Monk interview, 2015). The issues that the caucus brought up in Question Period then became the foundation for its press releases for the day to the national media and communications targeted at regional media outlets. Staff from the Leader's Office would give the media advanced notice of the NDP's questions in an attempt to persuade them to include the NDP in their stories. They even looked for ways to break news in Question Period such as asking the government about a minister's "ethnic media strategy" mistakenly sent to NDP MP Linda Duncan as opposed to Conservative MP John Duncan. Layton's staff thought that good performances in Question Period would bolster the party's profile with the national press and regional reporters who would eventually cover the party during election campaigns (Ibid.).

Planning began with a Question Period team of six staff members who met early in the morning to pitch ideas to each other and come up with a tentative list of questions. As opposed to having Question Period reflect the personal concerns of MPs, the main goal of the team was to have clips of Layton on one or more of the national stories of the day coming out of the House of Commons. Simply put, they wanted Layton to be seen by voters. After their early morning meeting, the Question Period team would meet with the house leader and one of his or her staff to confirm the lineup of questions as well as which MPs would be asking the questions. The lineup would always begin with Layton's questions on what was hoped to be the national story of the day, after which other MPs would ask questions on regional subjects or questions related to their areas of critic. Staff in the Leader's Office kept a spreadsheet of which MPs asked questions on which topics to ensure a good balance of theme, gender, region, and language.

In addition, the caucus stopped meeting daily when the House of Commons was in session and began to meet twice a week on Monday and Wednesday. At these meetings, the Question Period lineup was presented to the caucus by Kathleen Monk, the head staffer on the Question Period team. MPs were allowed to provide comments on and criticisms of the lineup and to suggest their own questions for consideration. Halfway through Layton's leadership, the practice of having MPs orally suggest their questions to the whole caucus ended, and instead they were required to "pitch" their questions to the Question Period team by email prior to caucus meetings (Monk interview, 2014). After the Monday and Wednesday caucus meetings, Layton and the house leader would confer in private to finalize the lineup of questions. If it was not a Monday or Wednesday, the final decisions on the Question Period lineup were simply made by the Question Period staff in consultation with the house leader and her or his staff. Once the Question Period lineup of questions was set, it was sent out by email to all of the MPs' offices. The Question Period team then wrote the questions themselves, and the MPs who had been chosen to ask them were required to practise in front of the Question Period team.

Private members' bills by NDP MPs could be controversial and draw voter and media attention away from the main narratives that political operatives in the Leader's Office attempted to construct. Unlike in the McDonough era, private members' bills were negotiated between staff from the Leader's Office and MPs during Layton's time as leader. A strict "no surprises" policy was implemented, stating that MPs were required to have all of their private members' bills shared with the staff in the Leader's Office and other MPs for their reactions before the bill was tabled (Godin interview, 2014). Staff from the Leader's Office could then work to dissuade MPs from presenting bills that could result in negative media coverage and the wrong signals being sent to voters. Staff in the Leader's Office also began to suggest private members' bills to MPs in an attempt to persuade them to present bills that fit with the party's broader legislative strategy (Monk interview, 2014). Such negotiations between staff in the Leader's Office and individual MPs took on greater importance once a lottery system for private members' bills was introduced.[1] If an MP was lucky enough to win a place high in the order of precedence as a result of the lottery, that MP had to meet with political operatives in the Leader's Office to discuss how best to use the opportunity. Although MPs ultimately retained the right to introduce any private member's bill that they desired, there was pressure from and "back and forth" with the Leader's Office staff about the content of the bill and the strategy for its introduction (Ibid.).

Over Layton's time as leader, the Leader's Office grew in size and scope as the number of seats that the NDP won gradually increased with each election. A larger Leader's Office translated into greater control of the activities of MPs by the Leader's staff. The enlarged influence of the Leader's Office was partly the result of increased resources and partly the result of Layton's team of political operatives wanting to set the strategic goals of the caucus and to ensure that their directives were followed. The growing number of MPs after each election proved that Layton and his team were on the right track.

For example, when it came to the use of parliamentary mailing privileges by the caucus, the Leader's Office took over responsibility from MPs' staff for so-called 10 percenters – flyers generally mailed in opposition-held ridings in a quantity equivalent to 10 percent of the voters in the NDP MPs' riding. The contents of these 10 percenters were largely devised by the Leader's Office even though the flyers were sent out on behalf of individual MPs. Reflective of the narrowcasting of postmodern campaigning, staff in the Leader's Office created a program to use Statistics Canada data and consumer survey data to target 10 percenters to certain demographic groups. The lessons learned from this exercise were applied to subsequent federal election campaigns (Gillespie interview, 2014).

Layton's stated goals during his leadership campaign included creating better connections between the NDP and social movements, raising the profile of the party in Quebec, and modernizing the organization of the party. His attempt to create issue-based committees made up of unions, social movement representatives, and caucus members ultimately fizzled, and responsibility for outreach to stakeholders was transferred to party headquarters. However, the efforts of the Leader's Office to increase the party's profile in Quebec were more successful. Following the 2004 election, Layton hired Pierre Ducasse as his special adviser on Quebec issues within the Leader's Office to conduct research and brief the leader and caucus. Ducasse also began outreach to civil society groups in Quebec, particularly on the NDP's federal budget demands (Ducasse interview, 2014). With Mulcair's by-election win in Outremont in 2007, more francophone staff were brought into the Leader's Office to create Quebec-specific materials that were not just translations of press releases written by anglophone staffers (Ibid.). Reflecting a greater orientation toward francophone Quebec voters, this team of francophone staffers began to develop media and communications strategies for Layton and Mulcair aimed at discrediting the Bloc Québécois and finding issues that could appeal to soft nationalist francophone voters (Newman interview, 2014).

In terms of national media, Layton's staff identified two immediate challenges: the NDP was largely irrelevant and invisible, and the media strategy of the caucus lacked focus (Capstick interview, 2015; Heath interview, 2015). Being the fourth party in the House of Commons meant that the NDP was routinely not included in news stories about the major issues of the day. With their political market orientation toward voters, the caucus and leader needed a focused media strategy to ensure that the party was "getting into the face of voters" on a regular basis (Heath interview, 2015). One of the first moves of Layton's communications team, in particular Jamey Heath, was to stress to both caucus and staff the distinction between "useful" topics and "important" topics (Capstick interview, 2015; Dorse interview, 2015; Heath interview, 2015). For example, fighting AIDS in Africa was undoubtedly an "important" topic to individual MPs, but it was not "useful" in getting the NDP included in national media stories, and it was not a top-of-mind issue for many voters. The Leader's Office began to direct the media strategies of MPs by suggesting subjects that they should pursue. MPs also received training from Layton's staff on how to create earned media hits that would be useful to the overall goals of the party, and the media appearances of MPs were tracked by the Leader's Office. The quantitative analysis of media appearances allowed the Leader's Office to make more "evidence-based" decisions to predict which topics would succeed in getting coverage and which topics would likely be ignored (Capstick interview, 2015). Starting in 2009, a staff person was dedicated to aiding MPs to earn media coverage in their home ridings that would be heard in neighbouring ridings that the party was targeting in the next election (Soule interview, 2015).

The initial strategy for Layton was to place him on a punishing media schedule and say yes to almost any media request (Capstick interview, 2015; Dorse interview, 2015). Layton even went on Pot TV with marijuana activist Marc Emery to affirm NDP support for the legalization of marijuana (a position later softened in NDP platforms to decriminalization). Layton's team also adopted a political market orientation toward competitors. The team choreographed various stunts to garner media attention, such as asking which flags were being flown on the ships owned by Prime Minister Paul Martin's shipping company and holding a press conference on Thanksgiving when other parties were taking a break (Capstick interview, 2015; Heath interview, 2015). The NDP was the first federal party to set up stand-alone websites specifically to attack opponents, now a common practice (Dorse interview, 2015). Research conducted by the Leader's Office also moved away from policy analysis and toward "opposition research" or "oppo research" such as finding old quotations from government ministers that contradicted their current stances (Ibid.). At the same time, researchers in the Leader's Office explored the backgrounds of MPs and Layton himself to ensure that the caucus was not blindsided if opponents dug up something embarrassing (Ibid.). This emphasis on oppo research was in line with the emerging practices of all of the parties in the House of Commons in the 2000s (Marland 2016, 191–94).

Eventually, Layton's media team became more experienced and more adept at sorting through and rapidly responding to media requests. Reflecting a political market orientation toward competitors, a pool of money for access to information requests was created, and researchers in the Leader's Office began to keep detailed records of patronage appointments, promises made but broken by Conservatives, and controversial statements from Liberal Party leadership candidates (Dorse interview, 2015). Layton's staff came increasingly to understand how to recognize media cycles before they happened, create new narratives in the media, and target reporters who would give them the best opportunity to achieve their strategic goals (Capstick interview, 2015; Monk interview, 2014). In the process, the staff developed a reputation for being able to feed quality stories to national media outlets in a timely and friendly manner that would then be relayed to voters (Ibid.).

Timing was important to Layton's success in garnering greater media attention than previous NDP leaders. Unlike the staff of Alexa McDonough or Audrey McLaughlin, the staff of Jack Layton benefited greatly from media opportunities related to the minority governments of the day. All of a sudden, how the NDP voted in the House of Commons could have massive implications for national politics. The Leader's Office sought to maximize opportunities granted by the newfound relevance of the party. In particular, the NDP purposefully withheld its support for budgets, throne speeches, or votes of confidence to generate media speculation on its next move (Heath interview, 2015; Monk interview, 2014). As described in detail in books by Jamey Heath (2007) and Brian Topp (2010), two high-profile instances of this strategy occurred when the NDP forced the Liberal Party to make changes to the 2005–06 federal budget in exchange for caucus support and when the NDP joined the Liberal Party and the Bloc Québécois in proposing a coalition government to replace the Harper government in the fall of 2008. The operations of the Leader's Office became increasingly centred on deal making with other parties, election timing, and using NDP votes in the House of Commons to force the government to make policy changes – all of which thrust the party into the sight lines of voters (Broadbent interview, 2014).

Following postmodern campaigning's emphasis on branding, the overarching goal of the Leader's Office was to use the minority governments to create a new brand for the NDP and Layton. Interviewees noted that early in Layton's leadership he was perceived somewhat like a "used car salesman," and the NDP was written off by national media as irrelevant and trying to sell something that voters did not want or care about (Capstick interview, 2015; Comartin interview, 2014; Heath interview, 2015). Staff in the Leader's Office took advantage of the attention to the party provided by the instability of minority governments to construct a new brand for Layton as a statesman who "could get things done and fix Ottawa" (Heath interview, 2014). They tried to draw a "direct line between voting for the NDP and getting something done" (Ibid.). Layton matured into the "optimistic fighter" who could be negative in terms of condemning Ottawa as being broken but positive in terms of proposing concrete solutions to the problems facing Canada (Capstick interview, 2015; Comartin interview, 2014; Heath interview, 2015; Soule interview, 2015).

As mentioned, an important tradition in the NDP caucus had been a separation of the activities of party headquarters staff and Parliament Hill staff.

The changes in campaign financing rules meant that the rising share of the popular vote for the NDP had greatly increased the resources of party headquarters. The branding of Layton and the strategies pursued by political operatives within the Leader's Office were formulated in close consultation with staff at party headquarters. In response to the need to be ready for an election at almost any time because of the minority government situation, a senior campaign team composed of top campaign officials from party headquarters met weekly with staff from the Leader's Office to assess election readiness and to coordinate the NDP's legislative strategy with emerging campaign themes (McGrane 2011, 94). To reinforce the caucus' political market orientation toward voters, polling and focus group research done by the party were shared with officials in the Leader's Office to inform their decision making. For instance, polls and focus groups were used to understand how media relations staff in the Leader's Office could frame Layton's brand and image in their communications (Capstick interview, 2014). Similarly, reflecting the embrace of electoral market segmentation, polling data indicated to researchers in the Leader's Office that they should look for environmental issues that targeted NDP/LPC switchers in Ontario and Atlantic Canada and ethics issues to appeal to NDP/CPC switchers in Western Canada (Dorse interview, 2015). Similarly, around 2010, a researcher for Quebec was hired to look for issues that could appeal to NDP/BQ switchers (Ibid.).

The synchronization of House of Commons strategy and election strategy was reinforced by an increased tendency for staff employed at party headquarters to become employed by the Leader's Office and vice versa. Long-time MPs also noticed an increase in staff from party headquarters on Parliament Hill and a reduced influence of union representatives in caucus meetings (Davies interview, 2014; Godin interview, 2014; Martin interview, 2014; Stoffer interview, 2014). The party president and the national director began to participate regularly in caucus meetings to report on election preparations and internal polling and to explore ways to coordinate legislative activities with election goals (Davies interview, 2014; Godin interview, 2014). For instance, several of the commitments contained in the 2008 NDP platform were first proposed as opposition bills in the House of Commons (Erickson and Laycock 2009, 112). The exchange of information and personnel between Parliament Hill and party headquarters was important in ensuring that both parts of the party's operations in Ottawa were dedicated to postmodern campaign tactics and a political market orientation toward voters and competitors.

The move away from an external political market orientation as the political arm of labour slowly took hold within caucus operations. A combination of Layton coming in as NDP leader, Kerwin retiring as CLC political action director, and party financing laws banning union donations gave impetus to rethinking the role of labour in the functioning of the caucus (Mallett interview, 2014). Danny Mallett, Kerwin's replacement, was more an observer of caucus meetings than a participant in them. He still gave short reports, but he did not intervene in discussions on Question Period lineups or how to vote on particular bills (Mallett interview, 2014; Monk interview, 2014). An NDP MP was also no longer assigned to attend CLC executive meetings.

In many ways, the increased size of the caucus following the 2011 election and the ascension of Mulcair as leader cemented how the caucus and the Leader's Office had come to operate during the Layton era. The direction in which Layton and his team had been taking the caucus with their reforms turned out to be well suited to the large caucus that emerged from the 2011 election and fell under Mulcair's leadership in early 2012. Major adjustments in how the caucus functioned before and after that election simply were not needed.

Mulcair continued Layton's prime ministerial style of leadership by acting as the primary spokesperson for the party and deciding on the consensus of caucus following debate, after which a united front in public was considered imperative (Cullen interview, 2014; Dewar interview, 2014; Masse interview, 2014). Indeed, the four MPs from the "Class of '97" still in the House of Commons as the 2015 election approached noted a gradual change in the caucus regarding the tendency among MPs to freelance and upstage the leader (Davies interview, 2014; Godin interview, 2014; Martin interview, 2014; Stoffer interview, 2014). They argued that neither the leader nor the caucus during the later Layton era and the early Mulcair era would have accepted MPs who devised their own policy positions and broke ranks on whipped votes. According to these four MPs, a change in the culture of the caucus reflecting a political market orientation toward voters took place. Freelancing gradually came to be considered by the caucus as an unforgivable practice that generated negative stories in the media that hurt the NDP's credibility and chances of eventually forming the government. In this sense, there was little tolerance of freelancers. Four MPs who publicly disagreed with the caucus following the 2011 election felt compelled to sit as independents or join other parties after doing so.[2] There was only one instance in the Forty-First Parliament (2011–15) of an NDP MP remaining in the caucus after voting against the party line on a whipped vote, and that instance occurred under the interim leadership of Nycole Turmel on a vote on the abolition of the long gun registry (Harris interview, 2016). In that instance, the MP nonetheless received the harsh punishment of losing his portfolio and being barred from making members statements.[3] There was no instance of an MP voting against the caucus position on a whipped vote during Mulcair's time as leader in the lead-up to the 2015 election. Other parties exhibited similarly tight discipline – a 2013 analysis found that the most rebellious MP in the House of Commons still voted with his party 99 percent of the time (Curry and Thompson 2013).

Caucus meetings were evidently much larger following the 2011 election, and this necessitated setting up a room that resembled an NDP convention or union convention, with a table at the front consisting of the leader, the caucus chair, and the house leader, with MPs sitting in rows and lining up to use standing microphones placed among them. Despite the different setup of the room, the processes of formulating topics for Question Period and determining the subjects of private members' bills remained fundamentally intact (Davies interview, 2014; Godin interview, 2014). One important change was the advent of the Legislative Committee. Even with the caucus of thirty-seven MPs, Layton was able to maintain McDonough's practice of having the critic speak first to a bill in front of the entire caucus, then allowing debate, and finally making a decision collectively on whether to support the bill or not (Godin interview, 2014). After the 2011 election, a subcommittee of caucus called the Legislative Committee would meet immediately after Wednesday caucus meetings to discuss bills coming before the House of Commons. Although all MPs were invited to stay for the meeting, generally they stayed only if there was a bill in which they were particularly interested (Godin interview, 2014; Martin interview, 2014). Generally, from fifteen to twenty MPs were present (Davies interview, 2014). At the meeting, the critic for the area in which the bill fell spoke to the one-page report that they had devised in consultation with the Leader's Office containing a recommendation on how to vote. The critic took questions, and the MPs present generally endorsed the position presented by the critic. The caucus position on the bill was then sent out by email from the Leader's Office (Ibid.).

The result of this new process was less caucus debate on bills, less scrutiny of the critic's work by the caucus as a whole, and greater willingness of MPs to accept the positions of the Leader's Office (Davies interview, 2014; Stoffer interview, 2014). Unlike in the past, not every MP could have a say on every bill or strategic decision (Ibid.). As such, MPs became less "generalist" and more "specialist" since they were not obliged to weigh in on every bill (Martin interview, 2014; Masse interview, 2014). With less legislative business to discuss, caucus meetings were reduced in length to one hour and forty-five minutes and held only on Wednesday mornings (Martin interview, 2014; Masse interview, 2014).

Whereas the party president and the national director continued to report to the caucus from the front table at the Wednesday meetings, the CLC representative lost the right to speak after 2011 (Davies interview, 2014; Godin interview, 2014). At that time, the CLC began to send a junior staff person to the weekly NDP caucus meetings who stood at the back of the room, and MPs were generally unaware of his or her presence (Davies interview, 2014; Martin interview, 2014). Similarly, by 2011, the expectation that MPs attend all Federal Council meetings was gone. Instead, two relatively junior MPs were designated as caucus representatives to those meetings (Ibid.). As a result of these changes, there was much less oversight of caucus activity by labour and party members, reflecting a move away from an external and member political market orientation.

Coordination between the Office of the Leader of the Official Opposition and party headquarters continued in a similar fashion under Mulcair, and on occasion OLO staff went on leave from the Leader's Office to work at party headquarters (Soule interview, 2015). The most noticeable difference between the Mulcair OLO and the Leader's Office prior to the 2011 election was that the former was much better resourced because the NDP had 100 seats and formed the official opposition. The single person in the Leader's Office prior to the 2011 election responsible for a certain function morphed into an entire department of staffers in Mulcair's OLO. Separate departments for operations, leader affairs, opposition research, and human resources were created, and the communications and policy department grew in size and budget (Moran interview, 2014). A department for stakeholder relations was also created within the OLO as opposed to being housed in party headquarters. Compared with the Layton Leader's Office, the Mulcair OLO was able to research thoroughly and respond to all issues that emerged as well as to branch out into the deeper analysis of economic and fiscal policy not possible before (Ibid.). The OLO no longer had to choose between doing political research on other parties and policy analysis – it now had the resources to do both. Communications and media relations could also be expanded to cover more regional media markets, provide rapid responses to and intensive analyses of specialized issues, and monitor ethnic media (Soule interview, 2015; Watkins interview, 2015). The number of francophones and staff dedicated to Quebec issues was greatly increased as well (Bélanger interview, 2014; Watkins interview, 2015). These increased resources within the OLO allowed longer-term visioning. This planning capacity was evident in the lead-up to the 2015 election when the OLO was able to launch pre-election campaigns based on well-researched policy announcements such as a national child-care program or a federal minimum wage of fifteen dollars per hour (Moran interview, 2014; Watkins interview, 2015). In summary, the Mulcair OLO was able to embrace postmodern campaigning and a political market orientation toward voters and competitors to an even greater extent than the Layton Leader's Office had prior to the 2011 orange wave, partly because of the expanded financial resources that came with 100 seats and official opposition status.

The NDP and Question Period

Another important source of data is composed of questions asked by NDP MPs in Question Period as recorded in Hansard. To examine the NDP's performance in Question Period, I have compiled a data set containing all of the 18,701 questions asked by NDP MPs in the House of Commons during the Thirty-Seventh to Forty-First Parliaments (2001–15). In addition to the texts of the questions, the questions have been coded by date, parliamentary session, and questioner. Each question was also assigned a topic code using the *Canadian Policy Agendas Data Codebook* (Penner, Blidook, and Soroka 2006; Soroka, Penner, and Blidook 2009). The same research assistant coded all of the questions to ensure that there were no problems associated with intercoder reliability (i.e., two or more research assistants coding in different ways).[4] As an additional step to ensure the accuracy and reliability of this analysis, I randomly selected 1,800 questions (approximately 10 percent of the data set) and coded them myself to ascertain whether there was any discrepancy between the research assistant's coding and my own interpretation of the data. Since I agreed with 97 percent of the coding of the student research assistant in the randomly selected segment of the data set, the quality of the assistant's work is assured.

In terms of continuity over the period that I am examining, Table 3.1 illustrates that some topics were consistently unpopular. Of the twenty-five possible topics, about fifteen garnered somewhere between 0 percent and 5 percent of the NDP's questions across the five Parliaments. The low priority placed on intergovernmental relations and constitutional/national unity issues might reflect a lack of interest in the NDP caucus but also a lack of controversy in these areas during the Martin and Harper governments. Education is not formally within federal jurisdiction, so the opportunities for questions on this topic by the NDP caucus were limited. In line with "issue ownership theory," described in detail in Chapter 5, one might expect the caucus to emphasize typical "left-wing" issues ideologically important to it while neglecting "right-wing" issues less ideologically significant to it and typically considered to be used by right-wing parties for electoral advantage. Interestingly, issue ownership theory is not a good guide for my analysis. Over the five Parliaments that I examine, the NDP caucus did neglect some right-wing issues such as energy, crime, and technology, but it also paid attention to banking, commerce, employment, and defence. Moreover, left-wing issues such as social welfare, minorities, housing, and Aboriginal affairs were not disproportionately prominent in the NDP's Question Period strategy across the five Parliaments.

The variation over time in Table 3.1 is more interesting. Because of the rules of the House of Commons, the NDP asked a much larger number of questions as the official opposition in the Forty-First Parliament compared with the other Parliaments. In fact, the party asked more than double the number of questions in the Forty-First Parliament than it asked in the previous four Parliaments. However, more questions did not mean that the party covered more topics in that Parliament. Even though the NDP caucus had many fewer questions under the leadership of McDonough in the Thirty-Seventh Parliament, it spread those limited questions over more topics than in subsequent Parliaments.

In fact, the most striking finding of Table 3.1 is the growing importance of the topic of government operations and corruption within the Question Period strategy of the NDP caucus. In the pre-Layton era, the caucus devoted only 8 percent of its questions to that topic. As the decisions on Question Period topics shifted away from individual MPs and toward staff in the Leader's Office, the number of questions devoted to the topic grew considerably – over 25 percent of the NDP's questions during Layton's time as leader. Turmel's and Mulcair's leaderships accelerated this trend,

TABLE 3.1

Topics of NDP questions in Question Period, Thirty-Seventh to Forty-First Parliaments

Topic	37th (June 2001 – May 2004) (%)	38th (Oct. 2004 – Nov. 2005) (%)	39th (Apr. 2006 – Sept. 2008) (%)	40th (Nov. 2008 – Mar. 2011) (%)	41st (June 2011 – Aug. 2015) (%)	Average of 37th to 41st Parliaments (%)
Government operations and corruption	8	25	20	23	37	23
Labour, employment, and immigration	7	7	6	14	13	10
Defence	8	6	13	8	10	9
International affairs and foreign aid	13	9	8	8	4	9
Environment	7	12	11	7	5	8
Health	10	10	5	6	3	7
Banking, finance, and domestic commerce	3	3	6	7	2	4
Agriculture and forestry	8	2	3	2	2	3
Aboriginal affairs	2	2	5	3	5	3
Transportation	7	0	1	2	4	3
Social welfare	1	4	4	2	2	3
Foreign trade	5	3	3	1	1	3
Civil rights, minority issues, and multiculturalism	2	3	2	3	2	2

Macroeconomics	6	3	1	0	2
Community development and housing issues	2	3	2	2	2
Intergovernmental relations and internal trade	1	3	1	3	2
Energy	2	1	3	2	2
Law, crime, and family issues	1	1	1	2	1
Culture and entertainment	1	0	3	1	1
Space, science, technology, and communications	2	0	1	1	1
Fisheries	2	0	1	1	1
Education	1	1	1	0	1
Constitutional and national unity issues	0	2	1	0	0
Provincial and local government administration	0	0	0	1	0
Public lands and water management	0	0	0	0	0

NOTE: Number of questions: 37th = 1,335; 38th = 643; 39th = 1,677; 40th = 2,227; 41st = 12,819.

with 37 percent of more than 12,000 questions in the Forty-First Parliament being dedicated to the topic, heavily reported in the media and likely to garner the attention of voters. Indeed, the focus on scandal and corruption appears to have been a direct consequence of the team of Question Period staffers who tried to anticipate the national news story of the day as opposed to letting MPs ask questions on their own pet issues.

Although Table 3.1 illustrates several interesting trends in the NDP's questions in Question Period from 2001 to 2015, it is necessary to dig a little deeper to understand fully the evolution of the caucus toward a greater voter political market orientation. Table 3.1 indicates that the two categories in which the NDP asked the most questions during the Thirty-Seventh Parliament were international affairs (13 percent) and health (10 percent). Looking closely at the data set reveals that the international affairs category contained questions that spanned a number of global issues, such as the Iraq War, instability in the Congo, generic drugs for Africa, and the case of Maher Arar.[5] Similarly, the party's questions on health care involved diverse topics such as safe injection sites, privatization of health care, and increased transfers to the provinces. However, international affairs and health care were far from being the party's exclusive focus in Question Period. Seven other categories garnered between 5 percent and 8 percent of the questions. In categories broadly related to the economy, the NDP asked about mad cow disease, the softwood lumber dispute with the United States, the labelling of genetically modified food, the Canadian Wheat Board, Employment Insurance, corporate tax havens, higher taxes on the wealthy, and financial aid for the auto industry. The category of foreign trade contained a bevy of questions condemning free-trade agreements such as NAFTA, the WTO, and the Free Trade Area of the Americas. In the transportation category, there were many questions on stricter standards for the airline industry (particularly limits on supplementary fees) and the need for greater investment in public transit. On the environment, the NDP focused on the Kyoto Protocol and better regulation of toxic waste disposal. The category of defence contained many questions on whether Canada should join the American missile defence scheme and a small number of questions on the replacement of the aging *Sea King* helicopters. There was a relatively small number of questions on corruption even though there was no lack of scandal during this period. Indeed, Ottawa was beginning to be subsumed by the sponsorship scandal triggered by the auditor general's report as well as testimony regarding the scandal in front of the Public Accounts Committee. Nonetheless, the

NDP did not ask many questions about the emerging scandal. Indeed, in the Thirty-Seventh Parliament, the party devoted as many questions to the government about studying proportional representation, a topic decidedly not at the top of voters' minds at the time (Marzonili 2004), as it did to the sponsorship scandal, which ended up being very important to voters in the 2004 election (Clarke, Kornberg, and Scotto 2009a).

The potpourri of topics explored Question Period by the NDP during the Thirty-Seventh Parliament confirms the recollections of interviewees, recounted in the section above, that the party's strategy lacked focus in the early 2000s. In fact, the tradition of allowing MPs to bring Question Period topics to the entire caucus led to questions on a wide range of topics and created no overarching theme. The processes of Question Period encouraged such heterogeneity because individual MPs simply brought whatever topics were on their minds to daily caucus meetings, and no single group tracked the questions or attempted to devise strategies across several Question Periods. Most importantly, the NDP caucus did not use market intelligence in the form of polls and focus groups to discern which issues were important to voters. In short, the political market orientation of the caucus was both internal, toward the concerns of MPs, and external, toward the issues brought to MPs by party members, unions, or citizens' groups.

In the three minority Parliaments during which Layton was leader, there was a gradual narrowing of the focus of the NDP during Question Period. In Table 3.1, we can see that ten topics comprised 5 percent or more of the party's questions in the Thirty-Seventh Parliament. When Layton took over as leader in the Thirty-Eighth Parliament, only five topics comprised 5 percent or more of the party's questions. The NDP caucus focused more on corruption and government operations, with a quarter of all its questions falling into that category. With the Gomery Inquiry on the sponsorship scandal in full swing, the NDP devoted many questions to the hearings since they were captivating voters' attention. However, questions in this category also dealt with broader ethical and operational critiques of the Liberal government pertaining to patronage appointments, lobbyists, reports of the auditor general, concerns of the ethics commissioner, and a general lack of respect for the will of Parliament. This broader focus perhaps reflected the view of staff in the Leader's Office that Stephen Harper and Gilles Duceppe were dominating coverage of the Gomery Inquiry and that the NDP needed to find something unique to add to the conversation on Liberal corruption heading into the 2006 election (Heath interview, 2015). NDP questions in other areas during the Thirty-Eighth Parliament were more focused than in the past and used more catchphrases. For instance, the questions on defence and foreign affairs relied heavily on opposing the "George Bush foreign policy agenda," whether defined as the weaponization of space or disrespect for the privacy rights of Canadian customers of American companies embodied in the Patriot Act. Similarly, the NDP's questions on health care mostly revolved around "credit card medicine," the term frequently used to describe the privatization of Medicare. The NDP dedicated almost all of its questions in the environment category to climate change by tying the Liberal Party's lack of progress on meeting its Kyoto Protocol obligations to smog in Canadian cities and the government's refusal to endorse the NDP's "practical" suggestion of improving fuel efficiency for passenger vehicles. Questions in the labour, employment, and immigration category frequently used Walmart as a symbol of the declining wages and lower labour standards of low-income Canadians. The use of such catchphrases reflected how staff in the Leader's Office were now writing the questions in a consistent manner as opposed to the diversity of language that naturally resulted when MPs wrote their own questions in the absence of an overarching framework.

In the Thirty-Ninth Parliament, the Layton-led NDP caucus faced a Conservative Party minority government in its first term; the Liberal Party had been relegated to the official opposition benches. There was once again a focus on government operations and corruption, that category being responsible for 23 percent of the NDP's questions to the new Harper government. The main theme of those questions was that Conservative scandals had replaced Liberal scandals and that the Conservative government had failed to live up to its election promise to do away with Liberal corruption. The NDP frequently accused the Conservative government of cronyism, of breaking Elections Canada regulations, and of attempting to cover up the Mulroney-Schreiber Airbus affair.[6] The New Democrats further accused the Conservatives of not fully implementing the recommendations of the Gomery Inquiry and of not enacting appropriate whistle-blower protection legislation.

We can also see a tighter focus and a simpler message in the NDP's questions in other areas. The 13 percent of questions that fell within the defence category almost exclusively focused on critiques of the Afghanistan mission for its unclear timelines, uncertain purposes, treatment of detainees, and need to balance combat with objectives related to reconstruction, diplomacy, and peace building. It was during this Parliament that Layton earned the moniker "Taliban Jack" in the media for his suggestion that a comprehensive peace process had to bring all of the combatants to the negotiating table, including representatives from the Taliban. The NDP's questions on foreign affairs generally tried to portray the Conservative Party as the puppet of Bush in his agenda that included disrespecting human rights in the name of counterterrorism and sacrificing Canadian interests in softwood lumber. On the environment, the NDP's message in Question Period boiled down to accusing the Conservative government of refusing to put forth a plan to reduce greenhouse gas emissions because it did not believe in the science behind climate change and was beholden to the oil industry. In the NDP's questions on economic matters, the focus was on the Conservative government's inaction in creating and protecting jobs, whether the lack of financial aid to manufacturing industries, cuts to seasonal unemployment insurance benefits, or inadequate immigrant credential recognition. There were also a number of questions on Conservative government cuts to corporate taxes when companies were turning around and raising banking fees or cellular telephone fees (two ideas that made their way into NDP election platforms). In the area of health, the emphasis on the NDP's ideological opposition to privatization as an affront to Canadian values was reduced in favour of a focus on the simpler messages of lower-cost prescription drugs and the shortage of doctors and nurses.

When facing the second Conservative Party minority government in the Fortieth Parliament, the NDP caucus focused on jobs, government corruption, and government incompetence. A full 14 percent of the NDP's questions fell into the labour, employment, and immigration category. The questions in this category were devoted almost exclusively to pointing out the number of jobs lost in the 2008–09 recession and condemning the government for not doing more on job creation and helping unemployed workers. A further 6 percent of the NDP's questions were in the banking, finance, and domestic commerce category and focused on consumer protection issues such as bank and credit card fees as well as the prevention of foreign takeovers of Canadian companies that could result in job losses.

The NDP once again emphasized – 23 percent of questions – government operations and corruption. New Democrats accused Conservatives of unethical behaviour, including patronage appointments, illegal fundraising, and using public resources for partisan purposes. The strident language and the use of simple language and concrete examples reflected a greater political market orientation toward voters. For instance, in 2009, Mulcair, then an MP, declared that

> four years ago today the Prime Minister promised that if elected, he would do things differently than the sleazy Liberals. No more patronage appointments; the Conservatives have made over 1,000. A parliamentary budget officer; they are trying to starve him. No more cronyism; dozens of Conservative lobbyists, thousands of contracts. No more Senate stuffing; 1-800-Mike Duffy. All that they have changed is that we now have the Conservative logo on the same old Liberal sleaze. (Hansard, April 11, 2009)

Even the NDP's questions under the defence and international affairs and foreign aid categories were centred on the unethical cover-up of the mistreatment and possible torture of detainees by the Canadian military in Afghanistan.

The NDP's perennial call for 0.7 percent of gross domestic product dedicated to international aid was replaced by questions on the Conservative minister's decision to override her bureaucrats' decision to fund an organization that supported boycotting Israeli goods. The New Democrats further accused the Conservatives of mismanaging the purchase of various pieces of military equipment and brought up the cases of veterans unhappy with how they had been treated by the Department of Veterans Affairs. Similarly, while the NDP continued its push for broad implementation of the Kyoto Protocol in its questions on the environment, it began to use specific examples of improperly completed environmental assessments and environmental disasters followed by the media such as oil spills. When it came to health care, the party shied away from commenting on funding of the system or on privatization, preferring to focus on the shortages of health professionals and on particular examples of the effects of those shortages. For instance, one NDP MP stated that

> yesterday, the lack of emergency resources took an absurd turn. Overcrowding in the Royal Columbian Hospital resulted in patients being treated at Tim Hortons. The Conservative government needs to order a double-double on the double and to wake up and

smell the health care crisis in this country. Will the Conservatives listen to New Democrats on public health care to ensure folks are not being treated in a donut shop? (Hansard, March 1, 2011)

By early 2011, Layton was already foreshadowing the party's eventual election slogan by reciting a litany of ethical breaches by the Conservative government and examples of its mismanagement of programs, leading to his pronouncement in the House of Commons that "no wonder so many Canadians feel that something is broken in Ottawa" (Hansard, March 10, 2011).

Following the 2011 election, the NDP was the official opposition without Layton at the helm and faced a majority Conservative Party government. Interestingly, this new situation for the NDP and its new leader did not bring about much change in the party's Question Period strategy. To even a greater extent, its strategy was dominated by topics related to corruption and ineptness in government operations. Nearly 5,000 questions were asked by the NDP in this category during the Fortieth Parliament. In particular, Mulcair grilled the Conservative government about the Duffy-Wright affair.[7] A closer look at the data set reveals that Mulcair and other NDP MPs devoted approximately 2,000 questions to this affair from when the story broke in May 2013 to the end of the Forty-First Parliament in August 2015. Most of these questions were asked by Mulcair himself, who adopted a short and direct style of questioning the prime minister that played well on national news, on which air time is limited. For example, he asked "Mr. Speaker, when did the Prime Minister first speak with Nigel Wright about Mike Duffy's expenses?" and then sat down again (Hansard, June 28, 2013). Mulcair was dubbed the "Prosecutor-in-Chief" by the media (Kennedy 2015). The NDP also asked about several cases of departments that mismanaged public money, federal scientists disallowed to speak to the media, travel expenses submitted by ministers, and electoral fraud by the Conservatives.

In other areas, the NDP caucus during the Forty-First Parliament also followed a game plan in Question Period similar to that of the Layton era. Questions from New Democrats deplored Canada's high unemployment rate and repeatedly called on the Conservatives to introduce a "real job creation plan" that would "kickstart" the economy. In the area of defence, the NDP focused on the "boondoggle" of cost overruns in the purchase of *F-35* fighter jets from an untendered contract and on the personal stories of veterans and their mistreatment by the government. A small shift in questions on the environment occurred as NDP MPs stressed the international embarrassment that Canada's lack of action on climate change was creating; they also began to emphasize the green jobs that could be created in the process of lowering greenhouse gas emissions. There was a continued line of questions, however, on the Conservatives' weakening of environmental assessment and habitat protection laws.

The changes to the Question Period strategy made by Layton and continued by Mulcair were an important part of the moderation and modernization of the NDP. The focus of the party in Question Period was on talking to voters through the filter of national media. The NDP caucus thus began to ask questions in fewer areas and concentrated on topics prominent in the media, such as scandals, the combat mission in Afghanistan, and the economic recession. When the staff in the Leader's Office took over writing the questions, the language became more consistent, biting, and urgent and less academic in an attempt to get the attention of "average Canadians." There was a concerted effort to make the questions more concrete by using particularly egregious and specific examples of the government's lack of compassion or wealth of incompetence as opposed to trying to deal with broader or systemic problems. Themes developed over consecutive Question Periods and foreshadowed promises and criticisms brought up during subsequent election campaigns. Finally, there was an emphasis on offering solutions to problems as opposed to just criticizing the government of the day. Often questions to ministers were prefaced with comments about NDP ideas that had been presented on the subject, such as an independent appointment commissioner to reduce patronage, Layton's climate change bill that introduced hard targets for greenhouse gas emissions, and a $4,500 tax credit for each job created by an employer. For the NDP caucus, the focus of questions asked in Question Period became the voter at home watching national news and the development of narratives that could help the party to win more seats in the next election as opposed to the concerns of individual MPs on a large variety of issues.

Parliamentary Activity of NDP MPs in 2014

To assess the parliamentary activity of MPs in the NDP caucus that formed the official opposition following the 2011 election, I recorded interviews with fifty-eight MPs, representing 60 percent of the caucus, from March to December 2014. MPs were guaranteed that their identities would be kept anonymous, and the interviews were transcribed in the language in which they were conducted (either English or French depending on the preference of the MP). The similarity of the demographic makeup of the interview sample and the demographic composition of the caucus meant that no weighting was necessary.[8]

One section of these interviews used open-ended questions designed to understand how NDP MPs approach their parliamentary activities. It asked about the types of organizations with which they meet, whom they consider their strongest allies in their ridings, how they communicate with voters inside and outside their ridings, who crafts their communications, and what they consider to be the determining factor of how they vote in the House of Commons. The responses to these questions allowed me to explore key aspects of the moderation and modernization of the NDP such as the influence of the Leader's Office, which organizations MPs interact with, and the role that the "party line" plays in their decisions on how to vote on bills.

After the interviews were transcribed, the textual data were coded using NVivo 10. Instead of starting with a predetermined list of codes to be forced on the data, I performed "open coding," a line-by-line reading of the interview transcripts, to generate themes and categories suggested by the participants themselves (Glaser 2004, 14; Saldana 2009, 81–85). There was no limit to the number of themes and categories that could emerge, and this process allowed the identification of recurring patterns in the data without reference to any preconceived ideas.

The results of this open coding are contained in Table 3.2, which illustrates the percentage of MPs in the interview sample whose answers contained any length of text coded under a certain code. For instance, in the table, 34 percent of the NDP MPs interviewed mentioned business groups when asked an open-ended question about which groups they had met with over the past month. Since some MPs were more descriptive and verbose in their answers than others, it did not matter if the MP talked about the subject embodied in the code for one sentence or two paragraphs. What mattered was that the MP mentioned the topic. To keep the size of the table manageable, codes related to a subject that appeared in the answers of three MPs or fewer were eliminated.

Since the NDP was once considered to be the political arm of labour, one might expect that its MPs would meet frequently with unions and rank them as their strongest allies. However, the external political market orientation of the caucus was not dominated by unions. Instead, NDP MPs from the 2014

TABLE 3.2

Parliamentary activity of NDP MPs, 2014

Question	Very popular responses (%)	Somewhat popular responses (%)	Less popular responses (%)
What types of organizations have you met with over the past month?	business groups (34), community groups (34), unions (29), lobbyists (26)	environmental groups (17), health sector (17), seniors' groups (14), agricultural groups (10), food banks (10), municipal government (10), women's groups (10)	arts groups (9), university sector (9), Aboriginal groups (7), housing groups (7), youth groups (7)
What types of organizations do you consider to be your strongest allies in your riding?	community groups (40), unions (31), ethnocultural communities (21), antipoverty/housing organizations (19), business groups (19)	Environmental groups (17), seniors' groups (14), arts community (9)	Aboriginal groups (7), family support groups (7), youth groups (7)
How do you communicate with your constituents in your riding?	mail (95), social media (57), community events (48)	earned local media (29), door-to-door canvassing (22), telephone calls (22), town halls and other events such as barbecues (21), email and electronic newsletters (19)	paid local print advertising (10), one-on-one meeting with constituents (9), website (7)
How do you communicate with Canadians outside your riding?	social media (38), earned national media (34)	stakeholder meetings (26), mail (24), email (22), House of Commons work (17)	National conferences (9), national tour in critic area (9), telephone calls (9), website (9)
Who crafts your communications?	my staff (91), central communications department (OLO or caucus office) (85)	myself (67)	critics' offices (16)
When deciding how to vote on a bill, what is the most important factor in your decision?	position of critic, caucus, leader, and party (88)	personal values and personal judgment on merits of the bill (41), desires of constituents in my riding (36)	views of all Canadians (9)

caucus met with a large variety of organizations and cited them as allies within their ridings.

Just 29 percent of NDP MPs spontaneously thought of unions when asked about which organizations they had met with over the past month. The most frequently mentioned type of organization was actually business groups (34 percent). They indicated that these business groups often came from their particular riding, city, or region. In addition, 26 percent of MPs reported having met with unspecified "lobbyists" when they were in Ottawa, a category largely dominated by business interests as well. When it came to groups that the MPs considered to be allies in their ridings, unions were a popular response at 31 percent, but the category of business – including groups such as local chambers of commerce and small businesses – were mentioned by 19 percent of the MPs. Notably, 21 percent of Quebec MPs and 44 percent of ROC MPs mentioned unions as allies in their ridings, indicating that most Quebec unions have traditionally supported the Bloc Québécois or remained nonpartisan and that English Canadian unions have had a stronger tradition of backing the NDP.

When asked about their allies and recent meetings, NDP MPs also commonly responded, simply, "community groups." The popularity of this response was driven by Quebec MPs, over half of whom mentioned unspecified "groupes communautaires" when asked about their recent meetings. In Quebec, groupes communautaires refer to an array of nongovernmental and not-for-profit organizations that rely partially on volunteer labour and have social missions such as increasing literacy, helping the homeless, or protecting the rights of senior citizens. Among ROC NDP MPs, 16 percent mentioned unspecified community organizations. Not surprisingly, then, 55 percent of Quebec NDP MPs mentioned groupes communautaires among their allies as opposed to 20 percent of ROC NDP MPs, who mentioned community-based organizations, local citizens' groups, and community organizations. Yet ROC MPs were more likely to mention ethnocultural communities among their allies compared with Quebec MPs. ROC MPs and Quebec MPs equally mentioned antipoverty/housing organizations as their allies.

In the somewhat popular and less popular responses on the questions concerning allies and recent meetings, we can see a wide array of groups represented in Table 3.2. The MPs reported meeting with organizations as diverse as agricultural groups, municipal government officials, women's groups, and health sector groups. The MPs listed some allies that could characteristically be considered left wing, such as environmental groups, Aboriginal groups, and the arts community. However, some allies mentioned likely would not have a specific ideological bent, such as seniors' groups, youth groups, and family support groups.

It is also interesting to note the types of groups mentioned infrequently or not at all in terms of recent meetings and allies. Only one MP mentioned religious groups as an ally, and only three MPs mentioned meeting with religious groups in the past month. Veterans and legions were mentioned by three MPs as allies, similar to the number of MPs mentioning women's groups, unemployed workers, cooperatives, and academics as allies. Finally, no Quebec MP mentioned meeting with groups concerned about protection of the French language or any group that could be considered nationalist, such as the Société Saint-Jean-Baptiste.

In terms of postmodern campaign techniques, NDP MPs mentioned an interesting mix of what could be referred to as traditional and nontraditional means of communication with their constituents and with Canadians living outside their ridings. Given the relatively generous mailing program provided to all MPs by the House of Commons, it is no surprise that nearly every MP mentioned mass mailings of printed flyers or newsletters to their constituents as a primary means of communication. However, several other "old-fashioned" ways of communicating were also mentioned, such as telephone calls, face-to-face meetings, community events, town halls and barbecues, and door-to-door canvassing. Given the small advertising budgets of MPs, earned local media such as press releases and news conferences were much more popular than paying for ads in newspapers. No MP mentioned paid television or radio ads, which were probably too expensive. In terms of newer ways of communicating with constituents and other Canadians, social media (particularly Facebook) were the most popular, mentioned by 57 percent of the MPs, followed by 19 percent who mentioned that they had email lists of voters within their ridings and Canadians living outside their ridings. Other means of narrowcasting – such as electronic town halls, text messaging, robocalls, online petitions, and internet advertising – were barely mentioned. When asked about their communications with Canadians outside their ridings, the MPs also talked about a mix of nontraditional means (e.g., social media and email lists) and traditional means (e.g., earned national media, stakeholder meetings, national tours, national conferences, and work in the House of Commons).

The last two questions in Table 3.2 were designed to get a sense of central control of the parliamentary activities of NDP MPs and the extent of the party's adoption of the postmodern campaign tactic of moulding the party to its leader and an overarching leader/party brand. When asked about who crafts their communications, the MPs described a collaborative interplay among their staff, themselves, and the OLO or caucus office. Unsurprisingly, almost all of the MPs mentioned that their paid staff in either Ottawa or local constituency offices took some responsibility for drafting and coordinating communications. Furthermore, 67 percent of the MPs mentioned that they played direct roles in writing and editing their communications. However, 85 percent of the MPs mentioned that a central body such as the OLO or the caucus office played a role in creating a template, providing content, and approving what was written. Indeed, a news story from the *Globe and Mail* in late 2013 found that 86 of 100 NDP MPs' websites were created by a central service from the OLO that used a common template and a common NDP logo, thus creating a consistent feel and brand across the web presence of almost the entire caucus (Hannay 2013). In contrast, the websites of Conservative Party MPs did not follow a common template, only 20 percent of their websites displayed the party's logo, and 75 percent did not even mention the party by name.

There is a relatively robust literature in Canada (Blidook 2012; Carey 2009; Docherty 1997; Kam 2009) on MPs' views on democratic representation and their records on voting for and against their parties that draws from a wider international literature in this area (Beer 1969; Eulau and Wahlke 1978). To simplify this literature, there is significant debate on the extent to which MPs, in their parliamentary activities, place primary importance on the desires of voters in their ridings, their own opinions, the positions of their parties, or some combination of these three considerations. To explore the views of NDP MPs on this matter, I asked them about the most important factor in the decision to vote in favour of or against a bill before the House of Commons. The response of almost all of the MPs was the position of their party. Although not shown in Table 3.2, a deeper analysis indicates that 40 percent of the MPs mentioned the party line as their only consideration in deciding how to vote on bills, and another 48 percent cited the position of the party as one of the factors determining their decisions. MPs described how they trusted the advice of the leader and critic, how they felt obliged to respect the will of the caucus after debate on the particular bill, how they wanted their activity to conform to the policies of the party as formed at conventions, and how they wanted to represent the platform on which they were elected. They also expressed the need for the caucus and the party to remain united in what they perceived to be hostile media and political environments.

Much less popular responses were the personal judgments of the NDP MPs and the desires of their constituents. The survey found that 41 percent of the MPs cited factors such as correspondence of the bill with their own values or personal assessments of the ability of the bill to improve society. Just over a third of the MPs mentioned the opinions of their constituents when asked about how they decided to vote on bills. Additional calculations revealed that 21 percent of the MPs reported that personal judgment and party line were their two primary considerations, and 20 percent indicated that the desires of their constituents and the party line were their most important considerations. In both cases, the MPs stressed how they firmly believed that the party's position consistently corresponded with their own values or what they believed to be their constituents' desires. In very few cases (only 12 percent) did the MPs rely exclusively on their personal judgments and/or their perceptions of their constituents' desires with no reference to the party line.

In many ways, the results of the open coding of the final two questions in Table 3.2 illustrate how the independence of NDP MPs was eroded by the postmodern campaign tactics of branding and presidentialization (i.e., moulding the image of the party to the image of its leader). In postmodern campaigning, there is an overarching brand that intertwines the brand of the party with that of the leader. The activities of MPs must reinforce the larger leader-party brand – "Jack Layton's New Democrats" or "Tom Mulcair's NDP." MPs who develop their own personal brands by Svend Robinson–like freelancing are not tolerated. It was the job of political operatives in Mulcair's OLO to ensure that communications from MPs' offices reinforced the party-leader brand, hence the need for collaboration between MPs' staff and central staff described by MPs in developing their communications. Similarly, MPs who take positions on bills that contradict the position taken by the leader can undermine the consistency of the party-leader brand. Reflective of the commitment to leader-centric and brand-centric postmodern campaigning, a culture within the NDP caucus had developed by 2014 that stressed the importance of presenting unified positions on bills before the

House of Commons. Constituents' desires and the MP's own values were secondary considerations.

Conclusion

The operations and functions of the NDP caucus went through a transformation from 2000 to 2015 that helped create the "new NDP," which increased its political market orientation toward voters and competitors and adopted postmodern campaign tactics. As this transformation in political marketing took place, the level of order and discipline rose, and political operatives in the Leader's Office became much more involved in directing the daily activities of MPs. Changes to campaign financing rules and a larger share of the popular vote increased resources at party headquarters and diminished the influence of labour on the party, thus affecting NDP operations on Parliament Hill. The party's key external stakeholder, unions, played a diminished role in the functioning of the NDP caucus, and election preparations made by party headquarters became intertwined with parliamentary activities. Also, as public subsidies aided the party in winning more seats, the resources that the NDP received for its parliamentary operations and the Leader's Office grew. Interestingly, the larger the NDP caucus became, the more unified and focused it became. A higher level of coordination among MPs was attained through stricter processes, created by political operatives, that all MPs were required to follow and a subsequent shift of power away from MPs and their staff and toward staff within the Leader's Office.

By 2015, the small and unruly caucus of independent thinkers and freelancers that McDonough had faced was long gone. Gradually, the NDP leader and his staff had been able to achieve military-like control over their army of MPs to deploy them in such a way as to achieve common strategic goals. MPs who operated within an established command structure were much less likely to work at cross-purposes or do things that did not fit with the goals of the Leader's Office and the overarching party-leader brand. However, to achieve such a high level of coordination among such a large group of people meant that MPs had less independence and less power. In the quest to moderate and modernize its political marketing, the NDP chose discipline and order over freedom and discretion for MPs.

The changes to the political marketing of the federal NDP were apparent in the evolution of its campaign strategies in the six federal elections from 2000 to 2015. Political operatives played a primary role in pushing forward the moderation and modernization of the NDP. These operatives, as opposed to individual MPs or groups of party members, were the driving force in determining campaign goals, tactics, and positions in relation to competitors. They devised bold and risky strategies in their efforts to make the NDP a major player in federal elections instead of a party whose campaign could be easily ignored by voters and the media.

4
Dare to Dream: Campaign Strategies, 2000–15

This chapter examines the campaign strategies of the federal NDP, as conceived by political operatives at party headquarters, during the six federal elections held between 2000 and 2015. It defines campaign strategies as consisting of three elements: goals, tactics, and market positioning. The concept of market positioning is adopted from the framework created by Patrick Butler and Neil Collins (1996) in which political operatives adopt one of four positions in relation to the political market that they are facing: market leader, market challenger, market follower, or niche marketer.

Using a combination of semi-structured interviews with staff who worked on these campaigns and content analysis of the party's television commercials and news releases with NVivo 10, I assess the campaign strategies of the NDP in these elections and explore how political operatives evaluated the successes and failures of their strategies. The NDP followed a cautious niche marketer strategy in 2000 consistent with a member political market orientation and rudimentary electoral market segmentation. Under Jack Layton's leadership, political operatives devised bold and risky strategies in the 2004, 2006, 2008, and 2011 elections reflecting a tilt in political market orientation toward voters and competitors as they dared to dream about forming an NDP government, and they became more sophisticated in their electoral market segmentation (an important element of postmodern campaigning). Agency and changes to party financing rules remained important in the emergence of the "new NDP" during this time period. Agents (i.e., NDP operatives) decided to move toward a market follower position and then a market challenger position focused on winning government with Layton as prime minister. In carrying out their strategies, the agents used increased financial resources gained through changes to party financing rules to take several well-researched and well-calculated risks that ended up placing the NDP as the frontrunner going into the 2015 election. With better financial resources, political operatives were able to understand clearly the market position of the NDP in the context of strategic voting, minority Parliaments, and multiparty competition, exhibiting a political market orientation toward competitors and voters. However, the agents who had been risk takers in previous elections devised a cautious market leader strategy based on framing the 2015 campaign as a two-way race between New Democrats and Conservatives and presenting the NDP as the party of "safe change." This strategy was gradually overtaken by a series of campaign events that allowed the Liberals to emerge at the end of the 2015 campaign with unstoppable momentum toward forming a majority government, leading to questions about whether moderation and modernization of the NDP can really take it all the way to power.

Campaign Strategy: Goals, Tactics, and Market Positioning

I define a campaign strategy as a political campaign's stated internal goals, its articulation of tactics to achieve those goals, and its market positioning. These three elements are determined by agents, generally political operatives gathered around the leader, prior to the beginning of the campaign.

First, no matter how the party is polling and how many seats the party currently holds, any political operative at the beginning of a campaign will say with a straight face that the goal is to win the election and form the government. Although this is always the ultimate goal, political operatives are more realistic in their assessments of the political environments in which they operate. If their party is already in government, then the operatives will set goals beyond just winning a majority such as breaking into a region where they have been unsuccessful or holding on to seats that they won by narrow margins in the previous election. If their party is very unlikely to win the election, then the operatives will set modest goals such as winning the leader's seat or increasing the party's percentage of the popular vote. In both cases, the operatives are future oriented. In this sense, the goals of political operatives are simply where they want their party to be positioned at the end of the campaign. The operatives for the weak party hope to create the building blocks required for the party eventually to form the government, whereas the operatives for the strong party look for ways to strengthen it further to continue to win elections well into the future.

Second, tactics are the activities carried out by the party to achieve its stated internal goals. Generally, tactics are divided into two categories: air game and ground game. The ground game is the party's campaign in local ridings that identifies supporters and gets them out to vote. From the perspective of an operative in a party's central campaign, ground game tactics often involve the deployment of resources. Given the party's universe of voters (i.e., the voters within an electorate who would actually consider voting for the party), how many seats and which seats should the political operative target? The stakes are high. Target the wrong seats, and precious resources are wasted. Target the right seats, and the chances of gaining seats go up. In contrast, the air game involves communicating the party's policy offerings in its platform, the image of its leader, and other key messages in its ads and news releases that generate earned media. Given the limited time accorded to the party in the media and limited advertising space, decisions must be made about which opponents to attack, how to attack them, and which issues to address. The air game also involves decisions about when and where to advertise as well as which medium to use (e.g., television, radio, internet, newspapers) and where to send the party's leader.

Third, an important part of a party's air game, and to a lesser extent its ground game, is market positioning as first developed by Butler and Collins, who conceived of Western democracies as "mature markets [in which] ... patterns of competitive behaviour among participants are established" (1996, 27). Political operatives position their party in a particular way in relation to the electoral market that they face. Market positions signal to voters how the party sees it role in the polity. In their discussion of market positioning, Butler and Collins outline four potential positions: market leader, market challenger, market follower, and niche marketer. Parties that choose a market leader position are usually parties that had the largest number of votes in the previous election, parties in government, or parties that have a large lead in public domain polling. A market leader will claim that it is in first place and try to maintain its position by expanding the total market (i.e., encouraging previous nonvoters to vote for it), stealing voters away from its opponents, or preventing its base of voters from migrating to other parties. A market challenger is not necessarily the party in second place. Rather, there can be several market challengers, and they are distinguished by aggressively pursuing the goal to become the market leader. The market challenger explicitly claims that it is in the running to become the market leader, even if polls or past election results do not support that claim. The party will directly attack the market leader to steal its votes, attack competitors of similar size to dislodge their voters, or target the voters for smaller opponents.

Cooperation can also be a tactic as a market challenger can try to manage its rivalry with other parties to prevent direct competition and vote splitting or to cultivate postelection cooperation in the form of a coalition government or another power-sharing arrangement.

Market followers and niche marketers are generally parties not seen as viable candidates to form the government, nor do they explicitly claim to be contenders for the government. Market followers still run country-wide campaigns and address a broad range of issues, but they are aware of their limited appeal to a wide cross-section of voters. As opposed to trying to become the market leader and form the government, they try to increase their share of the popular vote, establish the relevance of their leader, and expand the number of regions in which they are competitive. They often claim that they can have impacts on national politics despite their small sizes by holding the balance of power in a minority Parliament or influencing the agenda of a majority government. Niche marketers do not entertain notions of forming the government either. Instead, they have small shares of the popular vote, and their support is highly concentrated in a particular region or among a specific segment of voters. Their goal is to form a long-term relationship with a targeted set of voters by running on a narrow set of issues and by focusing their resources on limited geographical areas, thereby ensuring the viability of the party over several elections. Unlike market followers, niche marketers do not attempt to run national campaigns, raise their national profiles, or comment on a wide range of issues facing the country.

The point of this discussion is that campaign strategy is largely determined by agency and is a good indication of the political market orientation of a party. Using the information that they possess and their personal evaluations of the political landscape, political operatives choose their interrelated goals, tactics, and market positioning. An operative who adopts a market leader position will have a much different set of goals and tactics than an operative who adopts a niche marketer position. Evidently, there are risks and rewards in all campaign strategies, and political operatives have to guess how voters will react to their chosen strategies before an election campaign begins. For instance, the reward for a niche marketer to push policies that appeal to voters outside its loyal base might be winning a higher number of seats. Yet there is a risk that voters in its loyal base feel that they are being abandoned and look to another party. Believability is also an important consideration. A party polling in single digits with only two seats in the House of Commons could try to position itself as a market challenger ready to topple the government. The risk is that voters will simply ignore the party because they find its claim foolish, but the reward is that this positioning might give the party momentum, and the resulting excitement might lead to better electoral results than in the past.

Campaign strategy is intimately related to a party's political market orientation and its attempts to achieve electoral market segmentation. On the one hand, the goal of a party with an internal political market orientation (i.e., toward members) might be to represent faithfully the ideology of its members and loyal supporters on the national stage during an election. This party sees the electorate as being based on relatively stable voting behaviour and high partisan attachments, and it engages in little electoral market segmentation beyond identifying the concerns of its loyal supporters, generally already well known. On the other hand, the goal of a party with a political market orientation toward voters might be to attract the support of certain voters who do not usually support the party by researching their needs and desires. In terms of tactics, a party with an external political market orientation toward stakeholders might focus on highlighting its alliance with a particular group in society, such as a church, a labour organization, or the business community. In this instance, electoral market segmentation is rudimentary in assuming that the leaders of these groups represent the views of their members and relying on the leaders of these groups to transmit the party's message to the group's members. Conversely, a party with a political market orientation toward competitors might place strategic voting at the forefront of its tactics in the air game. In this example, political operatives are keenly aware of how voters in this segment of the electoral market pay attention to public domain polling and then seek to vote in a way that brings about their desired outcome.

As we can see, market positioning is intertwined with political market orientation and the sophisticated electoral market segmentation inherent in postmodern campaigning. The contrast between a niche marketer and a market leader provides a good example. A niche marketer is likely to have a member political market orientation that focuses on defending the interests and ideologies of its members and loyal supporters, a segment of the electoral market that it understands well and can easily identify. A market leader would have a political market orientation toward competitors who seek to steal market share from it, and it needs comprehensive electoral market segmentation in order to understand which of its supporters are susceptible to appeals from other parties.

Below I examine two sources of data to understand the campaign strategies adopted by the NDP over the six federal elections from 2000 to 2015. First, I use interviews with political operatives from each of these campaigns to ascertain their goals, tactics, and market positioning and how they evaluated the risks and rewards associated with their campaign strategies. The interviews also revealed how these agents evaluated the success of the campaign once it was over and whether they thought that certain campaign events had worked well or not with their campaign strategy. These interviews were semi-structured, and I relied on handwritten notes (as opposed to recordings) to ensure that the participants remained candid. The chapters on these NDP campaigns in the *Canadian Federal Election* series also provide valuable context for my analysis of the interview data (Erickson and Laycock 2009; McGrane 2011, 2016; Whitehorn 2001, 2004, 2006).

Second, political operatives leave traces of their campaign strategies in the form of advertisements and news releases. I gathered all of the news releases and television commercials of the NDP during the six federal elections held between 2000 to the 2015. I also gathered the radio advertising for the 2000 election when the NDP relied heavily on that medium. I subsequently transcribed these news releases and commercials. Adopting a technique that I have employed elsewhere (McGrane 2011, 2016), I performed open coding of the transcripts of news releases and television commercials using NVivo 10 to analyze their main themes. As opposed to looking at mentions of particular topics, I was interested in how much space was devoted to particular themes. Since words are always at a premium in political news releases and commercials, the amount of space devoted to different themes yields insights into the campaign strategies of the political operatives who crafted the communications. The amounts of space provided for the various themes were calculated through what NVivo 10 calls "percentage coverage," based on the number of characters coded under a particular theme divided by the total number of characters in the source that one is examining. For instance, I was able to calculate that 55 percent of all the characters in NDP news releases during the 2000 election focused on health care. Importantly, I allowed the same passage of text to be coded with more than one code, so the percentage coverage of the themes added together is higher than 100 percent.[1] This NVivo 10 analysis provides a valuable way to supplement and verify the data contained in the semi-structured interviews, thereby enhancing our understanding of the NDP's campaign strategies.

The NDP as a Niche Marketer: The 2000 Election

Political operatives understood the difficult position of the NDP when the 2000 election was surprisingly called by Prime Minister Chrétien only three and a half years into his second mandate to take advantage of what he perceived to be a set of weak opposition parties (Clarkson 2001). The NDP's internal polling showed its national support hovering around 10 percent, and its leader was neither well known nor particularly popular (Blakeney interview, 2015; Nystrom interview, 2015). Indeed, public domain polling at the time found that only 6 percent of all Canadians chose Alexa McDonough as the best prime minister, just barely ahead of Bloc Québécois leader Gilles Duceppe (Whitehorn 2001, 120). Moreover, the NDP had limited financial resources for its campaign (Bélanger interview, 2014; Fraser interview, 2014). The primary goal of the NDP in the 2000 election was to keep the seats that it held and maybe add a few more (Blakeney interview, 2015; Dick Proctor interview, 2015). Even in its most optimistic estimations, the party never envisioned winning more than thirty-two seats (Whitehorn 2001, 120).

The tactic to meet this modest goal was to be a niche marketer. Partly because of weak finances, NDP operatives decided to run the campaign like a series of simultaneous by-elections within the party's niches of support in certain parts of five provinces (Nova Scotia, Ontario, Manitoba, Saskatchewan, and British Columbia) (Fraser interview, 2014). This tactic had led to some success for the party in the 1997 election as its seat total rose from nine to twenty-one (see Whitehorn 1997). The party also displayed a member political market orientation. Instead of comparing its leader with other leaders or bringing up a broad range of issues, the NDP focused on loyal voters who cared deeply about publicly funded health care and strong local representation. Indeed, NDP incumbents who ran in the 2000 election recall stressing their own records as MPs and their own experience more than promoting McDonough's qualities as a leader (Bill Blaikie interview, 2015; Nystrom interview, 2015; Dick Proctor interview, 2015). At the same time, agents hoped that the focus on health care, an issue on which the party's basic and infrequent polling indicated that the NDP was trusted, could maintain the loyalties of voters in these regions and prevent them from defecting to the governing Liberals (Blakeney interview, 2015; McDonough interview, 2015). Indeed, health care was the only issue that New Democrats could be said to "own." The rewards of targeting these regional niches was

TABLE 4.1

Coverage of themes in 2000 NDP news releases and English television/radio commercials

News releases (%)	English television and radio commercials (%)
Health care (55); attack Chrétien and Liberals (53); end tax cuts for banks and big corporations (16); invest surplus (8); attack Day and Alliance (7); environment (6); postsecondary education (6); child care (5); free trade (5); agriculture (4); diverse slate of NDP candidates (3); women's issues (3); youth's issues (3); NDP team (2); Employment Insurance (2); attack Clark and PCs (2); housing (2); ethics (2); poverty (2); First Nations (1)	Health care (46); NDP team (37); attack Chrétien and Liberals (25); invest surplus (17); end tax cuts for corporations, banks, and rich (14); attack Day and Alliance (10); environment (2)

that the party's limited financial resources were not wasted on ridings where there was no chance of winning the seat, and the party already knew about voters in targeted ridings through the work of local MPs, so little needed to be spent on additional research (Blakeney interview, 2015). Indeed, the NDP relied on the impressions of local MPs, as opposed to regular polling (that was expensive for the party), for the market intelligence that it used for its simple electoral market segmentation. The risks for the NDP were low visibility for the national campaign and not building up the party as a major player in Canadian politics in the long term (Whitehorn 2001, 120).

Reflecting the member political market orientation of the NDP at the time, the news releases analyzed in Table 4.1 comprise a potpourri of issues important to party members and loyal supporters, such as protecting the environment, opposing free-trade agreements, and increased spending on postsecondary education, child care, and housing. Issues such as job creation, the economy, the military, and crime that might be of less interest to NDP members are not mentioned. We can see that the party overwhelmingly concentrated on promoting health care and attacking the Chrétien government in its news releases. Often the two codes dovetailed as the New Democrats attacked the Liberals over their decreased spending on health care while presenting their own plans for more investment in home care and a national drug insurance program (i.e., Pharmacare). There were also several mentions of the Chrétien government not doing enough to stop the creeping privatization of Medicare and concerns about the hidden intentions of the Canadian Alliance to introduce American-style "two-tiered health care" in Canada. To pay for the increased health care spending, New Democrats stressed that they would invest the government's surplus in health care in contrast to the Liberals, who would "squander" the surplus on tax cuts for large corporations and banks. The news releases rarely highlighted McDonough's personal attributes or referred to her strong leadership qualities. Rather, they preferred to point out the NDP's strong legacy on Medicare with phrases such as "New Democrats have a life-long commitment to health care" (November 24, 2000) and the need to prevent privatization so as not to jeopardize the accomplishments of "Tommy Douglas and other pioneers who created Medicare in Canada" (November 23, 2000).

Given its regional targeting and weak finances, the NDP spent 40 percent of its advertising budget on radio and television ads in its niche markets (Whitehorn 2001, 23). No television commercials were produced in French, and no television commercials ran on a Canada-wide basis. The focus on local NDP candidates was more evident in television and radio commercials than in news releases. After repeating the party's promises on health care, the surplus, and corporate tax cuts, the ads ended with a tagline about sending a "strong team" of New Democrats to Ottawa to fight for better health care. McDonough barely appeared in the commercials (Whitehorn 2001, 123). The message of the ads was clear. Voting NDP within these regional niches of party strength was a way to send strong New Democratic MPs to Ottawa to be "the conscience of Parliament" and to keep the Liberals honest when it came to funding health care and preventing the privatization of Medicare.

Many in the NDP judged this campaign strategy to be unsuccessful since the party barely clung to official party status and saw its percentage of the popular vote fall. There was disappointment that the NDP lost good MPs in its regional niches, such as Nova Scotia and Saskatchewan (Nystrom interview, 2015; Dick Proctor interview, 2015). Interestingly, political operatives and incumbent MPs could not point to specific events in the campaign that hurt the party. In some ways, the campaign was uneventful for the NDP because it focused on a single and safe issue, and the national media virtually ignored the party when it came to major twists and turns in the campaign (Nystrom interview, 2015). The cautious market positioning as a niche marketer targeting precise areas of regional support had left the party out of the national campaign altogether. Therefore, when the election was over, there was a foreboding sense that the NDP was no longer a relevant player in federal politics (Bill Blaikie interview, 2015; McDonough interview, 2015).

The NDP as a Market Follower: The 2004 Election

The 2004 election was called in the midst of some considerable shifts in Canadian federal politics, such as Paul Martin taking over from Jean Chrétien, the sponsorship scandal, and the uniting of the Progressive Conservative Party and Canadian Alliance under Stephen Harper. The NDP's internal polling showed that its national support was somewhere between 10 percent and 15 percent and that Layton was not well known, particularly outside Toronto (Penner interview, 2015). It also showed that the Liberal Party was in a dominant position but that the newly formed Conservative Party was trending upward, particularly in Western Canada, where the NDP hoped to pick up seats (Ibid.). Given this context, some NDP operatives argued for concentrating their limited resources on twenty to thirty ridings, similar to the strategy that had been followed in 2000 and 1997 (Cox interview, 2015; Chris Watson interview, 2015). After much discussion, they decided to eschew the previous niche marketer position and move toward a market follower position. As opposed to targeting regional niches of support, the primary goal of the NDP in 2004 was to increase the national profile of the party and its new leader (Hébert-Daly interview, 2014). This goal signalled a political market orientation toward voters and competitors. NDP operatives thought that, if the party could win a significant number of new seats, including seats in every region, it would have momentum coming out of the campaign and could start to work toward convincing voters that it could be a contender for the government in future elections, displacing the Liberal Party as the pan-Canadian centre-left alternative to a Conservative Party government (Heath interview, 2015; Milling interview, 2015; Chris Watson interview, 2015). Winning in the neighbourhood of thirty seats could also give the NDP the balance of power if there was a new minority Parliament and ensure that voters knew about its activities in the House of Commons because the party would inevitably garner significant national media attention (Cox interview, 2015).

There were essentially two tactics to accomplish this goal. Given that quarterly allowances had boosted the finances of the NDP, it could afford to run more of a national campaign by putting resources into "next tier" ridings that the party thought it had a chance of winning in the future (Cox interview, 2015). Indeed, convincing voters that the NDP could eventually become a contender for the government required running competitive campaigns in every region of Canada, including Quebec, Newfoundland, and Alberta (Cox interview, 2015; Penner interview, 2015; Chris Watson interview, 2015). Roughly a year prior to the election, the party identified close to ninety ridings where it thought that potential for NDP gains existed and started to put resources into those ridings (Cox interview, 2015; Whitehorn 2004, 114). To reach voters in this large group of targeted and next tier ridings, the NDP ran a national television advertising campaign that ate up almost all of the party's advertising budget and was more expensive than past campaigns. The party had spent 54 percent of its advertising budget on television and 40 percent on local radio in 2000 in its regional niches of support, whereas in 2004 it spent 91 percent of its advertising budget a national television campaign (Whitehorn 2004, 120). As the party approached election day, the number of ridings that it targeted gradually decreased (Cox interview, 2015; Hébert-Daly interview, 2014). However, the initial focus on aspirational or next tier ridings across Canada represented greater sophistication in electoral market segmentation than that of the previous election, which had focused exclusively on regional niches.

The NDP's second tactic was to run a leader-centric campaign as opposed to an issue-centric campaign (Chris Watson interview, 2015). The basic and infrequent polling that the party had done in the past had found that the NDP was trusted on the issue of health care, and it remained a top-of-mind issue for many voters (Penner interview, 2015). Once again, to the extent that the party owned any issue, health care was that issue. However, the increased financial resources from changes to party financing rules were used to run more sophisticated focus groups and more comprehensive polling, and it was found that stubborn stereotypes of the NDP as a party prone to taxing and spending still stuck but that Layton was starting to connect with voters as someone whom they trusted to work hard for them (Hébert-Daly interview, 2014; Chris Watson interview, 2015). Given this situation, the political operatives decided to focus on building a national brand for Layton based on his commitment to traditional NDP issues such as health care while including a promise for a balanced budget and an emphasis on his new energy and positive tone (Ibid.). The idea was that the NDP would move away from running on a couple of issues (e.g., health care and corporate taxes) and build a campaign around Layton and his alternative vision of Canada embodied within a bouquet of issues important to Canadians. An internal NDP strategy document dated June 17, 2003, described Layton's brand as an "exciting scrapper ... He'll fight for you and your family on issues that matter."[2] Reflecting a greater political market orientation toward competitors, NDP operatives thought that Layton could appeal to soft Liberal Party voters by stating over and over that the Liberals always made promises to do progressive things to help Canadian families but still had not fulfilled these promises after being in government for over ten years, insinuating that Martin was really no different from Harper (Hébert-Daly interview, 2014). The focus on Layton's leadership also reflected the emphasis that postmodern campaigning places on having the party mould itself to its leader's brand.

There were certainly risks related to this market positioning of daring to dream about an eventual NDP government. Political operatives were keenly aware that they needed to win Layton's seat in Toronto and make a comeback in some of the regional strongholds to increase the party's seat count (Hébert-Daly interview, 2014). A higher seat total, as opposed to a higher share of the popular vote, was the key to ensuring that the NDP held the balance of power in the event of a minority Liberal Party government (Cox interview, 2015). Spending time, energy, and money on next tier ridings might not immediately increase the number of seats that the NDP held in the House of Commons – the returns on those investments in terms of seat gains might only be realized in future elections (Milling interview, 2015). Also, though the NDP had a well-established reputation on health care, Layton was unknown. Not only was he unfamiliar to most Canadians, but also he had never been in the House of Commons or run as a leader in a national campaign. There was no guarantee that he would perform well on the campaign trail. Given that he failed in two previous attempts to win a federal seat for the NDP in Toronto (1993 and 1997) and an attempt to be mayor of Toronto (1991), it might have been a safer bet to keep him close to home so that he could secure his own riding. The reward for following this strategy – the NDP re-establishing itself as a national political presence and force – was much more ethereal. It appeared to be a case of risking immediate short-term gains for relatively undefined success in the future.

Table 4.2 well illustrates the strategy of NDP operatives. The news releases focused on attacking Martin and the Liberals on a variety of issues, such as the privatization of health care, missile defence, climate change, and flags of convenience used by his shipping company. In an attempt to prevent NDP voters in Western Canada from being poached by the Conservatives, the

TABLE 4.2

Coverage of themes in 2004 NDP news releases and English television commercials

News releases (%)	English television commercials (%)
Attack Martin and Liberals (44); attack Harper and Conservatives (35); health care (19); environment (12); ethics (9); gay rights (8); military (7); municipalities (7); jobs (6); give a "central role" to NDP in Parliament (6); balanced budget (4); post-secondary education (3); women's issues (3); polls in NDP's favour (2); protect the CBC (2); attack Bloc Québécois (2); taxes (2); NDP has same values as Quebec (1); protect French language (1); democratic reform (1); seniors (1); First Nations (1); immigration (1); diverse slate of candidates (0.5); child care (0.5); agriculture (0.5); employment insurance (0.5)	Layton's leadership (66); attack Martin and Liberals (21); attack Harper and Conservatives (21); give a "central role" to NDP in Parliament (16); taxes (11); health care (7); environment (7); Bush's foreign policy (4); education (4); child care (1); ethics (1); pensions (0.4); "equality rights" (0.5)

New Democrats were alarmist in their attacks on Harper's "irresponsible" corporate tax cuts, his "hidden agenda" to undermine the CBC, and the social conservative tendencies of his caucus. The NDP talked about a wider array of issues than it had in 2000. Although health care was still the top issue in its news releases, the party also frequently discussed the environment, ethics, the military, federal funding of municipalities, jobs, and gay rights (in particular the party's stance in favour of same-sex marriage). In an attempt to get noticed, the NDP released its full platform on the third day of the campaign, May 26, 2004. The NDP's news release for that day stated that the platform contained a promise of "five straight balanced budgets," and Layton stated that "we know there's an expectation that budgets be balanced. If the money isn't there, we will change the timing of our proposals, so that we keep the budget balanced." In an effort to raise the party's national presence, Layton also visited Quebec in the first week of the campaign and insisted that the NDP held values similar to those of Quebecers and could act as a link between progressives in Quebec and English Canada in a way that the Bloc Québécois could not. Again, in an attempt to make the NDP relevant in the final days of the campaign, Layton argued that polls were looking favourable for the party and repeatedly asked voters to give it a "central role" in what could be a minority Parliament so that he could fight for issues that mattered to them and their families. In hinting at its future role as a deal maker with other parties, the NDP was playing the role of market follower by positioning itself to have influence in the House of Commons with the aim of building the credibility with voters that it needed to become a contender one day to form the government.

The NDP's leader-centric campaign was evident in its English television commercials. Although two French television commercials were produced featuring Pierre Ducasse and other Quebec NDP candidates, these commercials were not placed in heavy rotation (Whitehorn 2004, 120), and only the English commercials are analyzed in Table 4.2. Whereas McDonough was almost absent from the NDP's commercials in 2000, Layton was presented as the primary spokesperson for the party in the commercials in 2004. The ads featured him talking about his ideas and plans (as opposed to the party's ideas and plans) to take on a variety of issues important to Canadian families, such as better health care, a cleaner environment, and more affordable education. Layton also highlighted the NDP's promise to remove the GST from family essentials such as children's clothing. Much time in the ads was devoted to touting his attributes, such as being a "respected civic leader, with a record of achievement," and clippings from newspapers that praised Layton as a "smart tough cookie" and a "thrilling new figure."

Reflecting the improved electoral market segmentation that came with greater financial resources to undertake polls and focus groups, political operatives were better equipped to craft appeals to strategic voters in 2004 compared with 2000. In juxtaposition to Layton's positive attributes, the NDP painted Liberals and Conservatives with the same brush as disciples of Bush's foreign policy agenda, privatizing health care, untrustworthy, and beholden to corporate interests. The NDP's critique of Canada's two major parties as being one and the same was intended to make voters consider the need for the NDP to play a central role in a possible minority government, which would avoid handing a Liberal or Conservative majority government what NDP commercials referred to as "a blank cheque." This strategy was also a direct response to the Liberal Party strategy of demonizing Harper and then imploring NDP supporters to vote strategically. Indeed, the Liberals ran negative ads accusing Harper of having a scary secret agenda on abortion, Iraq, Quebec separatism, and the environment that went against Canadian values – a tactic intended to convince NDP voters to support the

Liberals to prevent a Conservative majority (Clarkson 2004, 48). With polls showing the Conservatives gaining enough popularity to form the government possibly, the Liberals warned NDP voters in their final commercial to "think twice, vote once," and then exhorted them to "choose your Canada" (Clarkson 2004, 51). Martin even made a plea to NDP supporters in the dying days of the 2004 election to vote Liberal because New Democrats and Liberals shared the "same wellspring of values," and only a vote for the Liberals could avoid a Conservative majority (Whitehorn 2004, 129). For his part, Layton tried to depict Martin as the same type of politician as Harper, in an effort to combat these Liberal strategic voting appeals (Penner interview, 2015). However, some operatives felt that Layton was not particularly successful in equating Martin with Harper, and this tactic did not prevent strategic voters from shifting their votes to the Liberals in the final days of the campaign (Ibid.).

The NDP campaign was successful in some respects but unsuccessful in others. Political operatives were pleased that Layton's national profile became firmly established. Voters' name recognition of Layton had increased from 66 percent at the beginning of the campaign to 86 percent by the end (Whitehorn 2004, 115). The party's share of the popular vote nearly doubled from 8.5 percent to 15.7 percent, and this share increased in every province except Saskatchewan. This increase in the popular vote meant a massive increase in the quarterly allowances allotted to the party following the election. Still, operatives were disappointed with campaign events at which Layton stumbled, showing his lack of experience. They pointed to his using overheated rhetoric when he claimed that Martin was personally responsible for the death of a homeless man because he had cut housing programs, and his opposition to the Clarity Bill when he visited Quebec that was publicly rebuked by both Blaikie and McDonough. These missteps reflected poor preparation by Layton and his staff and insufficient consultation between the leader and his caucus. Although the NDP's proposal to impose an inheritance tax was thought to be innocuous, it caught the attention of the media as Layton struggled to explain it, and it ended up reinforcing the negative tax and spend stereotype that the party's promise of balanced budgets was supposed to address (Cox interview, 2015; Penner interview, 2015).

Most importantly, the party was able to increase its standing in the House of Commons by only five seats. Although Layton did win his seat in Toronto, the NDP lost its remaining two seats in Saskatchewan and dropped one of its three seats in Nova Scotia. Political operatives were particularly disappointed that the party was unable to pick up Trinity–Spadina, where Olivia Chow, Layton's wife, was running (Heath interview, 2015). The most upsetting element of the results was the inability of the party to translate its increased share of the popular vote into seats in the House of Commons, meaning that the NDP was two seats short of holding the balance of power in the minority Parliament. It appears that positioning itself as a market follower had forced a trade-off. The NDP had regained a national profile and a level of national support that it had not enjoyed since the 1980s, leading to larger quarterly allowances from Elections Canada, but not concentrating all of its resources on its niches of strength might have cost it more substantial seat gains.

The NDP as a Market Follower with a Focused Ground Game: The 2006 Election

Unlike in past campaigns, when the timing of the election had always been thrust on the NDP, the party actually had some control over when the 2006 election would be called. Despite having a caucus of only nineteen MPs and being the fourth party in the House of Commons, the NDP played a significant role in the brinkmanship that characterized the final year of the Thirty-Eighth Parliament (see Heath 2007). Belinda Stronach's defection to the Liberals effectively gave the New Democrats, along with independent MPs, the balance of power in the House of Commons. The NDP used this new-found power to force a series of amendments to the federal budget in May 2005 that deferred a planned series of corporate tax cuts in favour of a package of social and infrastructural spending (Heath 2007, 50–62). The party quickly branded the amendments as the "NDP's Better Balanced Budget," reflecting how the party was able to improve social programs while still balancing the books.

In the fall of 2005, the NDP publicly stated that its continued support for the minority government would depend on whether the Liberals made legislative changes to forbid the privatization of health care in the wake of the Supreme Court's decision in the *Chaoulli* case. When the Martin government appeared to be unresponsive on health care privatization, New Democrats effectively triggered an election by joining Conservative and Bloc Québécois MPs in voting for a nonconfidence motion in the aftermath of the first report of the Gomery Inquiry. Going into the election, the NDP had national support of just below 20 percent, and Layton was popular among the party's targeted voters (Whitehorn 2006, 94–95).

Given this context, NDP operatives devised three primary goals. First, the greatest nemesis of the party in federal politics had always been irrelevance. The party wanted to leverage its role in the brinkmanship of the House of Commons during the Martin minority government and the results that it delivered to Canadians in the federal budget amendments into greater national profiles for itself and its leader (Heath interview, 2015). Operatives wanted to ensure that the NDP went into the next Parliament and the next election as an important player in federal politics. In this sense, it wanted to position itself firmly as a market follower – having a national presence in federal politics but not being a contender to form the government. Second, the concept of next tier ridings was set aside for the 2006 election. Operatives instead emphasized re-electing the caucus, and, because of the party's increased financial resources to conduct small-scale polls, they knew the ten ridings that the NDP did not hold but had the best of chance of winning (Topp interview, 2015). Third, the NDP had been ill prepared for the strategic voting in 2004. In particular, political operatives thought that the Liberal Party stole NDP voters in the final days of the 2004 campaign when Martin claimed that the New Democrats and the Liberals had the "same wellspring of values" and that voting Liberal was the only way to prevent Harper from becoming prime minister. Operatives were determined this time to prevent a late-campaign migration of soft NDP voters away from the party based on the strategic voting arguments of the Liberals and their leader. This goal of preventing strategic voting reflected the political market orientation of the NDP toward competitors.

The most important tactic to achieve the goals of winning more seats and increasing the national profiles of both the party and the leader was what Brian Topp, director of the 2006 NDP campaign, called "big air, tight ground" (Topp interview, 2015; see also Lavigne 2013, 100–1). Before the writ was dropped and during the election period, the party poured the greater financial resources from the quarterly allowances into ten seats that it wanted to add to those that it already held (Milling interview, 2015). The improved finances of the party also allowed it to increase its national television advertising budget to almost $5 million from the roughly $1 million that it had spent on television in 2000 (Whitehorn 2001, 123; Whitehorn 2006, 102). The ads were more audacious and flashy in order for the NDP to remain prominent in the media as the campaign wound down (Milling interview, 2015). Displaying a political market orientation toward voters and greater financial resources for market testing, the national campaign adopted the tactic of having a clear and simple message based on a streamlined, well-rounded, and fully costed platform that did not include controversial stances such as an inheritance tax or opposition to the Clarity Bill (Milling interview, 2015; Topp interview, 2015).

The tactics against strategic voting were multifaceted. Whereas in 2004 the New Democrats had been almost equally critical of the Liberals and the Conservatives, in 2006 they decided to avoid demonizing Harper and focus on Martin and his Liberal government. In addition, the party tried to combat the idea that voting NDP was a wasted vote by continually pointing to the results that the party had attained for Canadians in the minority Parliament. Using electoral market segmentation techniques and better research paid for by the quarterly allowances from Elections Canada, the strategy culminated in isolating soft Liberal voters by having Layton ask them to "lend" their votes to the NDP in the election to teach the Liberals a lesson about their corruption and broken promises.

This campaign strategy carried some risks. First, it ignored the interests of some important stakeholders for the party. The strategy of focusing on the centrist Liberals and ignoring the right-wing Conservatives could leave the NDP open to public criticism from social movements and unions that it was not doing everything that it could to stop Harper from becoming prime minister. Also, refraining from critiquing the Conservatives could leave NDP voters in Western Canada susceptible to appeals from Harper's campaign. Moreover, the focus on a small number of ridings could endanger some of the overall gains that the party had made in 2004. Nonetheless, the reward was gaining a larger number of seats with which to weld influence in a minority Parliament and taking steps toward stopping the hemorrhaging of votes to the Liberals that had badly hurt the New Democrats in 2004 and in other elections.

As evident in Table 4.3, the overwhelming theme of NDP news releases during the 2006 election was attacking Martin and the Liberals. Often the attacks centred on Liberal corruption and the social conservatism of some Liberal MPs, but the NDP also highlighted what it claimed were broken promises by the Liberals in the areas of health care, seniors, infrastructure, and the environment. In contrast to the Liberals' record of broken promises and scandals, the NDP highlighted that it could get results for Canadians in Parliament, as it had during the minority government period from 2004 to 2005. We can also see that the party spent some days during the election talking about issues relatively new to it, such as crime, veterans, northern

TABLE 4.3

Coverage of themes in 2006 NDP news releases and English and French television commercials

News releases (%)	English television commercials (%)	French television commercials (%)
Attack Martin and Liberals (65); ethics (18); lend your vote to the NDP (12); health care (11); seniors (7); NDP results in the previous Parliament (6); attack Harper and Conservatives (6); crime (5); highlighting previous election results (5); education (3); veterans (3); vote NDP to provide balance to Conservatives (3); infrastructure (3); jobs (2); environment (2); women's issues (3); attack Bloc Québécois (2); balanced budget (2); child care (2); taxes (2); NDP has same values as Quebec (1); encourage Quebec to sign the Constitution (1); agriculture (2); arts and culture (2); northern Canada (1); youth issues (1); First Nations (1); immigration (1); diverse slate of candidates (1); equalization (1); NDP team (1); labour rights (1); democratic reform (0.5)	Attack Liberals (40); ethics (38); results for people in Parliament (35); lend your vote to the NDP (20); attack Conservatives (19); health care (9); jobs and skills training (6); seniors (3); end corporate tax giveaways (4); education (2); American-style social values (0.5)	Attack Liberals (48); results for people in Parliament (39); ethics (27); lend your vote to the NDP (16); jobs and skills training (16); health care (13); attack Bloc Québécois (10); seniors (5); end corporate tax giveaways (4); education (1)

Canada, and arts and culture as well as highlighting its national unity plans, which included recognizing Quebec as a "nation" and initiating negotiations for the Quebec government to sign the Constitution. The NDP used only limited space in its news releases to attack the Conservative Party. And its attacks on Conservatives were less harsh than its attacks on Liberals. Typical of its approach to Conservatives was a line from a news release on December 17, 2005, when Layton visited Vancouver: "Stephen Harper is out of touch with the priorities of British Columbians, and [Conservatives] have been an ineffective opposition when it comes to delivering results for British Columbia."

In the final days of the campaign, the NDP was clearly worried about the segment of the electoral market prone to strategic voting. As party operatives had anticipated, the Liberals repeated their 2004 strategy of negative ads against Harper to scare NDP voters into supporting the Liberals in order to prevent a Conservative majority (Clarkson 2006, 49–51). As evidence that Liberals held values similar to those of New Democrats, the Liberals convinced Buzz Hargrove, president of the CAW, to appear on stage with Martin and call on his members to vote strategically for the Liberals (Clarkson 2006, 45). The tactic used by the NDP against strategic voting was to ask Canadians who had voted Liberal in the past to "lend" their votes to the NDP this time, and this tactic came out strongly in its news releases. Typical of this appeal was Layton's statement late in the campaign, on January 18, 2006, that

> the Liberal Party is about to enter an extended period in the garage for repairs. It's going to be busy dealing with its own issues, not with yours. So I'm asking you to switch your vote. To lend us your vote in this election, to send a tough, experienced, able, and determined team of New Democrats to Ottawa ready on the first day of the next Parliament to fight for working families.

NDP operatives hoped to set the agenda of the campaign's final weeks by focusing media attention on teaching the Liberals a lesson and on the possibility of a minority Parliament in which the NDP would hold the balance of power. The party also spent some time late in the campaign highlighting past election results to argue that only voting for an NDP candidate could defeat a Conservative or Liberal candidate, depending on the region that Layton was visiting. Finally, as the Conservatives gained some momentum in the final days of the campaign, the NDP sent out three news releases about how voting for it could "balance" a possible Conservative minority government.

In terms of the NDP's English television commercials, the main theme was an attack on the Liberals, particularly their record on ethics and cutting taxes for corporations. The commercials also emphasized the results that Layton and New Democrats could gain in Parliament and asked Canadians who had voted Liberal in the past to vote NDP now to punish the Martin government for its corruption and broken promises. Although issues were not the main points of the commercials, most did mention that Layton and the NDP would fight in the House of Commons for a trio of issues summed up in one commercial as "improv[ing] care for seniors, education for young people, and health care for families." Perhaps reflecting the rise of the Conservatives in the polls as the campaign progressed, the NDP commercials closer to Election Day attacked Harper and his party for seeking to privatize health care and for their US-style social conservatism – issues that the Conservatives did not want mentioned (Ellis and Woolstencroft 2006, 77–79). Although the commercials did not explicitly tout Layton's leadership qualities as in 2004, they did reflect that the NDP was once again running a leader-centric campaign. His image and voice were featured prominently, and the narrator talked about how "Jack Layton and the NDP" would get "results for people" and put "working families first."

Using the financial resources from public subsidies, the NDP did run more television advertising in French in Quebec in 2006 than in previous campaigns (Whitehorn 2006, 120). However, at this point in the party's evolution, the French commercials were simply translations of the English commercials, with a few lines attacking the Bloc Québécois for not getting concrete results for Quebec and omitting references to the Conservative Party. Besides this small difference, the themes of the French and English commercials were ostensibly similar.

Overall, political operatives could not point to any campaign event that threw them off their strategy. The NDP platform contained a large number of commitments, but none of its promises became overly controversial, and the media generally accepted the party's costing (Topp interview, 2015). One campaign event reinforced the political market orientation of the party toward voters. Eschewing the party's traditional tendency to stress poverty as a root cause of crime and focus on rehabilitation that appealed to party members, one part of the platform included a section on harsher sentences for gun crimes that the party thought coincided with voters' mood after the Boxing Day shooting of fifteen-year-old Jane Creba shocked Canadians and became an election issue (Heath interview, 2015). Unexpectedly, the NDP became a major player in the campaign when the RCMP confirmed in a letter to NDP MP Judy Wasylycia-Leis that the Liberal government was under criminal investigation for leaks on changes to its income trust policy. Besides placing the NDP at the centre of national media stories, the news confirmed the party's charges that the Liberals were unethical. High-profile efforts to encourage strategic voting in favour of the Liberals by the CAW and a group of social movements within the Think Twice coalition undoubtedly did not help the NDP campaign. However, unlike in 2004, political operatives thought that they had anticipated these efforts and put in place tactics designed to limit their damage (Ibid.).

The greatest success of the NDP campaign was that its focused ground game helped the party to hold on to all of the seats that it had held going into the election with the exception of one as well as adding eleven more for a total of twenty-nine. It had been able to position itself as a market follower by running a national advertising campaign while still concentrating on its ground game in regions where it had a chance of picking up seats. This success in winning additional seats meant greater resources for the party's House of Commons operations. However, the party's share of the popular vote increased only marginally from 15.7 percent to 17.5 percent, and its vote share in Quebec bumped up slightly from 5 percent to 7 percent. The NDP was still the fourth party in the House of Commons and could not legitimately claim that it was a contender for the government.

The NDP as a Market Challenger: The 2008 Election

With the NDP facing a Conservative government as opposed to a Liberal government, the 2008 federal election had a different context than those immediately preceding it. Along with the Bloc Québécois, the NDP had consistently voted against the Harper government in the Thirty-Ninth Parliament, forcing the Liberals to prop up the government as they went through the process of choosing a new leader and rebuilding the party after a decade in power. Besides reflecting the New Democrats' ideological opposition to the Conservatives' agenda, voting against the government indicated a political market orientation toward competitors since it was intended to remind voters of how the Liberals were complicit in keeping Harper as prime minister and shirking their duty as the official opposition (Erickson and Laycock 2009, 99). The message was that Layton and the New Democrats, and not Dion and the Liberals, were standing up to Harper and the Conservatives (Lavigne 2013, 147).

The Conservatives had passed fixed election legislation that set the date for the next election in October 2009. When Harper ignored this legislation and called the election for October 2008, the speculation was that he did so because he believed that the time was ripe for a Conservative majority despite his public declaration that the outcome of the election "in all likelihood" would be a minority government (Waddell 2009, 217–18). Indeed, the dominant media narrative as the campaign began was simply "can Stephen Harper get the majority that seemed within grasp but had eluded the Conservatives in the two previous campaigns?" (Waddell 2009, 217). Harper himself was careful not to use the words *majority government*, preferring to focus on the economy (Ellis and Woolstencroft 2009, 45–55). This dominant narrative set up a parallel narrative of competition among the four so-called centre-left parties (Liberals, New Democrats, Bloc Québécois, and Greens) over who could emerge as the main opposition to Harper to prevent a Conservative majority government (Erickson and Laycock 2009, 99). Public domain polling confirmed this picture of a crowded left, with the Conservatives polling around 35 percent (below the 40 percent that pundits thought was needed for a majority government) and the rest of Canadians split among the other four parties, with the Liberals appearing to be close to 30 percent, the New Democrats hovering around 15 percent, and the Greens and Bloc Québécois somewhere between 5 percent and 10 percent (Clarke, Kornberg, and Scotto 2009b, 280; Erickson and Laycock 2009, 107).

As in the 2004 and 2006 elections, the overriding goal of the NDP reflected a political market orientation toward voters – to increase the national profile of Layton and the party and lead voters to realize that it was an important player in federal politics. The focus on a higher national profile could well position the NDP in relation to its competitors in the next Parliament – which could be a minority Parliament – creating momentum that could help the New Democrats to supplant the Liberals as the main opposition to the Conservatives. To do so, the NDP needed to re-elect all of its incumbents and win some of the next tier seats (potentially twenty to thirty) that the party had identified through small-scale polling as having a reasonable chance of going NDP (Lavigne interview, 2014). Research showed that most of these next tier seats were clustered around a riding that the NDP either held or had almost won in the previous election. Claiming the key "must win" riding and doing well in aspirational ridings surrounding it became important goals of the campaign. Since these regional clusters of support were spread throughout the country (including Quebec), the hope was that these groups of seats would form the foundation for the New Democrats to take over from the Liberals as the national alternative to the Conservatives and leave the party with a large number of seats with which to be influential in the House of Commons after the election.

Using the financial resources garnered from public subsidies and improvements in its fundraising, the NDP undertook more sophisticated market research. With internal research showing Layton's approval ratings close to 60 percent but voting intentions for the party around 15 percent (Topp interview, 2015), a political market orientation toward voters dictated that the campaign become even more leader-centric than in the past. As Brad Lavigne, the communications director of the NDP campaign, put it, "the 2008 campaign was the first campaign where the NDP was completely defined by the leader" (Lavigne interview, 2014). The acronym NDP fell into disuse as party operatives styled communications by referring to "Jack Layton's New Democrats."

The most audacious part of the NDP's campaign strategy was the move away from a market follower positioning that sought to depict the party as an important player in federal politics but not as a contender to form the government. Despite public domain polling showing that the NDP was far from forming the government, holding only 10 percent of the seats in the House of Commons, political operatives decided to adopt a market challenger positioning that publicly put forth the notion that the party was a contender to form the government. In doing so, they decided to place Layton front and centre in the campaign and to have him declare at his campaign kickoff that he was running to be prime minister. They hoped that the audacious and novel idea of Layton as prime minister would become part of the broader campaign narrative.

This bold decision resulted from the party's internal polling and focus group data, which illustrated that Stéphane Dion was perceived as a weak leader and that potential NDP voters found it believable that Layton could be prime minister (Topp interview, 2015). Canadians in the soft Liberal voter segment of the electoral market thought it completely normal that Layton would run to win the election and questioned why else he would run (Lavigne interview, 2014). The frame that the NDP attempted to impose on the campaign was embodied in the title of its platform: *A Prime Minister on Your Family's Side, for a Change*. The NDP essentially decided to ignore the Liberal Party and instead focus on the contrast between the "new strong" that Layton represented and the "bad strong" that Harper represented (Ibid.). The frame of Layton as prime minister was also a way to address strategic voting. It pushed the message within the strategic voter segment of the electoral market that Liberals, with their weak leader and lack of party unity, were in irreversible decline, and the only way to prevent a Harper majority government was to vote for New Democrats so that Layton could become prime minister (Topp interview, 2015). The idea that Dion was a weak leader had been reinforced constantly by Conservative Party advertising both before and during the campaign (Ellis and Woolstencroft 2009, 45–55). So, in pursuing this strategy, the NDP hoped to benefit from the negative attack machine that the Harper Conservatives had built up. Furthermore, the NDP attack on the Liberals was logical to voters since the Liberals were clearly struggling with an unpopular platform whose centrepiece was a complex carbon tax scheme and the destabilizing presence of Michael Ignatieff and Bob Rae waiting in the wings should Dion fail (Jeffrey 2009).

To make Layton look prime ministerial, the party platform had to inoculate him against being seen by voters as a high-taxing and high-spending New Democrat with little sense of how government revenues worked (Erickson and Laycock 2009, 112; Milling interview, 2015). Inspired by the approach taken by the Gary Doer NDP government in Manitoba and the Lorne Calvert NDP government in Saskatchewan, the platform was costed using federal Department of Finance projections, promised no personal tax increases, pledged balanced budgets, and presented spending on new programs as slow and incremental (Anderson interview, 2011). Layton described the platform as embodying "a very measured step-by-step approach" (quoted in Erickson and Laycock 2009, 113). All of this branding of Layton as a potential prime minister was supported by expensive national television commercials as in previous campaigns.

When it came to tactics to win more seats in its regional clusters of support around the country, the NDP used a sliding scale to place more resources in ridings that it was closer to winning based on internal polling and fewer resources on ridings that it was unlikely to win (Lavigne interview, 2015). Though key ridings would get the most resources, adjacent ridings that had future potential would also get some resources. For instance, most of the NDP's resources went into St. John's East in 2008, but some resources were also placed in neighbouring St. John's South Pearl (Ibid.). One interesting decision was to send Layton almost exclusively to next tier ridings and not to have him visit incumbents. His visits would bring considerable local media attention to the NDP candidates and boost the morale of the party's local volunteers. The guiding ideas behind these tactics were to wean the party off the need to target incumbent seats, use most of its resources on seats that were potential pickups in the election, and give at least some resources to aspirational seats that the party could win in subsequent elections. Again the surgical deployment of resources in this manner was possible only because of more sophisticated small-scale polling paid for by per-vote subsidies.

There was considerable debate among staff at party headquarters concerning the decision to have Layton declare that he was running for prime minister (Lavigne interview, 2014; Milling interview, 2015; Topp interview, 2015). The obvious risk of this strategy was that the media and opposing parties would ridicule the idea of "Prime Minister Jack Layton" as laughable and unrealistic, leading voters to look away from the NDP. Leaving incumbents more to their own devices than in previous campaigns could also backfire, and the party could lose seats in close races in ridings that it held. However, establishing Layton as Harper's principal opponent could marginalize the Liberals, who had a weak leader. Incremental gains in the party's regional clusters of support could also form beachheads from which future gains could be made, leading the NDP to supplant the Liberals as the main opponent of the Conservatives in these areas.

As shown in Table 4.4, the news releases illustrated the NDP's strategy to attack Harper and the Conservatives directly as much as possible. Early in the campaign, Layton's attack on the Conservatives generally centred on accusing Harper of giving corporations a $50 billion tax cut instead of investing in health care, infrastructure, education, and environmental protection. As the threat of economic recession became the most important issue in later stages of the campaign, Layton repeated that Harper had done nothing to protect Canadian jobs. Indeed, the economy came to dominate NDP news releases in the last couple of weeks of the campaign, with Layton often commenting that his "top priority" was to protect the "savings, pensions, homes, and jobs" of Canadians.

Reflecting a political market orientation toward voters and competitors, the NDP had moved away from campaigning on a certain issue, such as

TABLE 4.4

Coverage of themes in 2008 NDP news releases and English and French television commercials

News releases (%)	English television commercials (%)	French television commercials (%)
Attack Harper and Conservatives (48); economy (27); Layton as PM (15); health care (10); environment (9); taxes (8); progressives united behind NDP (6); infrastructure (5); Aboriginal issues (5); attack Dion and Liberals (4); poverty (4); ethics (3); education (3); child care (3); agenda for British Columbia (3); willingness to work with other parties (3); crime (2); agriculture (2); arts and culture (2); respect for Quebec's uniqueness (2); attack Bloc Québécois (2); food inspection (2); military (2); northern Canada (2); women's issues (2); balanced budget (1); equalization (1); international trade (1); NDP team (1)	Attack Harper and Conservatives (70); Layton's leadership (62); health care (31); environment (15); economy (15); taxes (6); attack Dion and Liberals (4); poverty (1); child care (0.5)	Layton's leadership (48); attack Bloc Québécois (22); environment (20); attack Harper and Conservatives (18); Bush and Iraq War (6); economy (6); arts and culture (4); health care (3); same-sex marriage (2)

health care, that appealed to members and external stakeholders and toward campaigning on an idea that the party's research indicated appealed to voters. That idea was Layton himself. The party argued that Layton, compared with Dion, was the best choice for prime minister and that progressive voters needed to unite behind Layton to stop Harper. Even if Layton did not become prime minister on election night, he was the leader who would stand up to Harper in the House of Commons and be open to working with all parties to improve the lives of Canadians no matter what Parliament looked like after election day.

The thrust of the English television commercials was to set up a contrast between Harper and Layton. Harper's version of strong leadership included giving away billions in tax cuts to corporations, failing to protect Canadian jobs, cutting funding to health care, and damaging the environment. Layton's strong leadership encompassed improving economic growth by training people for the jobs of the future, hiring more doctors and nurses, and making polluters pay. The point of the commercials was not to show what the

NDP planned to do in certain policy areas but to highlight issues that raised a contrast between the leadership of Harper and the leadership of Layton (Topp interview, 2015).

In contrast to previous campaigns, the NDP used its improved finances to run a substantially different set of French commercials in Quebec based on extensive market research in that province and spent $1 million to ensure that the ads were seen (Erickson and Laycock 2009, 118). The commercials displayed a political market orientation toward competitors and better electoral market segmentation, and their target was the relatively large segment of BQ voters whose second choice was the NDP. Using a play on words, the most prominent theme to appeal to this segment was that a vote for the Bloc Québécois would do little to "débloquer les choses [unblock things]" when it came to important issues such as the environment, the economy, and health care. Layton was hailed as the leader of a party with seats outside Quebec who shared Quebecers' values and would fight to improve the everyday lives of voters. Hence, as secondary themes, the commercials attacked Harper and the Conservatives for their cuts to arts and culture, pro-Bush stances, and opposition to gay marriage. If Quebecers were realistic, they would see that a vote for the NDP had the power to change things, whereas a vote for the Bloc Québécois would accomplish little. Hence the NDP's slogan in Quebec: "Le pouvoir de changer [The Power to Change]." For its part, the Bloc Québécois spent the campaign insisting that its presence was needed in Ottawa to defend Quebec's interests and values and to prevent a Conservative Party majority government (Bélanger and Nadeau 2009, 142–44).

Political operatives pointed out that some campaign events played into their plans, whereas others were disruptive. As they anticipated, Dion struggled throughout the campaign, and the media narrative about how many seats the Liberals would lose in the final days of the campaign reinforced the message of the NDP that it could emerge as the national alternative to the Liberals and that Layton could play an important role in the next Parliament. The emergence of the economic recession as the central issue of the election at the midpoint of the campaign was unforeseen and foreboding considering the traditional weakness of the NDP on economic issues. The party struggled to find a message on the economy, and the message that good social programs could insulate voters from tough economic times was seen by political operatives as satisfactory if not excellent (Topp interview, 2015).

Overall, the results of the election were disappointing for the New Democrat operatives. Harper was not the type of Conservative leader who could engineer a country-wide wave of support like Diefenbaker or Mulroney, and the Liberals ran an uncharacteristically weak leader and campaign, leaving the door open for an NDP breakthrough. It was Layton's third campaign in four years, the NDP had spent more money than ever before, and operatives thought that they had ran a technically sound campaign (Lavigne interview, 2015; Topp interview, 2015). Yet the NDP's percentage of the popular vote remained virtually unchanged, and its total number of votes edged downward, meaning slightly lower per-vote subsidies. The party failed to make a breakthrough in Quebec, only rewinning Mulcair's seat, which it had won in a by-election the year before. The party did win eight additional seats compared with the number in 2006, including a seat in Alberta and a seat in Newfoundland, to bring even more resources to its House of Commons operations. However, NDP operatives had been hopeful that New Democrats and Liberals would win enough seats to make it possible to form a Liberal Party–NDP minority government with support from the Bloc Québécois (Lavigne 2013, 164–66). Instead, the NDP won very few of the next tier seats that its operatives believed could turn orange, and the combined Liberal Party–NDP seat total was nowhere near high enough to contemplate a minority government arrangement. The positioning as a market challenger had raised the national profiles of the NDP and Layton, but the party seemed to be destined to continue to struggle for relevance as the perennial fourth party in a minority Parliament.

The NDP as a Market Challenger Again: The 2011 Election
Whereas the Liberals propped up the Harper government until late 2009, all three opposition parties (including the NDP) voted with the Conservatives to keep the Harper minority government from collapsing at various times in 2010. In the lead-up to the 2011–12 budget, the Bloc Québécois and the Liberal Party announced their intention to try to bring down the government at the first available opportunity, whereas the NDP attempted to negotiate amendments to the budget, with the intention of increasing its time under the media spotlight and continuing to develop Layton's brand as an honest broker trying to get results within a fractious House of Commons (Monk interview, 2014). When the budget did not meet the demands of the NDP caucus, Layton essentially triggered an election by announcing that it would not support the budget. This decision was panned by pundits,

who predicted that the party would lose seats in the upcoming election because it would be blamed for defeating a popular budget, and fear about a potential Conservative Party majority would fuel strategic voting in favour of the Liberal Party (McGrane 2011, 81). Moreover, Layton was not in good health, and public domain polling showed the NDP as somewhere between 13 percent and 18 percent of the popular vote (Ibid.).

The NDP did not waver from its political market orientation toward voters and competitors, and the goals of the 2011 election were fundamentally similar to those for the 2008 election. Once again the ultimate goal was to increase the profile and relevance of the NDP in the eyes of voters and to position the party well against its competitors in what could be another minority Parliament. Political operatives aimed at a growth election in which they could build on the regional beachheads that the party had been developing across Canada to win as many next tier seats as possible (Bélanger interview, 2011; Monk interview, 2011). As in 2008, NDP operatives would focus the party's resources and the leader's tour on nonincumbent ridings (Lavigne interview, 2011; Monk interview, 2011). There was a hope that the seats would be evenly sprinkled throughout the country and that the party could beat the forty-four seats that it had won in 1988 (Anderson interview, 2014). The operatives believed that the party could win as many as ten seats in Quebec (Bussières interview, 2015). The total number of targeted seats, including those of incumbents, was about seventy (Anderson interview, 2011; Rotman interview, 2011). If the campaign went well, internal research showed, the party could attain as much as 25 percent of the popular vote (Lavigne interview, 2011).

In terms of tactics, political operatives used the greater financial resources gained through public subsidies and better fundraising to conduct extensive internal polling and focus groups, allowing for much more sophisticated electoral market segmentation than in past elections. Party research illustrated that the base of NDP voters in English Canada (roughly 20 percent of the ROC electorate) would remain loyal, and therefore the party should concentrate on what it dubbed "Layton Liberals." They were a specific segment of the ROC electorate. These voters had the Liberal Party as their first choice and the NDP as their second choice, and they were unsure about Ignatieff but trusted Layton (Anderson interview, 2014). Compared with the NDP's loyal supporters, Layton Liberals were generally older and male and did not react particularly well to class-tinged language such as "working families" (Ibid.). Although these voters were generally economically secure, they were anxious about how the recent economic recession would affect their savings, their quality of life, and their senior parents or their children heading into university (Anderson interview, 2011; Lavigne interview, 2011). They did not believe that the NDP could form the government, so they were susceptible to Liberal arguments about wasting votes on the party (Anderson interview, 2011). NDP agents thought that, as long as the New Democrats were seen as reasonably competent and not too "radical" compared with the Liberals, the difference in Layton Liberals' levels of trust between the two leaders could be used to sway these voters into the NDP column (Anderson interview, 2014). So the NDP's ballot box question would be targeted directly at Layton Liberals by asking "which leader do you trust to get things done for you and your family?" (McGrane 2011, 85).

Once again the NDP decided to position itself as a market challenger. A leader-centric campaign was planned that focused on Layton's ability to deliver results in Parliament and his positive attributes, such as trustworthiness, empathy, and determination, that research indicated appealed to the party's targeted segments of the electoral market (Monk interview, 2011). The party had spent large amounts of money from public subsidies and its improved fundraising on efforts to understand and hone Layton's brand and to prepare and script their leader for campaigns. As in 2008, Layton was presented as running for prime minister, and the phrase "Jack Layton's New Democrats" was used in favour of the acronym NDP on lawn signs and during television commercials (Anderson interview, 2011). In presenting Layton as the potential prime minister, the NDP attempted to undermine Liberal Party arguments about strategic voting and therefore showing a political market orientation toward competitors. Indeed, as NDP operatives had anticipated, Ignatieff began the campaign by emphatically stating that "there's a blue door and a red door in this election" and reminding NDP voters that they needed to support the Liberals to avoid a Harper majority government (Jeffrey 2011, 62). Early in the campaign, NDP strategists presented the party as a contender for the government, and later they presented messages about voters having a "choice," as opposed to Ignatieff's argument that voting Liberal was necessary to prevent a Harper majority government (Lavigne interview, 2011; Monk interview, 2011). The NDP platform cautiously opted for a balanced budget, no personal tax increases, and five "practical results" that could be realized in cooperation with other parties in a minority Parliament summed up as "hire more doctors and nurses, strengthen your pension, kick-start job creation, help out your family budget, and fix Ottawa for good." In introducing the platform, Layton claimed that, "as Prime Minister, I will work with others to get Ottawa working for you. And I will deliver results in the first 100 days. You can hold me to it" (quoted in McGrane 2011, 83). To reinforce his trustworthiness and to inoculate against his brand weakness of being a "tax and spend" politician, party spending would be slowly phased in (Lavigne interview, 2011), and Layton made statements such as the one on April 30, 2011: "I know we can't fix every problem. But we can take practical steps in the right direction."

NDP operatives decided that they could not ignore the Liberals as they had in 2008. They decided to attack the Conservatives early in the campaign to illustrate that New Democrat candidates could beat Conservative candidates in all regions of the country and that the NDP was a better "Harper fighter" than the Liberal Party (Monk interview, 2011). This tactic was intended to protect the party from strategic voting by showing Layton Liberals that the NDP was the only party that could stand up to Harper and that voting NDP meant defeating Conservative candidates and preventing a Harper majority (Ibid.). After this narrative was established, the NDP campaign began to draw direct comparisons between Layton and Ignatieff by asking voters: "Who can you trust to fight Harper?" (Anderson interview, 2014). At the same time, the NDP talked about how Ottawa was broken (a theme that it thought hurt both Liberals and Conservatives as the traditional parties) and how voting for Layton would bring results since he was willing to work with other parties in a minority Parliament if one was elected (Anderson interview, 2014; Lavigne interview, 2011). In terms of the type of agenda that they were trying to set, the hope of political operatives was to have the media focus on leadership qualities (Layton versus Harper and Layton versus Ignatieff) as opposed to policy issues.

The strategy in Quebec was similar in some respects but different in others. The NDP would not overtly critique the Bloc Québécois because party research indicated that doing so would be akin to attacking Quebec and could offend voters who had the Bloc Québécois as their first choice and the NDP as their second choice (Anderson interview, 2014). The party's internal polling showed that support for the Bloc Québécois was trending downward and that Layton was popular among francophone Quebecers (Bélanger interview, 2011). The emphasis would be on Layton, along with his team of Quebec candidates, working with other parties to fix Ottawa and ensure that Quebec values were represented there. Coming down the stretch to election day, the NDP hoped that the election would be covered as a competition between Liberals and New Democrats over which party could be the alternative to a Harper government and that such coverage could drive Bloc Québécois voters to vote strategically for the NDP (Anderson interview, 2014).

All of this strategizing about the NDP's position vis-à-vis its opponents in English Canada and Quebec illustrates that the party had fully adopted a political market orientation toward competitors. The risks of this strategy and this orientation were familiar by now to the NDP's political operatives. Presenting the NDP as a contender for the government and Layton as a candidate for prime minister could lead to ridicule by the media and opponents. Focusing on next tier seats could endanger the seats of incumbents in tough local fights. Going hard after the Conservatives early in the campaign could end up driving voters to the Liberals if they became convinced of the merits of strategic voting. Moreover, refraining from attacking the Bloc Québécois left the door wide open for Duceppe to define his party as the only true opposition to Harper in Quebec and for the NDP to be ignored (Lavigne interview, 2011). Indeed, for the first half of the campaign, Duceppe repeated the message that only the BQ could defend Quebec's interests and that only a vote for the BQ could prevent a Conservative Party majority (Bélanger and Nadeau 2011, 119–23). Yet substantial gains in next tier seats could be made if the NDP's primary centre-left opponents ran poor campaigns and if the NDP could remain competitive and head into the final days of the campaign with momentum (Monk interview, 2014).

As indicated in Table 4.5, NDP news releases in 2011 focused closely on Layton's leadership. Most of the policies were announced as "Layton's plan" as opposed to the "NDP's plan." Often the news releases emphasized that Canadians could trust Layton to get results. For instance, a news release late in the campaign, on April 20, 2011, declared that "Jack Layton says Canadians can trust him to fix health care, and as Prime Minister, he will deliver results within the first 100 days." To accentuate the contrast between Harper and Layton, the news releases attacked the Conservatives on their ethics and their broken promises on health care in favour of giving tax breaks to "large profitable companies shipping Canadian jobs overseas" (March 30, 2011). The idea was clearly that Harper had broken Ottawa and that Layton could be trusted to fix it.

TABLE 4.5

Coverage of themes in 2011 NDP news releases and English and French television commercials

News releases (%)	English television commercials (%)	French television commercials (%)
Layton's leadership (33); attack Harper and Conservatives (30); momentum (14); health care (10); affordability (10); ethics (8); attack Ignatieff and Liberals (7); seniors (6); NDP team (6); Ottawa is broken (5); NDP campaign technology (5); infrastructure (4); small business (3); HST (3); environment (3); pensions (2); crime (2); MP absenteeism (2); military (2); jobs (2); agriculture (2); northern Canada (2); diverse slate of candidates (2); veterans (2); women's issues (2); workers' safety laws (2); working together (1); taxes (1); only NDP can defeat Conservatives (1); child care (0.5)	Layton's leadership (27); attack Harper and Conservatives (25); attack Ignatieff and Liberals (16); ethics (12); Ottawa is broken (5); health care (5); affordability (5); small business (4); pensions (2); working together (1)	Ottawa is broken (22); Layton's leadership (18); NDP team (12); protecting French (10); working together (8); environment (8); Afghanistan/ peacekeeping (5); affordability (3); health care (3)

The news releases brought up a variety of issues, and no particular issue was dominant. Indeed, Table 4.5 shows that the NDP discussed issues not usually associated with the party: protecting small business, helping veterans, increasing military spending on building naval ships (to respond to disasters, protect Canada's shorelines, and support peacekeeping), and fighting crime by hiring more police officers, preventing gang recruitment, and establishing tougher sentences on home invasions and carjackings. Reflecting a political market orientation toward voters, party strategists thought that it was important to focus on these traditionally non-NDP issues because voters expected a potential prime minister to have a well-rounded set of policies (Monk interview, 2011). Although the strategists knew that New Democrats had trouble competing with Conservatives and Liberals on the issue of macroeconomic stability, they believed that the NDP should not run away from the economy and that microeconomic or "pocketbook" issues could resonate with voters (Lavigne interview, 2011). Table 4.5 illustrates an emphasis on affordability, touted as the selling point of policies such as taking the GST off home heating, reversing the recent imposition of the HST in British Columbia and Ontario, capping credit card fees, and establishing regulations to make it easier for consumers to unlock their cell phones.

The NDP was more proactive in trying to convey a sense of momentum in its 2011 news releases compared with those of previous campaigns. News releases referred to the cutting-edge campaign technology that the party was deploying and commented on the improvement of the party's position in public domain polling, particularly in Quebec. The final news releases of the campaign often commented on the party's momentum while frequently referring to how Layton wanted to "work together" to make change. Political operatives acknowledged that the principal purpose of that theme was subtly to suggest that the NDP was open to working with other parties in a minority Parliament to get results, thereby undercutting the strategic voting argument that change could come only by voting for the Liberals, who had a realistic chance of forming the government (Anderson interview, 2011; Lavigne interview, 2011). However, party strategists also mentioned that leaving the phrase "working together" undefined played to their advantage as the campaign came to a close because the phrase had different meanings for different people. For some, it meant the NDP's openness to cooperation in a minority Parliament; for others, it meant Quebec and English Canada working together, new NDP voters and traditional NDP voters working together, average Canadians working together to defeat Harper, Layton working with voters, or simply an end to the political brinkmanship in Ottawa (Ibid.).

The NDP's English television commercials sought to reinforce its main messages concerning Layton's trustworthiness, working together, and giving voters a choice. In the last line of the final NDP commercial of the 2011 campaign, Layton used a combination of short and simple sentences shouted in front of a cheering crowd of supporters: "Together we can do this. You know where I stand. You know I'm a fighter. And I won't stop until the job is done." The commercials were clear that voters could trust neither Harper nor Ignatieff, but they could trust Layton. Commercials early in the campaign featured attacks on Harper about letting a Tim Hortons be used as a temporary emergency ward, cutting the taxes of a company that moved jobs to the United States, and impending fraud charges against senators whom he had appointed. Later in the campaign, commercials accused Ignatieff of flip-flopping on various issues and having the worst attendance record of all

MPs in the House of Commons. As opposed to choosing the Liberals as the lesser of two evils, voters could trust Layton as a viable alternative, and commercials implored voters not to believe the Liberals that they did not have a choice. In one commercial, Layton declared that "people will try to tell you that you have no choice but to vote for more of the same. But you do have a choice." Although health care was mentioned in the ads, economic matters were more prominent. Layton claimed that he would "target investments to small businesses and those actually creating jobs here in Canada," enhance pensions for seniors, and "give your pocketbook a break." The emphasis on the economy was intended to protect against negative "tax and spend" stereotypes of the NDP and to strengthen its standing with voters who were still feeling the effects of the 2008–09 economic recession (Lavigne interview, 2011).

The NDP's French commercials were different from the party's English commercials. The most striking difference was that, except for a single mention of Harper's cuts to arts and culture, the commercials refrained from directly attacking opponents. Epitomized by the image of a hamster running on a wheel, the main thrust of the French commercials was that Ottawa was broken and that important issues facing Quebec were being neglected. Although it was not stated clearly, the commercial insinuated that the Bloc Québécois could not change this situation given its inability to form the government and work with other parties (Anderson interview, 2014; Monk interview, 2011). Layton, whose party could be part of the government in a minority Parliament, could deliver results for Quebec that Duceppe and the BQ could not. In the commercials, Layton was portrayed as a "sympathique [good-natured]" politician who represented "Quebec" values, such as pacifism, environmental sustainability, and protection of the French language. These issues had been identified by the party's polling and market research on francophone Quebec (Anderson interview, 2011). By working together, Layton and Quebec voters could fix Ottawa. Working together here meant that Layton would work with his team of NDP MPs from Quebec, with ROC voters who hoped to prevent a Harper majority government, and with other parties in a minority Parliament. Mulcair was featured in the commercials as a representative of the NDP's Quebec team instead of having all of the commercials focus on Layton, as was the case in English Canada.

For the most part, political operatives were pleased with how campaign events played into their strategy. The defection of an NDP candidate to the

Liberals during the first week of the campaign had the potential to reinforce strategic voting arguments, and the initial public domain polls showed the NDP mired at about 15 percent of national support (Lavigne 2013, 209–15; Turcotte 2011, 207–9). However, the operatives stuck with their plans, and nothing happened in the crucial second part of the campaign to throw the party off its strategy. After the party's platform and candidates were scrutinized with little resulting controversy, the NDP's preparation and market-testing of its leader paid off as Layton had good performances during *Tout le monde en parle* (a popular Quebec talk show) and in both the French and the English leaders' debates (McGrane 2011, 91–92). Layton even had some memorable unscripted moments such as enthusiastically cheering a Montreal Canadiens goal during a live hit from a bar in Quebec and rousing crowds by raising his cane over his head following his speeches (Anderson interview, 2014). As the campaign entered its final weeks, strong polling numbers in Quebec gave the party a sense of momentum and undercut Liberal arguments about strategic voting. This momentum reinforced the operatives' planned ads for the end of the campaign that focused on visuals of Layton delivering emotionally charged lines (Lavigne interview, 2011).

The NDP also benefited from the fact that it had been almost completely ignored by its opponents during the early and middle portions of the campaign. With the NDP surge occurring so late in the campaign, the other parties were caught off guard and had little time to respond. In fact, the Conservatives had disbanded their NDP opposition research unit before the campaign started and hastily had to put together commercials about the "socialist threat" posed by a Layton-led coalition government with the Liberals (Ellis and Woolstencroft 2011, 37–38). The Liberals were completely unprepared for the NDP surge (Jeffrey 2009, 69). Despite polls showing that the NDP was quickly gaining in popularity, the Liberals decided to stick with the strategy that they had devised before the campaign, which consisted of attacking the Conservatives and touting their own platform that "speaks to Canadian families" (Ibid.). The Bloc Québécois began the campaign by criticizing Conservatives and Liberals as one and the same because of their weak defence of Quebec's interests, but the BQ had refrained from the attacking the NDP, which it did not regard as a "real competitor" (Bélanger and Nadeau 2011, 119). Duceppe was forced to rethink quickly the BQ's tactics in the final week of the campaign. The party suddenly began to argue that the election was no longer about blocking a Conservative Party majority government but about keeping the sovereignist dream alive in the face of Layton's ambiguous constitutional stance and about preventing a team of very inexperienced Quebec NDP candidates from being sent to Ottawa to defend the province's interests (Ibid., 125–26). NDP strategists thought that these attacks on Layton in the last week of the campaign did not make much of a difference because they appeared too late, and the party had been building up the Layton brand over several elections, so he could withstand a one-week attack (Lavigne interview, 2011).

Although the Conservatives won a majority government, NDP operatives were ecstatic with the results of the 2011 election. Positioning the party as a market challenger and adhering to a political market orientation toward voters and competitors had worked. Overall, the NDP's share of the national popular vote had increased from 18.2 percent to 30.6 percent, meaning large increases in the party's public subsidies over the next four years of the majority Harper government. The party increased its seat total in English Canada from thirty-six to forty-four, narrowly beating its former best election result, when it had won forty-three seats outside Quebec in the 1988 election. Moreover, those forty-four seats were spread throughout almost all of the English Canadian provinces. The party's percentage of the popular vote increased in every English Canadian province except Newfoundland and Labrador, and its share of the popular vote in English Canada increased from 20.3 percent to 26.4 percent. In an incremental fashion, the NDP was gaining next tier seats and votes in English Canada.

There was nothing incremental, however, about the results in Quebec. An "orange wave" swept over the province, and the NDP took a remarkable fifty-nine seats, including many seats that it did not expect to win. The party's share of the popular vote in Quebec surged from 12.1 percent to 42.9 percent. This historic breakthrough ensured that the NDP became the official opposition and would have greater resources for its parliamentary operations than at any other time in its history. The 2011 election also represented the first time in the history of the CCF-NDP that its seat total and popular vote surpassed those of the Liberal Party, which fell into third place with only thirty-four seats and 18.9 percent of the popular vote. The risks that NDP strategists had been taking since Layton had become leader in 2004 finally paid off, and the NDP had been resurrected from being an afterthought in Canadian politics to being a contender for the government with one of the most popular political leaders in Canada.

The NDP as a Market Leader: The 2015 Election

The NDP entered the 2015 election in an unprecedented position. It was the official opposition and had a solid base of seats in Quebec. Internal research showed that there was a strong desire for change among approximately two-thirds of the electorate, growing weary of a Conservative Party government heading into its tenth year of office (Lavigne interview, 2015). The NDP was well financed, and its top operatives were well experienced, many of them working in their third or fourth election for the party. Although the New Democrats had been mired in third place behind the Liberals and the Conservatives for much of 2014, their support rose steadily during the first half of 2015 as the Liberals slipped into third place, with about 20 percent of the popular vote, and the Conservatives remained steady at 30 percent (Coletto 2016). Harper did respect his government's fixed election date legislation and called an election for late October, but he surprised his opponents and the media by dropping the writ on August 6 instead of waiting until after Labour Day, resulting in a seventy-eight-day campaign, the longest in recent Canadian history. On the day that the campaign began, public domain polling indicated the strong likelihood of an NDP minority government (Ibid.). One poll even found that the NDP's support was at 39 percent and that Mulcair was the most preferred prime minister, and it projected that the NDP was only ten seats short of a majority government (Forum Research 2015). The poll put Conservatives and Liberals well behind New Democrats at 28 percent and 25 percent, respectively.

Given that its internal polls confirmed the public domain polls, the goal of the NDP was to form the government and ensure that Mulcair became prime minister (Bélanger interview, 2015; Lavigne interview, 2015). In short, the party positioned itself as a market leader that would rise to power by defending the market share that it had recently acquired. The party ambitiously targeted 170 seats, including all of the seats that it had won in the previous election and approximately seventy additional seats, enough to form a one-seat majority government given a 338-seat House of Commons (Lavigne interview, 2015; Lucy Watson interview, 2015). Thus, though the political operatives were actually targeting a minority NDP government, they were prepared to aim at a majority NDP government if the campaign went really well (Ibid.).

In Quebec, the NDP was solidly in first place in internal polling at the beginning of August, and that polling showed that Mulcair was far more liked and trusted than Harper, Trudeau, or Duceppe (Rebecca Blaikie interview, 2015; Gébert interview, 2015). It appeared to be a relatively safe bet that Quebec could be relied on as the party's regional stronghold and that a block of seats from the province could be the anchor of the first-ever NDP federal government (Ibid.). However, since the party had won fifty-nine of seventy-five seats in Quebec in 2011, there were few additional seats left to claim. Importantly, the seventy additional seats that the NDP was targeting were almost all in English Canada, and almost all were held by Conservatives. It had to be this way. The New Democrats had placed second to the Conservatives in many ridings in English Canada in 2011, and the Liberals had won only twenty-seven seats outside Quebec in 2011 (Bélanger interview, 2015). Assuming that Quebec voters stayed loyal to the NDP, the road to an NDP minority government would go through Conservative-held ridings in English Canada. In practice, this strategic calculation meant that Mulcair's tour would spend a disproportionate amount of time in the battleground provinces of Ontario and British Columbia in ridings held by Conservatives (Bélanger interview, 2015; Gébert interview, 2015).

Two primary tactics were devised to meet the goals of the NDP. First, the party sought to present itself as a government-in-waiting and "safe change." Reflecting a political market orientation toward competitors, NDP strategists feared that the Conservatives would use their large advertising budget to paint the NDP as too risky to trust as the government during the final two weeks of the campaign (Lavigne interview, 2015). Incumbent governments in recent provincial elections in British Columbia and Ontario had effectively used the message "don't vote for us because you like us, vote for us because we are safe and the official opposition is risky," as their campaigns were ending (Ibid.). The NDP decided not to run television commercials in August and to save its advertising budget for September and October to combat the potential barrage of Conservative attack ads about the risk that an NDP government would pose (Fortin interview, 2015; Lavigne interview, 2015). At the same time, the NDP's research, comprehensive because of the party's improved finances, indicated that many voters thought that Justin Trudeau was a risky choice for prime minister because of his inexperience (Lavigne interview, 2015; McGrath interview, 2015). During the past two elections, the NDP had benefited from the Conservative Party's attacks on Dion and Ignatieff. In 2015, the Conservatives ran pre-election advertising claiming that Trudeau was "just not ready," and NDP strategists saw an opportunity to present their party as "safe change" compared with the "risky change" that voting Liberal would bring (Ibid.). NDP operatives thought that the key to winning the election was a particular segment of the English Canadian electoral market: voters who wanted change, lived in Conservative-held ridings, but hesitated between New Democrats and Liberals, dubbed NDP/LPC switchers by the operatives (Lavigne interview, 2015). The research done by the operatives suggested that the NDP would be able to win over these English Canadian voters by promising that its version of change was safe and secure. Hence, the NDP slogan "change that's ready" was unveiled in late 2014, and the party used that slogan extensively in its pre-election advertising. Use of the slogan foreshadowed what the operatives wanted to be the ballot box question of the election: "Which party is ready to bring change to Ottawa?" (Lavigne interview, 2015; Soule interview, 2015).

Creating a safe change/government-in-waiting frame for the election encompassed several elements. NDP research showed that Mulcair was seen by the NDP/LPC switcher segment of the electoral market as a serious politician, reassuring and capable, in contrast to Trudeau, seen as a political neophyte (Bélanger interview, 2015; Lavigne interview, 2015; McGrath interview, 2015). The Mulcair brand was a simple one: experienced leadership (Ibid.). Mulcair was portrayed as the type of leader who could manage a $2 trillion economy and be trusted to handle international crises at three in the morning as Canadian families slept (Lavigne interview, 2015; Lucy Watson interview, 2015). Reflecting the presidentialization of postmodern campaigning, the acronym NDP was replaced with the phrase "Tom Mulcair's NDP."

Political operatives also did not want any doubt to arise about whether the NDP had enough candidates who were "cabinet material" (Soule interview, 2015). So they organized what they called the "B tour," a series of news conferences for the national press that featured prominent NDP candidates (Linner interview, 2015; Lucy Watson interview, 2015). Unlike in past campaigns in which Layton announced all of the party's policies, these candidates were tasked with making announcements on certain platform commitments. To be seen as a government-in-waiting and safe change, research indicated, the NDP needed to mitigate negative stereotypes of its brand, such as overspending, overtaxing, and being bad for the economy (Lavigne interview, 2015; Moran interview, 2015; Soule interview, 2015). As in past campaigns under Layton, the NDP stressed that it would not raise personal taxes, be committed to a balanced budget in every year of its mandate, and focus on an array of policy areas instead of just "NDP issues" such as social programs and environmental protection. The party would commit to creating new and relatively expensive social programs in areas such as child care and prescription drug insurance, but the funding for such programs would be gradually phased in (Moran interview, 2015; Watkins interview, 2015). These considerations of how voters saw the NDP and its brand indicated that the party had fully adopted a political market orientation toward voters.

The NDP's second tactic to achieve its goals was to try to set the agenda of the campaign and to have the media focus on a two-way race between New Democrats and Conservatives. As the campaign entered its final days, the NDP had to be seen as the sole credible alternative to the Conservative government, and Mulcair had to be seen as the only safe choice to replace Harper as prime minister (Bélanger interview, 2015; Lavigne interview, 2015; McGrath interview, 2015). It was decided that the NDP campaign would intensely criticize the Conservatives and refrain from attacking the Liberals. Strategic voting had been the bane of the NDP for years, but in 2015 its political operatives hoped that it could be used in their favour. With the assumption that the Liberals would gradually fade away during the campaign, the narrative of a two-way race between New Democrats and Conservatives would set up strategic voting appeals at the end of the campaign (Bélanger interview, 2015; Lavigne interview, 2015; Linner interview, 2015). The strategic voting arguments of the Liberals could finally be used against them: a vote for the Liberals would be a wasted vote, and if one wanted to get rid of Harper then one had no choice but to vote NDP. Direct attacks by the NDP on Trudeau and the Liberals would only give their campaign credibility and undermine the narrative of the two-way NDP–Conservative Party race (McGrath interview, 2015). There were also fears of blowback from NDP/LPC switchers; attacking the Liberals and Trudeau might only help the Conservatives. In the many focus groups that had become possible with the party's more robust financial position, the NDP's targeted voters tended to be slightly offended and come to the defence of Trudeau when presented with NDP attacks on him (Ibid.). Based on feedback from these focus groups, the operatives decided that critiquing Trudeau, with whom many voters in important segments of the English Canadian electoral market felt that they had personal connections, could backfire on the NDP in the heated context of an election campaign (Ibid.). Instead, the operatives decided that the NDP's air game would exclusively attack Harper and to focus Mulcair's tour on Conservative-held ridings

(Bélanger interview, 2015). By attacking the Conservatives only, the NDP was signalling to NDP/LPC switchers in Conservative-held ridings in English Canada that it was the party best positioned to beat Conservative incumbents and repair the damage that the Harper government had done (Ibid.). As the long campaign came to an end and the NDP had momentum because it was leading in the polls, anti-Conservative voters would flock behind New Democrats' version of "ready" and "safe" change to eject Harper from power (Ibid.). As in 2011, all of this planning around strategic voting and how the NDP should treat its opponents indicated a political market orientation toward competitors as opposed to party members or external stakeholders.

In the elections that the NDP had run under Layton, the risks of its strategies centred on being too ambitious and daring. In adopting what could have been seen as a classic front-runner strategy, there was the possibility that the NDP under Mulcair was playing it too safe. The party positioned itself as a market leader, but perhaps its support was too soft to merit that positioning. Potentially, the cautious tone of the NDP campaign would not motivate voters and fail to underscore the urgency of defeating the Harper government. The idea of Mulcair's best quality being his experience lacked emotional punch and spoke more to voters' heads than to their hearts (Lavigne interview, 2015; Linner interview, 2015; Soule interview, 2015). The NDP was relying on the rationality of voters instead of trying to excite them. Although attacking the Liberals ran the risk of giving them credibility and alienating some NDP/LPC switchers sympathetic toward Trudeau, failing to attack them could allow them to hang around and remain a viable agent of change as the campaign progressed.

For their part, the Liberals decided to run a large amount of advertising in August to showcase their young and energetic leader and their positive message of being the party of "real change" (Jeffrey 2016, 72–75). If the Liberals were not eliminated as an agent of change by the final weeks of the campaign, then the two-way race that the NDP strategists envisioned would never materialize. Indeed, not attacking the Liberals and focusing on strategic voting appeals could leave the impression that there were no substantial differences between Liberals and New Democrats (Linner interview, 2015). Also, the NDP's constant attack on how Harper was so destructive for Canada could actually reinforce the Liberals' messages about the need for drastic and bold change (Rebecca Blaikie interview, 2015; Lucy Watson interview, 2015).

Another risk involved Quebec. Realizing that its base of voters in Quebec was not well established, the NDP could have concentrated its strategy on protecting its Quebec stronghold by making specific appeals to Quebec voters and ensuring that Mulcair spent much of his time there. Interestingly, the party's message in Quebec was almost the same as its broader national message (Rebecca Blaikie interview, 2015). The research of the political operatives found that, like English Canadians, Quebecers were looking for a credible and well-prepared agent of change to replace Harper, and they saw Mulcair as the leader who had the most experience and was the most ready to get the job done (Rebecca Blaikie interview, 2015; Gébert interview, 2015; Soule interview, 2015). The campaign in Quebec was designed to be leader-centric and light on policy or what could be considered "Quebec issues." As in the rest of the country, the NDP refrained from attacking the Liberals in Quebec so as not to give them credibility. But the party also refrained from attacking the Bloc Québécois in order to maintain the narrative of a Conservative-NDP race (Ibid.). NDP strategists relied on a well-organized ground game to win over Quebec as opposed to looking for specific issues that resonated with Quebec voters or sending Mulcair frequently to Quebec to defend NDP seats (Rebecca Blaikie interview, 2015; Gébert interview, 2015).

However, the rewards of the NDP strategy in the 2015 campaign were equally obvious. If the Quebec base held with a strong ground game, then the overall NDP strategy aimed at wooing NDP/LPC switchers in Conservative-held ridings in English Canada could lead to the party forming government for the first time in its history. With the NDP leading in national polls, there was no need to spook these swing voters by proposing ambitious ideas that would inevitably reinforce negative "taxing and spending" and "bad for the economy" stereotypes of the party that had come up so often in internal focus groups and polls (Soule interview, 2015). Rather than scare off these voters telling both pollsters working for the party and pollsters working for the media that they were intending to vote for the NDP, it made more sense to reassure them (Lavigne interview, 2015).

As shown in Table 4.6, the NDP news releases for the 2015 election illustrate that the party operationalized several parts of its planned strategy. Its team of candidates played a large role in the news releases. Earlier releases offered examples of local NDP MPs who fought for their constituents in the House of Commons, whereas later releases featured candidates who made important policy announcements and attacked Harper and Trudeau.

TABLE 4.6

Coverage of themes in 2015 NDP news releases and English and French television commercials

News releases (%)	English television commercials (%)	French television commercials (%)
Attack Harper and Conservatives (31); NDP team (28); attack Trudeau and Liberals (27); Mulcair's leadership (20); economy and protecting middle class (16); environment (10); health care (10); time for a change (9); Trans-Pacific Partnership (TPP) (8); fiscal responsibility (8); foreign affairs (6); ethics (7); infrastructure (4); seniors (3); child care (3); Aboriginal issues (3); strategic voting (2); small business (2); immigration (2); taxes (2); tourism (2); youth issues (2); northern Canada (2); pensions (1); crime (1); housing (1); democratic reform (1); disabilities (1); agriculture (1); Bill C-51 (1); respect for science (1); poverty reduction (1); post-secondary education (1); protecting CBC/Radio-Canada (1); sports (1); women's issues (1); Employment Insurance (1); transgendered rights (1); veterans (1); arts and culture (0.5); internet freedom (0.5); natural disaster protection (0.5)	Attack Harper and Conservatives (46); Mulcair's leadership (40); ethics (31); economy and protecting middle class (13); attack Trudeau and Liberals (13); TPP (9); environment (8); health care (3); strategic voting (2); time for a change (2); youth issues (2); child care (1); seniors (1)	Ethics (41); attack Harper and Conservatives (40); Mulcair's leadership (25); attack Trudeau and Liberals (14); English Canada following 2011 orange wave in Quebec (13); economy and protecting middle class (9); environment (8); strategic voting (4); time for a change (3)

NOTE: Bill C-51 or the *Anti-terrorism Act* was a bill passed by the Harper government in 2015. Critics claims that it did not adequately protect the human rights and the privacy of Canadian citizens from abuses of Canadian and American spy agencies. The NDP voted against the bill, while the Liberals voted for the bill after the Conservatives accepted some of their amendments.

Although NDP strategists noted that the national media covered the B tour less as the campaign worn on (Linner interview, 2015), the party continued heavily to promote its "cabinet material" candidates well into the second half of the campaign. Along with promoting the cabinet-in-waiting, the news releases consistently promoted Mulcair as the prime minister-in-waiting. Most of the party's policies were announced as "Tom Mulcair's plan," and there were frequent references to Mulcair as an experienced, strong, and principled leader. Often the NDP candidates on the B tour argued that he had the experience to be prime minister and explained how his plans were important for solving Canada's problems.

The NDP was also concerned about mitigating negative stereotypes, a key part of its political market orientation toward voters. According to Table 4.6, the issue discussed the most by the party was the economy and protecting the middle class. Typical of this theme, a news release in the middle of the campaign, on September 17, 2015, stated that the NDP was committed to "creating more jobs by targeted support for small business, infrastructure, manufacturing, and innovation. Combined with investing in skills training, Tom Mulcair's plan will grow a stronger middle class – and a stronger middle class means a stronger Canada." There was also an emphasis on fiscal responsibility and how the NDP platform was fully costed and realizable with a small increase in the corporate tax rate rather than raising the personal tax rates. The party also talked about a wide range of issues not traditionally considered NDP issues, such as crime, tourism, sports, veterans, and preparation for natural disasters to show voters that Mulcair would be a well-rounded prime minister.

A political market orientation toward competitors was evident. Indeed, the most prominent shift in the NDP's strategy during the 2015 election involved altering the targets of attack as the campaign came to a close and the Liberals surged in popularity. In the first half of the campaign, the party focused on attacking the Conservatives, particularly for their ethical lapses and their failure to stand up for the middle class and engineer economic growth. There was initially much emphasis on how it was time for a change of government so that Mulcair could repair the damage done by Harper, and NDP news releases rarely mentioned the Liberals. In contrast, the Liberals' earned media strategy attacked both Conservatives and New Democrats with almost equal vigour (Jeffrey 2016, 79–81). When the Liberals refused to fade away, as NDP operatives had anticipated, the party was forced to criticize Liberals alongside Conservatives. The NDP criticisms of the Liberals were varied: their lack of an overall plan because Trudeau was inexperienced, fiscal irresponsibility, deep cuts to social programs, insulting small-business owners, support for Bill C-51, failure to set greenhouse gas emissions reduction targets, and the Trans-Pacific Partnership. One NDP operative noted that his party had trouble "landing punches" on Trudeau (Soule interview, 2015), and this frustration might have been reflected in the wide array of criticisms that it threw at him. Perhaps because of the massive amount of money that the Liberals had put into branding Trudeau and placing him at the centre of their campaign (Jeffrey 2016, 72–75), NDP operatives were simply unable to find a criticism that really stuck to him as the campaign wound down.

The rise of the Liberals' popularity forced the NDP to become more focused on maintaining the support of its loyal base of voters. It is possible to discern a shift in emphasis in news releases to more traditional NDP issues such as health care, the environment, and free-trade deals (in particular the TPP) in the final two weeks of the campaign. In terms of the TPP, the NDP came out strongly against what it characterized as a secretive deal negotiated by Harper and supported by Trudeau that would weaken environmental laws, raise the prices of prescription drugs, hurt the auto sector, undermine supply management in the dairy industry in Quebec, and increase the surveillance of Canadians as they surfed the internet. With the Liberals' popularity rising to ever higher levels, NDP strategists were evidently not worried about any damage to their brand inflicted by stridently opposing a trade deal supported by most of Canada's business community.

Similar differences in messaging between the start and the end of the campaign can be seen in the NDP's English commercials. Early in the campaign, these commercials attempted to set up a clear two-way NDP–Conservative Party race. They attacked Harper and the Conservatives primarily on ethical failings and secondarily on doing little to combat recent job losses and protect Canada's middle class. In contrast to Harper, Mulcair was portrayed as a serious and experienced politician who came from a middle-class background and had a plan "to give our kids a better start in life, ensure our young people get the opportunities they need, and seniors get the benefits they deserve," as he put it in one commercial. The narrative was simple: it was time for a change, and Mulcair was ready to be prime minister. This message was supposed to set up strategic voting arguments about only the NDP being able to defeat Harper later in the campaign (Bélanger interview, 2015; Lavigne interview, 2015; McGrath interview, 2015). When the two-way race did not emerge, the NDP strategy in English television advertising was altered. The commercials still mentioned that Mulcair "needs just 35 more MPs to stop Harper, Liberals need 100," but more time was devoted to critiquing Trudeau on ethics and highlighting issues on which strategists thought New Democrats had a comparative advantage over Liberals, such as climate change and the TPP (Bélanger interview, 2015).[3]

The NDP did not devise a different set of tactics for francophone Quebec. Table 4.6 illustrates that the themes in the party's French and English commercials were very similar. Indeed, for the most part, the French commercials were simply translations of the English commercials during the 2015 election. The one exception was a French commercial released during the last two weeks of the campaign that featured Mulcair speaking about how English Canada was preparing to follow the orange wave in Quebec in 2011 as images of Layton, Rachel Notley, and himself were shown. Although strategic voting was not mentioned, the connotation of the commercial was clearly that the NDP was the party that could unite English Canada and Quebec in order to remove Harper from power.

Overall, NDP operatives thought that their strategy was overtaken by several campaign events. A longer than anticipated campaign allowed the Liberal Party to spend heavily on television advertising in August to showcase Trudeau, and the party inched up in the polls since the NDP was not running any television advertising at the time (Lavigne interview, 2015). The Liberals also harshly critiqued the New Democrats, who concentrated their attacks on the Conservatives (Lavigne interview, 2015; Soule interview, 2015). In particular, Mulcair's refusal to have a debate on women's issues because Harper would not attend it was used by the Liberals to portray Trudeau as more "feminist" than Mulcair (McGrath interview, 2015; Moran interview, 2015; Lucy Watson interview, 2015). Moreover, the unprecedented five leaders' debates and sustained media exposure given to Trudeau over the three-month campaign gave the Liberals the time to build up their leader's credibility (Lavigne interview, 2015). In short, a long campaign did not end up working in the NDP's favour. Since the party was still in the lead in most polls at Labour Day, some political operatives thought that they had won the "first campaign" in August but lost the "second campaign" in September and October (Bélanger interview, 2015; Lavigne interview, 2015).

Although the NDP withstood media scrutiny of its ability to field a slate of candidates from which a cabinet could be drawn, the end of the summer saw a protracted controversy over the party's policies. Because of the party's front-runner status, the media became fixated on the most minute details of party spending initiatives, such as the fifteen-dollar-a-day child-care program, and how they were to be financed (Linner interview, 2015). NDP operatives indicated that reporters became very interested in whether provincial governments would buy in to the party's plans or resist them (Watkins interview, 2015). Questions about how the NDP intended to pay for its campaign promises increased once the party dedicated itself to balanced budgets and the Liberals stated that they would run deficits (Soule interview, 2015; Watkins interview, 2015). The NDP was forced to defend itself against the counterintuitive claim that it was positioned to the right of the Liberal Party (Moran interview, 2015; Lucy Watson interview, 2015). NDP strategists had expected this level of scrutiny and had the resources in place to deal with it, yet they thought that they were spending too much time explaining and defending their plans as opposed to setting the agenda (Watkins interview, 2015; Lucy Watson interview, 2015).

The release of the NDP's costing document of its platform in the middle of September set off another round of scrutiny, with media and pundits focusing on how unforeseen circumstances in the future, such as the dropping price of oil, might affect spending plans given the party's commitment to balanced budgets (Linner interview, 2015; Watkins interview, 2015). The Liberal war room was only too happy to repeat these criticisms (Liberal Party of Canada 2015). NDP strategists strongly believed that, though the Liberals could get away with proposing deficits, the New Democrats could not. Given the negative stereotypes about the NDP evident in their market research, political operatives concluded that proposing deficit spending would lead to damaging charges that an NDP government would engage in "out of control spending" and lead Canada toward economic ruin (McGrath interview, 2015; Soule interview, 2015; Watkins interview, 2015). Also, the NDP had been running on balanced budgets since 2006. To change plans in 2015 would have been considered a flip-flop (Ibid.). The decision was made to defend vigorously the party's position on fiscal responsibility through a complex three-part argument: 1) new spending would be financed through new revenues coming from a higher corporate tax rate; 2) the federal government had posted a $1.9 billion surplus in the 2014–15 fiscal year, so going into deficit to pay for the expansion of social programs was unnecessary; and 3) Canadians had to remember that Saskatchewan CCF Premier Tommy Douglas had introduced Medicare while running seventeen consecutive balanced budgets (Watkins interview, 2015; Lucy Watson interview, 2015).

The release of the NDP's costing document coincided with a court ruling allowing women to take their citizenship oaths while wearing the niqab, and the Conservatives vowed to appeal the court's decision within 100 days of being re-elected (McGrane 2016, 103–5). NDP strategists pointed to the niqab ruling as a major setback for their campaign in Quebec. In March 2015, the party had opposed the ban on the niqab at citizenship ceremonies, and strategists considered opposing the ban "to be a position of principle for the party and the leader" (Linner interview, 2015). The niqab issue came to dominate francophone media in Quebec over the last two weeks of September (McNeney 2015). NDP polling showed the party's support in Quebec dropping 17 percent over three days, and some NDP candidates even stopped going door to door to avoid the backlash (Bélanger interview, 2015; Rebecca Blaikie interview, 2015; Gébert interview, 2015; Soule interview, 2015).

The NDP's opponents in Quebec reacted quickly. The Bloc Québécois and the Conservative Party quickly began to use an Ipsos poll from March 2015 indicating that 91 percent of Quebecers supported banning the niqab at citizenship ceremonies to claim that the NDP was out of touch with Quebecers' values (McGrane 2016, 103). Eventually, the entire BQ campaign became devoted to how Mulcair and the NDP were unwilling to stand up for Quebec values, using the niqab controversy and the NDP's stance in favour of the Energy East pipeline as prime examples (Bélanger and Nadeau 2016, 123–26). The Conservatives also began to promote their opposition to the niqab at citizenship ceremonies in their targeted ridings around Quebec City, and Harper even went as far as to state that a re-elected Conservative government would follow the Quebec government's lead on reasonable accommodation, leading to speculation about whether the Conservatives would deny federal government services to Canadians wearing a niqab (Ellis 2016, 49–50).

By late September, NDP strategists realized that a perfect storm had beset their campaign, and how they had positioned their party was now awkward given the recent dynamics of the election. The party had been put on the defensive over how it would pay for its programs given its commitment to balanced budgets, and its position on the niqab debate had led to questions about the solidity of its Quebec stronghold. The niqab debate had also helped the Conservatives to regain their footing since they were able to direct attention away from corruption and unethical behaviour associated with the Mike Duffy trial (Bélanger interview, 2015). Moreover, the Liberal campaign continued to surge as doubts about Trudeau's readiness to be prime minister waned. Mulcair had done well in the four debates in September, but so had Trudeau, Harper, and Duceppe (Moran interview, 2015; Turcotte 2016).

NDP strategists began to notice a troubling feedback loop in their internal polling, also reported in public domain polling (Rebecca Blaikie interview, 2015; Lavigne interview, 2015; Moran interview, 2015). The drop in NDP support in Quebec over the niqab controversy had created a dip in the party's national numbers. This drop seemed to send a signal to NDP/LPC switchers in English Canada, particularly in Ontario, that the NDP might not be the party best positioned to defeat the Conservative Party, and the NDP's national numbers dropped further as English Canadian voters shifted to the Liberal Party. Then, when voters in Quebec saw the NDP's national numbers dropping further, they were once again less likely to support Mulcair's party.

In short, the two-way NDP–Conservative Party race narrative was not developing in the home stretch of the campaign as planned. Public domain polling heavily reported in the media showed a two-way Liberal Party–Conservative Party race as the NDP began to slide into third place nationally (Lavigne interview, 2015; Linner interview, 2015; Moran interview, 2015). Indeed, compared with the Liberal Party, both mentions of the NDP and positive coverage of the NDP in Canadian newspapers declined in October (McNeney 2015). NDP strategists had planned for their strategic voting arguments down the stretch to hurt the Liberals and had saved their advertising budget for the last two weeks of the campaign to combat Conservative scaremongering about a potential NDP government (Bélanger interview, 2015; Lavigne interview, 2015). In fact, the opposite occurred as "anybody but Harper" voters concluded that the Liberals were best positioned to topple the Conservatives, that Trudeau was not so risky after all, and that voting NDP might be a "wasted vote" (Ibid.). The barrage of Conservative Party negative ads aimed at the NDP never did come as the Conservatives focused their attacks on the Liberals as the campaign came to a close (Soule interview, 2015). The Conservative plan had been to focus advertising juxtaposing the judgment of Harper with the judgment of Trudeau and hope that the Liberal leader would falter in an exceptionally long campaign (Ellis 2016, 37). NDP polling, along with public domain polling, showed the party's support spiralling downward in the final days of the campaign as the Liberals gained unstoppable momentum toward a majority government (Bélanger interview, 2015; Lavigne interview, 2015; McGrath interview, 2015).

On election night, the NDP's share of the popular vote dipped to 19.7 percent and its seat total plunged to forty-four. It experienced massive seat losses in Quebec and lost all of its seats in Atlantic Canada and three-quarters of its seats in Ontario. The results in Western Canada were less disastrous, with the party holding on to its two seats in Manitoba and its one seat in Alberta and picking up three seats in Saskatchewan, where it had not won a seat since 2000. The party also moved from twelve to fourteen seats in British Columbia, even though its percentage of the popular vote there declined.

Political operatives were extremely disappointed with the outcome. Although the party had positioned itself as the market leader, its support in Quebec and English Canada was much softer than the operatives realized (Moran interview, 2015). NDP strategists indicated that their ground game was relatively effective, but how they positioned their party and how they relayed its overall message were poor, resulting in little momentum going into October, and support for the party melted away (Lavigne interview, 2015; McGrath interview, 2015; Lucy Watson interview, 2015). They thought that the Liberals' organization had been faster and more nimble, whereas they had been slow to react and were constantly on the defensive as campaign events unfolded (Rebecca Blaikie interview, 2015; McGrath interview, 2015; Watkins interview, 2015; Lucy Watson interview, 2015). Some regretted that there were few Quebec-specific messages (Rebecca Blaikie interview; Gébert interview, 2015; Soule interview, 2015), and others pointed out that the NDP needed to attack the Liberal Party aggressively in August instead of running a cautious campaign focused on the shortcomings of the Harper government (Moran interview, 2015). Some political operatives thought that the New Democrats pushed fiscal responsibility too hard, giving the Liberals the opportunity to paint themselves as agents of bolder change than the New Democrats (McGrath interview, 2015; Moran interview, 2015). Despite their disappointment that their strategy did not work as planned, they did point out that the NDP was in much better shape coming out of the 2015 election in terms of seats and popular votes than at any time in its history, excluding the 2011 election (Soule interview, 2015). Reasons for optimism included that the party was well funded, professional, and relatively unified and maintained a base of sixteen seats in Quebec (Rebecca Blaikie interview, 2015; Fortin interview, 2015; Linner interview, 2015; Lucy Watson interview, 2015). Yet the most interesting part of the NDP campaign in this election is that the strategists did not end up having all of the answers. Their risky campaign strategies from 2004 to 2011 brought the NDP to the brink of power. Even though their research indicated that a cautious approach was the best route to take in the 2015 election, it ended up backfiring. Moderation and modernization had brought the NDP close to forming the government, but this transformation of the party did not take it all the way.

Conclusion

In some ways, the story of the NDP's campaign strategies was about chasing dreams and taking risks. Given the tough political situation and its limited financial resources, the NDP adopted a cautious and defensive strategy in the 2000 election aimed at protecting the seats that it held in its regional niches of support. The key innovation of Layton's team of political operatives was their willingness to take risks and set lofty goals such as forming the government. These risks were well researched and well calculated, and they were carried out by professionals. Undoubtedly, the party's greater financial resources after changes to party financing rules paid for the expensive research and salaries of the professionals who commissioned the research and put its findings to good use. Thus, the NDP campaign strategies in the Layton era were not only the product of the party's increased financial resources but also the result of decisions made by agents (i.e., political operatives) about how to deploy those newfound resources.

An important part of the moderation and modernization of the NDP under Layton was a political market orientation toward voters and competitors, and the party's campaign strategies definitely reflected this shift. Tilting toward voters and competitors dovetailed with putting power in the hands of professional operatives to shape the party's communications using formal market intelligence and an assessment of the party's position in key segments of the Canadian electoral market leading to the creation of the "new NDP." An orientation toward voters and competitors and sophisticated electoral market segmentation required surgical precision by agents to choose the issues that appealed to targeted voters and to frame those issues within the complex context of multiparty competition, minority Parliaments, and strategic voting. On the other hand, a member political market orientation would have entailed involving party members in policy development, using them as sources of informal market intelligence, and soliciting local input when devising national strategy. Similarly, an external political market orientation would have sought the public approval of stakeholders (e.g., unions or social movements) and the incorporation of their organizations into campaign structures.

Although the tilt toward voters and competitors provided opportunities for political operatives to think outside the box and take risks in campaign strategies (e.g., having Layton state that he was running to be prime minister in 2008), it also resulted in moderation of NDP ideology. Similar to the political marketing of New Labour under Tony Blair (Scammell 2007; White and De Chernatony 2002), political operatives used market research to discover the negative stereotypes holding the party back and the phrases and policies displeasing to targeted segments of the electoral market. Their discoveries resulted in a moderation of NDP platforms in areas such as the inheritance tax and pushed the party to talk about issues such as crime and veterans as opposed to free trade and labour rights. A political market orientation toward competitors meant that the NDP's policies had to be constantly juxtaposed with those of its opponents. For example, the promise of a balanced budget was meant to attract Layton Liberals who were unsure about Ignatieff but could be turned off by the NDP's purported lack of fiscal responsibility. The NDP thus adopted a moderate version of social democracy, which will be examined in greater detail in the next chapter.

5
Continuity and Change: The Ideology and Policies of the NDP

New approaches to political marketing of the federal New Democratic Party also affected its ideology from 2000 to 2015. The revolution in its political marketing in these years entailed the adoption of an ideology and policies that represented a moderate version of social democracy. However, as opposed to an unadulterated move to the centre and an abandonment of the principles of social democracy, the ideological moderation of the "new NDP" was a mixture of continuity and change.

My analysis of the NDP's ideology is primarily based on the party's platforms during elections and surveys of NDP members, MPs, and potential voters. An examination of surveys of NDP members administered in 1997 and 2015 shows that their basic political values remained fundamentally similar. A quantitative and qualitative exploration of the federal NDP and Liberal Party election platforms from 2000 to 2015 illustrates that those of the NDP continued to place a strong emphasis on issues related to increasing equality, and the party maintained a number of policy positions that were distinctively social democratic and different from the centrism of the Liberals. At the same time, professionalization and an emphasis on maintaining the purity of an overarching party-leader brand inherent in postmodern campaigning led to greater ideological moderation of the NDP. Political operatives and their strategies emanating from more comprehensive market intelligence financed by public subsidies had much influence on the platforms of the party. Reflecting a greater political market orientation toward voters, the platforms gradually began to frame policy ideas more practically and downplayed policy areas where the party's positions could be controversial within the context of an election campaign and turn off key segments of the electoral market. A side-by-side comparison of the NDP and Liberal Party platforms depicts that the number of similar commitments made by the two parties grew from 2000 to 2015, reflecting that the NDP had a greater political market orientation toward competitors intended to steal soft Liberal voters.

An analysis of surveys of NDP members, MPs, and potential voters uncovers some interesting findings. The moderate version of social democracy of NDP members and MPs in 2015 encompassed viewing economic growth and environmental protection as equal priorities, being in favour of trade agreements that did not harm human rights, protecting existing Crown corporations as opposed to creating new ones, and questioning the need to increase taxes and spending rapidly. Interestingly, when NDP MPs and members displayed less moderate ideological positions related to deficits, social conservatism, and social democratic principles to gain power, this lack of moderation brought them in line with the ideas of potential NDP voters. A deeper analysis of the NDP MPs' responses illustrates their caution and adherence to incrementalism in achieving social democratic change so as to give voters time to get used to an NDP government – an idea in line with the strategies of political operatives.

The Political Values of NDP Members

An important source of data on the federal NDP's ideology has been surveys of its members by scholars such as Alan Whitehorn, Keith Archer, David Laycock, Lynda Erickson, and Maria Zakharova. These scholars have worked with the party to mail surveys to its members or to administer surveys to delegates during NDP conventions. I also worked with party headquarters in Ottawa to administer an online survey to party members. To what extent was there a moderation of the political values that they held between 2000 and 2015?

To answer this question, Erickson and Laycock provided me with data from their 1997 survey of 1,490 NDP members from British Columbia, Saskatchewan, Manitoba, and Ontario. Their survey was mailed to randomly selected members, members of all riding association executives, provincial council members, and current and former MPs and MLAs in those provinces. Although their data are not weighted by region, they note that "the sample distribution is a reasonable reflection of party size in each province" (Erickson and Laycock 2002, 306). The sample design and method of my data from 2015 and their data from 1997 are quite dissimilar. Nonetheless, their data are the only available data on NDP members' ideology in the period around 2000, so I will use them to give an approximation of their ideology at the time.

TABLE 5.1

NDP members' values of collectivism/individualism (conflicting statements) in 1997 and 2015

Statements	Mean (1997)	Mean (2015)	SD (1997)	SD (2015)
0 = Individuals should take more responsibility for providing for themselves; 1 = The state should take more responsibility to ensure that everyone is provided for.	0.63	0.71	0.27	0.23
0 = In the long run, hard work usually brings a better life; 1 = Hard work doesn't generally bring success; it is more a matter of luck and connections.	0.51	0.58	0.30	0.27
0 = People can only accumulate wealth at the expense of others; 1 = Wealth can grow so that there is enough for everybody.	0.62	0.62	0.31	0.30
0 = There should be greater incentives for individual effort; 1 = Incomes should be made more equal.	0.69	0.72	0.30	0.24
0 = Private ownership of business and industry should be increased; 1 = Government ownership of business and industry should be increased.	0.63	0.66	0.25	0.23

I replicated ten questions from the Erickson and Laycock 1997 survey on my 2015 survey. The first set of questions is the level of agreement with two conflicting statements on a seven-point scale. For ease of interpretation, the data have been converted into scores of 0 to 1. Table 5.1 reports the mean and standard deviation for each set of conflicting statements. As we can see, these questions present the respondent with two conflicting statements in order to explore the underlying values of NDP members regarding collectivism versus individualism.

Despite the difference in sampling methods and the eighteen-year interval between the surveys, the results are remarkably similar. These two surveys provide no evidence that there has been a large-scale change in values among NDP members from 1997 to 2015. There is limited evidence that their values have shifted slightly to the left because of the greater level of agreement that the state should "provide for everyone" and that "success is a matter of luck as opposed to hard work." NDP members in both 1997 and 2015 unsurprisingly leaned to the left-wing or collectivist positions on these questions. However, in both time periods, there appears to have been a healthy

TABLE 5.2

NDP members' values measured with reference to public policies in 1997 and 2015

Statements*	Mean (1997)	Mean (2015)	SD (1997)	SD (2015)
To control costs, some services should be removed from Medicare for those who can afford to pay for such services themselves.	0.22	0.22	0.29	0.28
Much of the talk about "welfare abuse" is exaggerated.	0.74	0.78	0.28	0.28
Hiring people because they are women or members of a visible minority undermines the principle of merit.	0.40	0.34	0.31	0.29
When faced with a difficult fiscal situation, the government should cut its own expenditures by reducing the size and cost of the government.	0.56	0.43	0.29	0.30
When faced with a difficult fiscal situation, the government should increase revenues by raising the income taxes of wealthy Canadians.	0.84	0.80	0.20	0.25

* 0 = strongly disagree; 0.25 = disagree; 0.5 = neutral; 0.75 = agree; 1 = strongly agree

diversity of values. The mean ranges from 0.51 to 0.72, and the standard deviation falls between 0.23 and 0.30. Although NDP members are definitely collectivist in their values, there are differences in their levels of collectivism. Not all members have the same values.

Another indication of ideology is positions on government policies. Erickson and Laycock also included questions on their 1997 survey that explored the ideology of NDP members by presenting them with specific public policy situations. Members were asked to indicate their level of agreement with certain statements on a five-point scale. The statements dealt with affirmative action, the alleged abuse of social assistance, the cost of Medicare, and budgeting in a time of limited government revenue. Once again the data in Table 5.2 have been converted into scores of 0 to 1 to ease interpretation.

One is struck once more by the similar results of the surveys in 1997 and 2015. The means on most of the questions in Table 5.2 are almost the same. The one exception, that party members in 2015 were somewhat less likely to agree that governments should cut their expenditures in difficult fiscal situations, illustrates that members in the 2015 survey leaned slightly more to the left than did members in the 1997 survey. Compared with Table 5.1, there was greater consensus on certain policy questions – raising the taxes of the wealthy, delisting services in Medicare, and abuse of social assistance being exaggerated. However, the standard deviations are between 0.20 and 0.30 on these two questions, indicating a diversity of opinions among members of both eras. Nonetheless, both tables provide evidence that the values of NDP members in 1997 and 2015 were fundamentally similar. If anything, there might have been a slight movement to the left.

NDP and Liberal Party Platforms, 2000–15

Although political parties take policy positions for a variety of reasons, the congruence of a policy position with a party's ideology is always an important consideration. Another source of data for the examination of NDP ideology is the policy commitments that the party took in its platforms in the six elections from 2000 to 2015. Platforms are subject to intense internal negotiations and constitute authoritative statements of party policy and thus ideology during campaigns (Robertson 1976). Although platforms are undoubtedly useful for understanding a party's ideology, the question for political scientists is how to analyze these documents. Recently, the most popular way to analyze Canadian federal parties' platforms has been to apply the RILE method (Cochrane 2015, 152–58; Koop and Bittner 2013, 320–21; Pétry 2015, 145) pioneered by researchers involved with the Comparative Manifesto Project (Budge et al., 2001). This quantitative method involves content analysis – assigning passages of text certain codes and then aggregating the codes to identify patterns. The RILE coding scheme is generally based on calculating how much space a party devotes to various issues considered typically left wing or right wing (e.g., welfare state expansion is a left-wing issue, whereas law and order comprise a right-wing issue). Based on their coding schemes, Canadian researchers found that NDP platforms moved to the centre of the political spectrum and closer to the RILE scores of the Liberal Party during the time that Jack Layton was leader. However, the method adopted by these researchers has a fundamental drawback. It is summative and does not specify how NDP platforms moved to the centre under Layton or how Liberals and New Democrats became ideologically more similar.

So I decided to deviate from the RILE method. I created a catalogue of all of the commitments contained in the Liberal Party and NDP platforms from the six elections from 2000 to 2015. In total, I catalogued 1,378 NDP commitments and 1,141 Liberal commitments that I classified into sixteen policy areas: arts and culture; consumer protection; crime and justice; deficit/debt; democratic reform; economic policy; environment; federalism; foreign affairs; infrastructure; labour policy; military; social policy; taxation; trade; and women and minorities. The analysis of this catalogue is broken up into two sections. First I examine the evolution of NDP platforms, and then I explore the differences and similarities between NDP and Liberal platforms. Since I did all of this coding myself, there is no need to report intercoder reliability scores or to use a quality assurance check on the work of a student research assistant. The coding is a result of my own interpretation of the platform data.

The basis of the RILE technique is issue ownership theory (Budge and Farlie 1983; Budge, Robertson, and Hearl 1987; Pétry 2015), which holds that parties devote more space in their platforms to policy areas for which they have a reputation of competence. It is also argued that parties allot more space to policy areas ideologically important to them. So we can expect that a party drifting to the right will devote more space to issues such as crime, economic policy, and the military and less space to issues such as social programs, the environment, and women's issues. Table 5.3 contains a basic description of NDP platforms from 2000 to 2015 using the catalogue and allows us to see the policy areas that the party emphasized. All of the social policy issues are grouped into one category, as are the issues related to minorities and women. I made this decision to keep the size of the table manageable and because, according to issue ownership theory, mentions of these social policy issues and any policy related to a minority and women indicate a left-wing direction taken by a political party.

Table 5.3 illustrates that the number of commitments that the NDP made in various policy areas was consistent over the time period that I examined. For the most part, the percentage devoted to a certain policy in any one platform does not stray too far from the average for that policy area when the six platforms are taken together. The dominant themes of NDP platforms during this period are consistently what might be considered left-wing issues such as social policy, women and minorities, and the environment.

However, the influence of the campaign strategies adopted by political operatives is apparent. These operatives adopted a political market orientation toward voters in wanting the NDP to have policies in all areas of federal government activity to show voters that the party was ready to govern. Thus, there are some small but noteworthy variations in Table 5.3. Commitments

TABLE 5.3

Policy commitments by category, 2000–15 NDP platforms

Category	2000 (McDonough) (%)	2004 (Layton) (%)	2006 (Layton) (%)	2008 (Layton) (%)	2011 (Layton) (%)	2015 (Mulcair) (%)	Average
Arts and culture	2	2	4	6	10	3	5
Consumer protection	3	3	1	8	6	6	5
Crime and justice	4	5	10	7	5	5	6
Deficit/debt	0	2	1	1	1	1	1
Democratic reform	3	4	9	3	3	11	6
Economic policy	8	14	13	10	9	11	11
Environment	14	13	13	11	8	10	11
Intergovernmental relations	2	3	2	2	1	1	2
Foreign affairs	6	9	4	8	5	4	6
Infrastructure	4	2	2	2	4	3	3
Labour policy	5	4	2	2	0	3	3
Military	4	2	1	3	8	8	4
Social policy*	20	16	21	15	24	17	19
Taxation	7	3	2	2	1	2	3
Trade	6	3	1	3	0	1	2
Women and minorities**	12	16	15	18	16	14	15

NOTES: Number of policy commitments: 2000 = 169; 2004 = 262; 2006 = 162; 2008 = 328; 2011 = 171; 2015 = 286.

* Social policy includes health care, child care, education, poverty reduction, unemployment insurance, pensions, and housing.

** Minorities include Indigenous people, official language minorities, immigrants, ethnocultural groups, gays and lesbians, and disabled Canadians.

in policy areas classified as right wing by issue ownership theory become more prominent. In particular, the number of commitments related to crime increased noticeably in 2006 and 2008, and there was a marked increase in the number of commitments regarding economic policy in Layton's first two elections as leader. There was also a slight decrease in the number of commitments to the environment in 2011 and 2015 compared with Alexa McDonough's last election as leader in 2000. We can also see a gradual increase in the number of commitments related to the military and consumer protection along with a reduction in the number of commitments on trade, taxation, and labour in later elections. Overall, later NDP platforms were better balanced in terms of addressing all policy areas of the federal government compared with earlier platforms.

However, what if NDP platforms devoted more space to what is traditionally considered a right-wing issue but talked about that issue in a distinctly left-wing manner? Similar to the RILE technique, Table 5.3 shows that the NDP devoted more space to talking about the military in its platforms but does not indicate what the party actually proposed. Perhaps the party explained how it would drastically reduce spending on the military – a left-wing proposition indeed. Ultimately, we need to examine more closely the NDP platform commitments to explore the moderation of party ideology.

Further qualitative exploration reveals that some elements of NDP platforms from 2000 to 2015 were consistent. All of these platforms featured an activist state that would intervene in the economy through granting tax credits to companies that create jobs, creating orderly marketing in agriculture, restricting foreign takeovers, developing industrial strategies for priority sectors, and offering various subsidies to promote a green economy. With the exception of the suggestions in the 2004 platform of new Crown corporations to invest in renewable energy and manufacture prescription drugs, the creation of new public enterprises was not mentioned in the NDP platforms. Yet all of the platforms committed to expanding existing Crown corporations such as Canada Post and VIA Rail and vowed to prevent any privatization of the health care system. The NDP's ideas on infrastructure repeatedly stressed giving municipalities additional federal revenues to fund better public transit systems. The party's policies on women and minorities were consistent in their advocacy of establishing better pay equity and greater funding for women's groups, ensuring more family reunification for immigrants, recognizing Indigenous self-government, increasing funding for on-reserve education, and creating more government programs for disabled

Canadians. In intergovernmental affairs, there was a constant message of creating frameworks for national standards that nonetheless respected the autonomy of Quebec. Given the party's consistency in these policy areas, we can see that there was continuity in its ideology over this period.

However, on other policies, there were shifts that indicated ideological moderation driven by political operatives as they adjusted the NDP's political market orientation toward voters. The party's arts and culture policies initially focused on better funding for the CBC and encouraging Canadian content. Later platforms supplemented these ideas with programs that focused on artists as businesspeople or self-employed workers such as incentives to improve their incomes and a variety of tax credits. The party's consumer protection policies expanded as well. The 2000 platform focused on the labelling of genetically modified foods, a way to help consumers make environmentally conscious purchases. In contrast, platforms in the Layton and Mulcair eras looked at consumer protection through the lens of lowering the cost of living with policies aimed at decreasing fees for credit cards, cell phones, internet service, and banking. The consumer protection planks were intended by NDP operatives to show how the party could make a real and immediate difference in voters' lives. Consumer protection was a "pocketbook" issue intended to increase the party's credibility on the economy, which research found to be its greatest brand weakness.

Importantly, there were shifts in how the NDP platforms dealt with deficits. These shifts were driven by market research, financed through the per-vote public subsidy, indicating that the party had a negative "tax and spend" stereotype attached to it. The 2000 platform was opaque on whether the party would run a deficit but noted that it would pay for expanding social programs without adding to the national debt. The 2004 platform promised balanced budgets except in "years of extreme revenue shortfalls and disasters and acts of God." Subsequent platforms were clearer and firmly committed to a balanced budget in every year of NDP government. In terms of social policy, Layton's platforms maintained a strong commitment to expanding social programs, but their scope was circumscribed. A few examples of the differences between the 2004 and 2011 platforms will suffice: creating 200,000 new child-care spaces a year was reduced to 25,000 new spaces a year; reducing tuition by 10 percent and freezing it at that level were changed to making postsecondary education "more affordable" through increased transfer payments to provinces; establishing pharmacare (a publicly funded prescription drug insurance program for all Canadians) was replaced by an "aggressive" review of drug prices and hiring more doctors and nurses; and developing a ten-year strategy to build 200,000 new public housing units was reduced to a vague commitment to "new funding for affordable and social housing" and restoring funding to the residential rehabilitation assistance program.

In terms of the need to be seen as pragmatic and reassuring to voters, the NDP altered the far-reaching nature of its ideas in certain areas without completely abandoning the impetus for immediate action. The party dropped some of its more ambitious democratic reforms, such as lowering the voting age to sixteen and designating seats for Indigenous people in the House of Commons. However, under Layton and Mulcair, the party did remain committed to establishing a mixed-member proportional representation electoral system, abolishing the Senate, and restricting the power of the prime minister and lobbyists. Similarly, in foreign affairs, the NDP dropped some of its more daring ideas that could scare off voters and hurt Layton's reputation for pragmatism, such as creating a "Tobin tax" (a small tax on all international monetary transactions) and forgiving the debts of developing nations, but maintained a commitment to more conventional ideas such as increasing foreign aid to 0.7 percent of Canada's GDP.

Further moderation of the NDP's policies took place in the areas of taxation, the environment, the military, and crime. Earlier platforms stressed rehabilitation, restorative justice, and the underlying causes of crime, such as poverty. In contrast, the 2011 and 2015 platforms pledged tougher punishments and more police officers, which voters easily understood as directly reducing crime. On the environment, earlier platforms were stringent in calling for moratoriums on certain types of economic activity (e.g., new development of the oil sands) and completely removing government subsidies from the nuclear sector. Later platforms focused on softer ideas for a cap-and-trade system as well as research on green technology and renewable energy that could not be construed as hurting the economy. Although the NDP consistently advocated higher corporate taxes from 2000 to 2015, it did back away from its insistence on raising taxes on Canadians with higher incomes through initiatives such as an inheritance tax after that idea became controversial in the 2004 election. The party also backed off from disallowing meals and entertainment expenses as tax write-offs. Instead, it began to advocate lowering taxes on small businesses as a way to promote economic growth. When it came to the military, earlier NDP platforms put forth minimal and vague ideas of a stronger commitment to peacekeeping and increasing the pay of members of the Armed Forces. By 2011 and 2015, the platform on the military had evolved considerably by identifying three priorities (peacekeeping, natural disaster relief, and defending Canada) and putting forth specific plans for purchasing more military equipment and improving services for Canadian veterans.

The NDP platforms in 2000 and 2004 had a relatively strong emphasis on labour policy, with suggestions for anti-scab legislation, better benefits for part-time workers, new national holidays, and a federal minimum wage. Similarly, echoing its 2000 platform, the NDP called in 2004 for the replacement of "undemocratic, corporate-driven trade deals" such as NAFTA and the WTO with fair trade agreements. However, the 2011 platform mentioned neither labour policy nor trade policy.

Finally, there were certain policy areas where ideological moderation during the Layton years was somewhat undone by Mulcair in the 2015 platform. It contained two throwbacks to the party's earlier promises of a national child-care program and a national pharmacare program: it promised 1 million child-care spaces over eight years at fifteen dollars a day and boldly claimed that an NDP government would work toward universal public drug coverage that would lower prescription drug costs by 30 percent. Labour and trade policies also resurfaced in 2015. The NDP platform that year clearly committed to ensuring that trade agreements improved social, environmental, and labour standards in partner countries. The party also came out strongly against the Trans-Pacific Partnership during the final two weeks of the 2015 election campaign because it feared a loss of jobs in the dairy and auto sectors. The 2015 platform also pledged not only to repeal several pieces of labour legislation passed by the Harper government but also to introduce anti-scab legislation and a federal minimum wage of fifteen dollars per hour. These bolder moves were based on a political market orientation toward competitors as New Democrats attempted (perhaps unsuccessfully) to be seen as more progressive than Liberals, the alternative agent of change away from the Conservatives. However, these revisions should not be seen as a reversal of ideological direction, and most of the 2015 platform was consistent with the 2011 platform.

Overall, an examination of NDP platforms from 2000 to 2015 illustrates a moderation of party ideology driven by political operatives who moved the party to a greater voter and competitor orientation. Later platforms dealt more with what might be considered right-wing issues such as the military and the economy in an attempt to show voters that the NDP had a plan for all parts of federal government activity. The party quietly removed many of its ambitious left-wing policies and downplayed its stances in the areas of labour, deficits, and trade, where its views could be controversial and unpopular among voters. There was a change in the tone of NDP platforms as well. The number of commitments involving "national" strategies, plans, and standards was steadily reduced and replaced with commitments introduced by expressions such as "a practical first step toward" and "as finances permit" to reinforce the Layton-NDP or Mulcair-NDP brand of pragmatism and incrementalism.

However, it is not accurate to suggest that the party's ideology went through a wholesale transformation and movement toward the centre. Social policies and policies related to women and minorities continued to make up large portions of the party's platform. Commitments to promoting economic equality, expanding social programs, and deepening Canada's liberal rights regime endured. The 2011 platform, under which the NDP made its historic electoral breakthrough, was not a radical departure from previous party platforms during the 2000s. Indeed, the catalogue that I have compiled reveals that approximately 70 percent of the policies in the 2011 platform can be found in the 2000, 2004, 2006, and 2008 platforms. Rather than a complete makeover of the party's ideology, the 2011 platform, devised by political operatives, narrowed the party's focus and selected the most realizable and practical suggestions from previous platforms.

It has been asserted that the NDP gradually drifted toward the centre during the Layton and Mulcair years until it was almost indistinguishable from the Liberals (Carroll 2005; Conway 2016; Evans 2012). What should be made of this claim? The only genuine way to analyze the similarities and differences between Liberal and NDP platforms from 2000 to 2015 is a qualitative, side-by-side comparison. Table 5.4 depicts the number of Liberal and NDP commitments in the catalogue that were similar. Admittedly, the analysis is subjective. In cases in which the two parties made the exact same promise, the coding was straightforward (e.g., restoring Canada Post's home delivery service in 2015). Most cases were less clear-cut. For instance, in 2011 the Liberals promised a "gradual increase of the defined benefits" of the Canada Pension Plan (CPP), whereas the New Democrats committed to the "eventual goal" of doubling CPP benefits. The NDP's promise is noticeably more generous and precise. However, the two promises would move the federal government in the same general direction (i.e., gradually enhancing CPP benefits), so I considered them to be similar. Furthermore, unless the gap

TABLE 5.4

Commitments in NDP platforms similar to those in LPC platforms by category, 2000–15

	2000	2004	2006	2008	2011	2015
Arts and culture	0	0	1	4	4	4
Consumer protection	0	0	0	2	4	1
Crime and justice	3	1	4	2	0	3
Deficit/debt	0	1	0	1	0	1
Democratic reform	0	3	0	0	1	13
Economic policy	2	2	5	5	1	8
Environment	2	1	5	11	7	12
Intergovernmental affairs	0	1	0	1	0	0
Foreign affairs	1	3	0	3	3	3
Infrastructure	1	1	0	0	4	4
Labour policy	0	0	0	0	0	1
Military	0	2	0	0	6	10
Social policy*	4	7	4	6	15	10
Taxation	1	1	2	1	2	3
Trade	0	0	0	0	0	0
Women/minorities**	3	6	7	12	10	16
Total	17	29	28	48	58	89

NOTES: Total number of NDP commitments: 2000 = 169; 2004 = 262; 2006 = 162; 2008 = 328; 2011 = 171; 2015 = 286; total number of LPC commitments: 2000 = 108; 2004 = 106; 2006 = 213; 2008 = 239; 2011 = 183; 2015 = 292.

* Social policy includes health care, education, poverty reduction, unemployment insurance, pensions, and housing.
** Minorities include Indigenous people, official language minorities, immigrants, ethnocultural groups, gays and lesbians, and disabled Canadians.

was large, I coded commitments as similar if the two parties wanted to increase funding in a certain area but disagreed on how much funding should be increased.

The most striking element of Table 5.4 is that the number of NDP commitments similar to LPC commitments increased substantially from 2000 to 2015. Indeed, by 2015, I was able to identify almost ninety similar commitments compared with seventeen in 2000, and there was a consistent increase in the number of similar commitments across the six elections. The symmetries between the two parties grew the most in the areas of social policy and women/minorities. There was also increasing similarity in economic

FIGURE 5.1

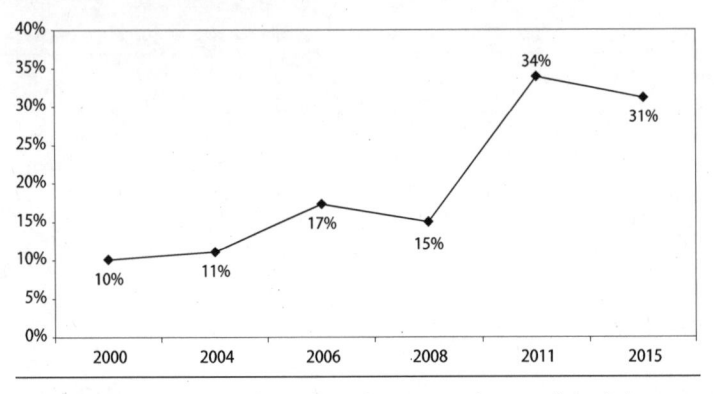

Percentage of NDP platform made up of commitments similar to those in LPC platform, 2000–15

```
40%
35%                                          34%
30%                                                 31%
25%
20%
15%              17%
                         15%
10%     10%  11%
 5%
 0%
      2000  2004  2006  2008  2011  2015
```

Sources: NDP and LPC platforms from the 2000 to the 2015 federal elections

policy, the environment, infrastructure, the military, and arts and culture. However, there was almost no similarity throughout this period on questions of labour policy, trade, and intergovernmental affairs. The two parties also did not display much similarity in their platforms on democratic reform until the 2015 election.

It is clear from Figure 5.1 that NDP platforms became increasingly similar to LPC platforms over this period. The figure illustrates the percentage of the NDP platform similar to the LPC platform. Whereas about 10 percent of the NDP platform was made up of commitments similar to those in the LPC platform in the early 2000s, in 2006 and 2008 it rose to about 15 percent. Strikingly, Figure 5.1 illustrates that, during the later years of the Harper Conservative government (the 2011 and 2015 elections), over 30 percent of the NDP platform was made up of commitments similar to those in the LPC platform.

A brief look at the actual commitments in the platforms enables us to understand better the convergence between the two parties. In the 2000 election, New Democrats and Liberals agreed on two important issues. First, the NDP vowed to decrease the middle-income tax bracket to 23 percent, and the LPC pledged to reduce it to 22 percent. Second, the NDP pledged to increase federal transfers for health care to 25 percent of total spending for health care in Canada, and the LPC made the more precise promise to increase federal transfers by $18.9 billion over five years. Both parties also wanted to halt health care privatization by strictly enforcing the Canada Health Act. The other similarities were committing more financial resources to research and development in the private sector, public transit, national parks, official language minorities, debt relief for developing countries, the child tax benefit, and the fight against organized crime.

The 2004 election followed a similar pattern, with the important similarities between the two parties centring on health care and personal income taxes. The parties agreed on the importance of closing the "Romanow gap," the investment needed to move the federal government from funding roughly 19 percent of health care to funding 25 percent. Both parties wanted to continue to index personal income tax brackets and credits that had been recently phased in while reducing Canada's debt-to-GDP ratio. There was growing agreement in other areas of social policy, such as a national homecare program, increased funding for affordable housing, a new public health agency, and partnerships with provincial governments to create more licensed child-care spaces. In terms of urban affairs, both parties were in favour of increasing the gas tax transfer to municipalities and giving cities a greater role in intergovernmental relations. Common ground was also evident when it came to generic drugs for developing countries, the fight against HIV/AIDS in Africa, more resources for peacekeeping missions, whistle-blower legislation, and the salaries of soldiers.

In 2006, the NDP and the LPC again agreed on personal income taxes by proposing to increase the basic exemption for all taxpayers and to reduce the rate of the lowest bracket. With the negotiation of the Canada Health Accord with the provinces, federal funding for health care was not a contentious issue in the 2006 election. However, there was growing agreement between the NDP and the LPC in policy areas other than social issues. The New Democrats' calls for mandatory minimum sentences for gun offences, anti-gang programs, more funding to combat smuggling, and restricting handgun ownership mirrored the Liberals' crime platform. Certain aspects of the New Democrats' economic policy – such as increased funding for research and development in the auto sector, cutting red tape for small businesses, higher income support for farmers, and enhanced Canada-US border infrastructure – were similar to proposals made by the Liberals. The environmental commitments of the NDP might have been more aggressive than those of the LPC, but they were similar in pointing the federal government in the direction of retrofitting homes and buildings to reduce energy consumption, increasing the ethanol content of gasoline, providing more money for public transit, and expanding the protection of wildlife habitat. Finally, the immigration and Aboriginal policies of the two parties had several symmetries. Both parties wanted to eliminate the landing fee for new immigrants, allow more temporary foreign workers and international students to become permanent residents, and invest greater resources in immigrant settlement and credential recognition. The LPC and the NDP also agreed on a basic package of Aboriginal policies, including the need for more skills training, targeted health programming, and on-reserve water treatment infrastructure.

Although the similarities between the two parties were still dispersed throughout their platforms, we can see a basic pattern of growing symmetry in their platforms during the final years of the Chrétien government and the two years of the Martin government. By the 2006 election, the agreement between the two parties on a limited number of taxation and social policies had morphed into a broader convergence, including aspects of their environmental, criminal, economic, Aboriginal, and immigration policies. The 2006 election campaign was the one in which control of the platform was removed from volunteers and placed more firmly in the hands of political operatives at NDP headquarters who thought that previous party platforms had been too expansive and ambitious. These operatives crafted a platform close to that of the governing Liberals to peel away their soft voters. So the ideological moderation of the NDP in 2006 had its roots in the attempt by agents, in this case political operatives, to tilt the NDP toward its competitors.

The election of Stephen Harper and the Conservatives in 2006 and the sharing of the opposition benches by New Democrats and Liberals led to even more commonalities in the platforms of the two parties. In 2008, most of the similarities concerned the environment, women/minorities, and arts and culture. Under the leadership of Stéphane Dion, the LPC platform was centred on environmental issues, leading to convergence with the NDP platform on topics such as establishing greenhouse gas emissions targets of 25 percent of 1990 levels by 2020, developing stricter energy efficiency standards in building codes, retrofitting homes for low-income families, banning bulk water exports, creating green bonds, and designing an east-west electricity grid to reduce reliance on coal. Both parties pledged more resources to eliminate the backlog in immigration applications and to reverse the Harper government's closure of Status of Women offices, and the LPC and NDP platforms on Aboriginal policy emphasized ratifying the United Nations Declaration on the Rights of Indigenous Peoples, implementing Jordan's Principle to reduce jurisdictional wrangling over responsibility for Aboriginal children, seeking Aboriginal input on climate change policy, and increasing funding to preserve Indigenous languages. In 2008, the two parties also came to greater agreement on their arts and culture policies by promising to increase the film tax credit, establish income averaging for artists, and create stronger Canadian content rules. In other areas, the level of agreement between the parties remained similar to that of the pre-Harper era.

It was during the 2011 and 2015 elections that the similarity between the NDP and LPC platforms reached its zenith. In both elections, just over 30 percent of the NDP platform was made up of commitments similar to those in the LPC platform. Although not shown in Table 5.4, it is also possible to calculate the percentage of the LPC platform that comprised commitments also found in the NDP platform – 32 percent of the 2011 LPC platform and 30 percent of the 2015 LPC platform made up of commitments similar to NDP promises. In short, approximately one-third of the platforms of the two parties in 2011 and 2015 were relatively similar. Furthermore, it would be superficial to chalk up the growing similarity to a common desire to roll back the most conservative parts of the Harper government's agenda. A closer examination reveals that slightly less than one-fifth of the similar commitments in the 2011 and 2015 elections entailed simply undoing something that the Harper government had done (e.g., restoring the long-form census).

If we deal with the platforms from the 2011 and 2015 elections together, then we can see that the symmetry between the New Democrats and Liberals was driven by the policy areas where there had already been agreement. In terms of social policy, both parties committed to increasing the Guaranteed Income Supplement for seniors, expanding CPP benefits, coordinating bulk purchasing of prescription drugs by provinces, raising grants for low-income postsecondary students, and investing more in affordable housing. On the environment, there was a shared commitment to establishing stricter environmental assessments of industrial projects, reducing subsidies to the oil and gas sector, making large investments in green infrastructure, developing renewable energy, promoting clean technology, and retrofitting older buildings. In terms of taxation policy, the NDP and LPC concurred on cancelling the accelerated capital cost allowance for oil sands production, opposing income splitting, and providing more resources to combat tax evasion. Although there was only limited similarity on economic policy in 2011, the two parties had several comparable proposals in 2015, such as reducing the small-business tax rate, increasing resources for export promotion, creating more work placements for young Canadians, and reinstating labour-sponsored venture capital tax credits. The points of agreement between the two parties in the 2011 and 2015 elections in the areas of women and minorities and arts and culture were substantially similar to those in 2008.

What is interesting about the 2011 and 2015 elections is the similarity between New Democrats and Liberals in policy areas where they had not been close in the past. By the earlier 2010s, the parties had come to agreement on the basic priorities of Canada's military: ending the combat mission in Afghanistan, cancelling the *F-35* jet fighter contract, enhancing services for veterans, emphasizing peacekeeping, and bolstering disaster relief capacity. The two parties' infrastructure plans stressed more investment in public transit, wastewater treatment, cultural facilities, and flood mitigation. In foreign affairs, Liberals and New Democrats were in broad agreement on prioritizing climate change, working toward a two-state solution in the Israel-Palestine conflict, creating higher standards of corporate responsibility for Canadian companies operating abroad, establishing parliamentary oversight of national security operations, and ratifying the United Nations Arms Trade Treaty. In terms of labour policy, both parties agreed to eliminate laws recently passed by the Conservative government to force unions to disclose publicly all of their financial activities and to remove automatic certification for workers in federally regulated sectors (Bills C-377 and C-525). Finally, Liberals and New Democrats were far apart on democratic reform for most of the period examined here. However, in 2015, they agreed on a whole host of reforms to counteract what they condemned as the Harper government's lack of respect for Canadian democracy. These reforms ranged from banning government advertising deemed partisan to disallowing omnibus bills to giving federal government scientists more freedom to share their research publicly.

In summary, we can see that the number of parallel positions between New Democrats and Liberals grew in this period. Much of the strategy of NDP operatives during the Layton and Mulcair years was predicated on attracting former Liberal voters, particularly if they were inclined to vote strategically. In this sense, the increase in similarity between the NDP and its chief opponent should be seen as evidence of the party's growing political market orientation toward competitors. Ideological equivalence with the Liberals' platform was designed by political operatives as a way for New Democrats to steal soft Liberal voters.

Nonetheless, the discussion above should not be taken to argue that the LPC and the NDP converged toward the same centrist ideology. By the end of the period examined here, roughly 70 percent of LPC and NDP platforms was still different. Within this large portion of these platforms, there are important differences that point to the NDP as a social democratic party and the LPC as a more centrist party. As I have argued elsewhere (McGrane, 2019), multiple examples from the 2015 NDP and LPC platforms prove this point. The New Democrats argued for higher corporate taxes, whereas the Liberals concentrated on reducing personal income taxes for all but the top 1 percent of taxpayers. The NDP promised two key universal expansions of the welfare state: a national child-care program at fifteen dollars a day and a publicly owned insurance scheme for all Canadians that would lower prescription drug costs by 30 percent. The Liberals pledged a means-tested monthly allowance to spend on child-care costs if parents desired as well as bulk purchasing hoped to lower prescription drug costs by an unidentified amount. The New Democrats pledged to remove interest on all student loans, and the Liberals promised to delay student loan repayment until the student made $25,000 per year. Although the LPC platform was silent on public ownership, the NDP committed to preventing private-public partnerships for municipal infrastructure projects, expanding Crown corporations such as VIA Rail, and restoring the Canadian Wheat Board. The Liberals vaguely promised to allow provinces to set their own frameworks on greenhouse gas emissions, whereas the New Democrats promised to enforce a pan-Canadian cap-and-trade system that would put a price on carbon and reduce emissions by 34 percent of 1990 levels by 2025. Key differences were also seen in labour policy and trade policy, such as the NDP's proposals for a federal minimum wage, anti-scab legislation, and opposition to the Trans-Pacific Partnership not echoed in the LPC platform.

Finally, regarding the much-publicized fiscal policies of the two parties during the 2015 election, the NDP platform insisted that its increases in corporate taxes would generate enough revenue to cover its spending promises and avoid deficits, whereas the LPC planned to go into deficits to pay for its promises of personal income tax cuts and increased infrastructure spending. During the election, this difference in the two parties' platforms generated stories in the media about the New Democrats being outflanked on their left by the Liberals (Kohut 2015).

In reality, the situation was much more complex. Keynesian ideas of deficit financing and demand stimulation had been popular in the federal NDP during the postwar era and up to the late 1990s. The party gradually moved toward a greater insistence on not running a deficit during Layton's time as leader. In many ways, this was a sign of ideological moderation as a stronger sense of fiscal responsibility meant that the party prudently wanted to create new programs that it could afford and to avoid the "tax-and-spend" stereotype that its research showed stuck to it in voters' minds. However, fiscal responsibility is not completely alien to the Canadian social democratic tradition, and Keynesian ideas were contested historically by a certain element of the CCF-NDP. A strain of Canadian social democratic thought characterized by the Saskatchewan CCF-NDP had always insisted on fiscal discipline. Following the ideas of the Fabian Society, Tommy Douglas consistently argued that it would be folly to run up public debt because tax revenue would end up being siphoned off to bankers in the form of debt servicing charges instead of being used on programs that could aid citizens. Similar to the 2015 federal NDP platform, the CCF government in Saskatchewan increased taxes on businesses and individuals to create new universal social programs without running a single deficit during the seventeen years that Douglas was premier. Subsequent Saskatchewan NDP premiers, such as Allan Blakeney and Roy Romanow, followed a similar course of action and raised taxes to finance social program expansion instead of running deficits (McGrane 2014). So the federal NDP's insistence on avoiding deficits under Layton and Mulcair, though a sign of ideological moderation, should not be seen as evidence that the party had somehow abandoned social democracy by promising to be fiscally responsible or was importing right-wing ideas that were completely alien to Canadian social democratic traditions.

The NDP's Internal Left-Right Spectrum

Given the continuity and change within the NDP's ideology mapped out above, it is fruitful to analyze the ideology of NDP MPs, members, and voters in 2015. Such an examination will ascertain the extent to which the moderation advocated by NDP operatives seeped into the ideology of party members and MPs by 2015. I can also compare the ideology of members and MPs to Canadians who were potential NDP voters in the 2015 federal election.

To perform this examination, I employed a unique research design. The same seven questions outlined in Table 5.5 were asked to NDP members in the online survey described in Chapter 2 and the survey of NDP MPs described in Chapter 3. The same questions were asked to potential NDP voters during the first two weeks of the 2015 election campaign through a randomly selected internet panel of voters over eighteen administered by the survey companies SOM in Quebec and Probit in English Canada. In these surveys, voters were asked "for each of the following *federal* parties, can you tell us whether you will certainly vote for that party, will probably vote for that party, would consider voting for that party, will probably not vote for that party or would never vote for that party?" (emphasis in original). The same seven questions asked to NDP MPs and members were then asked to potential NDP voters, defined as those who indicated that they would certainly or probably vote, or consider voting, for the NDP. The resulting sample size for potential NDP voters was 2,612 in Quebec and 1,987 in English Canada. According to these surveys, potential NDP voters, what political operatives refer to as the "NDP universe," represented 63 percent of the Quebec electorate and 60 percent of the English Canadian electorate during the early part of the 2015 federal election campaign.[1]

The seven questions asked to NDP members, MPs, and potential voters were based on the assumption that it would be uninteresting to ask these respondents, for example, if they believed in the large-scale privatization of Medicare. The vast majority would likely be opposed to it. Rather, it is more interesting to focus on areas of potential disagreement within the party and among potential voters that constitute an internal left-right political spectrum. The seven survey questions were thus devised to encapsulate this internal political spectrum. Each question contains two conflicting statements. One statement represents a position that could be considered on the right wing of the NDP, whereas the other statement represents a position that could be considered on the left wing of the NDP. Respondents were asked to place themselves on a scale from 0 to 10, where 0 is complete agreement with the left-wing statement and 10 is complete agreement with the right-wing statement.

Table 5.6 depicts the mean for each group of respondents as well as the standard deviation for each set of conflicting statements. Given the alphas reported in the table, it was possible to create an index for all seven questions for potential NDP voters and members. This index indicates the respondent's overall position within the NDP's internal left–right political

TABLE 5.5

Statements measuring NDP's internal left-right spectrum

Topics	Left-wing position (0 on the scale)	Right-wing position (10 on the scale)
Public ownership	The NDP should push for the creation of new Crown corporations and forms of public ownership.	The NDP should focus on protecting and improving our existing federal Crown corporations as opposed to creating new ones.
Trade agreements	Canada should refrain from signing new free-trade agreements because they reinforce the control of large corporations over our economy.	Canada should negotiate new free-trade agreements with other countries as long as those agreements respect human rights, environmental laws, and labour laws as well as promote economic growth.
Environmental protection	Environmental protection should be prioritized over economic growth.	Economic growth and environmental protection are not mutually exclusive. They should be equal priorities.
Taxing and spending	An NDP government should immediately raise taxes and quickly increase government spending.	An NDP government should maintain taxes at current rates and restructure government spending.
Social conservatism	The NDP should not shy away from taking progressive stances on moral issues even if it means turning off socially conservative voters.	Society changes its values slowly on moral issues that concern religion and the traditional family, and the NDP must be cautious not to be too aggressive on such matters.
Deficits	An NDP government should increase investment in social programs even if it means increasing short-term deficits.	An NDP government should ensure that its spending on social programs does not create any budget deficit.
Principles versus power	The NDP should never sacrifice its social democratic principles in the pursuit of power.	The NDP might occasionally have to compromise its principles in order to win the government.

spectrum. Perhaps because of the small sample size, the alphas for NDP MPs are too low to ensure reliable indices, so they were not calculated. The 0 to 10 scale has been converted into a 0 to 1 scale for ease of interpretation.

Several aspects of this table deserve comment. First, what could be called ideologically moderate NDP positions on these questions would normally fall closer to the right-wing positions within the party or those on the scale used in Table 5.6. In this sense, we can see that MPs in both Quebec and English Canada displayed generally moderate positions that leaned toward seeing economic growth and environmental protection as equal priorities, being in favour of trade agreements that did not harm human rights, and protecting existing Crown corporations as opposed to creating new ones. For the most part, the views of NDP members were slightly to the left of those of NDP MPs on these three indicators but not overwhelmingly against more moderate positions. The only mean to fall under 0.5 on these three indicators was the opinion of ROC members concerning how trade agreements "reinforce the control of large corporations over our economy," and that was 0.44. Similarly, with a mean closer to the midpoint, MPs and members were skeptical of having an NDP government "immediately raise taxes and quickly increase government spending." On other questions, MPs and members took what could be considered less moderate positions. There was a willingness to entertain short-term deficits and progressive stances on moral issues by both members and MPs. On the question of power versus principles, the general opinion among both MPs and members appeared to be that the party should never sacrifice its "social democratic principles" in the pursuit of forming the government. But it is interesting to note that, with a mean of 0.47, MPs from English Canada were an outlier on this question.

The standard deviations for the seven sets of conflicting statements presented to NDP members and MPs were rather high. So we should be careful in asserting that there was a consensus position on any of the topics. This diversity of opinions reflects a healthy debate within the NDP on what it means to be left wing or a social democrat and mirrors the diversity of values discussed above.

Another interesting way to examine the ideological moderation of the NDP is to explore the distance between the ideologies of its members and MPs and those of potential voters. An ideologically moderate party would illustrate a political market orientation toward voters by having an ideology close to those of its targeted voters – that is, those voters within its universe.

TABLE 5.6

Means of statements of NDP's internal left-right political spectrum with standard deviation in parentheses (NDP members, MPs, and potential voters, 2015)

	ROC members	ROC MPs	ROC voters: Certain	ROC voters: Probable	ROC voters: Consider	QC members	QC MPs	QC voters: Certain	QC voters: Probable	QC voters: Consider
Statements	Mean (SD)	Mean (SD)	Mean (SD)	Mean (SD)	Mean (SD)	Mean (SD)	Mean (SD)	Mean (SD)	Mean (SD)	Mean (SD)
Public ownership	0.53 (0.31)	0.62 (0.21)	0.59 (0.28)	0.63 (0.22)	0.67 (0.22)	0.62 (0.28)	0.57 (0.30)	0.73 (0.28)	0.74 (0.27)	0.73 (0.28)
Trade agreements	0.44 (0.35)	0.70 (0.29)	0.49 (0.32)	0.57 (0.31)	0.63 (0.30)	0.56 (0.33)	0.78 (0.21)	0.65 (0.34)	0.68 (0.30)	0.67 (0.32)
Environmental protection	0.56 (0.36)	0.66 (0.37)	0.59 (0.34)	0.59 (0.31)	0.66 (0.31)	0.58 (0.36)	0.67 (0.32)	0.67 (0.38)	0.71 (0.33)	0.68 (0.33)
Taxing and spending	0.50 (0.31)	0.55 (0.15)	0.56 (0.28)	0.60 (0.25)	0.69 (0.25)	0.61 (0.31)	0.55 (0.33)	0.77 (0.28)	0.79 (0.25)	0.79 (0.27)
Deficits	0.31 (0.27)	0.38 (0.26)	0.30 (0.25)	0.40 (0.26)	0.51 (0.29)	0.40 (0.30)	0.38 (0.28)	0.50 (0.35)	0.50 (0.33)	0.54 (0.34)
Social conservatism	0.33 (0.29)	0.28 (0.23)	0.29 (0.30)	0.36 (0.27)	0.43 (0.29)	0.38 (0.30)	0.31 (0.28)	0.55 (0.35)	0.50 (0.34)	0.52 (0.35)
Principles versus power	0.36 (0.30)	0.47 (0.34)	0.37 (0.27)	0.43 (0.26)	0.50 (0.27)	0.34 (0.29)	0.25 (0.29)	0.39 (0.33)	0.41 (0.31)	0.39 (0.31)
Sample size	1980	25	430	670	887	460	33	592	810	1210
Index of seven statements	0.43 (0.19)	–	0.45 (0.17)	0.51 (0.16)	0.58 (0.16)	0.50 (0.20)	–	0.61 (0.19)	0.62 (0.18)	0.62 (0.18)
Alpha of seven statements	0.7195	0.586	0.7453	0.7198	0.6510	0.7125	0.401	0.7127	0.6695	0.6387

For English Canada, the means in Table 5.6 illustrate that NDP members were more left wing than voters certain to support the party and NDP MPs, but the gap was not overwhelmingly large. The biggest differences occurred between members and voters considering supporting the party. Predictably, members were firmly to the left of voters whose support for the NDP was not completely confirmed. In fact, the configuration that repeats itself in Table 5.6 is that members, certain voters, probable voters, and voters willing to consider the NDP line up perfectly from left to right with members on the left and voters willing to consider the NDP on the right. For their part, MPs aligned themselves closer with potential voters than with members on most of the seven indicators. On questions of public ownership, trade agreements, environmental protection, taxing and spending, and power versus principles, the mean position of English Canadian NDP MPs was closer to that of probable voters or voters willing to consider voting NDP than to that of party members. When it came to deficits and social conservatism, MPs were closer to certain and probable voters and a bit further away from those who would consider voting for the party. Overall, the findings confirm that there was a left-right structuring of how the federal NDP related to English Canadian society in 2015. Party members were on the left end of the spectrum, voters who would consider voting for the party were on the right end, and MPs, certain voters, and probable voters landed somewhere in the middle.

Similar to English Canada, in Quebec NDP members, certain voters, probable voters, and voters willing to consider the party lined up from left to right, with members on the left and voters willing to consider the party on the right. However, Quebec MPs were positioned somewhat to the left of Quebec members on five of the seven indicators (public ownership, taxing and spending, deficits, social conservatism, and principles versus power). This created some distance between MPs and potential voters on these five issues. However, when it comes to the two remaining issues (trade agreements and environmental protection), the mean of the MPs lines up well with that of potential voters. So, in Quebec, members were slightly better aligned ideologically with potential voters than with MPs – the opposite of the situation in English Canada.

There is one important commonality in the results of surveys in Quebec and English Canada. The mean scores for NDP MPs and members in both English Canada and Quebec gravitate toward less moderate positions on the questions concerning deficits, social conservatism, and principles versus power and toward more moderate positions on the other questions. Interestingly, potential NDP voters in English Canada and Quebec illustrate the same pattern. They are also immoderate concerning deficits, social conservatism, and principles versus power. This finding illustrates an important point. There was a political market orientation toward voters among NDP members and MPs leading into the 2015 election: when they were immoderate, they were immoderate on the same issues as voters. This is not to say that this congruence was necessarily a conscious decision by NDP politicians and activists. But it does illustrate an alignment of the thinking of NDP politicians and activists with that of voters who support the party and a reluctance to stray too far from what they think. In this sense, the thinking of both NDP members and MPs shows signs of a political market orientation toward voters.

Finally, it is important to look for ideological divisions between Quebec and English Canada in the surveys. The ideological unity of the Quebec and ROC segments of the NDP caucus is noteworthy. There is little evidence that the Quebec segment of the NDP caucus was any more left wing than the ROC segment. The small exception is that Quebec MPs were more idealistic than their ROC colleagues, believing that the NDP should never sacrifice its "social democratic principles" in the pursuit of forming government. Likewise, there does not appear to be an ideological chasm between NDP members in Quebec and the ROC, though on certain issues (e.g., public ownership, trade agreements, taxing and spending, and deficits) the former were positioned slightly to the right of the latter. Overall, voters within the NDP universe in Quebec were further to the right than voters within the NDP universe in the ROC. In particular, voters who were certainly or probably supporting the party in Quebec were noticeably to the right of certain and probable ROC voters on all of the indicators with the exception of the question on principles versus power.

Interestingly, ROC voters considering voting for the NDP were to the left of their counterparts in Quebec, though only by a small gap. Importantly, there appears to be more ideological diversity within the NDP's English Canadian universe of voters compared with its Quebec universe of voters. In Quebec, there was relatively little ideological distance between certain, probable, and possible NDP voters. In English Canada, voters who were certain to support the party were considerably to the left of voters who were considering whether or not to vote NDP.

NDP MPs were asked to elaborate on where they placed themselves on the internal left–right political spectrum. After the interviews were transcribed, the textual data were coded using NVivo 10. I used the coding scheme described in Chapter 3. Instead of starting with a predetermined list of codes, I performed "open coding," a line-by-line reading of the interview transcripts to generate a list of themes and categories suggested by the participants themselves. The results of this open coding are contained in Table 5.7, which illustrates the percentage of MPs whose answers contained any length of text coded under a certain code. For instance, 13 percent of the MPs interviewed mentioned that trade could help developing countries when asked to elaborate on where they placed themselves on the scale concerning trade agreements. To keep the size of the table manageable, I eliminated codes related to a subject that appeared in the answers of three or fewer MPs.

There is certainly evidence in Table 5.7 that affirms the ideological moderation of NDP MPs. Although a commitment to public ownership is a hallmark of social democracy (McGrane 2014), the clear preference of MPs (86 percent) was the protection and improvement of existing Crown corporations as opposed to the creation of new state-owned enterprises that could prove to be controversial within the context of an election. MPs were particularly interested in strengthening Canada Post, CBC/Radio Canada, VIA Rail, and federal public housing programs (presumably through the Canadian Mortgage and Housing Corporation), all of which they felt were being undermined by the Harper government. As one MP put it,

> Je pense qu'on a suffisamment de travail de réinvestissement à faire avec qu'est-ce qui existe déjà en ce moment, que ça serait mettre un peu la charrue devant les bœufs de vouloir prendre des sociétés nouvelles alors que celles qu'on a sont en mauvais état [I think that we have enough work already to reinvest in what exists right now, it would be putting the cart before the horse to want to create new state-owned corporations when the ones we have are in such a bad state].

In contrast, a relatively small number of MPs gave precise ideas of sectors in which new forms of public ownership should be created (e.g., health care and natural resources).

When it came to free-trade agreements, the concerns that the NDP raised in the early 2000s about trade liberalization undermining Canadian sovereignty

TABLE 5.7

Open coding of NDP MPs' textual responses to internal left-right spectrum questions, 2015

Statements	Very popular responses (%)	Somewhat popular responses (%)	Less popular responses (%)
Public ownership	General need to improve and protect existing Crown corporations (86)	Improve Canada Post (19); improve CBC/Radio Canada (16); need for public ownership in energy/natural resources sector (14); improve VIA Rail (14)	More public ownership needed but precise example not given (10); more public housing (9); more public health care (7)
Trade agreements	Better/fairer free-trade agreements (95); trade good for economic growth (95)	Concerned about increased investor rights (18); must sign agreements only with countries that respect human rights (18); trade helps developing countries (13)	Fearful of the loss of Canadian jobs (7); concerns about supply management (7); concerns about energy security (5)
Environmental protection	Economic growth and environmental protection go together (82)	Need for stronger environmental reviews of industrial projects (15); need to protect the planet for future generations (13)	Fearful of consequences of pipelines and oil sands (7); need to protect jobs (5); seriousness of climate change (5); social licence (5); future economic growth might need to be limited to protect the environment (5)
Taxing and spending	Increase corporate taxes (67); re-evaluate current government spending (42)	No increases to personal income taxes (26); spend more on social programs (25); open to increasing personal income taxes on the wealthy (21); stop unnecessary subsidies for business (particularly the oil sector) (21); need to go slowly in first NDP mandate of the government (16)	Stop offshore tax havens (12); spend more on economic development (11); become free of NDP's "tax and spend" brand (7); decrease small-business taxes (7); reduce taxes on individuals (7); review military spending (7)

Deficits	Short-term deficits permissible to reinvest in social programs (69); spending on social programs creates long-term savings and economic growth (40)	New social programs must be affordable (17); raise corporate tax revenues to avoid deficits (16); Keynesian idea of balancing the budget over the business cycle (10)	Restructure total spending to increase spending on social programs while holding the line on deficits (9); fearful of high interest charges endangering the fiscal health of Canada (5)
Social conservatism	Need to be true to our convictions and values (64)	Social conservatives do not vote NDP in any case (20); should not compromise on human rights (18); be cautious because social mores change slowly (18); moral issues are complicated, and NDP approach should change depending on the issue (18)	Have a strong stance on moral issues but avoid controversy by not talking about such issues (7); majority of Canadians support NDP stances on moral issues (5); must be careful not to risk electoral success of the NDP (5)
Principles versus power	Balance seeking power and upholding our convictions (53); foremost, be true to our beliefs (39)	Need to move slowly when implementing change (21); being too radical means never winning government and never getting results (18)	Canadians will rally behind NDP values (9); if people vote for social democrats, give them social democracy (7)

and aggrandizing corporate control were notably absent from MPs' responses. MPs believed that increasing international trade was a fundamental part of creating economic growth for Canada. Some even specified that trade with Canada helped developing countries as well. However, there was an equally strong sentiment that free-trade agreements should not undermine social democratic values. As one MP explained, "rule of law, environmental standards, human rights, so we've put together a template of what we would need to see in a free-trade agreement, that we could support. And if it meets those basic criteria, then by all means we should expand our international trade through trade agreements." The responses of only a small number of MPs reflected the party's positions of the early 2000s by arguing that free-trade expands investors' rights (e.g., Chapter 11 of NAFTA), causes job losses, undermines supply management, and endangers energy security.

The idea that economic growth and environmental protection go hand in hand was popular among NDP MPs. They lauded the growth opportunities related to green innovation and were adamant that environmental degradation eventually undermines economic growth because pollution is expensive to clean up and can eventually render land unusable. Representative of this category, one MP stated that, "if you take environmental protection seriously enough, you're creating a new kind of economy that may actually be more prosperous and productive." Hence, several MPs stressed the need for stronger environmental regulations and reviews. Interestingly, mentions of the need to limit economic growth to ensure environmental protection and direct attacks on building more pipelines and expanding Alberta's oil sands were rare.

MPs were asked two questions regarding the federal government's budget. First, on the question of immediately raising taxes and spending or maintaining current tax rates and restructuring spending, the proposal to raise corporate tax rates that Mulcair had made in late 2013 was particularly popular. Raising corporate taxes was seen as a way to increase spending on new social programs in the areas of child care, health care, and poverty reduction. However, Mulcair's promise not to increase "personal taxes" (quoted in Fekete 2013), also made in late 2013, was less popular and mentioned by only 26 percent of MPs. In fact, 21 percent of MPs (mostly from English Canada) expressed openness to increasing personal income taxes on the wealthy. This emerged as a point of difference in late 2013 between Tom Mulcair and Linda McQuaig, a high-profile NDP candidate in a downtown

Toronto riding (Raj 2013). Ideas from earlier NDP platforms – such as reducing the use of offshore tax havens and eliminating subsidies for the oil sector – were mentioned by several MPs, even though neither idea had been discussed by Mulcair or made it into the 2015 platform. A handful of MPs from Quebec were in favour of reducing personal taxes, particularly for low- and middle-income earners. Although this idea was not part of the 2015 platform, decreasing small-business taxes, mentioned by 7 percent of MPs, was part of it. Finally, 42 percent of MPs stated that more money on social programs could be spent without drastically raising taxes by reviewing the spending priorities of the Harper government. As one MP argued,

> c'est des détails dans un budget, par exemple c'est ... 10 000 là qui est mal dépensé, un 20 000 là. Ça fait que quand tu les regroupes tous ensemble bien ça fait des millions puis des milliards. Avant d'aller augmenter les impôts, je pense qu'il faut aller faire le ménage dans toutes les dépenses [it is in the details of the budget, for example there is ... $10,000 poorly spent here and $20,000 poorly spent there. When you group that all together, it makes millions and billions. Before increasing taxes, I think that we have to clean up our spending].

The example most often cited by NDP MPs was reallocating military funding to social programs. Often mentions of restructuring spending dovetailed with MPs' insistence that the NDP would slowly ramp up spending in its first mandate and the need to combat the "tax and spend" label frequently pinned on the party – evidence that MPs had internalized the branding analyses by the political operatives at party headquarters.

These interviews with NDP MPs were completed prior to the announcement early in the 2015 campaign that the party intended not to run a deficit in any of its four years of government. Yet data from the interviews shows that MPs were open to running short-term deficits immediately to repair at least part of the extensive damage that they thought the Harper government had inflicted on social programs. One MP's response was typical:

> Actuellement pour en revenir à ce que je disais sur l'héritage qu'on va avoir du pouvoir, des dix ans de pouvoir conservateur, puis du pouvoir libéral précédemment, il y a eu des pertes énormes en

matière d'entente de transfert entre le fédéral et les provinces en matière du programme d'assurance-emploi qui a été ravagé. Alors c'est évident qu'on ne pourra pas attendre, à strictement parler, à maintenir un équilibre dans le budget pour faire les changements dans ces programmes-là. [To come back to what I was saying earlier about what we will inherit when we come to power after ten years of the Conservatives in power and the Liberals being in government before them, there have been enormous decreases in federal transfer payments to the provinces, and the Employment Insurance program has been ravaged. As such, we cannot wait, strictly speaking, to have a balanced budget to make changes to those programs].

Often the MPs' arguments about short-term deficits involved referencing the idea of "social investment" (Jenson and Saint-Martin 2003): spending on social programs can lead to long-term savings by lowering health care and social assistance costs as well as to future economic growth by creating an educated population that can compete in the knowledge-based economy. Some MPs also explicitly referred to the Keynesian idea that short-term deficits are needed to ride out economic downturns. Despite the views of many of the MPs interviewed, the thinking that short-term deficits can pay for immediate public investments to push economic growth became more associated with the Liberals as opposed to the New Democrats during the 2015 election. The NDP official position during the 2016 campaign that social spending should be slowly increased and covered by increases in corporate taxation to avoid deficits, was mentioned by only a handful of MPs.

When it came to the question of social liberalism, a strong majority of NDP MPs was firm that the party should be true to its convictions and values on moral issues. For some MPs, the party's stances on moral issues (they mentioned abortion, gay rights, euthanasia) involved nonnegotiable human rights. Other MPs pointed out that social conservatives do not vote NDP in any event, so there is little to lose by taking firm stances on moral issues. As one MP succinctly put it, "les conservateurs sociaux ne sont pas vraiment notre public cible, je crois, à la base. Alors, je pense qu'il faut qu'on reste près de nos valeurs et qui ont est [Social conservatives are not really our target audience, I believe. As such, I think that we should stay close to our values and who we are.]" Other MPs were more nuanced in their responses, stating the need to be cautious because public opinion on moral issues changes slowly and arguing that the NDP should be aggressive on some moral issues and restrained on others. However, MPs who counselled excessive caution on moral issues to safeguard the NDP's electoral success were a small minority.

Finally, MPs were asked a broad question on whether the NDP should ever sacrifice its principles to attain power or whether occasional compromise is necessary to win the government. The largest group of MPs interviewed could be described as cautious. They talked about the need to balance seeking power and upholding principles and alluded to the necessity of occasional compromise in the pursuit of power. There were frequent mentions of moving slowly to implement change and an overriding sentiment that being too radical or ideological would prevent the NDP from cooperating with other parties to get results for Canadians and even block the party from forming the government and being able to really transform Canadian politics.

Overall, the ideological moderation of NDP MPs involved a large dose of caution and adherence to the idea of incrementalism in achieving social democratic change. This overarching idea was consistent with the pragmatic "safe change" branding that political operatives ultimately adopted for the Mulcair NDP in the 2015 election. It showed a political market orientation toward voters in its commitment to move slowly to allow voters time to get used to an NDP government and a political market orientation toward competitors in being careful not to give opponents ammunition to reinforce negative stereotypes about the NDP brand. According to the MPs interviewed months prior to the 2015 election and before the release of the NDP platform, the first steps of an NDP government would include strengthening existing public enterprises, signing free-trade agreements that respected human rights, promoting the green economy, and gradually ramping up spending on social programs by using revenue from a small increase in corporate tax. Despite a general consensus on moving slowly and incrementally, there was still substantial continuity with NDP values and past stances in the textual answers of MPs to these questions. The need for aggressive stances on moral issues was affirmed as a matter of fundamental human rights. Progressive taxation (whether through corporate taxes or individual taxes) would build up the fiscal capacity needed to construct an expanded welfare state. Environmental protection remained a high priority, and there was no mention of privatizing public enterprises. The MPs' answers illustrated a cautious and moderate social democracy, not a sprint toward the centre that abandoned the traditional social democratic values of the party.

Conclusion

Ultimately, the notion that the "new NDP" abandoned its socialist roots and moved toward the centre during the Layton and Mulcair years (Carroll 2005; Conway 2016; Evans 2012; Palmer 2016) is too simplistic. The ideological evolution of the NDP from 2000 to 2015 was actually more nuanced, complex, and multilayered. There was ideological continuity in terms of the stable values of NDP members and persistent platform differences between the centrist Liberal Party and the social democratic NDP. At the same time, the NDP did move toward a moderate version of social democracy that increased its political market orientation toward voters and competitors. With the growing power of political operatives and the influence of market research funded by public subsidies, the NDP gradually oriented its ideology toward voters by downplaying policy areas in which its positions could be controversial and abandoning some of its more ambitious ideas that could reinforce negative stereotypes of its brand. At the same time, moving away from these ideas displayed a competitor orientation since the rejection of such policies took away ammunition that could be used by opponents to attack the party. Indeed, the growing equivalence between NDP platforms and LPC platforms represented an attempt to steal soft Liberal voters, reflecting more sophisticated electoral market segmentation.

Interestingly, it appears that the voter orientation prescribed by political operatives at party headquarters was shared, to a certain extent, by NDP members and MPs. By 2015, the ideology of members and MPs displayed an impressive congruence with the ideology of the party's universe of voters that made up roughly 60 percent of the Canadian electorate. In the next two chapters, I look more closely at the attitudes and behaviours of NDP voters from 2000 to 2015. I use voter surveys from the Canadian Election Study from 2000 to 2011 to analyze English Canada and surveys done by Ipsos-Reid in Quebec immediately following the federal elections in 2006, 2008, and 2011. I then analyze the 2015 Canadian Federal Election Panel Survey on Social Democracy, a custom survey of voters in anglophone Canada and francophone Quebec. This custom survey used a random sample of the same voters surveyed at the beginning of the 2015 federal election campaign and immediately following that election. The examination of voter behaviour gives us an appreciation of how the moderation and modernization of the political marketing of the NDP were received by voters and explains the party's rise to official opposition and its subsequent fall back to its traditional position of being the third party in the House of Commons.

6
Stealing Market Share: Electoral Market Segmentation and the NDP, 2000–11

The creation of the "new NDP" was accompanied by a period of unprecedented electoral success for the party. After one of its worst electoral performances in the 2000 election, the party incrementally improved its seat totals and popular vote percentages to become the official opposition in the House of Commons in 2011. Indeed, the resounding success of the NDP in the 2011 election affirmed the wisdom of going down the road of moderation and modernization that Layton and his team of political operatives had began to travel following the upheaval within the party at the beginning of the 2000s.

To gain a better understanding of how voters reacted to the moderation and modernization of the NDP, I use data from voter surveys to trace the evolution of NDP support in both the ROC and Quebec. The concept of electoral market segmentation helps to explain the success of the NDP during the Layton years, in particular how it built up to its surprising breakthrough in the 2011 election. The evidence suggests that the electoral success during the Layton years should not be attributed to Canadians becoming ideologically more left wing, "NDP issues" becoming more important to Canadians, or certain sociodemographic groups predisposed to supporting the NDP voting in greater numbers than in the past. Rather, the electoral success during Layton's time as leader can be explained by the party's ability to steal market share from the parties ideologically closest to the NDP (the Liberal Party and the Bloc Québécois). The voter surveys administered in the elections between 2000 and 2011 illustrate that the NDP stole market share from the Liberal Party in sixteen segments of the English Canadian electoral market and from the Conservative Party in only two segments. In the Quebec electoral market, the NDP stole market share from the BQ in sixteen segments, the Liberal Party in thirteen segments, and the Conservative Party in eight segments.

So the electoral success of the "new NDP" during the Layton years that culminated in its breakthrough in the 2011 election was a combination of its own prowess and the weakness of its principal opponents on the centre-left: the LPC and BQ. It was a mixture of good fortune and working hard and working smart to take advantage of that good fortune. The moderation and modernization of the NDP prescribed by political operatives and financed by new public subsidies enhanced the ability of the party to target soft LPC and BQ voters as support for those parties crumbled during the later 2000s when they ran substandard campaigns and the popularity of their leaders sagged. In English Canada, the Liberals' choice of unpopular leaders and struggle to define the party dovetailed with the New Democrats' emphasis on Layton, their increased presence in the public consciousness because of minority Parliaments, the moderation of their language, and the discipline of their caucus to allow strategists to present the NDP as a credible alternative to the LPC in order to push the Conservatives out of power. The roles of the NDP and Layton in brokering cross-party compromises during the string of minority governments in the late 2000s certainly made the party more present in Quebec media, but there was something more happening. The Quebec electorate was becoming fatigued with Gilles Duceppe and the BQ in the later 2000s but remained wary of both the Conservatives and the Liberals. NDP operatives had done research that pointed to the potential for their party in Quebec and started making significant investments in the province shortly after the 2004 election in terms of Layton's time, paid advertising, media relations, Quebec-specific policies, and a professional campaign structure. When the Quebec electorate suddenly shifted during the 2011 campaign to look for alternatives to the BQ and LPC, the "new NDP" was ready to take advantage of this shift and created a sense of momentum that eventually swept over the province.

Incremental Growth: The NDP in English Canada, 2000–11

As we can see in Table 6.1, the NDP incrementally increased its number of votes and its percentage of the popular vote in the ROC from the 2000 election to the 2011 election. There was a large jump in its popular vote from 2000 to 2004 and then a stabilization in 2006 and 2008 before another noticeable increase in 2011. There was also steady improvement in the party's seat count throughout this period. The Conservatives experienced similarly strong growth in seat total and popular vote during this period as well, whereas the Liberals consistently lost seats and popular vote. Indeed, in

TABLE 6.1

NDP votes in the ROC, 2000–11

Federal election	Popular vote for the NDP (%)	Total number of votes for the NDP	Voter turnout (%)	Seats won by the NDP
2000	11.0	1,030,257	59.9	13
2004	19.4	1,968,976	60.8	19
2006	20.8	2,313,196	64.7	29
2008	20.3	2,074,190	57.6	36
2011	26.4	2,881,546	60.3	44

SOURCE: Elections Canada.

English Canada, the Liberals dropped from 136 seats in 2000 to 27 seats in 2011, and their share of the popular vote decreased from 40 percent to 20 percent.

What explains the steady growth of the NDP's popularity in English Canada in the 2000s? To answer this question, I examine data from the Canadian Elections Studies (CES) for 2000, 2004, 2006, 2008, and 2011. It does not appear that the success can be explained by voters becoming more left-wing during this period. For instance, I was unable to find evidence that English Canadians became noticeably more favourable to government intervention in the economy or more generous social programs from 2000 to 2011. There was also little evidence that voters who might have been predisposed to voting NDP were voting in greater numbers in the 2000s compared with the 1990s. There was not a large spike in voter turnout during this period, and there were no reports of NDP-friendly voters such as women, atheists, or union members who turned out at higher rates than in the past. The work of Clarke and his collaborators does not show an increased salience of issues in which the NDP could have had an advantage (Clarke, Kornberg, and Scotto 2009a, 2009b; Clarke et al., 2011). In fact, issues of the economy and corruption gained importance during this period as opposed to social policy issues on which the NDP might have been more trusted. Rather, the primary reason for the success of the party in English Canada was that it stole electoral market share from the Liberals from 2000 to 2011 as their popularity crumbled because of poorly ran campaigns, problems defining themselves and their policies in ways that Canadians could understand, and unpopular leaders.[1]

Using CES data, Figures 6.1a, 6.1b, and 6.1c break down the voting patterns of respondents according to which of the three major parties they reported supporting in the previous election. For example, Figure 6.1a shows that 64 percent of NDP voters in the 2000 election recalled voting for the party in the 1997 election, 20 percent recalled voting for the LPC, and 17 percent recalled voting for the CPC. In this sense, the NDP "lost" almost 40 percent of its 1997 voters to the other two major parties in 2000, contributing to the party's disappointing results in that election.

One important finding evident in Figure 6.1a is that, from 2000 to 2008, the NDP did a poor job of preventing its supporters in the previous election from migrating to its opponents. Compared with 2000, the NDP did a slightly better job maintaining its supporters from the previous election in 2004 and 2006 (roughly 75 percent remained loyal to the party in those two elections). However, in 2008, the NDP ran into trouble again, with both the Liberals and the Conservatives attracting more previous NDP voters than in the past two elections. The Green Party's vote in English Canada spiked upward to nearly 8 percent in 2008 compared with 2006, when it received 4.5 percent of the vote in English Canada. Although not depicted in Figure 6.1a, the CES data illustrate that the NDP was slightly hurt by the rising Green Party vote in 2008, losing 11 percent of its 2006 voters to the Greens in the 2008 election. So some of the success of the NDP in English Canada in 2011 could be attributed to its enhanced capability to maintain its voters from

FIGURE 6.1A

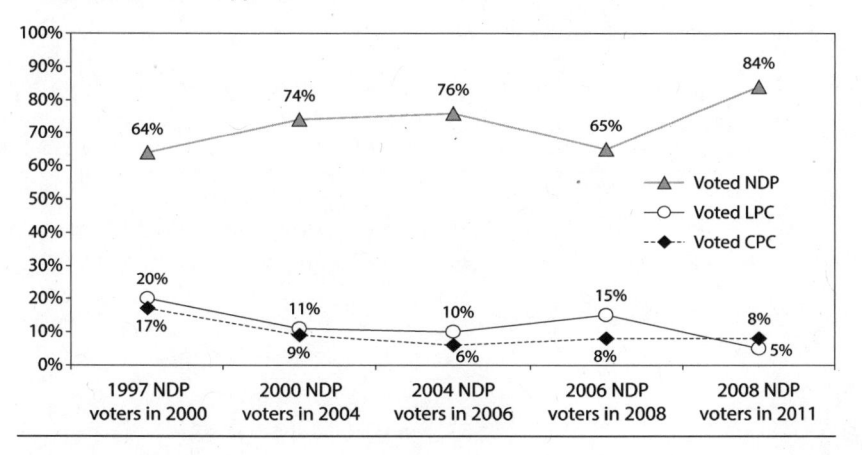

Parties NDP voters supported in the 2000–11 federal elections, ROC

Figure 6.1b

Parties LPC voters supported in the 2000–11 federal elections, ROC

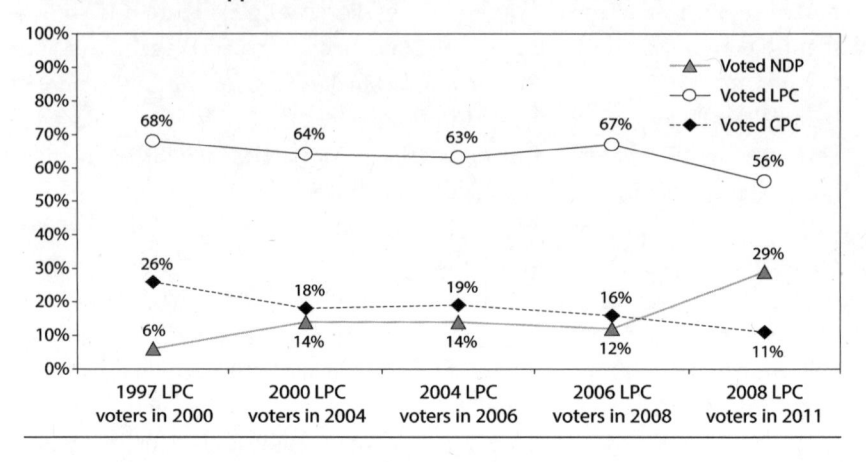

	1997 LPC voters in 2000	2000 LPC voters in 2004	2004 LPC voters in 2006	2006 LPC voters in 2008	2008 LPC voters in 2011
Voted LPC	68%	64%	63%	67%	56%
Voted CPC	26%	18%	19%	16%	11%
Voted NDP	6%	14%	14%	12%	29%

Figure 6.1c

Parties CPC voters supported in the 2000–11 federal elections, ROC

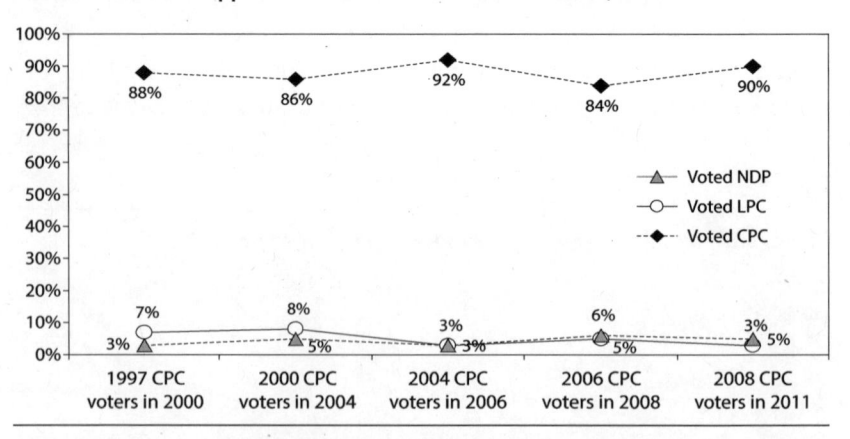

	1997 CPC voters in 2000	2000 CPC voters in 2004	2004 CPC voters in 2006	2006 CPC voters in 2008	2008 CPC voters in 2011
Voted CPC	88%	86%	92%	84%	90%
Voted LPC	7%	8%	3%	6%	3%
Voted NDP	3%	5%	3%	5%	5%

NOTES: *N* for 2000 = 1,370; *N* for 2004 = 1,890; *N* for 2006 = 2,027; *N* for 2008 = 2,510; *N* for 2011 = 1,993; *N* for all elections = 9,790. For the 1997 and 2000 elections, "Voted CPC" is the combined number of Reform/Canadian Alliance and Progressive Conservative voters.

SOURCE: Canadian Elections Studies (2000–11).

the previous election. Figure 6.1a illustrates that the NDP maintained the support of 84 percent of its 2008 voters in English Canada in the 2011 election, whereas other parties were largely unsuccessful in attracting voters who reported voting NDP in 2008.

Another interesting feature of these three figures is evidence that the NDP's success throughout the 2000s was not predicated on stealing market share from the Conservative Party. Figure 6.1c shows that, in the five elections examined, no more than 5 percent of CPC voters from the previous election switched their votes to the NDP. The figure clearly shows that the Conservatives did an extraordinarily good job during the 2000s of maintaining their supporters from the previous election and ensuring that they did not migrate to other parties. Undoubtedly, the ability of the CPC to maintain its supporters from the previous election was part of its rise to power in the 2000s. Conversely, the failure of the LPC to keep its supporters from the previous election from migrating to other parties led to its electoral weakness. Considering that the Liberals dropped from 40 percent of the popular vote in 2000 to 20 percent in 2011 in English Canada, attracting former Liberal supporters was the perfect opportunity for the NDP to increase its vote totals. Indeed, the reason behind the success of the NDP during the 2000s was that it gained prowess at attracting soft Liberal supporters as the decade progressed. Figure 6.1b illustrates that, in the 2000 election, only 6 percent of LPC voters from the previous election decided to change their support to the NDP. The figure then shows that in the 2004, 2006, and 2008 elections the NDP was able to convince from 12 percent to 14 percent of LPC supporters from the previous election to vote for it. In the 2011 election, the "Layton Liberal" strategy of NDP operatives really bore fruit, with nearly 30 percent of 2008 Liberal supporters going to the New Democrats.

In summary, Figures 6.1a, 6.1b, and 6.1c indicate that the NDP's electoral success in the 2000s in English Canada should be understood through the lens of its increased ability to steal overall market share from the Liberals and its enhanced ability to maintain its own share of the market from the previous election. However, these figures deal only with the overall market shares of the NDP, CPC, and LPC from election to election. They do not attempt to explain which segments of the LPC's market share the NDP stole. For instance, did a noticeably larger portion of female LPC voters compared with male LPC voters switch to the NDP? Were left-wing LPC voters more likely to migrate to the NDP than right-wing LPC voters? Answers to such questions will expand our understanding of how the moderation and modernization of the NDP positioned the party in relation to certain segments of the English Canadian electoral market.

Following political market segmentation techniques (Smith and Hirst 2001) and literature on Canadian voter behaviour (Blais et al., 2002; Clarke, Kornberg, and Scotto 2009a; Gidengil et al., 2012), I have devised just under thirty different segments of the English Canadian market. These segments range from the sociodemographic, based on where voters live and central characteristics of their identities (e.g., sex and religion), to the psychographic, based on voters' underlying values, loyalties to particular political parties, opinions of particular party leaders, and perceptions of the Canadian economy. I show that in sixteen segments of the English Canadian electorate (e.g., male voters, those who favoured government intervention in the economy, and those who disliked the sitting prime minister), the probability of voting NDP went up, whereas the probability of voting LPC went down. On the other hand, there were only two examples of a segment in which the probability of voting NDP increased and the probability of voting CPC decreased.

To elaborate this argument, I use CES samples from the ROC for each election from 2000 to 2011. I perform an analysis similar to that in *Dominance and Decline: Making Sense of Recent Canadian Elections* (Gidengil et al., 2012, 188). The dependent variable is vote choice limited to the three major parties – did the respondent vote NDP, LPC, or CPC? For the 2000 election, I considered CPC voting to be the combination of Canadian Alliance and Progressive Conservative voters in the sample. Using multinomial logistical regression, I ran two consecutive models on the ROC CES sample for each election. My first model predicts the probability of voting NDP, LPC, or CPC when it is assumed that all voters have the maximum of a single characteristic – for example, all voters are women, all voters have the highest level of market liberalism possible, or all voters like Jack Layton at 100 on the likeability scale. My second model predicts the probability of voting NDP, LPC, or CPC when it is assumed that all voters have the minimum of the same single characteristic – for example, all voters are men, all voters have the lowest level of market liberalism possible, or all voters like Jack Layton at 0 on the likeability scale. In both cases, all of the other independent variables are held at their means. The difference in the probabilities produced by the two models indicates the impact that a certain variable had on voting NDP, LPC, or CPC, everything else being equal. For example, in Table 6.2, a visible minority voter in the ROC had a 40 percent higher probability of voting for the LPC in 2000 than a non–visible minority voter, and being a visible minority had no statistically significant impact on the probability of voting for the NDP. However, by 2011, a visible minority voter in the ROC had a 14 percent higher probability of voting for the LPC than a non–visible minority voter and a 14 percent higher probability of voting for the NDP than a non–visible minority voter. Clearly, the LPC had lost part of its market share of visible minority voters to the NDP.

For each election, six blocs of independent variables were created from literature emanating from the CES (Blais et al., 2002; Fournier et al., 2013; Gidengil et al., 2012). Congruent with this literature and its use of the bloc recursive model, these six blocs are loaded on top of each other. The theoretical reason behind how the blocs are loaded into the models is that the variables more likely to pre-exist the voting decision and be found before the campaign even begins are loaded first, whereas the variables closer to the actual voting decision are loaded last. Table 6.2 contains the results of my model, including only a bloc of sociodemographic variables: region, gender, age, religion, union membership, visible minority status, and education. Table 6.3 shows the results of the model when sociodemographic variables and variables related to the underlying values of the respondent are included. Underlying values are measured by indices related to a respondent's openness to accommodating Quebec, feelings about the closeness of ties between Canada and the United States, beliefs about government intervention in the economy, level of social conservatism, sentiment that the federal government treats one's province "worse" than others, and cynicism about politics in general. Table 6.4 includes variables related to the standard CES questions concerning partisanship as well as underlying values and sociodemographic variables.[2] Table 6.5 adds two retrospective economic perspectives (feelings about one's personal finances and an evaluation of the strength of Canada's economy over the past year) on top of the variables related to partisanship, underlying values, and sociodemographic features. Since specific issues discussed during the various campaigns were different, a cross-election analysis of "hot-button" issues is not possible. Such an issue in one election might not be discussed at all in the next election. So I used policy preferences as an "issues" bloc. In particular, questions related to respondents' views on the appropriate level of corporate taxation, personal taxation, immigration, and federal spending on defence, education, health care, the environment, and social assistance were used. Table 6.6 includes positions on these issues in addition to economic perspectives, party identification, values, and sociodemographic variables. Finally, Table 6.7 illustrates the full model, which includes leadership evaluations in addition to the five previous blocs analyzed. Leaders were evaluated using a "feeling thermometer" from 0 to 100, where 0 is "really dislike" and 100 is "really like." The exact wording of the CES questions used is contained in Appendix B. The raw results of the multinomial logistical regressions are found in Web Appendix 1. The tables below report only the differences in probability for each independent variable when it is at its minimum and its maximum and all of the other independent variables are held at their means.

If the probability of voting for one party based on a certain characteristic grows in correspondence with a decline in the probability of voting for another party based on the same characteristic, we can establish that one party was stealing market share from the other party in that segment of the ROC electorate. For example, if the probability of Catholics voting for the NDP consistently increased from 2000 to 2011 while the probability of Catholics voting for the LPC consistently decreased and the probability of Catholics voting for the CPC stayed the same, then this finding constitutes evidence that the NDP stole market share from the LPC among English Canadian Catholics during the five elections of the 2000s. Examining the changes in the probability of voting for the three major parties in this manner across these five elections allows me to evaluate how the moderation and modernization of the NDP positioned the party within the English Canadian electoral market. I can gain an understanding of the extent to which the NDP was stealing market share from its competitors and in which segments of the market those transfers were taking place.

The overall pattern in Table 6.2 is that the New Democrats stole market share from the Liberals during the 2000s while maintaining their strength in certain sociodemographic segments of the ROC electorate where they traditionally did well. In terms of regional voting, it appears that the NDP was a party of the English Canadian periphery in 2000–08. The probability of voting for the NDP was greater for Atlantic residents than Ontario residents in 2000, 2006, and 2008, and a Western Canadian was six points more likely to vote for the NDP than an Ontarian in 2008. In 2011, Western and Atlantic Canadians were neither more nor less likely to vote NDP than Ontarians. This trend indicates the growing strength of the party in Ontario

TABLE 6.2

Sociodemographic variables, 2000–11 federal elections, ROC

	2000 NDP	2000 LPC	2000 CPC	2004 NDP	2004 LPC	2004 CPC	2006 NDP	2006 LPC	2006 CPC	2008 NDP	2008 LPC	2008 CPC	2011 NDP	2011 LPC	2011 CPC
Atlantic[a]	0.11	-0.16	0.06	0.05	-0.03	-0.02	0.10	-0.07	-0.03	0.12	-0.10	-0.11	0.08	0.03	-0.05
West[a]	0.04	-0.24	0.20	0.03	-0.18	0.14	0.04	-0.20	0.15	0.06	-0.18	0.12	0.03	-0.16	0.14
Female	0.06	0.05	-0.11	0.04	0.00	-0.04	0.06	0.03	-0.09	0.07	0.00	-0.07	0.04	0.01	-0.06
Under 35[b]	-0.02	0.03	-0.01	0.05	-0.02	-0.03	0.02	0.07	-0.09	0.07	-0.04	-0.02	0.01	0.08	-0.08
Over 54[b]	-0.01	0.05	-0.04	-0.06	0.05	0.01	0.00	0.07	-0.06	-0.01	0.04	-0.03	0.00	0.09	-0.09
Catholic[c]	0.04	0.22	-0.26	0.04	0.14	-0.17	0.04	0.09	-0.12	0.05	0.12	-0.17	0.08	0.05	-0.12
No religion[c]	0.19	0.09	-0.28	0.16	-0.02	-0.17	0.16	0.06	-0.22	0.14	0.16	-0.31	0.17	0.09	-0.26
Visible minority	-0.06	0.40	-0.34	-0.00	0.22	-0.21	-0.04	0.27	-0.24	0.03	0.15	-0.18	0.14	0.14	-0.28
Did not finish high school[d]	0.08	-0.01	-0.07	0.11	-0.03	-0.08	-0.01	-0.07	0.08	0.11	0.01	-0.11	0.02	-0.02	0.01
University graduate[d]	0.05	0.01	-0.05	0.00	0.06	-0.06	0.02	0.04	-0.06	-0.02	0.14	-0.12	0.02	0.10	-0.12
Union member	0.03	0.05	-0.08	0.10	-0.01	-0.10	0.11	-0.03	-0.07	0.13	-0.04	-0.09	0.16	-0.02	-0.14

NOTES: N for 2000 = 1,174; N for 2004 = 1,523; N for 2006 = 1,697; N for 2008 = 1,770; N for 2011 = 1,705; N for all elections = 7,869; shaded = $p \leq 0.05$.

a = reference category is Ontario; b = reference category is from thirty-five to fifty-four years old; c = reference category is Protestant or other religion; d = reference category is completed high school, completed college, or completed some university.

(the reference category), mostly at the expense of the LPC, which saw a weakening of its grip on Ontario, particularly compared with the 2000 election. Table 6.2 also indicates that the NDP vote became more male in the 2011 election. Whereas being female increased the probability of voting NDP in the 2000, 2006, and 2008 elections by roughly six points, English Canadian women were neither more nor less likely to vote NDP in 2011. Looking at bivariate statistics, we can see that the NDP's gender gap – defined as the difference between the percentage of English Canadian women voting NDP and English Canadian men voting NDP – declined in 2011 to only 2 percent, whereas it had been 6 percent to 7 percent in previous elections in the 2000s.[3] Although these effects seem to be slight, we must remember that the male/female division is the most important in any electorate. Approximately half of any electorate are women, whereas a significantly lower percentage would be nonreligious, Catholic, university graduates, and so on. The NDP's ability to do better among English Canadian male voters in 2011 was an important part of its success in that breakthrough election.

When it comes to religion, the NDP enjoyed a similar advantage among nonreligious voters compared with the other parties in the 2000s. It did not increase its advantage over competitors when it came to the nonreligious. However, the Liberals' large advantage among Catholic voters declined steadily from 2000 to 2011. As Fournier and colleagues (2013, 881) note in their analysis of the 2008 and 2011 CES data, "the propensity for Catholics to vote Liberal, already weak in 2008, vanished completely in 2011, marking the first federal election since 1965 where this relationship is not observed." The CPC and the NDP appeared to benefit from the diversification of the Catholic vote during the 2000s. The probability of a Catholic voting CPC improved from -0.26 in 2000 to -0.12 in 2011. Furthermore, whereas English Canadian Catholics were not more likely to vote NDP in elections from 2000 to 2008, they were eight points more likely to vote NDP in 2011 than non-Catholics. Similarly, the Liberals were particularly strong among visible minority voters in English Canada in the early 2000s. A visible minority English Canadian voter was neither more nor less likely to vote for the NDP in 2000, but in that election he or she was forty points more likely to support the LPC than a non–visible minority voter. By 2011, the picture had changed, with visible minority voters being equally likely to vote NDP (0.14) or LPC (0.14). The NDP had clearly decreased the LPC's advantage among visible minorities in English Canada.

When we look at union membership, we see a noticeable transformation. In 2000, union members were unlikely to vote Conservative, but they were not more likely to vote either Liberal or New Democrat. By 2011, union members were sixteen points more likely than non-union members to vote NDP. Indeed, CES data show that 14 percent of English Canadian union members voted NDP in 2000, whereas 44 percent voted LPC. In 2011, 37 percent voted NDP, and 21 percent voted LPC. One sociodemographic group with which the LPC gained some advantage over the NDP during the 2000s was university graduates, more likely to vote for the former party in both the 2008 and the 2011 elections.

Overall, moderation and modernization appear to have broadened the NDP's base of support. The large advantages that the Liberals had over the New Democrats with several sociodemographic groups in 2000 had been slowly diminished by 2011. As the coalition of voters that brought Jean Chrétien to victory slowly crumbled when the LPC started running lacklustre campaigns, the NDP was able to press its advantage. Indeed, it appears that part of its electoral success stemmed from its improved prowess in attracting voters from sociodemographic groups who had been habitual Liberal supporters in the early 2000s – Ontarians, Catholics, visible minorities, and union members. New Democrats were also able to maintain a strong base of support among nonreligious voters and to bring more male voters to their side. Thus, part of the story of the electoral success of the NDP in the 2000s is having its popularity more evenly distributed throughout the electorate by the 2011 election and eroding some of the traditional bases of Liberal support. The investments of political operatives in using Layton to attract more Liberal voters from Ontario and more Liberal male voters appeared to have paid dividends.

There is no evidence in the CES that the English Canadian electorate became noticeably more left wing, continentalist, pro-Quebec, cynical, or regionally alienated during the 2000s. For instance, the mean of the market liberalism index that I constructed ranged from 0.46 to 0.48 out of 100 for all the elections examined. This finding helps us to understand why NDP operatives chose not to push the party's ideology and policies to the left. It reflects a political market orientation toward voters because pushing the party to the left risked alienating it from a comfortably centrist English Canadian electorate.

To understand how the New Democrats stole market share from the Liberals, it is more instructive to look for changes in the voting patterns of

English Canadians with low levels and high levels of these values. Table 6.3 depicts the results for the underlying values bloc of independent variables. The more positive the number in the table, the more likely voters with high levels of these values voted for that party. Conversely, the more negative the number in the table, the more likely voters with low levels of these values voted for that party.

If we look at voters in the ROC who leaned toward accommodating Quebec, then we can see that the NDP closed its gap with the LPC. Pro-Quebec voters were twenty-five points more likely to vote LPC in 2004 and neither more nor less likely to vote NDP. By 2011, pro-Quebec voters in the ROC were twenty-two points more likely to vote NDP and thirty-seven points more likely to vote LPC while being fifty-nine points less likely to vote CPC. Possibly, this finding speaks to the growing credibility of the NDP on national unity issues throughout this period and its being seen as a competitor to the LPC as English Canada's "party of national unity." Interestingly, the New Democrats' electoral base in the ROC became slightly more continentalist over the 2000s. In 2000, the NDP dominated the market of those skeptical of further integration with the United States, whereas the probability of voting for the LPC did not fluctuate with a voter's continentalism. As the Liberal Party moved from being the government to being the opposition, a shift occurred. ROC voters skeptical of continentalism split between the NDP and the LPC, whereas procontinentalist voters shifted to the CPC. By 2011, an English Canadian voter with the lowest level of anticontinentalism was nineteen points less likely to vote NDP but forty points less likely to vote LPC. It appears that, as the NDP moderated itself by talking less about trade and opposition to free-trade agreements, it was seen as more attractive to some pro-American voters. In a rare instance of the NDP stealing market share from the CPC, Table 6.3 illustrates that the increase in pro-American voters who supported the New Democrats in 2011 coincided with a slight decrease in pro-American voters who supported the Conservatives. At the same time, the NDP was still able to maintain some support among anti-American voters even if the LPC had eroded that market share somewhat.

ROC voters with low levels of market liberalism and low levels of moral traditionalism were evidently potential NDP voters. The positions taken by the NDP were congruent with increased government intervention in the economy to create wealth redistribution and a socially liberal outlook on gay rights and women working outside the home. However, the problem for the

TABLE 6.3

Underlying values variables, 2000–11 federal elections, ROC

	2000			2004			2006			2008			2011		
	NDP	LPC	CPC	NDP	LPC	CPC	NDP	LPC	CPC	NDP	LPC	CPC	NDP	LPC	CPC
Accommodation of Quebec	0.06	-0.16	0.10	-0.01	0.25	-0.25	0.18	-0.05	-0.13	0.15	0.42	-0.57	0.22	0.37	-0.59
Continentalism	-0.32	0.09	0.24	-0.25	-0.40	0.64	-0.29	-0.35	0.64	-0.32	-0.36	0.68	-0.19	-0.40	0.59
Market liberalism	-0.27	-0.28	0.55	-0.37	-0.07	0.44	-0.42	-0.20	0.62	-0.42	-0.19	0.61	-0.60	-0.01	0.62
Moral traditionalism	-0.24	-0.44	0.68	-0.41	-0.16	0.57	-0.39	-0.27	0.65	-0.28	-0.27	0.55	-0.35	-0.25	0.60
Political cynicism	0.11	-0.64	0.53	0.18	-0.67	0.49	0.28	-0.70	0.41	0.34	0.20	-0.54	0.32	0.30	-0.62
Regional alienation	0.00	-0.17	0.17	-0.08	-0.10	0.17	0.02	-0.05	0.03	0.06	0.10	-0.16	0.02	0.03	-0.05

NOTES: *N* for 2000 = 1,174; *N* for 2004 = 1,523; *N* for 2006 = 1,697; *N* for 2008 = 1,770; *N* for 2011 = 1,705; *N* for all elections = 7,869; shaded = *p* ≤ 0.05; sociodemographics and the underlying values bloc were included in the model, but only the results for the underlying values bloc are shown.

New Democrats was that many potential voters in English Canada with low levels of market liberalism and moral traditionalism voted for the Liberals in the 2000 election. The NDP could never improve its electoral performance if voters with whom it had ideological affinities were voting LPC.

Table 6.3 illustrates that a large transfer of market share from the Liberals to the New Democrats occurred among voters with low levels of market liberalism. In 2000, these voters were equally likely to vote for the NDP (-0.27) and the LPC (-0.28). However, by 2011, ROC voters with low levels of market liberalism were much more likely to vote NDP (-0.60), and voters' values concerning market liberalism did not affect their probability of voting LPC. Although not as dramatic, a similar story emerges with the moral traditionalism index. ROC voters with low levels of moral traditionalism were more likely to vote LPC (-0.44) than NDP (-0.24) in the 2000 election. By 2011, ROC voters with low levels of moral traditionalism were more likely to vote NDP (-0.35) as opposed to LPC (-0.25). As we can see, part of the electoral success of the NDP can be explained by its ability to convince more of its "natural voters" (i.e., those with low levels of market liberalism and moral traditionalism) to support it as opposed to voting LPC. This finding speaks to the success of political operatives in establishing the New Democrats as the left-of-centre governing alternative to the right-of-centre Conservatives in the segment of the ROC electoral market with left-of-centre values. Perhaps these voters came to believe that voting NDP, as opposed to voting LPC, was the best way to ensure that their values were reflected in federal politics. If so, then this shift of left-of-centre voters to the NDP is a good example of the party taking advantage of LPC weakness among these voters.

Considering that the NDP was in opposition throughout this period and that it had never formed the government, one group of voters that it had the potential to attract were those cynical about politics. These voters believed that political parties do not keep their promises and that politicians do not care what average people think, and they were generally dissatisfied with the state of Canadian democracy. Such voters are a natural clientele for any opposition party, particularly one that has never formed the government. However, in 2000, the NDP was not doing a good job attracting these cynics. ROC voters with high levels of political cynicism heavily favoured the CPC as opposed to the governing LPC in elections from 2000 to 2006. The CPC was thus the opposition party that dominated the market of cynics. After the Conservatives gained power, the New Democrats along with the

Liberals began to split the market of cynical voters. Table 6.3 shows that the NDP made gains among cynics when the LPC replaced the CPC as the official opposition. Although those with the highest level of political cynicism were only eleven points more likely to vote NDP in 2000, they were thirty-four points more likely to vote for the party in 2008 and thirty-two points more likely to vote for it in 2011. Perhaps because of their record of government, the Liberals were not able to dominate the market of cynics as the Conservatives had when they were the official opposition. The New Democrats were able to steal some cynics wary of the Conservatives when they were in government and not fully convinced that the Liberals were much different. Layton's promise (based on the research of political operatives) to bring new energy to politics and "fix Ottawa" might have attracted voters "fed up" with the two traditional parties and politics as a whole.

An opposition party could also base its appeal on representing a certain region of the country and fighting for the interests of that region. Table 6.3 provides some evidence that the Conservatives pursued this strategy in the early 2000s. Voters with high levels of regional alienation (i.e., strongly believing that the federal government treated their province worse than others) favoured the Canadian Alliance/Progressive Conservatives in 2000 and the Conservative Party of Canada in 2004. However, the federal NDP never made strong regional appeals – it would have gone against political operatives' strategy of presenting the party as the "national governing alternative" to the Liberals. Therefore, it makes sense that throughout this period the probability of voting NDP was not particularly affected by feelings of regional alienation in English Canada.

It is possible that increased electoral success for an opposition party can be predicated on growing its base of partisans over an extended period of time. However, there is little evidence in CES data that the NDP dramatically increased its number of partisans in English Canada. Despite the share of the popular vote in the ROC climbing to 26 percent for the party in 2011, according to Elections Canada, CES data illustrate that no more than 10 percent of the English Canadian electorate identified as "New Democrats" during the 2000s.[4] Liberal identifiers constituted somewhere between 20 percent and 25 percent of the English Canadian electorate during this period. Given its inability to grow its partisan base substantially, an alternative option for the NDP was to depend on Canadians to be "flexible partisans" (Anderson and Stephenson 2010, 20–21) and attempt to attract Liberal identifiers through its "Layton Liberal" strategy and the points of equivalence

TABLE 6.4

Party identification variables, 2000–11 federal elections, ROC

	2000			2004			2006			2008			2011		
	NDP	LPC	CPC	NDP	LPC	CPC	NDP	LPC	CPC	NDP	LPC	CPC	NDP	LPC	CPC
NDP ID	0.63	-0.15	-0.47	0.53	-0.23	-0.30	0.57	-0.05	-0.52	0.55	-0.08	-0.47	0.68	-0.09	-0.58
LPC ID	-0.03	0.47	-0.43	-0.09	0.48	-0.39	-0.05	0.42	-0.36	-0.06	0.47	-0.41	-0.01	0.40	-0.42
CPC ID*	-0.08	-0.44	0.52	-0.16	-0.36	0.52	-0.23	-0.35	0.59	-0.20	-0.31	0.52	-0.28	-0.21	0.49

NOTES: * For the 2000 election, the "CPC ID" is the combined number of Canadian Alliance identifiers and Progressive Conservative identifiers. N for 2000 = 1,174; N for 2004 = 1,523; N for 2006 = 1,697; N for 2008 = 1,770; N for 2011 = 1,705; N for all elections = 7,869; shaded = $p \leq 0.05$; sociodemographics, underlying values, and partisanship blocs were included in the model, but only the results for the partisanship bloc are shown.

TABLE 6.5

Economic perspective variables, 2000–11 federal elections, ROC

	2000			2004			2006			2008			2011		
	NDP	LPC	CPC	NDP	LPC	CPC	NDP	LPC	CPC	NDP	LPC	CPC	NDP	LPC	CPC
National economy	0.02	-0.04	0.02	-0.04	0.05	-0.01	-0.08	0.13	-0.05	-0.02	-0.08	0.10	-0.12	0.03	0.09
Personal finances	-0.05	0.11	-0.06	-0.01	0.01	0.01	0.06	0.08	-0.14	-0.02	-0.03	0.05	-0.15	0.00	0.15

NOTES: N for 2000 = 1,174; N for 2004 = 1,523; N for 2006 = 1,697; N for 2008 = 1,770; N for 2011 = 1,705; N for all elections = 7,869; shaded = $p \leq 0.05$; sociodemographics, underlying values, partisanship, and economic perspective blocs were included in the model, but only the results for the economic perspective bloc are shown. Sociodemographics, underlying values, partisanship, economic perspective blocs, issue positions, and leadership evaluation blocs were included in the model, but only the results for the leadership evaluations bloc are shown between the platforms of New Democrats and Liberals. Such a strategy made sense because the weakness of the Liberals as the 2000s progressed made LPC partisans question the wisdom of voting LPC even if they still identified as Liberal. Indeed, CES data illustrate that 64 percent of English Canadian Liberal identifiers voted LPC in 2011 compared with 86 percent in 2000.

Table 6.4 suggests that the NDP took advantage of the increasing disloyalty of Liberal identifiers. Liberal partisans were nine points less likely to vote NDP in 2004 and six points less likely to vote NDP in 2008, but by 2011 the variable of Liberal identifiers was not significant in explaining the likelihood of English Canadian voters supporting New Democrats. Bivariate evidence reinforces this point. In the 2004 election, approximately 10 percent of Liberal partisans voted NDP. In the 2011 election, 20 percent of Liberal partisans cast ballots for the NDP. Considering that approximately one-quarter of the English Canadian electorate identified as Liberal partisans, the ability of the NDP to steal more of them was consequential in terms of increasing its share of the popular vote. There is also some bivariate evidence that the NDP did a better job of ensuring that its partisans did not vote for other parties as the 2000s progressed.[5] However, the number of NDP identifiers in English Canada was so low, even in 2011, that it is doubtful such a small shift made much of a difference.

According to economic voting theory, voters punish the governing party by voting for opposition parties when they perceive that the economy is weak or when their personal finances have worsened (Anderson 2010; Happy 1986). A study of recent Canadian provincial elections has also shown that the main competitor to the governing party (i.e., the nonincumbent party that received the highest percentage of the popular vote in the election) benefits directly from negative economic perspectives, whereas they have no impact on the popularity of third parties and their leaders. The study concludes that "economic perceptions are important for the battle between the governing party and its primary challenger: they prime voters to like either the incumbent party and Premier, or like the government-in-waiting and the Premier-in-waiting" (McGrane, Berdahl, and Clavelle 2015, 92).

Because of the coding of questions, a minus sign in Table 6.5 indicates that feeling negative about one's finances or the Canadian economy increased the probability of voting for that party. Positive signs indicate that feeling optimistic about personal finances and the Canadian economy increased the probability of voting for that party. A close look at the table illustrates that the NDP in 2000 and 2004, as a third party, was not particularly adept at attracting the support of ROC voters pessimistic about their personal financial situations and the national economy. In fact, in those elections, economic perspectives did not influence vote choice for any party. In 2006, the LPC, as the incumbent party, did benefit when a voter had a positive perception of the national economy, and the likelihood of voting for the CPC, the main opposition party, increased in tandem with insecurity about one's own finances. The 2008 election was held in the midst of a severe global recession, and CES data illustrate that English Canadian voters had more negative outlooks on the national economy than in previous elections in the 2000s.[6] In line with economic voting theory, the LPC, as the primary opposition party, benefited from pessimistic views of the economy. An English Canadian voter who thought that the Canadian economy had become worse over the past year was nine points more likely to vote for the Liberals in 2008. The probability of voting for the New Democrats, who were a third party, was unaffected by economic perspectives.

By 2011, however, things had changed. The insistence of NDP operatives that the party talk about job creation, kick-starting economic growth, and pocketbook issues appears to have worked. In 2011, ROC voters who thought that their personal finances had become worse or not improved were more likely to vote for the NDP (-0.12). Similarly, in that election, ROC voters pessimistic about the state of the national economy leaned more toward the NDP (-0.15). Negative perceptions of Canada's economy or one's finances had no impact on the propensity to vote Liberal – a finding that highlights the weakness of the LPC campaign. We can see that the segment of the English Canadian electorate that had negative economic perceptions shifted to the New Democrats from the Liberals between 2008 and 2011. The English Canadian electorate as a whole was more optimistic about the national economy and personal finances in 2011 compared with 2008. So the impact of this bloc of independent variables on the NDP's success in 2011 might have been slightly muted. Nonetheless, the transfer of English Canadian voters disgruntled about the state of the economy from the Liberals to the New Democrats did contribute to the latter replacing the former as the primary alternative to the governing Conservatives in 2011.

Since controversial issues change in each election, it is not possible to track such issues across elections. However, CES data contain variables related to voters' opinions on general public policy issues such as appropriate levels of taxation, suitable levels of spending in various policy areas, and the optimal level of immigration. The more positive the number in Table 6.6, the more likely voters who wanted higher levels of taxation/spending/ immigration voted for that party. Conversely, the more negative the number in the table, the more likely voters who wanted lower levels of taxation/ spending/immigration voted for that party.

There is little evidence in CES data that English Canadians shifted left or right on these issues over the 2000s – hence helping to explain why NDP operatives did not move the party dramatically to the left in its platforms. The means of all the indices that comprise Table 6.6 remained relatively stable from 2000 to 2011. The one noticeable shift in public opinion was related to defence spending: English Canadians desired less spending on defence later in the decade than earlier in the decade.[7] In this sense, the electoral success of the NDP cannot be explained by English Canadian voters moving left on these issue positions and becoming ideologically closer to the party. Instead, the table provides further evidence that the NDP stole market share from the LPC: Liberals dominated the market of voters who wanted more taxes and spending in the early 2000s, and New Democrats were able to erode the strength of Liberals among such voters by the 2011 election.

In Table 6.6, we can see that, during the early 2000s, the NDP was an unattractive option for ROC voters tolerant of keeping personal income taxes the same or even raising them. In 2004 and 2008, the LPC enjoyed an advantage over the NDP among these voters. However, in 2011, the situation shifted, and the NDP gained a fifteen-point advantage with voters who supported taxes going up or remaining stable, and voters' opinions on the appropriate level of personal taxation were not a statistically significant indicator of voting LPC. On the question of increasing corporate taxes, we can also see that the NDP had little advantage over the LPC until the later 2000s. In 2006, voters who wanted to see corporate taxes raised or stay the same were 15 percent more likely to vote LPC. In 2008 and 2011, ROC voters who wanted corporate taxes to be raised or stay the same were significantly more likely to vote NDP, and their opinions on corporate taxes had no impact on their probability of voting LPC.

When it comes to spending, the clearest pattern that emerges in Table 6.6 pertains to the environment. New Democrats were at a disadvantage compared with Liberals among ROC voters who wanted higher environmental spending in the 2000, 2004, and 2008 elections. However, by 2011, ROC voters who wanted higher environmental spending were 17 percent more

TABLE 6.6

Issue position variables, 2000–11 federal elections, ROC

	2000 NDP	2000 LPC	2000 CPC	2004 NDP	2004 LPC	2004 CPC	2006 NDP	2006 LPC	2006 CPC	2008 NDP	2008 LPC	2008 CPC	2011 NDP	2011 LPC	2011 CPC
Personal taxes	0.07	-0.04	-0.03	-0.05	0.20	-0.15	0.00	0.08	-0.08	0.04	0.16	-0.20	0.15	0.00	-0.15
Corporate taxes	N/A*	N/A*	N/A*	0.03	-0.04	0.01	-0.03	0.15	-0.12	0.08	-0.01	-0.07	0.20	0.06	-0.27
Defence spending	-0.01	-0.17	0.18	-0.09	-0.11	0.20	-0.14	-0.07	0.21	-0.02	-0.15	0.17	-0.07	-0.04	0.12
Education spending	-0.03	-0.06	0.09	0.15	-0.02	-0.13	0.08	0.01	-0.08	0.12	0.08	-0.20	0.08	0.06	-0.14
Health care spending	-0.02	0.12	-0.10	-0.11	0.22	-0.11	-0.03	-0.03	0.05	0.08	-0.26	0.18	0.03	-0.04	0.01
Welfare spending	0.04	0.00	-0.03	0.01	0.02	-0.03	0.01	0.01	-0.02	0.04	0.08	-0.12	0.03	0.05	-0.08
Environment spending	0.06	0.20	-0.26	-0.03	0.14	-0.11	0.09	0.00	-0.17	-0.04	0.17	-0.13	0.15	-0.05	-0.10
More immigration	0.00	0.02	-0.02	0.06	-0.06	0.01	0.06	-0.03	-0.03	-0.02	0.02	0.00	0.03	0.08	-0.10

NOTES: * No question about corporate taxation rates was asked in the 2000 CES.
N for 2000 = 1,174; N for 2004 = 1,523; N for 2006 = 1,697; N for 2008 = 1,770; N for 2011 = 1,705; N for all elections = 7,869; shaded = $p \leq 0.05$; sociodemographics, underlying values, partisanship, economic perspective blocs, and issue positions blocs were included in the model, but only the results for the issue positions bloc are shown.

TABLE 6.7

Leadership evaluation variables, 2000–11 federal elections, ROC

	2000 NDP	2000 LPC	2000 CPC	2004 NDP	2004 LPC	2004 CPC	2006 NDP	2006 LPC	2006 CPC	2008 NDP	2008 LPC	2008 CPC	2011 NDP	2011 LPC	2011 CPC
NDP leader	0.36	0.04	-0.39	0.62	-0.36	-0.26	0.76	-0.09	-0.66	0.66	0.12	-0.78	0.73	-0.06	-0.66
LPC leader	-0.01	0.68	-0.68	-0.25	0.86	-0.61	-0.12	0.76	-0.63	-0.05	0.59	-0.54	-0.17	0.67	-0.50
CPC leader[a]	-0.23	-0.67	0.89	-0.21	-0.68	0.89	-0.43	-0.51	0.95	-0.33	-0.60	0.94	-0.64	-0.26	0.90

NOTES: a = for the 2000 election, "CPC leader" is the respondent's highest score given to either Stockwell Day or Joe Clark.
N for 2000 = 1,174; N for 2004 = 1,523; N for 2006 = 1,697; N for 2008 = 1,770; N for 2011 = 1,705; N for all elections = 7,869; shaded = $p \leq 0.05$.

likely to support the NDP. When it comes to defence, health care, and education spending, the patterns are less clear. Although the LPC had a clear advantage among voters who wanted higher health care spending in the 2004 election, it lost that advantage in subsequent elections. However, it does not seem that its losses within the segment of ROC voters who wanted higher health care spending helped the NDP. In fact, Table 6.6 indicates that the probability of voting CPC increased in 2008 if a voter wanted higher health care spending. Voters skeptical of the need to increase defence spending leaned toward the LPC in 2000 and seemed to split their votes between Liberals and New Democrats in 2004. They leaned toward the latter in 2006 and jumped back to the former in 2008 before not really flocking to any party in 2011. In terms of education spending, voters who wanted higher education spending were more likely to vote NDP in 2004 and 2008 but in no other election, and this variable did not influence the probability of voting LPC. Finally, for higher welfare spending and more immigration, these two variables were not found to be significant indicators of voting NDP or LPC.

Similar to the findings in Table 6.3 concerning underlying values, the ability of the NDP to attract former LPC voters who held left-of-centre positions on taxation and environmental spending speaks to the success of political operatives in presenting the party as a viable left-of-centre alternative to the Conservatives and to the weakness of the Liberal campaigns to hold on to these voters. Perhaps these voters came to see voting NDP as a means through which their policy preferences could be realized.

Layton's popularity has been pointed out as a critical factor of the NDP's electoral breakthrough in 2011 by both political scientists (Fournier et al., 2013) and media (Levitz 2011). Table 6.7 illustrates the impact of liking party leaders at 100 versus liking them at 0 when it comes to the probability of voting for the three major parties when all of the other variables in the previous blocs are held at their means. As we can see, the NDP was at a clear disadvantage in 2000 when it came to leadership evaluations. The problem was not that Alexa McDonough was disliked by the English Canadian electorate more than the other leaders. Her overall feeling thermometer score of 47 out of 100 in English Canada compared favourably with Prime Minister Chrétien's score of 52 out of 100 as well as the scores of Day and Clark, which hovered around 50 out of 100. The challenge for the NDP in 2000 was that liking McDonough did not necessarily mean that a voter would support the party or be pushed away from supporting its opponents. Indeed, those who really liked McDonough (100 out of 100) were neither more nor less likely to vote for the Liberals than voters who really disliked her (0 out of 100). Liking her did increase the probability of a ROC voter supporting the NDP – but only by thirty-six points. In contrast, liking Chrétien at 100 out of 100 increased the probability of supporting the LPC by sixty-eight points. Simply put, the NDP did not harvest as many voters out of the segment of voters that really liked its leader as it should have. Ultimately, it appears that many English Canadians who liked McDonough voted Liberal and, to a lesser extent, Canadian Alliance or Progressive Conservative.

Interestingly, CES data illustrate that Layton was never dramatically more popular than McDonough in English Canada. His feeling thermometers ranged from 47 out of 100 to 51 out of 100 in English Canada in the four elections during which he led the NDP. The difference during the Layton years was that the party did not relinquish to its opponents as many voters who liked its leader during those elections as it had in 2000. From 2004 to 2011, the probability of a ROC voter who liked Layton voting for the NDP fluctuated between 0.62 and 0.76.

To understand the enhanced ability of the NDP to translate liking its leader into voting for the party, it is useful to examine the party's prowess in attracting support from voters who disliked the sitting prime minister, an important segment of voters for any opposition party. Here we can see that the CPC was heavily favoured over the NDP among ROC voters who disliked the Liberal prime minister (either Jean Chrétien or Paul Martin) in the 2000, 2004, and 2006 elections. In many ways, the CPC was stealing market share from the NDP during these elections. As opposition parties, both were vying for voters who disliked the sitting prime minister, and the NDP was doing a particularly poor job of attracting voters who disliked him.

Once Stephen Harper became prime minister and the LPC became an opposition party, we see a different situation. In 2008, the LPC was the preferred party of ROC voters who disliked Harper. However, by 2011, voters who disliked him had a higher probability of voting NDP. Compared to a voter who liked Harper 100 out of 100, a voter who liked him 0 out of 100 was sixty-four points more likely to vote NDP and twenty-six points more likely to vote LPC in 2011. We see the New Democrats stealing a share of the market of ROC voters who disliked Harper from the Liberals during that election. As the official opposition, the Liberals could ill afford to lose market share among this segment of voters to the fourth party in the House of Commons, and this finding reflects the struggles of the LPC in the late 2000s.

The inability of Liberals to compete with New Democrats within the market of voters who disliked Prime Minister Harper was connected to their unpopular leaders in the 2008 and 2011 elections. Indeed, a key weakness of the LPC in the late 2000s was that it chose two unpopular leaders one right after the other. CES data illustrate that Stéphane Dion and Michael Ignatieff were substantially less popular than Chrétien and Martin among English Canadian voters.[8] The NDP used this situation to its advantage. McDonough had struggled to create a gap between her popularity and that of Chrétien. Among NDP voters in 2000, the mean of McDonough's feeling thermometer was 64 out of 100 compared with 50 out of 100 for Chrétien (a gap of fourteen points). Among LPC voters in 2000, the mean of McDonough's feeling thermometer was 48 out of 100 compared with 66 out of 100 for Chrétien (a gap of eighteen points). He was not that unpopular among NDP voters, and she was less popular than him among LPC voters. By 2011, the situation was much different: Layton was popular compared with Ignatieff among both NDP voters and LPC voters. Among the NDP voters in 2011, the mean of Layton's feeling thermometer was 68 out of 100 compared with 42 out of 100 for Ignatieff (a gap of twenty-six points). Among the LPC voters in 2011, the means of Layton's feeling thermometer and Ignatieff's feeling thermometer were the same – 57 out of 100. These bivariate statistics are reflected in Table 6.7. In the elections from 2000 to 2008, the level at which an English Canadian voter liked the LPC leader was not found to have a statistically significant impact on voting for the NDP. Disliking the LPC leader did not push voters toward supporting the NDP. However, in 2011, an English Canadian voter who liked Ignatieff at 0 out of 100 was seventeen points more likely to vote for the NDP than an English Canadian voter who liked Ignatieff at 100 out of 100. So in 2011 disliking Ignatieff was an important factor for voters who flocked to the NDP.

Overall, the CES data indicate that Layton was not more popular than McDonough in English Canada. He was more popular than McDonough had been with the voters who mattered the most – those who disliked the sitting prime minister. Also, among both NDP and LPC voters, he was more popular than McDonough had been compared with the LPC leader. These two findings illustrate the success of the "Layton Liberal" strategy and the extent to which it depended on a weak Liberal leader. McDonough faced a relatively popular sitting Liberal prime minister in 2000, as did Layton in 2004 and 2006. NDP operatives made the most of their good fortune when the Liberals chose Dion and Ignatieff as their prime ministers-in-waiting to replace the incumbent Conservative prime minister. The minority Parliaments between 2004 and 2011 had increased Layton's presence in the public consciousness, and NDP operatives used that increased exposure to position their leader as an honest broker in the House of Commons who would fight for everyday Canadians. The two lacklustre Liberal leaders provided the opportunity for the NDP to sell Layton as the prime ministerial alternative to voters who disliked Harper. In particular, the popularity of Layton compared with that of Ignatieff in 2011 allowed the NDP to steal a large number of voters who disliked the sitting prime minister from the LPC.

To summarize, the clearest explanation of the New Democrats' growing electoral success during the 2000s in the ROC appears to have been its ability to steal market share from the Liberals, who ran poor campaigns and had unpopular leaders later in the decade. In the six blocs of variables that I examined, I found sixteen examples of the NDP stealing market share from the LPC. There were almost no examples of the NDP losing market share to the LPC, and there were only two examples of the NDP stealing market share from the CPC (pro-American voters and political cynics). There were also no examples of the CPC stealing market share from the NDP.

The moderation and modernization of the NDP, conceived by political operatives and financed by quarterly per-vote public subsidies, positioned the party well in the English Canadian electoral market as the popularity of the Liberals waned during the 2000s. When we unpack where the NDP gained market share within several different segments, we can see how the party stole votes from the LPC in small increments to make large gains in the popular vote over an eleven-year period. Changes in the political marketing of the NDP appeared to give the party an enhanced ability to persuade soft Liberal voters in English Canada to support it. The emphasis on Layton's leadership, the use of the party's position within minority Parliaments to raise its public profile, the moderation of its policies, and the discipline of its caucus gave agents within the NDP the opportunity to present the New Democrats as a credible alternative to the Liberals as their popularity sank. In this sense, the process of the moderation and modernization of the federal NDP promoted by party operatives was ultimately successful during the elections when Layton was leader.

Building for a Breakthrough: The NDP in Quebec from 2006 to 2011

The NDP appeared to burst onto the Quebec political scene in 2011, seeming to come out of nowhere to sweep fifty-nine of the province's seventy-five

TABLE 6.8

NDP voting in Quebec, 2000–11 federal elections

Federal election	Popular vote for the NDP (%)	Total number of votes for the NDP	Voter turnout (%)	Seats won by the NDP
2000	1.8	63,611	62.4	0
2004	4.6	158,427	59.3	0
2006	7.5	276,401	63.1	0
2008	12.2	441,098	60.8	1
2011	42.9	1,630,865	62.0	59

SOURCE: Elections Canada (2000–11).

seats. Table 6.8 illustrates the evolution of NDP voting in Quebec during the 2000s. In 2000 and 2004, the party was simply not a factor in Quebec in federal elections, winning under 5 percent of the popular vote. However, its share did go up to 7.5 percent in 2006 even though it was not able to win a seat in the province. Then there was another improvement in fortunes in Quebec in 2008 when the party took a respectable 12.2 percent of the popular vote and won its first seat during a general election in that province. Evidently, the real breakthrough came with the "orange wave" in the 2011 election, but nonetheless the NDP had built up a small base of support within the Quebec electoral market in 2006 and 2008. Improvements in the party's popular vote and seat totals came in tandem with the waning popularity of its competitors, in particular the Bloc Québécois, which dropped from forty-nine seats and 38 percent of the popular vote in 2008 to four seats and 23 percent of the popular vote in 2011. Indeed, work by Quebec political scientists has described how the BQ struggled for relevance in the late 2000s as the desire for sovereignty waned, urgent issues related to the French language did not emerge, and voters became eager for change after voting BQ in several successive elections (Bélanger and Nadeau 2009, 2011; Gagnon and Boucher 2017). In addition, they have described a particularly weak campaign run by the BQ in 2011 that overestimated Quebec voters' affinities for Gilles Duceppe and their need to vote for the party as the only way to prevent a Conservative Party majority and defend the interests of Quebec. Their work has also noted the weakness in Quebec in the late 2000s of the Conservative Party, seen as being offside with "Quebec values," and of the Liberal Party, which struggled with the legacy of the sponsorship scandal and weak leaders. It is within this context of the relative weakness of the other major parties in Quebec that the NDP's surprise breakthrough in 2011 must be understood.

Considering the difficulties of the NDP in Quebec in the 2000 and 2004 elections and the lack of data available on the small number of NDP voters in those elections, it makes sense to start my analysis at the 2006 election. I analyze voter surveys to try to understand the party's modest improvement in Quebec between the 2006 and 2008 federal elections. More importantly, how do we explain the party's breakthrough in Quebec in the 2011 election? How does that explanation relate to the moderation and modernization of the political marketing of the NDP?

As in English Canada, there has been no evidence presented that sociodemographic groups in Quebec favourably inclined toward the NDP voted in greater numbers in 2011 compared with the previous two elections. It is also difficult to believe that Quebec voters as a whole moved markedly to the left in terms of their values or issue positions between the 2008 and 2011 elections. The more likely explanation is that the NDP stole market share from its competitors in the 2011 election. Two recent studies of the orange wave in Quebec point to this possibility. In their assessment of NDP voting in Quebec using CES data, Fournier and colleagues (2013) argue that, in 2011, the NDP was able to attract voters who had supported the BQ in 2008 who exhibited acceptance of state interventionism, moral liberalism, political disaffection, and regional alienation as well as 2008 BQ voters who wanted increased spending on health care, more spending on the environment, and higher corporate taxes. The NDP, in 2011, was also successful in attracting some "centrist and right-of-centre" Quebec voters who had supported the LPC and CPC in 2008 (Fournier et al., 2013, 893). Gauvin, Chhim, and Medeiros (2016) analyzed CES data from 2006 to 2011 as well as the platforms of the major political parties in those elections. They contend that, as BQ platforms moved away from the opinions of BQ voters on certain dimensions (social, economic, and federalism), the NDP was able to attract those voters.

The analysis below expands on previous work by exploring a new source of data that uses a vastly different set of questions and much larger sample sizes to study NDP voting in Quebec in 2006, 2008, and 2011. Specifically, I use data from Ipsos-Reid exit polls administered on the days of the 2006, 2008, and 2011 elections. The advantage of the Ipsos-Reid data set, compared with the CES data set used in previous studies, is that it contains a much larger sample of NDP voters in Quebec for the 2006 and 2008 elections.

Indeed, the CES data set contains fewer than 100 NDP voters in Quebec in the 2006 and 2008 elections.[9] The disadvantage of the Ipsos-Reid data set is that, though topics covered by the surveys were similar across the elections, the wording of the questions often changed, and some questions were included in certain years but not in others. The lack of consistent questions makes comparisons across elections more challenging. Furthermore, the Ipsos-Reid data set does not include some of the standard questions found in academic surveys (e.g., partisanship).

The first part of the Ipsos-Reid data set that needs to be explored is how it captures the voting histories of respondents. To deal with problems of recall, the questionnaire first asks respondents if they voted in the previous election and then if they remember which party they voted for in that election. The results, broken down by party, are depicted in Figures 6.2a–6.2d.

The first notable finding in Figure 6.2a is that the NDP did a poor job of maintaining the support of its voters from the previous elections in 2006 and 2008. In fact, it lost almost half of its voters from the previous elections. In 2011, the party did a much better job of attracting voters who had voted for it in the previous election. However, since the party attained only 12 percent of the popular vote in 2008, maintaining the support from its previous voters was only a small part of its success in 2011.

More important to understanding the orange wave in Quebec in 2011 was the behaviour of voters who had supported the BQ, CPC, and LPC in previous

FIGURE 6.2A

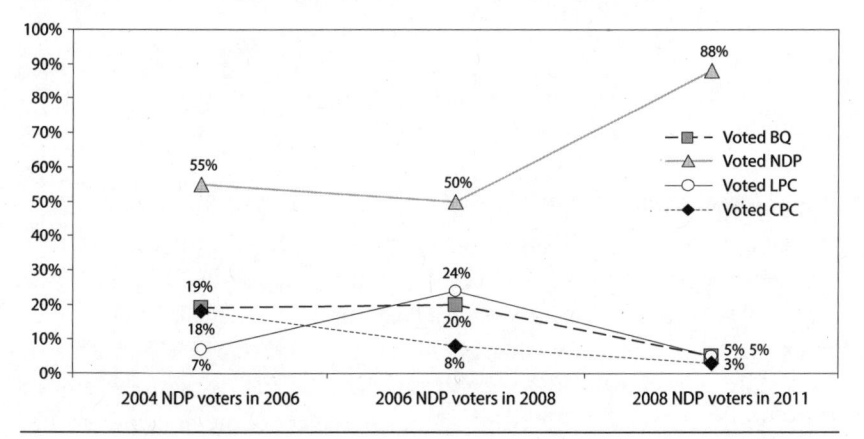

Parties NDP voters supported in the 2006–11 federal elections, QC

Figure 6.2b

Parties BQ voters supported in the 2006–11 federal elections, QC

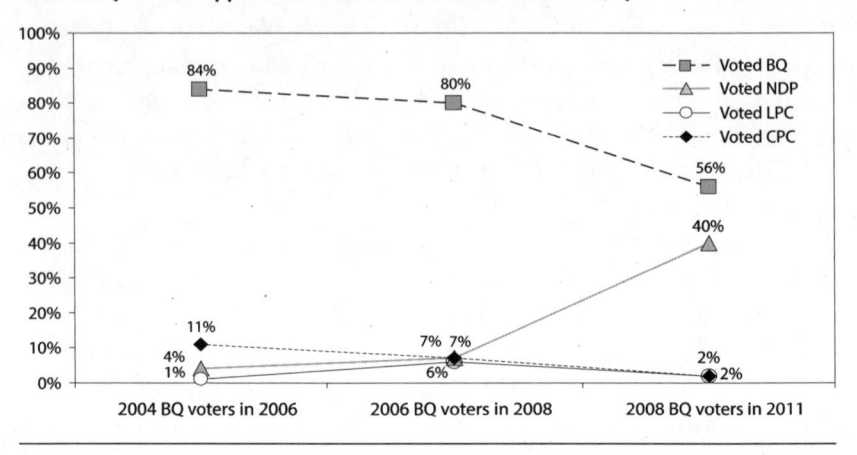

	2004 BQ voters in 2006	2006 BQ voters in 2008	2008 BQ voters in 2011
Voted BQ	84%	80%	56%
Voted NDP	4%	7%	40%
Voted LPC	1%	6%	2%
Voted CPC	11%	7%	2%

Figure 6.2c

Parties LPC voters supported in the 2006–11 federal elections, QC

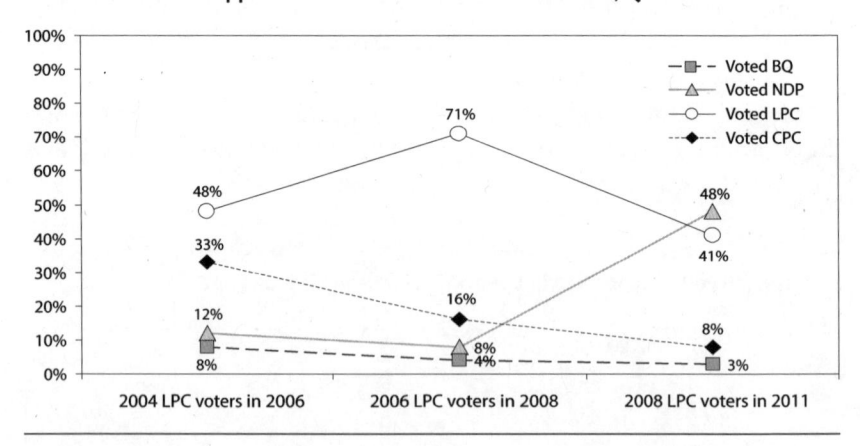

	2004 LPC voters in 2006	2006 LPC voters in 2008	2008 LPC voters in 2011
Voted BQ	8%	4%	3%
Voted NDP	12%	8%	48%
Voted LPC	48%	71%	41%
Voted CPC	33%	16%	8%

elections. We can see in Figure 6.2b that, in 2006 and 2008, the BQ did a very good job of ensuring that voters who had supported it in the past election voted for it again. In 2006, 84 percent of voters who recalled voting for the BQ in 2004 voted for the party once again. Similarly, in 2008, 80 percent of voters who reported supporting the BQ in 2006 did so again. However, in 2011, only 56 percent of BQ voters from the previous election voted once again for the party, with the NDP taking 40 percent of previous BQ voters.

Figure 6.2d

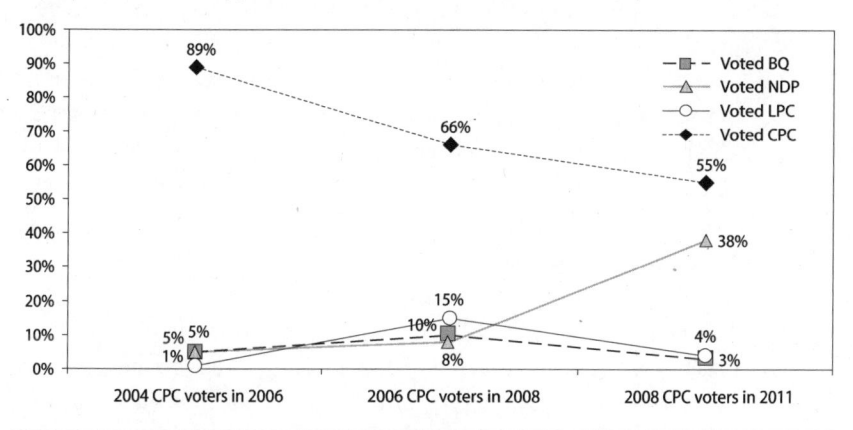

Parties CPC voters supported in the 2006–11 federal elections, QC

[Chart showing:
- 2004 CPC voters in 2006: Voted CPC 89%, Voted BQ 5%, Voted NDP 5%, Voted LPC 1%
- 2006 CPC voters in 2008: Voted CPC 66%, Voted NDP 15%, Voted BQ 10%, Voted LPC 8%
- 2008 CPC voters in 2011: Voted CPC 55%, Voted NDP 38%, Voted BQ 4%, Voted LPC 3%]

NOTES: N for 2006 = 7,274; N for 2008 = 6,678; N for 2011 = 7,869; N for all elections = 21,821.
SOURCES: Ipsos-Reid exit polls for 2006, 2008, and 2011 federal elections.

Figure 6.2c shows that, though the Liberals had lost a substantial portion of their previous voters in Quebec to the Conservatives in 2006, they did a better job of maintaining the support of their previous voters in 2008. Figure 6.2d illustrates that the Conservatives were the opposite: they were very good at keeping the support of their previous voters in 2006 but illustrated less prowess in this regard in 2008. The commonality between the LPC and the CPC is that they lost 48 percent and 38 percent of their previous supporters, respectively, to the NDP in 2011.

We can thus see that the major parties in Quebec lost almost an equal portion of their previous supporters to the NDP in 2011. However, the loss of BQ voters was a more important part of the orange wave since there were more BQ voters in 2008 than there were CPC or LPC voters. Indeed, Elections Canada reports that the BQ took approximately 40 percent of the popular vote in 2008, with the LPC taking 24 percent and the CPC taking 22 percent. So what explains this migration of voters, in particular from the BQ, to the NDP in 2011? Which segments of Quebec's electoral market demonstrated the highest propensity to move away from the BQ, LPC, and CPC and toward the NDP? How was this movement of voters related to the party's moderation and modernization?

The Ipsos-Reid data set provides the basis for an interesting evaluation of the NDP's ability to steal market share from the three other competitive parties that can be connected to the political marketing of the party. In Tables 6.9 to 6.14, the dependent variable is once again vote choice – which of the major parties (NDP, CPC, LPC, and BQ) the respondent voted for. Based on questions consistently asked for each election, six clusters of independent variables were identified, and they are similar to the blocs of variables used for English Canada. The first cluster contains variables related to the fourteen sociodemographic characteristics of the respondent: gender, sexual orientation, age, income, education, language, home ownership, marital status, religion, union household, born in Canada, rural/urban, region of Quebec, and employment status. The second cluster is made up of the respondent's general orientations using questions on perennial issues, such as sovereignty, same-sex marriage, government intervention in the economy, and general dislike of political parties. The next cluster comprises variables related to economic perceptions and whether the respondent believes that Canada is "headed in the wrong direction" or "on the right track." The fourth cluster deals with the issue that the respondent identified as the most important. The fifth cluster is made up of leader evaluations using the question of which leader the respondent thinks will do the "best job" of being prime minister. The sixth and final cluster contains variables about timing of the respondent's decision, his or her views on minority governments, and strategic voting (i.e., did the respondent vote for a party to prevent another party from winning?). The exact wording of all the questions is contained in Appendix B.

As in the previous section on English Canada, Tables 6.9 to 6.14 report the results of multinomial logistical regressions in which I run two models: one assuming that all voters have the maximum of a specific characteristic and one assuming that all voters have the minimum of a specific characteristic. The difference in the probabilities produced by the two models, when all other independent variables are held at their means, indicates the impact of a certain variable on voting NDP, BQ, LPC, or CPC, everything else being equal. Once again the clusters of variables are loaded on top of one another in the order indicated above. The first clusters are the variables more likely to pre-exist the voting decision and be found before the campaign begins, whereas the final clusters are variables closer to the actual voting decision. To round out the exploration, I analyze bivariate statistics from the results of some questions asked only in one or two of the exit polls examined.

Table 6.9 illustrates that the NDP became somewhat more adept at stealing market share from the BQ and, to a lesser extent, the LPC over these three elections in certain sociodemographic groups. The BQ and LPC had a clear advantage with voters in Montreal in 2006 and 2008. In 2008, the NDP became slightly more popular in Montreal, and by 2011 voters there were more likely to vote for the NDP than for any other party. A similar story emerges with female voters. They were four points more likely to vote BQ than male voters in 2006. In 2008, female voters were more likely to vote for the NDP or the LPC, and in 2011 the NDP asserted its advantage in this segment of the market, and female voters were more likely to vote for it than for the other parties. Indeed, the NDP had replaced the BQ as the party of choice among female voters in Quebec. In 2006, 51 percent chose the BQ, whereas 52 percent chose the NDP in 2011. Interestingly, the NDP gained popularity among gay voters – a much smaller segment of the electoral market – from 2006 to 2011 at the expense of the BQ and the LPC. In 2006, they were seven points more likely to vote BQ and seven points more likely to vote NDP. In 2008, they were six points more likely to vote LPC. By 2011, gay voters were eleven points more likely to vote NDP and neither more nor less likely to vote BQ and four points less likely to vote LPC. One segment in which the NDP did not improve its standing between 2008 and 2011 was among older voters. In both of those elections, voters over the age of fifty-four were approximately five points less likely than voters between the ages of thirty-five and fifty-four to vote NDP. It appears that older voters were less susceptible to the allure of the orange wave. Similarly, anglophone voters remained more likely to vote LPC and CPC as opposed to NDP, as in 2008. The NDP had a six-point advantage among francophone voters in 2011, but that advantage was outweighed by the BQ, which had a twenty-seven-point advantage among francophone voters.

Despite the effects outlined above, focusing on sociodemographics does not get us very far in explaining the NDP's breakthrough in Quebec in 2011. Gaining an advantage over both the BQ and the LPC among female, gay, and Montreal voters certainly helped the NDP, but the effects were slight and somewhat counterbalanced by the party's continuing weakness among older voters. There is no evidence that one or two sociodemographic groups moved massively more toward the NDP than other socio-demographic groups in 2011. In fact, striking in Table 6.9 is that relatively few sociodemographic variables were statistically significant in predicting the probability of voting NDP in 2011. Consistent with Gagnon and Boucher's (2017) theory that

TABLE 6.9

Sociodemographic variables, 2006–11 federal elections, QC

	2006 NDP	2006 BQ	2006 LPC	2006 CPC	2008 NDP	2008 BQ	2008 LPC	2008 CPC	2011 NDP	2011 BQ	2011 LPC	2011 CPC
Montreal	0.00	0.06	0.08	-0.13	0.03	0.11	0.08	-0.22	0.06	0.05	0.02	-0.13
Female	0.01	0.04	0.01	-0.07	0.03	0.01	0.03	-0.07	0.05	-0.02	0.00	-0.03
Under 35[a]	0.04	-0.02	-0.03	0.00	0.01	-0.02	-0.02	0.03	-0.01	0.01	0.00	0.00
Over 54[a]	-0.02	-0.07	0.04	0.04	-0.05	-0.03	0.02	0.06	-0.06	0.02	0.01	0.03
No religion	0.04	0.13	-0.06	-0.11	0.05	0.11	-0.07	-0.09	0.05	0.03	-0.04	-0.03
High school[b]	-0.02	0.04	-0.02	-0.01	-0.04	-0.01	0.02	0.04	-0.01	0.02	-0.02	0.02
University graduate[b]	0.02	0.02	0.01	-0.05	-0.03	-0.01	0.08	-0.04	-0.03	0.01	0.03	-0.01
Union household	0.02	0.11	-0.08	-0.04	0.01	0.08	-0.06	-0.03	0.00	0.05	-0.02	-0.02
Low income (0 to $39,000)[c]	0.02	0.03	0.00	-0.05	0.02	0.04	-0.02	-0.04	-0.03	0.01	0.05	-0.03
High income (over $80,000)[c]	0.02	-0.03	0.03	-0.02	-0.01	-0.03	0.00	0.04	-0.02	-0.02	0.04	-0.01
Immigrant	0.06	-0.27	0.16	0.05	0.00	-0.21	0.14	0.07	-0.03	-0.14	0.08	0.09
Gay	0.07	0.07	0.04	-0.17	0.02	0.05	0.06	-0.13	0.11	0.01	-0.04	-0.08
Renter	0.00	0.06	-0.01	-0.06	0.00	0.00	0.00	0.00	0.00	-0.01	0.00	0.00
Employed	-0.02	0.00	0.01	0.01	0.00	0.01	-0.02	0.01	-0.01	0.00	-0.02	0.02
Rural	0.00	0.06	-0.01	-0.06	-0.02	0.07	0.00	-0.05	-0.01	0.04	-0.03	0.01
Anglophone	N/A	N/A	N/A	N/A	0.01	-0.44	0.31	0.13	-0.06	-0.27	0.13	0.20

NOTES: N for 2006 = 7,274; N for 2008 = 7,376; N for 2011 = 8,780; N for all elections = 23,430; shaded = $p \leq 0.05$; a = reference category is from thirty-five to fifty-four years old; b = reference category is completed college or some university; c = reference category is between $40,000 and $79,000.

Quebecers tend to vote as a bloc, it appears that their movement toward the NDP was a general phenomenon consistent across all sociodemographic groups. For instance, according to Ipsos-Reid data, 40 percent of voters from union households and 40 percent not from union households voted NDP in 2011. The pattern repeats itself across the other independent variables. The proportion of NDP voters who were employed/unemployed, renter/owner, rural/urban, immigrant/nonimmigrant, high income/low income, anglophone/francophone, and high education/low education was relatively the same. In short, the NDP succeeded in creating a balanced set of supporters. It tended to be slightly more montréalais, female, and gay but balanced nonetheless.

Table 6.10 illustrates that, in 2006, the BQ had a dominant position in the segment of the Quebec electorate in favour of government intervention. A voter who agreed with the statement that the "government should do more to solve problems" was sixteen points more likely to vote BQ in that election than a voter who agreed with the statement that the "government is doing too many things that should be left to businesses and individuals." However, the BQ's advantage among these statists decreased in 2008, with both the NDP and the LPC eating into its market share. By 2011, a voter who agreed with government intervention was three points more likely to vote NDP and three points more likely to vote BQ but neither more nor less likely to vote LPC. A similar pattern emerges with the question on same-sex marriage. Unfortunately, Ipsos-Reid did not ask about same-sex marriage in 2008. But we can see in Table 6.10 that the BQ had a nineteen-point advantage among those who agreed with same-sex marriage in 2006, and the NDP had a twelve-point advantage with those who agreed with same-sex marriage in 2011. The BQ's loss of voters with left-of-centre general orientations indicates that the strategy of NDP agents of presenting Layton and the party as a way to realize progressive "Quebec values" might have worked. Perhaps these voters were persuaded that voting for the NDP, as opposed to supporting the BQ, which could never form the federal government, was the optimal way to ensure that their left-of-centre ideology would be reflected in federal government policy. Indeed, this is a good example of how the NDP was able to take advantage of a growing weakness of the BQ – its inability to create change in Ottawa despite holding a majority of Quebec seats in the House of Commons since 1993. The NDP was able to take advantage of the good fortune of francophone voters who had become tired of the BQ by the 2011 election.

TABLE 6.10

General orientation variables, 2006–11 federal elections, QC

	2006				2008				2011			
	NDP	BQ	LPC	CPC	NDP	BQ	LPC	CPC	NDP	BQ	LPC	CPC
Government intervention	0.02	0.14	0.01	-0.17	0.02	0.08	0.04	-0.14	0.03	0.03	0.01	-0.07
Same-sex marriage	0.07	0.19	0.01	-0.27	N/A	N/A	N/A	N/A	0.12	0.00	-0.02	-0.10
Antiparty sentiment	0.00	-0.05	0.06	-0.01	0.01	0.02	0.07	-0.10	-0.07	0.05	0.06	-0.03
Hard sovereignist*	-0.18	0.77	-0.25	-0.34	-0.13	0.74	-0.33	-0.28	-0.44	0.71	-0.12	-0.15
Soft nationalist*	-0.24	0.53	-0.17	-0.13	-0.05	0.52	-0.25	-0.21	-0.17	0.36	-0.07	-0.12

NOTES: N for 2006 = 7,274; N for 2008 = 7,376; N for 2011 = 8,780; N for all elections = 23,430; shaded = $p \leq 0.05$; sociodemographic variables and general orientation variables were included in the model, but only the results for the general orientation variables are shown.

* Hard federalist is the reference category.

Interestingly, there is no evidence that the electoral success of the New Democrats in Quebec was pushed by a general disgust with all political parties. From 2006 to 2011, between 30 percent and 35 percent of the Quebec electorate somewhat strongly or strongly agreed with the statement that "I don't really like any of the parties that we have to choose among in this election." These antipartisans were actually six to seven points more likely to default to the Liberals in the elections from 2006 to 2011. In rare cases of the NDP stealing market share from the CPC, the NDP gained voters who were pro-party in 2011. Table 6.10 shows that voters who disagreed that "I don't really like any of the parties that we have to choose among in this election" were ten points more likely to vote CPC and neither more nor less likely to vote NDP in 2008, but they were seven points more likely to vote NDP and three points more likely to vote CPC in 2011.

Some of the most impressive effects on the probability of voting for one of the four major parties in Quebec emanated from the variable related to sovereignty. To understand the segments of the electorate in Quebec in regard to sovereignty, it is useful to divide the electorate into three groups. Hard sovereignists answered "strongly support" to questions on sovereignty, whereas hard federalists answered "strongly oppose." Soft nationalists fall between these two extremes – they answered "somewhat support," "somewhat oppose," or "I don't know" when asked about sovereignty. Although there were certain differences in the questions asked, the electorate appeared to be split somewhat equally among the three categories in 2006, and in the later elections the hard sovereignist category had shrunk and the soft nationalist category had grown.[10] The movement of voters from the hard sovereignist to the soft nationalist category is consistent with the research of Quebec political scientists, who argue that the salience of the sovereignty issue waned in the late 2000s (Bélanger and Nadeau 2009, 2011; Gagnon and Boucher 2017).

The Ipsos-Reid data indicate that the NDP stole market share in all three segments of the electorate on the question of sovereignty. Between 2006 and 2011, the party stole market share from the BQ in the soft nationalist and hard sovereignist segments, and it further stole market share from the Liberals and the Conservatives in the hard federalist segment. To understand this conclusion more fully, I have created Figures 6.3a, 6.3b, and 6.3c, which depict a cross-tabulation of vote choice with the three categories related to support for sovereignty.

FIGURE 6.3A

Vote choice of hard sovereignists, 2006–11 federal elections, QC

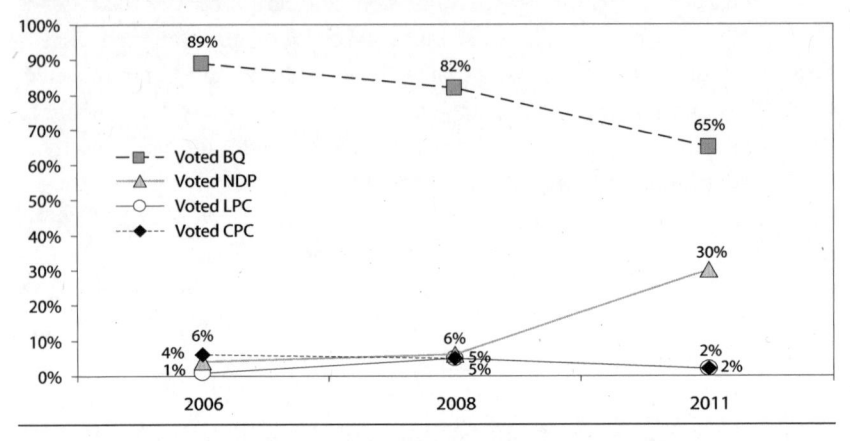

[Chart showing vote percentages for hard sovereignists across 2006, 2008, and 2011 federal elections:
- Voted BQ: 89% (2006), 82% (2008), 65% (2011)
- Voted NDP: 4% (2006), 6% (2008), 30% (2011)
- Voted LPC: 1% (2006), 5% (2008), 2% (2011)
- Voted CPC: 6% (2006), 5% (2008), 2% (2011)]

SOURCES: Ipsos-Reid exit polls for 2006, 2008, and 2011 federal elections.

FIGURE 6.3B

Vote choice of soft nationalists, 2006–11 federal elections, QC

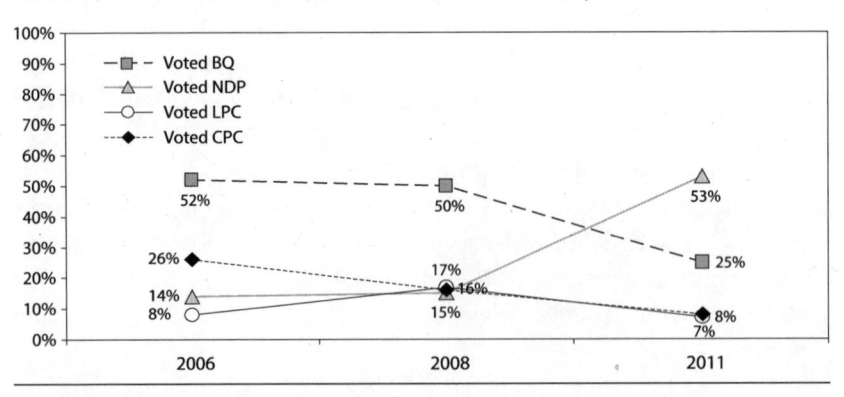

[Chart showing vote percentages for soft nationalists across 2006, 2008, and 2011 federal elections:
- Voted BQ: 52% (2006), 50% (2008), 25% (2011)
- Voted NDP: 14% (2006), 17% (2008), 53% (2011)
- Voted LPC: 8% (2006), 15% (2008), 7% (2011)
- Voted CPC: 26% (2006), 16% (2008), 8% (2011)]

SOURCES: Ipsos-Reid exit polls for 2006, 2008, and 2011 federal elections.

In 2006 and 2008, the BQ dominated the hard sovereignist and soft nationalist slices of the Quebec electoral market. We can see in Table 6.10 that hard sovereignists and soft nationalists were much more likely to vote BQ than hard federalists (the reference category). Figures 6.3a and 6.3b back up this finding – over 80 percent of hard sovereignists and about 50 percent of soft nationalists in 2006 and 2008 voted BQ. The CPC initially showed some

FIGURE 6.3C

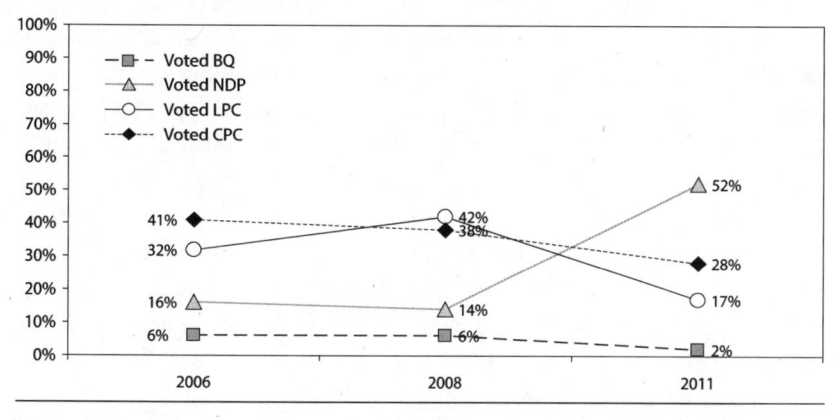

Vote choice of hard federalists, 2006–11 federal elections, QC

NOTES: N for 2006 = 7,274; N for 2008 = 7,376; N for 2011 = 8,780; N for all elections = 23,430.
SOURCES: Ipsos-Reid exit polls for 2006, 2008, and 2011 federal elections.

strength among soft nationalist voters compared with the other two federalist parties in 2006, but in 2008 the soft nationalist vote that did not go BQ split somewhat evenly among the three federalist alternatives. Hard federalists, whose vote choice is shown in Figure 6.3c, were clearly dominated by the Liberals and the Conservatives, who took roughly 80 percent of these voters in 2006 and 2008. These parties basically split the hard federalist vote between them in those elections. This splitting perhaps contributed to the BQ's ability to win roughly two-thirds of the Quebec seats in these elections with approximately 40 percent of the popular vote.

Unlike in the previous two elections, the hard federalist vote coalesced in the NDP in the 2011 election rather than split between the Liberals and the Conservatives. Although it is difficult to discern because hard federalist is the reference category, the findings of Table 6.10 indicate that hard federalists became less likely to support the CPC and the LPC and more likely to support the NDP between 2008 and 2011.[11] The bivariate analysis of the Ipsos-Reid data in Figure 6.3c is much easier to follow. It illustrates that in 2011 just over half of hard federalist voters coalesced to the NDP as the preferred antisovereignty party. It had effectively stolen a substantial share of the hard federalist segment from the CPC and the LPC as those two parties struggled to appeal to the Quebec electorate.

A similar coalescing took place with the soft nationalist vote previously dominated by the BQ. Figure 6.3b illustrates that the BQ, and to a lesser extent the Liberals and the Conservatives, lost shares of the soft nationalist vote to the NDP in 2011. As the issue of sovereignty decreased in salience and the BQ weakened, the party dropped from having about half of the soft nationalist vote in 2006 and 2008 to garnering only a quarter in 2011. Indeed, Table 6.10 illustrates that a soft nationalist voter was fifty-two points more likely to vote BQ in 2008 than a hard federalist, but that probability was reduced to thirty-six points in 2011. The percentage of soft nationalist voters supporting Liberals and Conservatives also decreased. The NDP, however, went from having approximately 15 percent of the soft nationalist vote in 2006 and 2008 to having 53 percent of that vote in 2011. Its prowess in prying soft nationalists away from the BQ was important because they were a growing segment of the electorate as the salience of the sovereignty issue diminished. The BQ lock on hard sovereignists – its core clientele – even loosened somewhat as the probability of a hard sovereignist compared with a hard federalist voting BQ declined from seventy-seven points in 2006 and seventy-four points in 2008 to seventy-one points in 2011. Using bivariate statistics in Figure 6.3a, we can see that 65 percent of hard sovereignists voted BQ in 2011 compared with 82 percent in 2008 and 89 percent in 2004. The percentage of hard sovereignists who voted NDP rose from 6 percent in 2008 to 30 percent in 2011.

Figures 6.3a, 6.3b, and 6.3c illustrate the success of NDP operatives in 2011 on the national question in Quebec. For soft nationalists and hard sovereignists, the operatives developed Quebec-specific policies such as applying Bill 101 in federal jurisdiction, adopting asymmetrical federalism that respects provincial jurisdiction by allowing the opting out of federal programs with compensation, and requiring future Supreme Court appointments to be bilingual (McGrane 2011, 92). Operatives also decided to advertise in Quebec in 2011 to a much greater extent than in previous elections. For hard federalists, NDP commercials portrayed the debate on sovereignty as an old and stale one that would only "block" (a play on the Bloc Québécois name) the progress of Quebec. In holding a middle ground of putting forth some concrete policies to accommodate Québécois nationalism and insisting that Quebecers move on from the sovereignist debate, the NDP effectively appealed to both sides of the national question and took advantage of the weakness of both federalist and sovereignist parties in the 2011 election.

In Table 6.11, a positive number means that voters who thought that Canada was headed in the wrong direction and that their personal finances were getting worse were more likely to vote for the party. Ipsos-Reid data show that approximately half of the Quebec electorate thought that Canada was headed in the wrong direction in each of the elections examined here. The table illustrates the proficiency of the BQ compared with the other opposition parties in this segment of the Quebec electorate in 2006 and 2008. In 2006, Quebec voters who thought that Canada was headed in the wrong direction were sixteen points more likely to vote BQ, and in 2008 they were twenty points more likely to vote BQ. Interestingly, the Conservatives, the primary opposition party to the governing Liberals in 2006, were likely to have Quebecers who thought that the country was on the right track vote for them. In 2008, the New Democrats and the Liberals did well among voters who thought that the country was headed in the wrong direction but not nearly as well as the BQ. In 2011, the situation changed. Not surprisingly, voters who believed that Canada was on the right track were nineteen points more likely to vote for the governing Conservatives. However, voters who thought that Canada was headed in the wrong direction coalesced in the NDP. These voters were twelve points more likely to vote NDP but only four points more likely to vote Liberal or BQ.

Although Ipsos-Reid did not ask about personal finances in the 2006 exit poll, the data set illustrates that approximately 20 percent of the Quebec electorate thought that their personal finances were in worse shape than a year before in 2008 and 2011. The BQ had an advantage among these voters in 2008. Voters pessimistic about their personal finances were eight points more likely to vote for the BQ and three points more likely to vote for the NDP in that election. Voters optimistic about their personal finances were more likely to vote Liberal or Conservative. In 2011, pessimistic voters were less likely to vote for the BQ than in 2008, and Liberals and Conservatives had lost their advantage completely with optimistic voters. However, neither optimists nor pessimists were more likely to vote for the NDP. So it appears that the party stole market share from the BQ among financial pessimists and market share from the LPC and the CPC among financial optimists. Perhaps NDP operatives convinced Quebec voters that supporting the party, which could affect government policy, as opposed to the BQ, was the way to stop Canada from heading in the wrong direction and to potentially improve voters' personal finances.

TABLE 6.11

Economic perception variables, 2006–11 federal elections, QC

	2006			2008				2011			
	NDP	BQ	LPC	CPC	NDP	BQ	LPC	CPC	NDP	BQ	LPC	CPC
Canada headed in wrong direction	0.04	0.16	-0.03	-0.16	0.07	0.20	0.11	-0.39	0.12	0.04	0.04	-0.19
Personal finances getting worse	N/A	N/A	N/A	N/A	0.03	0.08	-0.07	-0.04	-0.02	0.03	0.00	0.00

NOTES: N for 2006 = 7,274; N for 2008 = 7,376; N for 2011 = 8,780; N for all elections = 23,430; shaded = $p \leq 0.05$; sociodemographic variables, general orientation variables, and economic perception variables were included in the model, but only the results for the economic perception variables are shown.

TABLE 6.12

Most important issue variables, 2006–11 federal elections, QC

	2006				2008				2011			
	NDP	BQ	LPC	CPC	NDP	BQ	LPC	CPC	NDP	BQ	LPC	CPC
Health care voter	0.00	0.20	-0.04	-0.15	0.10	-0.04	0.00	-0.06	0.08	-0.05	0.00	-0.03
Corruption voter	-0.07	0.27	-0.11	-0.09	0.23	-0.09	-0.09	-0.05	0.07	-0.04	0.02	-0.05
Economy voter	-0.06	0.20	0.01	-0.13	0.02	-0.09	0.08	0.00	0.01	-0.06	0.02	0.03
Environment voter	0.16	0.08	-0.04	-0.21	0.07	-0.11	0.20	-0.16	0.09	-0.07	0.03	-0.06
Social program voter (e.g., pensions)	0.10	0.11	-0.03	-0.18	0.21	-0.10	-0.05	-0.06	0.15	-0.12	-0.01	-0.02

NOTES: N for 2006 = 7,274; N for 2008 = 7,376; N for 2011 = 8,780; N for all elections = 23,430; shaded = $p \leq 0.05$; sociodemographic variables, general orientation variables, economic perception variables, and most important issue variables were included in the model, but only the results for the most important issue variables are shown.

In the Ipsos-Reid exit polls, voters were given a list of issues and asked which issue "mattered most in deciding which party's candidate you voted for today?" Table 6.12 illustrates the probability of voting for the major parties in Quebec in relation to the five most popular top-of-mind issues. For instance, a respondent who identified health care as the most important issue would be referred to as a "health care voter" by NDP strategists, and that is the term used in the table. Although these five issues represented the top concerns of roughly two-thirds of voters, the salience of the issues varied across the three elections and is noted in the analysis of Table 6.12.

In 2006, the Ipsos-Reid data illustrated that the dominant issue was corruption (chosen by 22 percent) closely followed by the economy (chosen by 19 percent) and health care (chosen by 13 percent). In Table 6.12, we can see that the Bloc Québécois did well among voters who chose one of these three issues as their top issue. Those concerned about health care and the economy were twenty points more likely to vote BQ, and those concerned about corruption in the wake of the sponsorship scandal were twenty-seven points more likely to vote BQ. Conversely, voters concerned about these three issues were generally less likely to vote NDP, LPC, or CPC. The environment (chosen by 9 percent) and social programs such as child care and pensions (chosen by 9 percent) were less important issues in 2006. It was among these less important issues that the NDP showed some emerging strength within the Quebec electorate. Voters who chose social programs were ten points more likely to vote NDP and eleven points more likely to vote BQ. Those who chose the environment as the most important issue were sixteen points more likely to vote NDP and eight points more likely to vote BQ. Although voters in these two categories made up only one-fifth of the electorate, the popularity of the NDP among them did bode well for the future, and we can see why NDP operatives decided to put greater resources in Quebec after 2006 despite concrete results having yet to surface.

With the onset of the global recession, the economy was the central issue for approximately 30 percent of Quebec voters in the 2008 election according to the Ipsos-Reid data set. Other issues appeared to pale in importance. With the Liberals running on a "green shift" scheme that promised to reduce greenhouse gas emissions using a carbon tax, the environment became a top-of-mind issue for sixteen percent of the Quebec electorate. Health care was chosen by only 11 percent of voters, and social programs were chosen by another 8 percent. With no major scandal in the first two years of the Conservative government, corruption was simply a nonissue, and only 2 percent chose it as the most important.

The application of my model to the Ipsos-Reid data set from the 2008 election illustrates interesting findings. Despite winning forty-nine seats, it appears that the BQ had an underlying weakness when it came to top-of-mind issues. Voters who chose the economy as their most important issue were eight points more likely to vote LPC and nine points less likely to vote BQ. When it came to the environment, a voter who chose that issue as the most important was twenty points more likely to vote LPC and eleven points less likely to vote BQ. Simply put, on the two issues most frequently chosen by voters as their most important issues of the 2008 election, the BQ was bested by its rivals. The Conservatives' stress on a stable government to deal with the global recession might have appealed to some economy voters, and the Liberals' green shift might have attracted some environmentally conscious voters. On the two other issues less frequently chosen as respondents' most important issues, the NDP performed admirably to the detriment of the BQ and stole some of its share of these markets. Respondents who chose health care as their most important issue were ten points more likely to vote NDP and neither more nor less likely to vote BQ. Respondents who chose social programs as their most important issue were twenty-one points more likely to vote NDP and ten points less likely to vote BQ. As in 2006, voters who chose these two issues made up only one-fifth of the electorate. Nonetheless, it was encouraging to the NDP to be popular among Quebec voters concerned about social programs such as health care, child care, and pensions going into future elections and a sign of the underlying weakness of the BQ. This finding illustrates that NDP operatives were correct to be optimistic about the party's prospects in Quebec despite winning only one seat in the province in the 2008 election.

In 2011, the Ipsos-Reid data showed that no one issue dominated Quebec voters' consciousness. The economy was the most frequently chosen most important issue at 19 percent followed by health care (14 percent) and corruption (12 percent). The environment was chosen by 6 percent of voters as their most important issue, and social programs were chosen by 5 percent of voters. Once again the BQ was weak on top-of-mind issues. Choosing any of the five issues depicted in Table 6.12 as one's most important decreased the probability of voting BQ anywhere from twelve points to four points. With the exception of a small bump of 3 percent if the voter chose the economy as the top issue, the Conservatives also did poorly in 2011 among voters concerned about health care, corruption, or the environment. The likelihood of voting Liberal did not appear to be affected by the issues presented in Table 6.12.

In 2006 and 2008, the NDP performed well on issues chosen by a relatively small number of voters as their most important issues. The primary difference in 2011 was that the party showed strength on issues chosen by large numbers of voters. Table 6.12 illustrates that respondents who chose health care, corruption, or the environment as their most important issue were from seven to nine points more likely to vote NDP. Those who chose social programs as their top issue were fifteen points more likely to vote NDP. Overall, 37 percent of Quebec voters chose one of these four issues as their most important issue in the 2011 election. We can also find evidence that the NDP stole market share from the BQ and the LPC. Although corruption voters had a higher probability of supporting the BQ and a lower probability of supporting the NDP in 2006, when the sponsorship scandal was a headline issue, voters concerned about corruption in 2011 were seven points more likely to support the NDP and four points less likely to support the BQ. The LPC enjoyed a considerable advantage with environment voters in Quebec in 2008, and they were nine points more likely to support the NDP in 2011 and neither more nor less likely to support the LPC. Clearly, how NDP operatives chose to deal with top-of-mind issues, and the moderate policies that they chose to emphasize on those issues in 2011, were pleasing to many voters in Quebec.

On the economy, the key for the NDP was to neutralize this traditional weakness of the party brand. It is interesting that, unlike in the 2006 election, a voter who chose the economy as the top issue was neither more nor less likely to vote NDP in 2011. Also, the advantage that the CPC had among economy voters had diminished, and they were seven points less likely to vote BQ. In this sense, NDP operatives did not win over a large number of economy voters, but the party did not lose a disproportionate number either. New Democrats were able to do well with Quebecers on noneconomic issues and break even, so to speak, on the economy.

Layton's personal popularity has been noted as an important part of explaining the orange wave in Quebec (Fournier et al., 2013). However, less appreciated is the fact that Layton had an underlying popularity in Quebec prior to 2011 built up by paid advertising, his time spent there, and greater

TABLE 6.13

Leader evaluation variables, 2006–11 federal elections, QC

	2006				2008				2011			
	NDP	BQ	LPC	CPC	NDP	BQ	LPC	CPC	NDP	BQ	LPC	CPC
Layton best PM	0.18	0.03	0.03	-0.24	0.14	-0.08	-0.06	0.01	0.31	-0.16	-0.09	-0.05
Harper best PM	-0.09	-0.07	-0.09	0.26	-0.09	-0.24	-0.13	0.47	-0.26	-0.02	-0.04	0.33
Martin/Dion/Ignatieff best PM	0.08	-0.13	0.24	-0.19	-0.11	-0.17	0.34	-0.06	-0.27	-0.05	0.27	-0.04
Duceppe best PM	N/A	N/A	N/A	N/A	-0.08	0.20	-0.06	-0.05	-0.29	0.37	-0.05	-0.04
Leader voter	0.04	-0.12	-0.02	0.08	0.20	-0.15	-0.08	0.03	0.35	-0.22	-0.09	-0.04

NOTES: N for 2006 = 7,274; N for 2008 = 7,376; N for 2011 = 8,780; N for all elections = 23,430; shaded = $p \leq 0.05$; sociodemographic variables, general orientation variables, economic perception variables, most important issue variables, and leadership evaluation variables were included in the model, but only the results for the leadership evaluation variables are shown.

emphasis by the NDP on francophone media relations. Although the 2008 and 2011 Ipsos-Reid exit polls included Duceppe as a possible response to the question of which leader would make the best prime minster, the 2006 exit poll excluded him and included only Martin, Harper, and Layton as possible choices. When compared with only the other two federalist leaders in 2006, Layton was actually the most popular with the Quebec electorate according to Ipsos-Reid data: 44 percent chose Layton as the best prime minister compared with 33 percent for Harper and 23 percent for Martin. In 2008, the same question was asked, and the options of Gilles Duceppe, Elizabeth May, and "I don't know" were added alongside the leaders of the three main federalist parties. Even in this more crowded field, Layton was chosen by 35 percent of the Quebec electorate as the best prime minister, a score much higher than those of the other leaders.[12] His popularity in the Ipsos-Reid data supports the logic of the NDP operatives' decision to put additional resources in Quebec despite winning almost no seats there in the 2006 and 2008 elections.

Table 6.13 illustrates that, when it came to leadership, the problem for the NDP in 2006 and 2008 was not necessarily Layton's level of popularity. Rather, the challenge was threefold. First, voters who liked Layton were voting for other parties. In 2006, voters who chose him as the best prime minister were actually three points more likely to vote BQ or LPC. The situation improved slightly in 2008, and voters who chose him as the best prime minister were less likely to vote BQ or LPC. But these voters were only fourteen points more likely to vote NDP. Layton's popularity was helping the NDP but not to the extent that the popularity of Harper, Dion, and Duceppe was aiding their parties.

Second, the NDP was not doing well among voters who disliked the sitting prime minister. In 2006 and 2008, just over three-quarters of Quebec voters did not choose the sitting prime minister as the best prime minister. It was better for opposition parties to do well among the large segment of voters who did not like the sitting prime minister as opposed to the small segment of voters who liked the incumbent prime minister. Yet in 2006 a voter from the small segment of the electoral market who thought that Martin was the best prime minister was eight points more likely to vote NDP, which meant that a voter from the large segment of the electoral market who did not choose Martin as the best prime minister was actually eight points less likely to vote NDP. Conversely, the BQ and the CPC did better than the NDP among voters who did not like Martin. In 2008, the NDP's numbers among voters who did not like the incumbent prime minister improved slightly – voters who did not choose Harper as the best prime minister were nine points more likely to vote NDP. However, once again, the two other opposition parties did better in this segment of the electoral market.

Finally, in 2006, the NDP failed to attract voters who held that leadership was the most important factor in their voting decisions. In each of the Ipsos-Reid exit polls, respondents were asked "would you say that your vote today was mostly for your local candidate, mostly for their party leader, or mostly for their party's stand on the issues?" These "leader voters" (i.e., those who voted mostly based on the party leader) made up roughly one-quarter of the Quebec electorate in 2006 and 2008. In 2006, leader voters were four points more likely to vote New Democrat and eight points more likely to vote Conservative. However, the NDP did press its advantage more among these voters in 2008 – they were twenty points more likely to vote NDP and only three points more likely to vote CPC. Again this led to optimism among NDP operatives about their party's potential in Quebec.

Layton was the party's most important asset in Quebec, even if there were challenges in translating positive feelings about him into actual votes for the NDP. By sending Layton into Quebec and placing him at the forefront of the NDP's air game and earned media strategy there, party operatives seem to have resolved these challenges by the end of the 2011 election. On the day of the election, Layton was extremely popular in Quebec, with 54 percent of voters choosing him as the best prime minister compared with only 15 percent for Harper, 10 percent for Ignatieff, and 8 percent for Duceppe.

However, as the analysis above suggests, it was not enough for Layton to be the most popular choice as prime minister. Table 6.13 shows that, not only had he grown in popularity, but also NDP operatives were taking full advantage of that popularity to steal market share from their opponents. In 2011, the NDP did a much better job of harvesting votes from those who thought that Layton would make the best prime minister. For instance, 74 percent of these voters supported the NDP in 2011 compared with only 18 percent of these voters in 2006. In Table 6.13, we can thus see that a voter who chose Layton as the best prime minister was thirty-one points more likely to vote NDP in 2011 and much less likely to vote BQ, LPC, or CPC. More than in past elections, the NDP was able to prevent its opponents from winning votes within the relatively large segment of voters who thought that Layton would make a good prime minister. Indeed, the boost that he gave to the probability of voting NDP in 2011 was in line with the boost that the other leaders gave to their parties.

Another segment of voters with whom the NDP did better in 2011 were those who did not like the sitting prime minister. The percentage of voters in Quebec who thought that Harper would not make the best prime minister had increased from 78 percent in 2008 to 85 percent in 2011. Reflecting the weakness of both the BQ and the LPC, the NDP dominated those parties within the segment of the Quebec electorate who disliked the incumbent prime minister. In 2011, those voters were twenty-six points more likely to vote NDP but only four points more likely to vote LPC and neither more nor less likely to vote BQ.

Finally, perhaps because of Layton's surging popularity, the Quebec voters who stated that the leader was the most important factor in their voting decisions rose from 25 percent of the electorate in the past two elections to 41 percent in 2011. The NDP was able to persuade more of these voters to support it. Again a bivariate comparison with the 2006 election is illuminating. In 2006, only 13 percent of leader voters supported the NDP, whereas in 2011 72 percent supported the party. The multivariate statistics in Table 6.13 support this finding: leader voters were four points more likely to vote NDP in 2006, whereas in 2011 they were thirty-five points more likely to vote NDP and less likely to support the CPC, the BQ, or the LPC. Layton was popular in Quebec in 2011, and the segment of voters who thought that leadership was important came around to voting for the NDP instead of supporting its opponents. Notably, leader voters had shown a slight propensity to vote CPC in 2006 and 2008, but in 2011 they were four points less likely to vote CPC. This finding indicates that the Conservatives lost market share among leader voters to the New Democrats.

What accounted for Layton's remarkable popularity in Quebec? Unfortunately, Ipsos-Reid did not ask about specific leadership traits in 2006. However, eight questions were asked about these traits in the 2008 and 2011 exit polls. The questions put the leaders in direct competition with one another. Each respondent was asked this question: "Thinking about each of the party leaders, which leader best matches each of the following statements?" The respondent had to choose among Layton, Harper, Duceppe, May, Dion/Ignatieff, and "I don't know." The bivariate results broken down by leader are contained in Figures 6.4a and 6.4b. For example, in Figure 6.4a, we see that 33 percent of Quebec voters chose Layton as the most "inspirational" of the four leaders in 2008. The "I don't knows" have been removed

FIGURE 6.4A

Leadership traits, 2008 federal election, QC

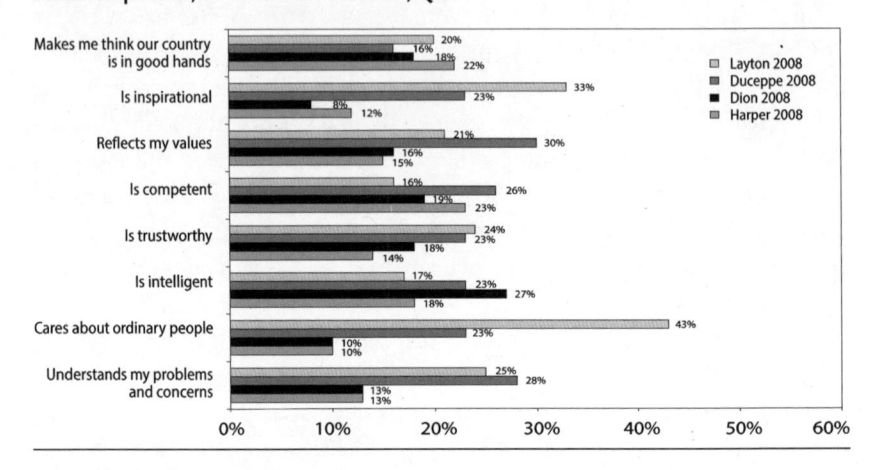

Trait	Layton 2008	Duceppe 2008	Dion 2008	Harper 2008
Makes me think our country is in good hands	20%	16%	18%	22%
Is inspirational	33%	23%	8%	12%
Reflects my values	21%	30%	16%	15%
Is competent	16%	26%	19%	23%
Is trustworthy	24%	23%	18%	14%
Is intelligent	17%	23%	27%	18%
Cares about ordinary people	43%	23%	10%	10%
Understands my problems and concerns	25%	28%	13%	13%

NOTE: $N = 7{,}376$.
SOURCE: Ipsos-Reid exit poll for 2008 federal election.

FIGURE 6.4B

Leadership traits, 2011 federal election, QC

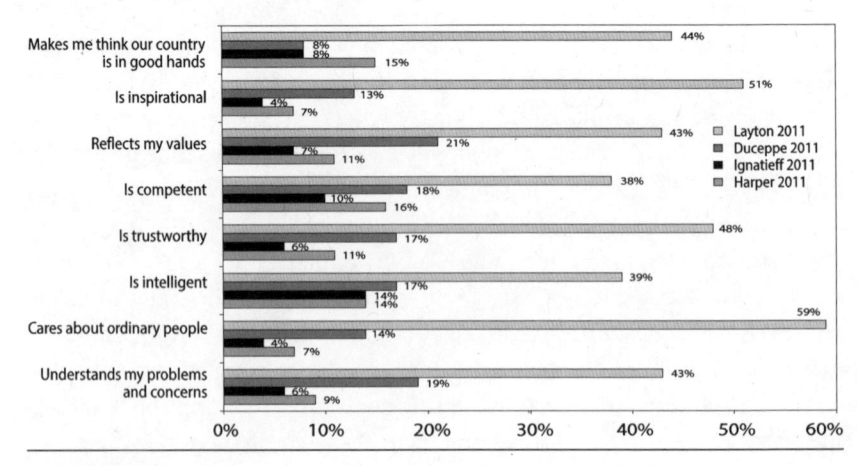

Trait	Layton 2011	Duceppe 2011	Ignatieff 2011	Harper 2011
Makes me think our country is in good hands	44%	8%	8%	15%
Is inspirational	51%	13%	4%	7%
Reflects my values	43%	21%	7%	11%
Is competent	38%	18%	10%	16%
Is trustworthy	48%	17%	6%	11%
Is intelligent	39%	17%	14%	14%
Cares about ordinary people	59%	14%	4%	7%
Understands my problems and concerns	43%	19%	6%	9%

NOTE: $N = 8{,}780$.
SOURCE: Ipsos-Reid exit poll for 2011 federal election.

to ensure that figures are uncluttered and that removal accounts for the percentages not adding up to 100 percent since about 10 percent or 20 percent of voters chose "I don't know."

Figure 6.4a illustrates the strengths of Layton's image in Quebec by 2008 and some weaknesses that still persisted. The greatest strengths were related to his character. Layton outshone the other leaders by a relatively large margin when it came to the leader whom voters believed cared about "ordinary people" and saw as "inspirational." Still, Duceppe was also popular in 2008. Layton beat Duceppe on being the most "trustworthy" leader by only 1 percent, and Duceppe did best on representing the "values" of Quebec voters and understanding their "problems and concerns." Perhaps this finding reflects a sentiment among Quebec voters in 2008 that Duceppe was "their guy" in Ottawa who would stand up for Quebec's interests. Interestingly, Layton came in second to Duceppe, ahead of the leaders of the other federal parties, in both reflecting the values of Quebec voters and understanding their concerns. Where Layton was the weakest was on traits pertaining to his competence. He was perceived as the least intelligent and least competent of the four leaders. On the trait of "makes me think our country is in good hands," Layton scored behind Harper and just slightly ahead of Duceppe and Dion. Overall, even though the NDP received only 12 percent of the popular vote in Quebec in 2008, Ipsos-Reid data illustrate that voters there admired Layton's character – they saw the NDP leader as caring, inspirational, and trustworthy. However, they had doubts about his competence and thought that Duceppe better understood Quebec's unique concerns.

By election day in 2011, Duceppe's popularity had waned after being the BQ leader in six consecutive federal elections, and the NDP was able to take advantage of voter fatigue with Duceppe as well as the unpopularity of Ignatieff. The Ipsos-Reid data from 2011, illustrated in Figure 6.4b, show that Layton was clearly the most popular leader among Quebec voters. The gaps between him and his closest competitor were 10 percent to 36 percent depending on the indicator. His image had also dramatically improved on every indicator between 2008 and 2011. Once again his greatest strength pertained to his character – approximately half of voters in Quebec saw Layton as the most trustworthy and inspirational leader, and nearly 60 percent believed that he was the leader who cared the most about ordinary people. Also, a strong plurality of voters (43 percent) now perceived Layton as the leader who best reflected their values and understood their problems and concerns. Most importantly, the NDP had corrected the weakness in his image in terms of competence. In 2011, approximately four of ten Quebec voters believed that Layton was the most competent and intelligent leader and thought that the country would be "in good hands." Given these findings, it appears that NDP operatives got his branding correct by stressing his qualities as a fighter and an honest broker in Ottawa who would get practical results for Quebec voters and represent their values in federal politics.

Layton's popularity in 2011 grew at the expense of the leaders of all three of the NDP's opponents, in particular the Bloc Québécois and the Liberal Party. According to the Ipsos-Reid data in Figures 6.4a and 6.4b, Harper's scores declined between 3 percent and 7 percent depending on the trait examined. In some ways, Harper was already unpopular in Quebec in 2008, and the 2011 election made him slightly more so. The larger decreases in popularity in the face of the Layton juggernaut related to the leaders of the BQ and the LPC. Duceppe's scores declined between 6 percent and 10 percent depending on the indicator between 2008 and 2011. More importantly, Duceppe was eclipsed by Layton as the leader who came in first in the categories of showing competence, reflecting the values of voters, and understanding the concerns of voters. The Ipsos-Reid data also depict the extent to which Ignatieff in 2011 was less popular than Dion in 2008 among Quebec voters. The scores for Ignatieff were 4 percent to 13 percent lower than those for Dion.

These findings point to the conclusion that NDP operatives' strategy of focusing on Layton's leadership in 2011 worked in Quebec for three reasons. First, it took advantage of an already unpopular prime minister in Quebec who engendered even more negative sentiments in 2011 than in previous elections. Second, the focus on Layton worked because it took advantage of the waning popularity of Duceppe and the inability of the Liberal Party to pick a leader more popular than Dion in Quebec (and he had not been that popular to begin with). Third, NDP operatives appeared to find a branding for Layton that fit with how Quebec voters saw him – honest, representative of their values, and able to get results in Ottawa.

Table 6.14 depicts the predicted probabilities of voting for the four major federal parties based on what can be termed "strategic considerations" once all of the other independent variables from the previous five clusters are included in my model. The first strategic consideration in the table is whether the respondent thought that the governing party and the sitting prime minister "deserved" to be re-elected. Evidently, these dissatisfied voters comprised

TABLE 6.14

Strategic consideration variables, 2006–11 federal elections, QC

	2006				2008				2011			
	NDP	BQ	LPC	CPC	NDP	BQ	LPC	CPC	NDP	BQ	LPC	CPC
Governing party/PM deserves to be re-elected	0.00	-0.19	0.32	-0.13	-0.08	-0.10	-0.27	0.45	-0.14	0.02	0.02	0.17
Strategic voter	-0.12	0.26	-0.01	-0.13	-0.18	0.41	-0.15	-0.08	0.13	-0.12	-0.02	0.00
Wants their MP in government	-0.02	-0.14	0.01	0.15	0.00	-0.15	0.12	0.04	0.10	-0.16	0.03	0.03
Wants a minority government	0.02	0.13	-0.01	-0.14	0.01	0.12	-0.09	-0.04	-0.04	0.09	-0.02	-0.02
Decided after the leaders' debates	0.09	-0.27	0.00	0.18	0.06	-0.20	0.14	0.00	0.17	-0.12	-0.04	-0.02

NOTES: N for 2006 = 7,274; N for 2008 = 7,376; N for 2011 = 8,780; N for all elections = 23,430; shaded = $p \leq 0.05$; sociodemographic variables, general orientation variables, economic perception variables, most important issue variables, leadership evaluation variables, and strategic consideration variables were included in the model, but only the results for the strategic consideration variables are shown.

a key segment of the Quebec electoral market for opposition parties. Reflecting a perennial dissatisfaction with the federal government in Quebec, roughly three-quarters of the electorate thought that the sitting prime minister and the governing party did not deserve to be re-elected across all three elections examined. We can see that the BQ in 2006 and the LPC in 2008 captured most of this important market segment. Voters who thought that the sitting prime minister did not deserve a majority were neither more nor less likely to vote for the NDP in 2006 and only eight points more likely to vote for it in 2008. However, in 2011, the party was able to steal from the BQ and the LPC a considerable number of voters who did not think that Harper deserved a majority government. In 2011, these voters were fourteen points more likely to vote NDP and neither more nor less likely to vote BQ or LPC.

Strategic voting was an important part of the strategies of NDP operatives during the Layton years. As we can see in Appendix B, strategic voters are defined in my analysis as respondents who reported that they were "trying to stop another party from winning and forming the government" as opposed to voting for the party that they thought "would offer the best government for Canada." In the elections that I examined, roughly 45 percent of the Quebec electorate was composed of strategic voters, so the concerns of NDP operatives about strategic voting were warranted. In both 2006 and 2008, the BQ dominated this segment of the Quebec electoral market. Strategic voters were twenty-six points more likely to vote BQ in 2006 and forty-one points more likely to vote BQ in 2008. The NDP, along with the other federalist opposition party (CPC in 2006 and LPC in 2008), did poorly among strategic voters in these elections. Indeed, strategic voters were twelve points less likely to vote NDP in 2006 and eighteen points less likely to vote NDP in 2008. In these elections, a strategic vote appeared to be a vote for the sovereignist party. These voters appeared to believe Duceppe's argument, outlined in Chapter 4, that voting for the BQ was the best way to prevent a Harper Conservative majority government. The NDP's weakness among strategic voters in 2006 and 2008 might have stemmed from their thoughts that voting for the NDP was a "wasted vote" as opposed to voting for the BQ, which could reduce the chances of a Harper majority government. Although the question was not replicated in subsequent Ipsos-Reid exit polls, the 2006 exit poll did ask respondents if they agreed that "a vote for the NDP in this election is really a wasted vote." Interestingly, 45 percent of all voters and 50 percent of strategic voters strongly or somewhat agreed with this statement.

It appears that NDP operatives' tactics to combat strategic voting worked much better in 2011 as opposed to previous elections. In a good example of stealing market share from its opponents, the NDP outperformed the BQ in this segment of the Quebec electorate in 2011. In that election, strategic voters were thirteen points more likely to vote NDP and twelve points less likely to vote BQ. Quebec strategic voters might have calculated that voting NDP, as opposed to BQ, was the best way to remove the Harper Conservatives from power. According to Ipsos-Reid data, 38 percent of NDP voters in Quebec in 2011 were willing on election day to bet $1,000 of their own money that the NDP would win their local riding.

Speculation that the three elections from 2006 to 2011 would result in a minority government was rampant prior to election day. Ipsos-Reid data illustrate that roughly 60 percent of Quebec voters in 2006 and 2008 preferred a minority government over a majority government. The variable of voters who wanted a minority government had no statistically significant effect on their probability of voting NDP in these elections. Rather, the BQ had a decisive advantage with these voters, thirteen points more likely to vote BQ in 2006 and twelve points more likely to vote BQ in 2008.

What Table 6.14 does not show, however, is that in 2006 and 2008 BQ voters were open to the participation of the NDP in a minority government and the prospect of Layton holding power. When presented with four possible minority government outcomes of the 2006 election, 45 percent of BQ voters chose a "Conservative-led minority supported by the NDP" as very or somewhat acceptable. The only more popular potential outcome for BQ voters was a "Conservative-led minority supported by the Bloc Québécois," with 76 percent finding it very or somewhat acceptable. Given the possibility of the LPC remaining in power, BQ voters were not enthusiastic about BQ-LPC or NDP-LPC minority government arrangements.[13] However, by 2008, BQ voters had apparently turned against the Conservatives and expressed a preference to see Layton as prime minister. Only 27 percent of BQ voters strongly or somewhat approved of the idea that Conservatives should "try to block a Liberal-NDP coalition by working out a deal with the Bloc Québécois that allows the Conservatives to govern with Bloc Québécois support." As an alternative scenario, the Ipsos-Reid exit poll asked respondents about their level of approval for Layton's statement during the campaign that he "might 'entertain' joining with the Liberals in a coalition to prevent the Harper Conservatives from forming the next government." A full 72 percent of BQ voters strongly or somewhat approved of Layton's idea. Furthermore, 55 percent of BQ voters preferred "Prime Minister Layton with Deputy Prime Minister Dion" as the outcome of such arrangements as opposed to 28 percent who preferred "Prime Minister Dion with Deputy Prime Minister Layton" and 17 percent who preferred "neither." Clearly, BQ voters in 2008 were comfortable with the prospect of the NDP in power and Layton as prime minister. This finding likely reflects waning confidence in the BQ as the only party that could defend the interests of Quebec in Ottawa.

In 2011, the BQ still did well with voters who wanted a minority government (a nine-point advantage). However, the desire in Quebec for a minority government in 2011 was somewhat tempered, with 45 percent of Ipsos-Reid respondents reporting that they wanted a minority government. The larger segment of the market was composed of voters who wanted a majority government. The NDP actually did better among these voters than any other party: four points more likely to vote NDP than voters who wanted a minority government. This finding is a reversal from the election in 2008, when voters who wanted a majority government were nine points more likely to vote LPC and four points more likely to vote CPC. So the NDP took away some of the market of voters wanting a majority government from the Conservatives and the Liberals in 2011.

Similarly, in 2006 and 2008, the Conservatives and the Liberals dominated the roughly 60 percent of the Quebec electoral market that wanted an MP from their local riding in the government. As expected, the BQ had an advantage with voters who believed that it was not important that their MP be in the government. The probability of voting NDP was unaffected by this variable in 2006 and 2008. However, by 2011, the situation had changed. Reflecting the weakness of the Liberals and the Conservatives, voters who wanted their MP in the government were ten points more likely to vote NDP and only three points more likely to vote CPC or LPC. Once again the New Democrats stole market share from the Liberals and the Conservatives: voting NDP was perceived by Quebec voters as a pathway to power in 2011. Voting for the New Democrats meant the possibility of having a local NDP MP in the government, whether a minority or a majority government. Voters seemed to know instinctively that BQ MPs could never be part of the federal government.

Finally, it is important to look at "late deciders," defined as voters who reported deciding which party to support after the leaders' debates, which generally took place in the middle of the campaign. Table 6.14 shows that the NDP did better among late deciders in 2011 compared with the two previous elections. Whereas the Conservatives held the advantage among late deciders in 2006 and the Liberals performed the best among late deciders in 2008, those voters were seventeen points more likely to vote NDP in 2011, and they were less likely to vote for the other three parties. Moreover, this segment of the Quebec electoral market had grown. According to the Ipsos-Reid exit polls, 35 percent of Quebec voters decided on which party to vote for after the debates in 2006, and 42 percent of Quebec voters made their decisions after the debates in 2008. In 2011, 49 percent of Ipsos-Reid respondents in Quebec reported deciding which party to support after the debates. Possibly because of Layton's strong performance in the French-language debate and on the Quebec talk show *Tout le monde en parle* that was aired after the debates, the NDP succeeded in stealing a share of the growing market of late deciders from the Liberals and the Conservatives in 2011.

The Ipsos-Reid data depict that political operatives were able to combat strategic voting by creating optimism in the NDP campaign in 2011 among Quebec voters that the party had a chance of forming the government or at least playing an active role in the government. They were able to create a sense of momentum for the NDP as a credible alternative for voters who wanted to oust Harper from power but had become tired of the BQ and were unimpressed by the LPC and its new leader. It is notable that 35 percent of NDP voters in Quebec in 2011 believed that the party would win the election. They preferred a majority NDP government, but Ipsos-Reid data illustrate that these voters were also in favour of a coalition government in which Layton was prime minister.[14] When asked about possible scenarios concerning the outcome of the election that did not include a NDP majority government, 87 percent of NDP voters in Quebec preferred a coalition government of New Democrats and Liberals as opposed to a majority government of Conservatives. Inclusion of the Bloc Québécois in a hypothetical coalition government changed little – 82 percent of NDP voters in Quebec preferred a coalition government of the BQ, NDP, and LPC as opposed to a majority CPC government. When asked whom they would prefer to see as the prime minister of such a coalition government, 90 percent of NDP voters chose Layton over Duceppe and Ignatieff. The goal of NDP voters in Quebec thus appears to have been to ensure that Layton became prime minister, in either a majority or a minority government. Investing resources in Quebec since 2004, political operatives cast Layton as a potential prime minister and a leader who could get practical results as part of the government. This tactic proved to be effective in combatting strategic voting in

Quebec. By 2011, voting for the BQ or the LPC could never "fix Ottawa" – Jack Layton was Quebecers' only hope.

Stealing Market Share toward Victory

The electoral success of the NDP during the Layton years can best be explained by the party's ability to steal market share from the Liberal Party and the Bloc Québécois in various segments of the Canadian electoral market. Table 6.15 summarizes the findings of this chapter in relation to English Canada.

The table shows very few examples of the NDP stealing market share from the CPC during the time period that I examined. Instead, the NDP stole market share from the LPC in sixteen segments of the English Canadian electoral market from 2000 to 2011. The probability of members of several important sociodemographic groups voting NDP went up, whereas the probability of members of those groups voting Liberal went down. Also, the NDP stole market share from the LPC in segments made up of left-of-centre voters. English Canadians who had political orientations that could

TABLE 6.15

Examples of stealing market share related to the NDP in the ROC, 2000–11

Examples of the NDP stealing market share from the LPC	Examples of the NDP stealing market share from the CPC	Examples of the LPC stealing market share from the NDP	Examples of the CPC stealing market share from the NDP
Ontarians; male voters; Catholics; visible minorities; union members; pro-Quebec orientation; low level of market liberalism; low level of moral traditionalism; Liberal partisans; negative retrospective perception of the national economy; wanting personal taxes to stay the same or go up; wanting corporate taxes to stay the same or go up; more spending on the environment; voters who liked the NDP leader; voters who disliked Prime Minister Harper	Pro-American voters; political cynics	University graduates; anti-continentalist voters	None

be considered left wing – such as low levels of market liberalism, low levels of moral traditionalism, and a willingness to accommodate Quebec – became more likely to vote NDP and less likely to vote LPC. Similarly, English Canadians who held left-wing positions on raising taxes and spending on the environment became more likely to vote NDP and less likely to vote LPC. By 2011, at least some Liberal partisans had started to vote for the New Democrats, and the NDP was doing better than the Liberals among voters who wanted to punish the Conservative government for a weak national economy. Leadership was crucial as well. It was not so much that English Canadian voters liked Layton more than they had liked McDonough. Rather, in 2011, the NDP was able to convince English Canadians who liked its leader to vote for it instead of the Liberals and captured a greater portion of the voter market that disliked Prime Minister Harper than the Liberals.

The NDP would not have had electoral success in English Canada if its competitors had been able to steal market share from it. Stealing market share is a zero sum game. If the NDP won a greater share of certain market segments but lost an equal share of other market segments, then it would have been no better off. However, we can see in Table 6.15 that the Liberals stole market share from the New Democrats in only two segments, and there are no examples of the Conservatives stealing market share from the New Democrats. So the success of the NDP in English Canada during the Layton years ends up being a story about political operatives positioning their party well to steal market share from the Liberals, who had poor campaigns and weak leaders, and preventing their own party's market share from being stolen by its competitors. By 2011, the hard work and innovative ideas of agents in the NDP, such as Layton and his team of political operatives, had paid dividends. By emphasizing Layton's leadership, taking advantage of opportunities provided by minority Parliaments to raise the profile of the NDP, moderating the party's language/policies, and having a disciplined caucus, the operatives were able to present the NDP as a credible alternative to the fading LPC and the party that could push the Harper Conservatives out of power.

Table 6.16 summarizes the findings of my examination of the Ipsos-Reid exit polls for Quebec in the 2006, 2008, and 2011 federal elections. Reflective of the orange wave in Quebec in 2011 being a landslide, it is not surprising that no party managed to steal market share from the NDP in that election. In any case, since the party received only 12 percent of the popular vote in 2008, there was not much market share to steal. Given the sudden surge of

TABLE 6.16

Examples of stealing market share related to the NDP in Quebec, 2006–11

Examples of the NDP stealing market share from the BQ	Examples of the NDP stealing market share from the LPC	Examples of the NDP stealing market share from the CPC	Examples of the CPC, LPC, or BQ stealing market share from the NDP
Montreal residents; female voters; gays; favoured government intervention; favoured same-sex marriage; soft nationalists; hard sovereignists; voters who thought that Canada was headed in the "wrong direction"; voters pessimistic about their personal finances; health care voters; voters who chose "social programs" such as child care and pensions as their most important issue; corruption voters; voters who thought that Layton would make the best prime minister; voters who disliked Prime Minister Harper; voters who thought that Harper did not deserve another majority; strategic voters	Montreal residents; gays; hard federalists; soft nationalists; voters who thought that Canada was headed in the "wrong direction"; voters optimistic about their personal finances; environment voters; voters who thought that Layton would make the best prime minister; voters who disliked Prime Minister Harper; voters who thought that Harper did not deserve another majority; voters who wanted a majority government; voters who wanted their MP in the government; late deciders	Voters who liked political parties; hard federalists; soft nationalists; voters optimistic about their personal finances; leader voters; voters who wanted a majority government; voters who wanted their MP in the government; late deciders	None

the party, it is obvious that it stole market share from all of the other major parties. The NDP stole market share from the BQ in sixteen segments of the Quebec electoral market from 2006 to 2011. In comparison, the NDP stole market share from the LPC in thirteen segments and from the CPC in eight segments.

The NDP stole market share from the BQ in two large sociodemographic groups (i.e., female voters and residents of Montreal) as well as among voters with "left-wing" orientations in terms of being socially liberal and favourable to government intervention in the economy. Similarly, voters concerned about what might be considered left-wing issues such as health care and social policy also became more likely to vote NDP and less likely to vote BQ. Although the BQ dominated the market of hard sovereignists and soft nationalists in 2006 and 2008, the NDP made headway into both segments at the expense of the BQ. Prior to the 2011 election, the BQ had performed well in the market of voters who felt negative about the overall direction of Canada and their personal finances as well as voters concerned about corruption, displeased with Harper as a prime minister, and prone to voting strategically in order to avoid a certain outcome. In 2011, dissatisfied voters and strategic voters swung away from the BQ and toward the NDP. Although they were voting against Conservatives and hoping to voice their displeasure with the state of the country, they were still voting for something. They were voting for Jack Layton as the prime minister. In 2006 and 2008, the BQ had done well among voters who thought that Layton would be the best prime minister. In the 2011 election, the NDP was able to convince voters who liked Layton and wanted to see him as prime minister, but had voted BQ, to vote NDP.

At first glance, the Liberals lost market share to the New Democrats in many of the same segments of the Quebec electoral market as the Bloc Québécois. The propensity to support the LPC of Montreal residents, gays, soft nationalists, voters dissatisfied with the overall direction of Canada, and voters displeased with Harper went down, whereas the propensity of these segments to vote NDP went up. Leadership was crucial as well. The Liberals held a share of the market of voters who thought that Layton would make the best prime minister in 2006 and 2008, but in 2011 these voters went to the New Democrats. There were also some important differences in the segments that the LPC lost to the NDP compared with the segments that the BQ lost to the NDP. The Liberals lost voters to the New Democrats in the hard federalist segment of the Quebec electoral market as well as the segments of environment voters and those optimistic about their personal finances. Most importantly, Liberals had always argued in Quebec that voting for them would ensure a stable majority government and give voters regional representation in the government. However, in 2011, the NDP turned those arguments upside down. Voters who wanted a majority government and their MP to be part of that government were more likely to vote NDP and less likely to vote LPC. They had been convinced by the momentum that the NDP had built as the 2011 campaign came to a close that their NDP MP could be part of the next government in Ottawa.

In 2011, Conservatives were more susceptible to having their market share stolen by New Democrats in Quebec than in English Canada. However, there were fewer segments in which the NDP stole market share from the CPC compared with the LPC and the BQ. Also, the Conservatives divided their losses to the New Democrats in most of these segments with the Liberals. We can see that the likelihood of voting Conservative went down and that the likelihood of voting New Democrat and Liberal went up in the following segments of voters: optimistic about their personal finances, wanted a majority government, wanted an MP in the government, soft nationalists, and hard federalists. Only in the segments of late deciders, voters who thought that leaders were important, and those who liked political parties did the Conservatives exclusively lose market share to the New Democrats in 2011, and often these losses were not great. As in English Canada, the story of the success of the NDP in Quebec in 2011 was not about stealing market share from the governing party but about stealing market share from its centre-left opponents that were also seeking to present an alternative to the governing party.

However, it would be a mistake to conclude that the NDP came out of nowhere in Quebec to break through in the 2011 election and that its success was merely a product of dumb luck – the political equivalent of being in the right place at the right time. There was an underlying strength of the NDP in Quebec in the 2006 and 2008 elections. Indeed, there are several examples of a faint foreshadowing of the orange wave in those two elections. In 2008, the NDP started to eat into the BQ's market share of voters who were socially liberal and desired state intervention. In both 2006 and 2008, the Ipsos-Reid data show that the NDP was popular among the one-fifth of Quebec voters who cited the environment and "social programs like childcare and pensions" as their most important issues. In 2008, the NDP stole market share from the BQ among voters who thought that health care was their most important issue. Layton was popular among Quebecers in the 2006 election, particularly compared with the leaders of the other federalist parties. The 2008 Ipsos-Reid data show that Layton beat all other leaders, including Duceppe, in being seen as the most empathetic, inspirational, and trustworthy leader in Canadian politics. Furthermore, between the 2006 and 2008 elections, the popularity of the NDP among Quebecers who disliked the incumbent prime minister improved slightly, and the NDP began to do better among voters who thought that leaders were the most important factor in their voting decisions. Perhaps most importantly, BQ voters in 2006 and 2008 were favourable toward the NDP participating in a minority government and favourable toward Layton being the prime minister.

The public subsidies provided to the NDP through quarterly allowances gave its operatives the financial resources to discover their party's underlying strength in Quebec when few others in Canada realized that it was there. Through sophisticated research funded by growing per-vote subsides, NDP operatives were able to "read the tea leaves" in Quebec prior to 2011 and see the party's budding strength in that province, not apparent if one looked only at election results. They saw the potential for the party in Quebec because of an overwhelming dislike of the Harper Conservative government, voter fatigue with the Bloc Québécois and Duceppe, and the unpopularity of the Liberals and their new leaders. The string of minority Parliaments had made the NDP and Layton more present in Quebec media despite holding almost no seats in the province, but the political operatives were not content to rely on media coverage of the brinkmanship within the House of Commons to reach out to Quebec voters. Despite some opposition within the party, agents within the NDP decided to send Layton to Quebec regularly, develop Quebec-specific policies, and invest more of the advertising, field organization, and media relations budgets in Quebec from 2004 to 2011. They also spent money on research to find the right brand for Layton in Quebec and the right message for the NDP in Quebec. When the Quebec electorate suddenly started to look for alternatives to the BQ and the LPC in order to get rid of the Harper Conservatives, the NDP was ready. Its operatives had the good fortune of a favourable political situation in Quebec in 2011, when their opponents were weak, but they also had the innovative ideas, willingness to take risks, and previous groundwork completed to take advantage of that situation. When they were able to gain momentum in Quebec in the middle of the 2011 campaign, they built on it toward a sweep of the province.

Conclusion

In many ways, the electoral success of the "new NDP" in the 2011 election represented an affirmation of the moderation and modernization of the party prescribed by its operatives and partially paid for by the creation of the public per-vote subsidy. With the slow crumbling of support for the Bloc Québécois and the Liberal Party, the audacious plans of Layton and his team positioned the party well to take advantage of the weakness of their left-of-centre opponents. Moderation of the party's ideology and language attracted soft LPC and soft BQ supporters. Party strategists used the increased clout of the NDP during a string of minority Parliaments to build Layton's image and to make the party more relevant in the minds of voters. Focusing on Layton's leadership to introduce Canadians to the NDP proved to be a sound tactic. The surgical precision needed to carry out this overall reorientation of the party required ensuring strong discipline of the caucus, moving away from being the political arm of labour, and concentrating power within party headquarters. These changes were now justified. Building the NDP in Quebec and strengthening regional beachheads in Alberta and Newfoundland paid off. The achievement of bringing the party to the status of official opposition in the House of Commons for the first time in its eighty-year history proved that the transformation of the political marketing the party since its disappointing results in the 2000 election had borne fruit.

Given that moderation and modernization of the NDP had set up its electoral success during the Layton years, the logical result of Mulcair's team continuing to follow that path would be the formation of the first federal NDP government in Canadian history. Indeed, the NDP started the 2015 campaign in a position to form at least a minority government and, if things went very well, even a majority government. Alas, it was not to be. Next I outline what went wrong and how the best-laid plans of NDP operatives failed to realize the long-hoped-for dream of the first NDP federal government in Canadian history.

7
Heartbreak: NDP Voter Behaviour and the 2015 Federal Election

October 19, 2015, was a heartbreaking night for New Democrats across Canada. The moderation and modernization, driven by the agency of NDP political operatives working with greater financial resources provided by the per-vote public subsidy, had placed the party in a position to form the government. The creation of the "new NDP" was leading toward the party winning power for the first time in its history. Despite a highly sophisticated campaign based on the latest postmodern campaign techniques and a political market orientation toward voters and competitors, the party was unable to take that final step, leaving its activists, politicians, and operatives with a simple question. What happened?

To answer that question, I examine the 2015 Canadian Federal Election Panel Survey on Social Democracy, a custom survey that captured the opinions of a random sample of voters during the first week of the 2015 campaign and immediately after the campaign ended. The same voters were surveyed in both waves to allow for an exploration of how their attitudes changed between the beginning and the end of the campaign. Mainly, the disappointing election results of the NDP can be attributed to its poor conversion rates: that is, voters who leaned toward the party at the beginning of the campaign did not end up voting for it. The principal reason for this failure to convert potential voters into actual voters was the inability of the NDP campaign, as designed by party operatives, to generate excitement. The wedge issues constructed by the operatives failed to capture the imaginations of swing voters, Mulcair's popularity sagged, the party platform was poorly communicated, and the party was not seen by voters as particularly "charming" or close to them on their most important issues.

If the electoral success of the NDP during the Layton years was predicated on stealing market share from the LPC and the BQ, the ability of those parties to steal back that market share caused the disappointing results for the NDP in 2015. When the momentum of its campaign stalled in the middle of September in both English Canada and Quebec after controversy over the party's position on the niqab and its insistence on simultaneously balancing the federal budget and increasing social spending, its opponents – running good campaigns – began to attract potential NDP voters, particularly among "late deciders" who waited until after Labour Day to decide which party to support. Potential NDP voters in English Canada who were late deciders flocked to the Liberal Party, which had run an effective campaign up to that point (Jeffrey 2016, 2017). These voters wanted to displace the Harper Conservatives, and they were impressed by Trudeau's leadership, the Liberal platform, and the party brand. In francophone Quebec, potential NDP supporters who were late deciders deserted the NDP and voted for the Liberals, Bloc Québécois, and to a lesser extent Conservatives. Some of the support for the Liberals among potential NDP voters in francophone Quebec might have been motivated by strategic considerations, yet it appears that these voters had simply become more impressed with the NDP's opponents as their campaigns progressed. Among potential NDP supporters, the likeability scores of Duceppe and Trudeau increased, the Liberals' platform was popular, the BQ and the LPC gained partisans, and the percentage of voters who reported the BQ or the CPC as the party closest to them on their most important issue increased. Ultimately, the campaign that NDP operatives had built around an experienced leader, safe change, and a two-way NDP-CPC race was simply unable to generate the momentum and enthusiasm needed to prevent potential supporters from migrating to competitors when campaign events unexpectedly turned against the party.

Failure to Convert: How the NDP Lost the 2015 Election

The research initiative that produced this book included the 2015 Canadian Federal Election Panel Survey on Social Democracy, internet-based polling done by SOM in Quebec and Probit in the rest of Canada. Breton and colleagues (2017, 1032) argue that "the internet mode should now be the default for election studies," and both companies have taken steps to construct internet panels of randomly selected respondents with no self-selection allowed. These companies were in the field during the first and second weeks of the campaign, from August 10 to August 20, 2015 (Wave 1), and then immediately following election day, from October 20 to October 30, 2015 (Wave 2). I have eliminated respondents who reported not voting in the federal election and respondents who did not fill out both waves of the survey. In the Quebec survey, I did not feel confident making conclusions about anglophones and allophones since relatively few completed both waves of the survey. Therefore, I decided to concentrate on comparing the two main electoral markets for the NDP in 2015: Quebec francophones and ROC voters. A "francophone" is defined as a respondent who reported having French as one of her or his mother tongues.[1]

When nonvoters and respondents who did not participate in both waves of the Probit survey are eliminated, there are 2,400 voters broken down as follows: Western Canada (750), Ontario (1,123), and Atlantic Canada (527). After nonvoters, respondents who did not participate in both waves of the survey, and respondents who did not have French as one of their mother tongues are eliminated, there are 1,931 francophone voters in the SOM Quebec sample broken down as follows: the Montreal Census Metropolitan Area that includes the Island and the Crown of Montreal (839), the Quebec City Census Metropolitan Area (316), and elsewhere in Quebec (776). Both data sets are weighted according to region, sex, age, and education using Statistics Canada population estimates from July 2015.[2]

Given the bivariate statistics from the two surveys, a relatively straightforward answer to the question of what happened to the NDP on election night in 2015 presents itself. The main reason that the NDP went from being a contender to form the government in August 2015 to being in third place after all the ballots were counted was poor conversion rates: the party was unable to convince voters who leaned toward it at the beginning of the campaign to vote for it. Simply put, it failed to convert potential voters into actual voters.

To understand this point, it is necessary to take a closer look at the polling done in August 2015. Public domain polling released in early August illustrated that the NDP was hovering just above or below the 35 percent mark using Canada-wide samples, whereas the CPC was polling around 30 percent and the LPC was polling just below 30 percent (Coletto 2016, 315). If everything went according to plan for the NDP during the campaign, then the party appeared to be headed for a minority NDP government. If things went really well for the party, then a majority NDP government was even imaginable. However, looking at national polls from early August 2015 does not allow us to understand how soft or hard the support for each party was: that is, the extent to which its voters were certain to vote for it or willing to consider voting for other parties. To capture the hardness or softness of

FIGURE 7.1

Certainty to vote for major parties in the rest of Canada, August 10–20, 2015

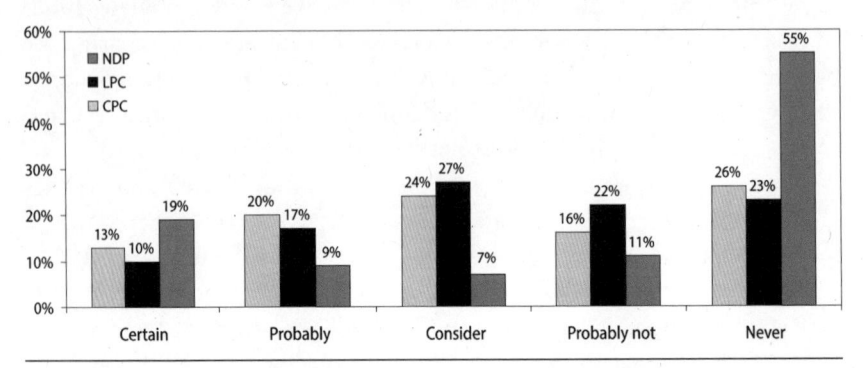

Category	NDP	LPC	CPC
Certain	13%	10%	19%
Probably	20%	17%	9%
Consider	24%	27%	7%
Probably not	16%	22%	11%
Never	26%	23%	55%

SOURCE: 2015 Canadian Federal Election Panel Survey on Social Democracy.

the support for each party, I devised a special question for the survey used for this book. The question was as follows: "For each of the following parties, can you tell us whether you are: certain to vote for that party, will probably vote for that party, would consider voting for that party, will probably not vote for that party, or would never vote for that party?" Figures 7.1 and 7.2 depict the results in both the rest of Canada and francophone Quebec.

As we can see in Figure 7.1, the NDP was doing well in English Canada at the beginning of the 2015 campaign, but its support was soft. Only 13 percent of voters in English Canada were certain to vote for the party, 20 percent were probably going to vote for the party, and 24 percent would consider voting for the party. The Liberal Party was in a similar position (10 percent certainly voting for it, 17 percent probably voting for it, and 27 percent considering voting for it). In fact, the gap between the first-place NDP and the third-place LPC in the national polls was somewhat illusory. If we define each party's pool of accessible voters as those who reported that they would certainly, probably, or possibly vote for a certain party, then the pool of accessible voters for the New Democrats stood at 57 percent of the English Canadian electorate compared with 54 percent for the Liberals. The Conservatives had the highest percentage of voters certain of voting for them even though their pool of accessible voters was only 35 percent of the English Canadian electorate.

Given the softness of support for the NDP and the LPC, it is not surprising that they were fighting for the same voters – NDP/LPC switchers, as NDP

FIGURE 7.2

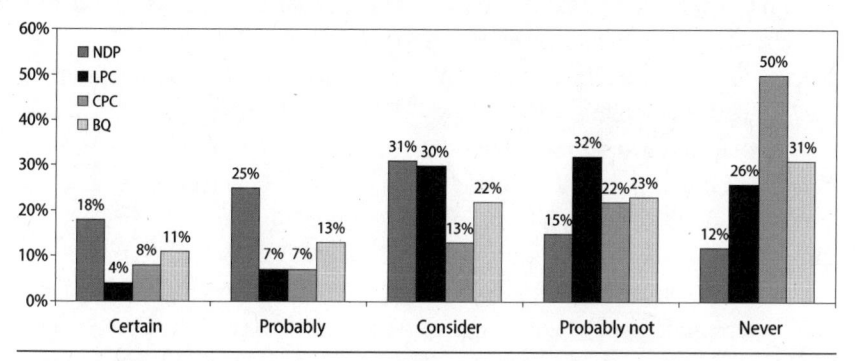

Certainty to vote for major parties in francophone Quebec, August 10–20, 2015

Certainty	NDP	LPC	CPC	BQ
Certain	18%	4%	8%	11%
Probably	25%	7%	7%	13%
Consider	31%	30%	13%	22%
Probably not	15%	32%	22%	23%
Never	12%	50%	26%	31%

SOURCE: 2015 Canadian Federal Election Panel Survey on Social Democracy.

operatives dubbed them. The best way to look at this situation is to examine the extent to which the NDP's pool of accessible voters considered voting for its opponents. Further analysis of the Probit survey data indicates that 69 percent of the NDP's pool of accessible voters in English Canada were certainly, probably, or possibly voting for the Liberals. In contrast, only 6 percent of the NDP's pool of accessible voters in English Canada were certainly, probably, or possibly voting for the Conservatives. So the fight for soft NDP supporters in English Canada was clearly a fight between the New Democrats and the Liberals.

In contrast to its competitors, the NDP was in strong shape during the first and second weeks of the 2015 campaign in francophone Quebec. Among francophone Quebecers, 18 percent said that they would certainly vote NDP, 25 percent responded that they would probably vote NDP, and 31 percent stated that they would possibly vote NDP. Only about 27 percent had either partially or completely closed the door on voting NDP. With 74 percent of the electorate being part of its pool of accessible voters, the NDP was clearly on its way to becoming the consensus choice of francophone Quebec on election day. The Liberal Party appeared to be in a difficult situation in francophone Quebec, with only 4 percent of voters stating that they would certainly vote LPC and only 7 percent of voters reporting that they would probably vote LPC. Yet Liberals could take some solace from the fact that 30 percent of francophone Quebecers would at least consider voting LPC. The Bloc Québécois was in better shape than the Liberal Party. Looking at Figure 7.2, we can see that 11 percent of francophone Quebecers stated that they were certain to vote BQ, 13 percent reported that they would probably vote BQ, and 22 percent indicated that they would consider voting BQ. The party's pool of accessible voters was at 46 percent (compared with 41 percent for the Liberals), and it had more support in the "certain" and "probable" categories than the Liberals. With 72 percent of francophone Quebecers stating that they would probably not or never vote CPC, the Conservative chances of making significant gains in francophone Quebec looked slim.

Yet the NDP's position in francophone Quebec was somewhat precarious. The party was popular, but it was vulnerable to attacks from all sides. Further exploration of the SOM data found that approximately 45 percent of the NDP's accessible pool of voters was also accessible to the Liberal Party and the Bloc Québécois. And 22 percent of potential NDP voters in francophone Quebec had yet to completely rule out voting for the Conservatives. Whereas the election in English Canada was clearly shaping up as a battle for the hearts and minds of NDP/LPC switchers, the situation was much more complex and fluid in Quebec. The NDP was in the lead, but its political operatives would have to wage a war on multiple fronts to fend off challengers from three sides.

Overall, the NDP was in a strong position at the beginning of the campaign, but its support was very soft in English Canada and somewhat soft in francophone Quebec. So what happened on election day in October? To answer that question, I calculated the conversion rates of the NDP. These rates are defined as the percentages of voters who were "certainly," "probably," or "considering" voting NDP in August who actually voted NDP on election day.

Looking first at English Canada, we can see in Figure 7.3 how the NDP was simply unable to convert potential voters in August into actual voters in October. The party even lost some of its certain voters in English Canada during the campaign. As the figure illustrates, 21 percent of English Canadian voters who reported that they would certainly vote NDP in Wave 1 ended up voting LPC. Even worse, 46 percent of voters who were probably voting NDP and 62 percent of voters who were considering voting NDP in Wave 1 actually voted LPC. Simply put, the New Democrats' potential support and even some of their certain support in English Canada melted away to the Liberals over the campaign. The fact that a fifth of voters who said that they were certain to vote for the NDP in August ended up voting for the LPC in October is testament to the effective campaign run by the Liberals. The

Figure 7.3

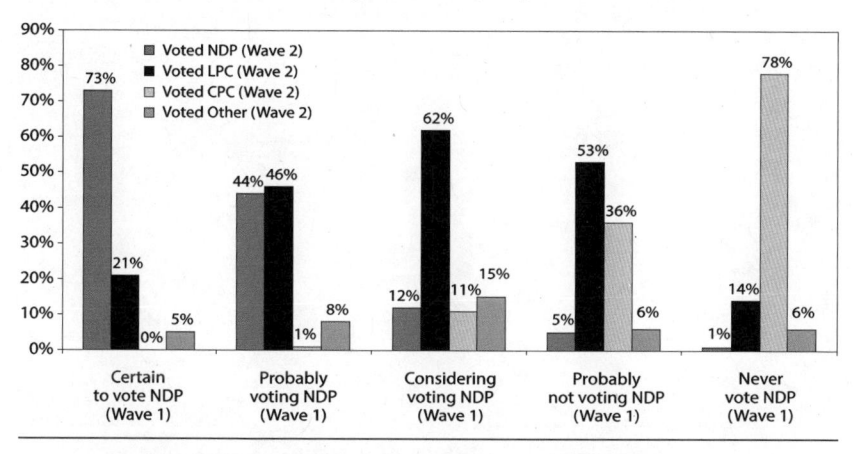

Conversion rates of the NDP in English Canada, 2015 federal election

Wave 1 category	Voted NDP (Wave 2)	Voted LPC (Wave 2)	Voted CPC (Wave 2)	Voted Other (Wave 2)
Certain to vote NDP	73%	21%	0%	5%
Probably voting NDP	44%	46%	1%	8%
Considering voting NDP	12%	62%	11%	15%
Probably not voting NDP	5%	53%	36%	6%
Never vote NDP	1%	14%	78%	6%

SOURCE: 2015 Canadian Federal Election Panel Survey on Social Democracy.

campaign, in the opinion of Brooke Jeffrey (2016, 72–83), was successful because of the Liberals' effective local organizing ground, the popularity of their leader, an innovative advertising campaign, a "credible but progressive" platform, and an articulation of the "Liberal values" that Canadians were yearning for after ten years of the Harper government. Indeed, Figure 7.3 shows that the Liberals were really the New Democrats' only adversary in English Canada since the Conservatives siphoned off no certain or potential NDP support during the campaign. NDP/CPC switchers almost did not exist.

The situation of the NDP in francophone Quebec was more complex than that in English Canada. But the bottom line remained the same: the party was unable to convert potential voters in August into actual voters in October.

Figure 7.4 illustrates that the NDP lost 20 percent of its certain voters, 16 percent of its probable voters, and 25 percent of voters who were considering it to the LPC during the campaign. Once again voters certain to vote for the NDP in August who voted LPC in October is evidence of an effective Liberal campaign.

Although the Liberal Party was the main beneficiary of the NDP's collapse in Quebec, the Bloc Québécois also benefited. Indeed, 7 percent of the NDP's certain supporters migrated to the BQ, as did 21 percent of its

Figure 7.4

Conversion rates of the NDP in francophone Quebec, 2015 federal election

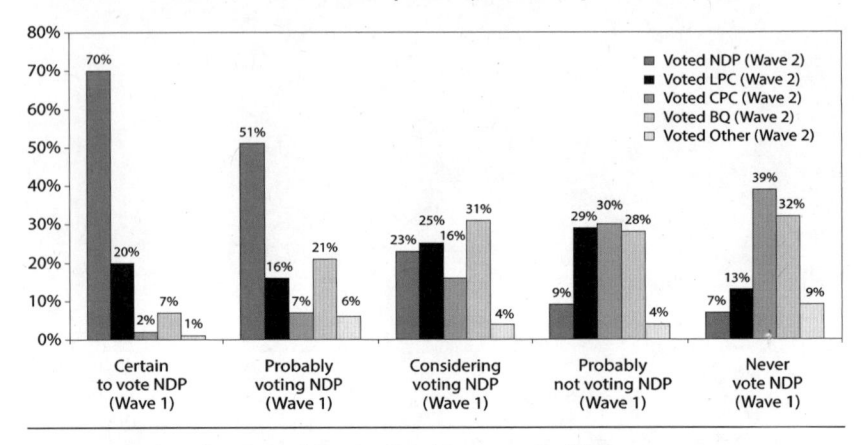

Wave 1 status	Voted NDP (Wave 2)	Voted LPC (Wave 2)	Voted CPC (Wave 2)	Voted BQ (Wave 2)	Voted Other (Wave 2)
Certain to vote NDP	70%	20%	2%	7%	1%
Probably voting NDP	51%	16%	7%	21%	6%
Considering voting NDP	23%	25%	16%	31%	4%
Probably not voting NDP	9%	29%	30%	28%	4%
Never vote NDP	7%	13%	39%	32%	9%

SOURCE: 2015 Canadian Federal Election Panel Survey on Social Democracy.

probable voters and 31 percent of voters who were considering the NDP. Even the Conservatives, though to a smaller extent, picked up some of the voters who had been accessible to the New Democrats at the beginning of the campaign.

These findings show the ability of both the BQ and the CPC to steal market share from the NDP as the campaign progressed and point to the somewhat underappreciated effectiveness of those parties' campaigns in Quebec in 2015. In the case of the BQ, part of this underappreciation stems from how the first-past-the-post system disadvantaged the BQ and advantaged the LPC in terms of final seat count that "helped to popularize the interpretation of the Liberals coasting to a spectacular victory in Quebec" (Bélanger and Nadeau 2016, 129). Even if the results for the BQ were weak compared with its heyday from 1993 to 2008, the party was not wiped off the political map. Indeed, it received 19 percent of the popular vote in Quebec as a whole and, as the SOM data illustrated, almost a quarter of the francophone vote. In fact, Bélanger and Nadeau (2016, 124–26) argue that the BQ succeeded in driving the dynamics of the federal campaign in Quebec by repeatedly bringing pipelines and the niqab controversy into the media spotlight. For its part, the CPC won twelve seats in Quebec, its best showing in the province since the reuniting of the right in 2003. This result illustrates that the Conservatives' message of protecting national security, promoting economic growth, and not interfering in provincial matters found at least some adherents in a province where the party struggled since Harper became prime minister (Bélanger and Nadeau 2016, 126; Ellis 2016, 53).

Solid, Converted, Lost, and Anti-NDPers

For the NDP, the story of the 2015 election was its failure to get voters accessible to it at the beginning of the campaign to vote for it at the end of the campaign. Who were the potential NDP voters who actually voted for the party? Who were the potential NDP voters who eventually voted for another party? Who were the voters who were never really in play for the party?

To answer these research questions, I divided the English Canadian and francophone Quebec electorates into four distinct categories. These categories are based on a combination of responses to questions asked in Waves 1 and 2 of the survey. In Wave 1, respondents were asked if they would certainly vote NDP, would probably vote for it, would consider voting NDP, would probably not vote for it, or would never vote NDP. In Wave 2, the same voters were simply asked which party they voted for in the election.

The first category is what I call a "solid NDPer." These respondents indicated that they would certainly vote for the NDP in Wave 1 and reported voting for the party in Wave 2. They constitute what NDP strategists commonly refer to as the party's "base." They are certain that they will vote for the NDP at the beginning of the campaign, and they come out faithfully on Election Day and do exactly that. Unfortunately for the party, its base did not make up a large portion of the English Canadian or francophone Quebec electorates in the 2015 election. According to my survey, only 10 percent of the English Canadian electorate and 13 percent of the francophone Quebec electorate could be classified as solid NDPers.

A somewhat larger portion of the English Canadian and francophone Quebec electorates in the 2015 election could be categorized as "converted NDPers." Such voters indicated that they would probably vote for or consider voting for the NDP in Wave 1 and then reported actually voting for the party in Wave 2.[3] These voters were up for grabs at the beginning of the 2015 campaign. They leaned toward the NDP or were open to voting for the party, but they also considered other parties. After weighing the alternatives, they did vote NDP. In the terms used by NDP operatives, these "swing voters" swung the NDP's way on election day. My surveys illustrate that these converted NDPers constituted 13 percent of the English Canadian electorate and 22 percent of the francophone Quebec electorate.

The most important category for my analysis is voters who could be classified as "lost NDPers." These voters indicated that they would certainly, probably, or consider voting for the NDP in Wave 1 and then reported voting for another party in Wave 2. In English Canada, these lost NDPers overwhelmingly ended up voting for the Liberals and to a much lesser extent for the Greens and the Conservatives. In francophone Quebec, the lost NDPers split three ways: 39 percent voted Bloc Québécois, 37 percent voted Liberal, and 17 percent voted Conservative. In many ways, the lost NDPers were the source of the heartbreak on election night. They had flirted with the NDP early in the campaign, inflating its numbers in national public domain polling. However, as the campaign progressed, they shifted away from the party and toward its competitors because of a weak campaign run by the NDP and strong campaigns run by its opponents. In the terms used by NDP operatives, these swing voters were "in play" for the party during the campaign but then swung to its opponents on Election Day. Ultimately, lost NDPers were a rather large segment of the electorate. According to my surveys, they made up 36 percent of the electorate in English Canada and 41 percent of the electorate in francophone Quebec. It was these voters who decided that the Liberals, rather than the New Democrats, formed government.

A final category of voters could be called "anti-NDPers." These voters indicated that they would probably not or never vote for the NDP in Wave 1 and followed through by reporting to have voted for another party in Wave 2. These voters were never in what NDP operatives referred to as the "NDP universe." That is, they were never really accessible to the party, and its strategists knew at the beginning of the campaign that the chances these voters would support their party were slim. In English Canada, my survey revealed, 64 percent of anti-NDPers voted for the Conservatives, and 30 percent voted for the Liberals. In francophone Quebec, they ended up supporting the Conservatives (36 percent) and the Bloc Québécois (33 percent) and to a lesser extent the Liberals (24 percent). It is important to realize that these voters were a formidable obstacle to the NDP in trying to form the government in the 2015 election, particularly in English Canada. After all, my surveys showed that approximately 40 percent of the English Canadian electorate could be classified as anti-NDPers compared with 24 percent in francophone Quebec.

What are the characteristics and opinions of voters who fell into the solid, converted, lost, or anti-NDPer category at the end of the 2015 election? To answer this question, I developed a multivariate model based on hypotheses about the characteristics and opinions associated with voters in these categories. The dependent variable in the model is not vote choice (i.e., which party the respondent voted for). Vote choice in the 2015 election, particularly voting for the Liberal Party, is examined in other research (Clarke et al., 2016; Clarke et al., 2017).

Rather, the dependent variable in the models below is the likelihood of a respondent falling into one of these four categories. Using established literature on voter behaviour in Canada (Blais et al., 2002; Cross et al., 2015; Fournier et al., 2013; Gidengil et al., 2012; Kanji, Bilodeau, and Scotto 2012; Roy and McGrane 2015), I devised a set of independent variables that could explain the probability of a voter being a solid, converted, lost, or anti-NDPer. Some of the data for these variables was collected only in the first wave of the survey, some was collected only in the second wave, and some was collected in both waves to allow for comparison. The wording and coding of all the questions that make up the independent variables within the model are in Appendix C.

As a starting point, my model includes sociodemographic characteristics of the respondent such as region, gender, education, and income. In response to particular campaign events or dynamics, it is possible that certain sociodemographic groups moved away from the NDP in large numbers during the 2015 campaign. I also inserted independent variables related to partisanship such as identifying as New Democrat, Conservative, Liberal, or Bloquiste and a question about which party the respondent supported in the previous federal election. Having a partisan attachment to the NDP or having voted for the NDP in a previous election might make a respondent less likely to move to another party over the campaign. The model includes variables measuring the underlying values of respondents. In particular, a market liberalism index was constructed to examine respondents' values about economic issues such as wealth redistribution and government intervention in the economy, and a postmaterialism index measured respondents' values about protecting the environment, women's place in society, and social conservatism. Similarly, the model includes questions about respondents' preferences in terms of appropriate levels of corporate and personal taxation as well as appropriate levels of federal government spending on health care, reducing poverty, fighting terrorism, arts and culture, and Indigenous peoples. It is possible that voters with more left-wing values (e.g., low market liberalism and high postmaterialism) and left-wing spending and taxing preferences (e.g., high taxes and high spending on social programs) were unlikely to move away from New Democrats and toward Liberals, Bloc Québécois, or Conservatives during the 2015 campaign. Perhaps respondents who wanted the federal government to spend more on fighting terrorism tended to be anti-NDPers. Respondents in francophone Quebec were asked about their opinions on sovereignty in Quebec with the expectation that voters who believed strongly in sovereignty would be anti-NDPers. In the surveys in both English Canada and Quebec, a retrospective question was asked on the performance of the Canadian economy over the past year. Potentially, respondents who thought that the economy was worsening were more likely to be lost or anti-NDPers given the weakness of the party's brand on economic issues.

On issues in the 2015 federal election, several different questions were asked. Following the work of Harold Clarke and his various collaborators (Clarke et al., 2009a), I asked respondents in both waves of the survey to identify the single issue most important to them in federal politics and the party closest to their position on that issue. A respondent who answered that the NDP was closest to him or her on the most important issue, particularly in the postelection survey, might be more likely to be a solid or converted NDPer. Respondents were also asked to what extent they agreed with the NDP positions on "wedge issues" between Liberals and New Democrats that political operatives had identified in the interviews with me used for my analysis of campaign strategies. These wedge issues included the NDP's positions against the TPP and Bill C-51 and for balanced budgets, a fifteen-dollar-a-day national child-care plan, universal pharmacare, and a cap-and-trade scheme to reduce greenhouse gas emissions. NDP operatives intended that these policy positions would create a stark contrast between the New Democrats and the Liberals. If these wedge issues worked well, then it was expected that those who agreed with NDP positions would be less likely to be lost NDPers and more likely to be converted NDPers. In essence, agreement with the NDP on these issues would have helped swing voters to support the NDP.

A question on the desirability of coalition governments was also included. My expectation was that, the more the respondent favoured a coalition government (the outcome that NDP operatives were informally aiming for), the more likely the respondent would be a solid or converted NDPer. Given the high profile of the niqab issue during the campaign, a question on it was included in the postelection survey with the expectation that lost NDPers disagreed with the NDP's position in favour of allowing niqabs to be worn at citizenship ceremonies. In the same vein, I included a general question in the postelection survey asking whether the respondent found major differences, minor differences, or no differences between the Liberals and the New Democrats during the campaign. Respondents who saw minor differences or no differences between the two parties might have been lost NDPers who went over to the Liberals as the campaign came to a close. In the postelection survey, respondents were also given a short description of the platform of each major party and asked to identify which party put forth the plan. Subsequently, they were asked to state their level of agreement with the plan on a scale of 0 to 10. Possibly, solid and converted NDPers were more likely to identify correctly the NDP's platform and more likely to agree strongly with it.

Given the large roles that strategic voting and momentum at the end of the campaign played in the tactics of NDP operatives, the model included variables related to these considerations. Respondents were asked in the postelection survey about when they made their voting decisions. Since Labour Day fell in the middle of the campaign, it was a good point at which to differentiate between early and later deciders. To discern if a respondent was a strategic voter, this question was asked: "When you were making up your mind how to vote, did you *very much* or *somewhat* prefer another party but decided against it because you thought that the party had little chance of winning? (emphasis in original)." Because of the Liberals' lead in public domain polling at the end of the campaign, lost NDPers might have been more likely to be late deciders and strategic voters. Also, given the importance that NDP operatives placed on building up good voter contact operations or their "ground game," respondents were asked which parties contacted them by "visiting your home, phoning you with a live person, phoning you with a recorded message, texting you, or e-mailing you." Voters contacted by the NDP might have been less likely to be lost or anti-NDPers.

The two final sets of independent variables in my model related to party leader and party brand. Respondents' evaluations of the major party leaders, measured in both Wave 1 and Wave 2, were based on a standard feeling thermometer in which 0 was "really dislike" and 10 was "really like." Evidently, lost and anti-NDPers were expected to have a low opinion of Mulcair and higher opinions of the other party leaders (particularly in the postelection survey). Based on Gareth Smith's (2009) work on "party political personality," the strengths of the brands of the major parties both at the beginning and at the end of the 2015 campaign were measured. Following Smith, the measurement of party brand entailed asking respondents how well five adjectives (honest, exciting, competent, charming, and tough) described the major parties. The responses were aggregated within a party brand index calculated for each party. Solid and converted NDPers would potentially hold a more favourable image of the NDP brand than lost and anti-NDPers.

To test these hypotheses, I used multinomial logistic regression to consider the impacts of all of these independent variables simultaneously on whether a voter was a solid, converted, lost, or anti-NDPer. Importantly, all of the variables are contained in the models presented below, unlike the analysis in the previous chapter, in which blocks of variables were loaded on top of one another. The results of the full multinomial logit model containing all of the variables and using anti-NDPer as the base outcome in the ROC and lost NDPer as the base outcome in Quebec are contained in Web Appendix 2. Unfortunately, multinomial logit models are difficult to interpret in their raw form. So I calculated the average marginal effects of the different variables on each of the possible outcomes – being a solid, converted, lost, or anti-NDPer. All of the marginal effects significant at the $p \leq$ .05 level are reported in Figures 7.5 to 7.12. Marginal effects are useful because they illustrate the extent to which a voter possessing certain characteristics and holding certain opinions leads to an increase or a decrease in the probability that the voter is a solid, converted, lost, or anti-NDPer. All of the variables for the models below were coded on a scale of 0 to 1. As such, the marginal effects in Figures 7.5 to 7.12 can be interpreted as illustrating the average marginal effect of moving from 0 to 1 for each independent variable on the probability that the voter is a solid, converted, lost, or anti-NDPer when all of the other variables in the model are held at their means. For instance, voters in the rest of Canada reporting that they did not have a religion increased the probability of being a solid NDPer by 2.1 points. Similarly, voters in francophone Quebec reporting that they did not have a religion decreased the probability of being an anti-NDPer by 7.2 points.

Solid NDPers: The Party's Loyal Base

Figure 7.5 paints a portrait of loyal NDP supporters who had their confidence shaken in their party during the campaign in 2015. These voters stuck with the party and voted for it, but they appeared to have lost some of their

FIGURE 7.5

Significant average marginal effects on the probability of being a solid NDPer in the ROC, 2015 federal election

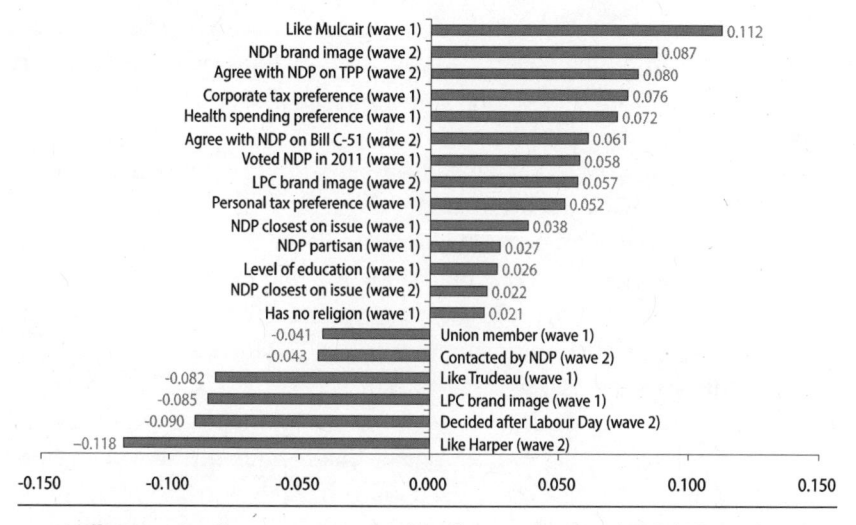

Like Mulcair (wave 1)	0.112
NDP brand image (wave 2)	0.087
Agree with NDP on TPP (wave 2)	0.080
Corporate tax preference (wave 1)	0.076
Health spending preference (wave 1)	0.072
Agree with NDP on Bill C-51 (wave 2)	0.061
Voted NDP in 2011 (wave 1)	0.058
LPC brand image (wave 2)	0.057
Personal tax preference (wave 1)	0.052
NDP closest on issue (wave 1)	0.038
NDP partisan (wave 1)	0.027
Level of education (wave 1)	0.026
NDP closest on issue (wave 2)	0.022
Has no religion (wave 1)	0.021
Union member (wave 1)	-0.041
Contacted by NDP (wave 2)	-0.043
Like Trudeau (wave 1)	-0.082
LPC brand image (wave 1)	-0.085
Decided after Labour Day (wave 2)	-0.090
Like Harper (wave 2)	-0.118

NOTE: Effects are significant at $p \leq .05$; number of wave in brackets behind name of variable, 1 = first wave and 2 = second wave.
SOURCE: 2015 Canadian Federal Election Panel Survey on Social Democracy.

enthusiasm. Reflecting the strength of the Liberal Party campaign, the esteem in which these solid NDPers held Trudeau and the Liberals increased even if they did not go as far as to vote LPC.

Solid NDPers in the ROC displayed characteristics that could be considered typical of long-time supporters of a political party. They were likely to have voted NDP in the previous election and to have made up their minds about supporting the party before the election started or early in the campaign. They were unlikely to be contacted by the NDP during the campaign period, a finding that could be explained by the party focusing its resources on contacting undecided voters.

In terms of partisanship, solid NDPers were likely to identify with the party in the first wave of the survey, but identifying with the party in the second wave did not have a statistically significant impact on being a solid NDPer. Bivariate statistics illustrate that the percentage of ROC solid NDPers who identified with the party dropped from 84 percent in Wave 1 to 74 percent in Wave 2, suggesting that some of them stopped being NDP partisans during the campaign. In a similar fashion, the NDP being the party closest to the voter on their most important issue had more impact on being a solid NDPer in the first wave of the survey compared with the second wave. This finding illustrates that some solid NDPers were no longer confident that their party was closest to them on their most important issue by the end of the campaign. Interestingly, the issues that rose in importance for solid NDPers between the beginning and the end of the campaign were the economy, health care, and electoral reform.

Feelings about party leaders ended up being more important for solid NDPers in the ROC at the beginning of the campaign compared with the end. Liking Mulcair and disliking Trudeau at the beginning of the campaign were among the most powerful indicators of being a solid NDPer in the ROC. However, by the end of the campaign, liking neither Trudeau nor liking Mulcair was a statistically significant indicator of being a solid NDPer. This finding does not mean that Trudeau was better liked among solid NDPers than Mulcair by the end of the campaign. Mulcair was rated at 9.11 out of 10 on the dislike-like scale at the beginning of the campaign for the solid NDPer category, but that number had fallen to 8.43 out of 10 by the end of the campaign. Reflective of the growing popularity of Trudeau throughout the campaign, the Liberal leader went the opposite way – his score rose from 6.20 out of 10 to 7.28 out of 10 among solid NDPers. So, even among the NDP's most loyal supporters, Trudeau gained popularity while Mulcair lost popularity. Indeed, by the end of the campaign, solid NDPers actually liked Trudeau more than converted NDPers. As for Harper, solid NDPers held him in even lower regard by the end of the campaign compared with the start, but this dislike did not seem to translate into any growth in popularity for Mulcair among this category of voters.

The NDP brand did show minor improvement between the start and the end of the campaign for solid NDPers – it went from a score of 3.67 out of 5 to 3.73 out of 5. Hence, the NDP brand from the postelection survey is a statistically significant indicator of being a solid NDPer. However, in the ROC, the LPC brand went from a negative indicator to a positive indicator of being a solid NDPer by the end of the campaign. Between the start and the end of the campaign, the brand score of the Liberals among ROC solid NDPers improved from 2.34 out of 5 to 2.90 out of 5. In particular, solid NDPers found the LPC to be much more "exciting," "competent," and "charming" at the end of the campaign compared with the start – a finding that confirms Jeffrey's (2017, 141–43) observations of the effective rebranding of the party following the difficulties of the Dion and Ignatieff years.

Although sociodemographic characteristics were not predominant in determining whether a voter fell into the solid NDPer category, Figure 7.5 does present some interesting findings. Given that past election studies have shown atheists to be more likely to vote NDP (Kay and Perrella 2012, 127; Wilkins-Laflamme 2016), it is not surprising that they were overrepresented among solid NDPers. Striking is that what might be termed the "working-class basis" of the NDP's solid support in 2015 did not seem to be strong. Indeed, union members were 4.1 percent less likely to be solid NDPers, and having a university degree increased the probability of being a solid NDPer by 2.6 percent, whereas income level was not significant.

The decision of NDP operatives to stress "NDP issues" such as the environment, social programs, and free trade as a way to counteract the Liberals' surge in popularity near the end of the campaign perhaps helped the party to shore up the support of loyal voters. Figure 7.5 illustrates that the NDP's strident opposition to Bill C-51 and the TPP appeared to resonate with core supporters in English Canada, as did its stances on raising corporate taxes and increasing health care spending. Although agreement with the NDP's pharmacare proposal was not significant in the model that produced Figure 7.5, the plan garnered enthusiastic support among solid NDPers, with approximately 85 percent indicating that they were "very favourable" to it. One exception should be noted here. Although the NDP promised during the 2015 campaign that it would not increase personal taxes, support for raising them (the Liberals proposed a tax on the wealthiest 1 percent of Canadians) was an indication of being a solid NDPer.

Figure 7.6 shows that solid NDPers in francophone Quebec displayed similar characteristics to solid NDPers in the ROC. Although they ultimately voted for the NDP, they appeared to be lukewarm toward the party by the end of the campaign, and they had gained an appreciation for the Liberals and their strong campaign.

At the outset of the campaign in 2015, solid NDPers in francophone Quebec displayed a high probability of liking Mulcair, being an NDP partisan, having a positive impression of the party brand, and reporting that the party was the closest to their position on their most important issue. They were also more likely to have made their minds up to vote for the NDP either before the campaign started or before Labour Day, and they had a

Figure 7.6

Significant average marginal effects on the probability of being a solid NDPer in francophone Quebec, 2015 federal election

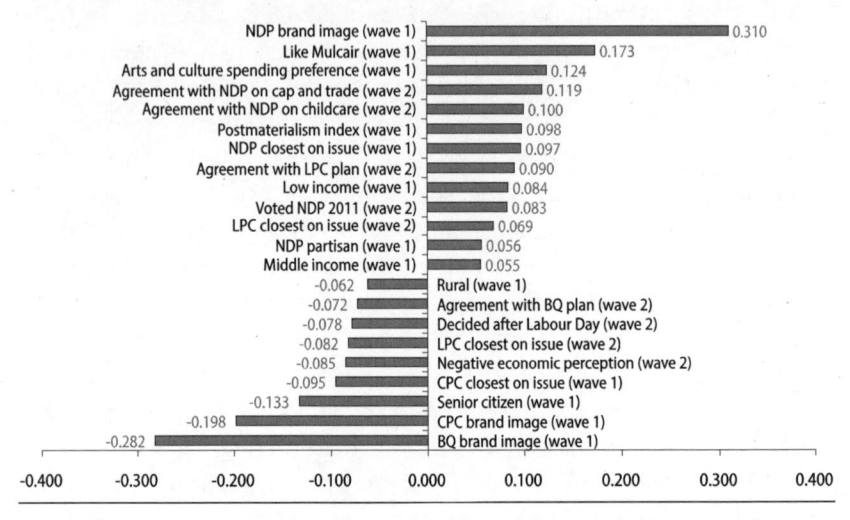

NDP brand image (wave 1)	0.310
Like Mulcair (wave 1)	0.173
Arts and culture spending preference (wave 1)	0.124
Agreement with NDP on cap and trade (wave 2)	0.119
Agreement with NDP on childcare (wave 2)	0.100
Postmaterialism index (wave 1)	0.098
NDP closest on issue (wave 1)	0.097
Agreement with LPC plan (wave 2)	0.090
Low income (wave 1)	0.084
Voted NDP 2011 (wave 2)	0.083
LPC closest on issue (wave 2)	0.069
NDP partisan (wave 1)	0.056
Middle income (wave 1)	0.055
Rural (wave 1)	-0.062
Agreement with BQ plan (wave 2)	-0.072
Decided after Labour Day (wave 2)	-0.078
LPC closest on issue (wave 2)	-0.082
Negative economic perception (wave 2)	-0.085
CPC closest on issue (wave 1)	-0.095
Senior citizen (wave 1)	-0.133
CPC brand image (wave 1)	-0.198
BQ brand image (wave 1)	-0.282

NOTE: Effects are significant at $p \leq .05$; number of wave in brackets behind name of variable, 1 = first wave and 2 = second wave.
SOURCE: 2015 Canadian Federal Election Panel Survey on Social Democracy.

high likelihood of having voted NDP in 2011. When it came to their opinions of the NDP's opponents in the pre-election survey, they were likely to have negative views of the BQ brand and the CPC brand and unlikely to report that the CPC or the LPC was the party closest to their position on their most important issue.

However, there is evidence that solid NDPers in francophone Quebec were less sure of their party by the end of the campaign and more attracted to the Liberals even if they did not vote for them. Claiming NDP partisanship, liking Mulcair, having the NDP as the party closest on one's most important issue, and holding a positive view of the NDP brand were significant indicators of being a solid NDPer in Wave 1 but not in Wave 2. Bivariate statistics allow us to discern the changes that took place. The percentage of solid NDPers who identified with the NDP dropped slightly over the campaign from 60 percent to 54 percent. At the same time, Mulcair's dislikelike thermometer for solid NDPers in francophone Quebec dropped from 8.31 out of 10 to 7.75 out of 10, whereas Trudeau's score improved from 4.22

out of 10 to 5.85 out of 10 – confirming that the rise of the Liberal leader's popularity was not confined to English Canada. Duceppe's and Harper's dislike-like thermometers among solid NDPers were relatively the same at the start and end of the campaign. Solid NDPers had a slightly more negative view of the NDP brand at the end of the campaign (3.61 out of 5) versus at the beginning (3.78 out of 5). Conversely, they had a more positive view of the LPC brand at the end of the campaign (3.11 out of 5) compared with the start (2.52 out of 5). The elements of the NDP brand that declined the most for solid NDPers in francophone Quebec over the campaign were seeing the party as "exciting," "charming," and "tough." Interestingly, these were the same elements of the LPC brand that increased the most during the campaign for solid NDPers in francophone Quebec, an indication of the Liberals' strong campaign.

One dramatic change in the attitudes of solid NDPers in francophone Quebec between Wave 1 and Wave 2 pertained to the variable of the party closest to the respondent on their most important issue. On this measure, 70 percent of solid NDPers reported that the NDP was the closest to their position on their most important issue in Wave 1 compared with 49 percent in Wave 2. Hence, this was a statistically significant indicator of being a solid NDPer only in Wave 1. The situation was much different for the Liberals and provides evidence for Jeffrey's (2016, 77–79) assertion that the LPC platform – "progressive but credible" – was designed to attract soft NDP voters. Only 2 percent of solid NDPers reported that the LPC was closest to them on their most important issue in Wave 1, but that grew to 21 percent in Wave 2. With the exception of the environment becoming slightly more important for solid NDPers, the issues among this category of voters remained relatively the same between the start and the end of the campaign, with growing the economy, improving social programs, and displacing Harper being top-of-mind issues. There is also some interesting evidence that solid NDPers in francophone Quebec were attracted to the LPC plan. Although agreeing with the NDP plan was not a statistically significant indicator of being a solid NDPer, a voter who fully agreed with the LPC plan (i.e., gave it a 10 on the 0 to 10 agreement scale) was 9 points more likely to be a solid NDPer than a voter who completely disagreed with the LPC plan (i.e., gave it a 0 on the 0 to 10 agreement scale). Indeed, the mean of solid NDPers' agreement with the LPC plan, 6.93 out of 10, was not far from their agreement with the NDP plan, 7.37 out of 10. It appears that loyal NDPers were only slightly more impressed with the NDP platform compared with the LPC platform.

When it came to issues and underlying values, there was a basic congruence between the NDP and its loyal supporters in francophone Quebec. An important indicator of being a solid NDPer there was a high level of postmaterialism, which corresponded with the NDP's feminist stance, environmentalism, and social liberalism. Perhaps related to their high level of postmaterialism, solid NDPers in francophone Quebec were likely to support the NDP's ideas for a national child-care program (which facilitated women's entry into the workforce), a cap-and-trade system to reduce greenhouse gas emissions, and a preference for spending more on arts and culture. However, there might have been one minor difference between the NDP and its loyal supporters in francophone Quebec. In contrast to NDP commercials during the 2015 campaign about the economic downturn under the Conservative government, solid NDPers were actually less likely to be pessimistic about the state of Canada's economy. Approximately half of them believed that the economy had "stayed the same" or "improved a little."

Finally, in terms of sociodemographics, solid NDPers in francophone Quebec were less likely to be senior citizens, more likely to be between forty-five and sixty-four, and more likely to live in the inner city core of an urban area than live in a rural area. Also, there did seem to be a "working-class basis" for solid NDPers in francophone Quebec compared with English Canada. In Quebec, compared with high-income francophones, low-income francophones were 8.4 percent more likely to be solid NDPers, and middle-income francophones were 5.5 percent more likely to be solid NDPers. Neither level of education nor union membership was significant.

Converted NDPers: The Party's "Swing" Voters

It would be unfair to say that the NDP converted no voters to its cause in the ROC during the 2015 election. As shown above, about 12 percent of the ROC electorate who were probably or considering voting NDP in mid-August actually did so on election day. It is therefore interesting to examine this slice of the English Canadian electorate who were not completely sure about voting NDP at the start of the campaign but had warmed up to the party by the end – that is, the voters who swung the NDP's way.

Figure 7.7 illustrates several interesting characteristics of converted NDPers in the ROC. Perhaps because atheists fell more into the solid NDPer category, not having a religion had a slightly negative effect on being a converted NDPer. Aside from religion, no other sociodemographic variable was found to have a statistically significant impact on whether a voter was

FIGURE 7.7

Significant average marginal effects on the probability of being a converted NDPer in the ROC, 2015 federal election

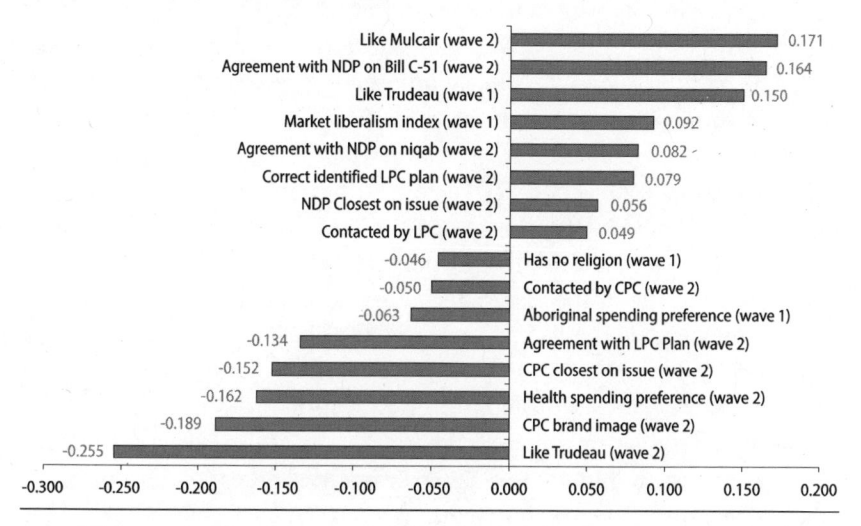

Like Mulcair (wave 2)	0.171
Agreement with NDP on Bill C-51 (wave 2)	0.164
Like Trudeau (wave 1)	0.150
Market liberalism index (wave 1)	0.092
Agreement with NDP on niqab (wave 2)	0.082
Correct identified LPC plan (wave 2)	0.079
NDP Closest on issue (wave 2)	0.056
Contacted by LPC (wave 2)	0.049
Has no religion (wave 1)	-0.046
Contacted by CPC (wave 2)	-0.050
Aboriginal spending preference (wave 1)	-0.063
Agreement with LPC Plan (wave 2)	-0.134
CPC closest on issue (wave 2)	-0.152
Health spending preference (wave 2)	-0.162
CPC brand image (wave 2)	-0.189
Like Trudeau (wave 2)	-0.255

NOTE: Effects are significant at $p \leq .05$; number of wave in brackets behind name of variable, 1 = first wave and 2 = second wave.
SOURCE: 2015 Canadian Federal Election Panel Survey on Social Democracy.

classified as a converted NDPer. Possibly reflecting the Liberals' effective ground game, which targeted soft NDP voters in English Canada (Jeffrey 2016, 63–65), those who reported having been contacted by the LPC increased their probability of being converted NDPers by 4.9 percent.

Views on party leaders were an important part of the success of the NDP among this group of voters. The defining feature of converted NDPers in the ROC was that, at the end of the campaign, they continued to like Mulcair, and their opinion of Trudeau had improved only slightly. So liking Trudeau in the second wave had a negative impact on being a converted NDPer in the ROC, and liking him in the first wave had a positive impact. Bivariate statistics illustrate this finding well. Among ROC converted NDPers, Mulcair's dislike-like thermometer was 7.69 out of 10 in August compared with 7.72 out of 10 in October. Between the start and the end of the campaign, Trudeau's dislike-like thermometer among ROC converted NDPers had climbed from 6.27 out of 10 to 6.94 out of 10. There were much larger increases in his popularity over the campaign in the solid NDPer category and, as we shall see, in the lost NDPer category. Also, there were relatively larger decreases in Mulcair's popularity in those categories. In short, the NDP was able to limit the increase in Trudeau's popularity while maintaining Mulcair's popularity in this segment of the English Canadian electorate.

Another success for the NDP among converted NDPers in the ROC was being the party closest to their most important issues at the end of the campaign. A voter who reported in the postelection survey that the NDP was closest to him or her on their most important issue increased the probability of being a converted NDPer by 5.6 percent. The most important issues for converted NDPers remained similar in both waves: the environment, the economy, the lack of democracy, and government dishonesty. And, when it came to specific wedge issues, agreeing with the NDP's position on the niqab and Bill C-51 increased the likelihood that a voter was a converted NDPer.

There is some evidence that converted NDPers in the ROC tended toward economic conservatism on measures pertaining to ideology. Strikingly, moving from the minimum to the maximum level of market liberalism increased the probability of being a converted NDPer by 9.2 percent. Also, the desire to spend less on health care and Aboriginal affairs was positively correlated with being converted NDPers. They appeared to be particularly aware of the Liberals' plan involving short-term deficits and raising taxes on the richest 1 percent of Canadians, but they did not agree with it. Whereas the mean of converted NDPers' agreement with that plan was 6.48 out of 10, the mean of solid NDPers' agreement with it was 7.00 out of 10, and the mean of lost NDPers' agreement with it was 7.42 out of 10. Although opinions on balanced budgets were not a significant indicator of being converted NDPers, my survey found that these voters were more in favour of balanced budgets than solid and lost NDPers.

Overall, the strategy adopted by NDP operatives for the 2015 campaign appeared to be effective among converted NDPers. The branding of Mulcair as safe and experienced change worked with this category of voters as they displayed a slightly improved opinion of him between the start and the end of the campaign and were less likely to have succumbed to what the *Toronto Star* dubbed "Trudeaumania 2.0" (Blatchford 2015). They trusted the NDP as the party closest to them on their most important issues. Given the NDP's insistence on a balanced budget and slowly phasing in spending on social programs, it is interesting that converted NDPers tended to be

Figure 7.8

Significant average marginal effects on the probability of being a converted NDPer in francophone Quebec, 2015 federal election

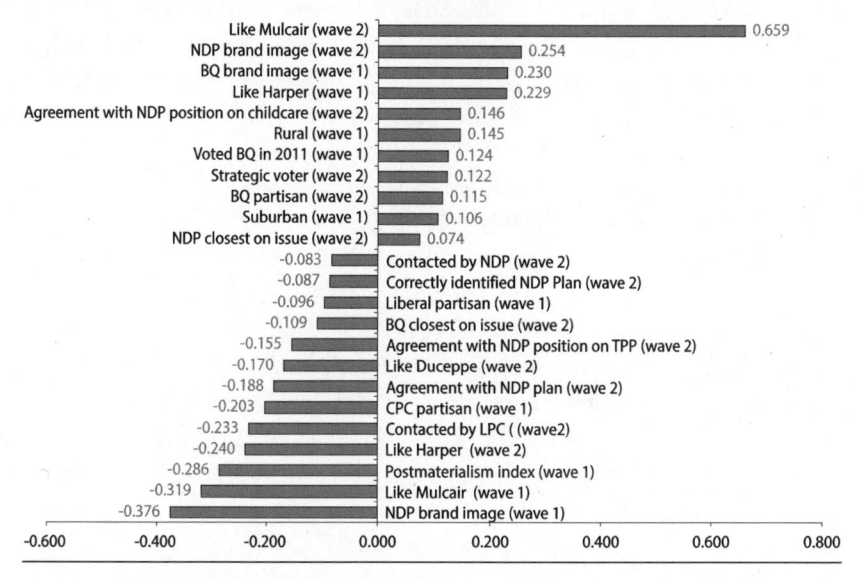

Like Mulcair (wave 2)	0.659
NDP brand image (wave 2)	0.254
BQ brand image (wave 1)	0.230
Like Harper (wave 1)	0.229
Agreement with NDP position on childcare (wave 2)	0.146
Rural (wave 1)	0.145
Voted BQ in 2011 (wave 1)	0.124
Strategic voter (wave 2)	0.122
BQ partisan (wave 2)	0.115
Suburban (wave 1)	0.106
NDP closest on issue (wave 2)	0.074
Contacted by NDP (wave 2)	-0.083
Correctly identified NDP Plan (wave 2)	-0.087
Liberal partisan (wave 1)	-0.096
BQ closest on issue (wave 2)	-0.109
Agreement with NDP position on TPP (wave 2)	-0.155
Like Duceppe (wave 2)	-0.170
Agreement with NDP plan (wave 2)	-0.188
CPC partisan (wave 1)	-0.203
Contacted by LPC ((wave2)	-0.233
Like Harper (wave 2)	-0.240
Postmaterialism index (wave 1)	-0.286
Like Mulcair (wave 1)	-0.319
NDP brand image (wave 1)	-0.376

NOTE: Effects are significant at $p \leq .05$; number of wave in brackets behind name of variable, 1 = first wave and 2 = second wave.
SOURCE: 2015 Canadian Federal Election Panel Survey on Social Democracy.

more economically conservative voters unexcited by the Liberal's deficit plan. Nonetheless, since they were impressed with the NDP's opposition to Bill C-51 and its position on the niqab at citizenship ceremonies, converted NDPers were socially liberal as well. Given that converted NDPers made up only 12 percent of the English Canadian electorate, the problem for NDP operatives was there were not enough of these socially liberal but economically conservative voters who appreciated Mulcair's leadership qualities for the party to make an electoral breakthrough.

Figure 7.8 illustrates the typical characteristics and opinions of converted NDPers in francophone Quebec. The evidence points to the conclusion that the NDP was in competition with the BQ for the support of converted NDPers.

In terms of partisanship, it is not surprising that Conservative and Liberal partisans were unlikely to be converted NDPers in francophone Quebec.

However, it is interesting that converted NDPers were likely to have a positive image of the BQ's brand in August and likely to have voted BQ in the 2011 election. Furthermore, BQ partisans in Wave 2 were 11.5 percent more likely to be converted NDPers. In fact, 24 percent of converted NDPers identified with the BQ in Wave 2, the same percentage of converted NDPers who identified themselves as New Democrats. These findings illustrate that some voters inclined toward the BQ supported the NDP by the end of the campaign in 2015.

So what convinced soft NDP voters in francophone Quebec, some of whom had affinities with the BQ, to vote NDP ultimately? Strategic voting might have been part of the story. Converted NDPers were 12 percent more likely to be strategic voters. Although the sample is small ($n = 134$), the bivariate evidence indicates that 56 percent of converted NDPers who voted strategically had the BQ as their preferred party, with 19 percent citing the Liberals, 17 percent citing the Greens, and 4 percent citing the Conservatives. Strategic voting actually helped the NDP in francophone Quebec, particularly in its competition with the BQ.

In addition to strategic voting, those who identified the NDP in the postelection survey as the party closest to them on their most important issues were 7.4 percent more likely to be converted NDPers. Indeed, bivariate statistics illustrate that 70 percent of converted NDPers in August, compared with 75 percent in October, said that the NDP was the party closest to them on their most important issues. Interestingly, the issues profile of converted NDPers between Wave 1 and Wave 2 did not change, with the economy, the environment, income inequality, and better social programs being the most popular issues.

The increase in Mulcair's popularity and the stability of the NDP brand were also important factors in increasing the probability that a voter in francophone Quebec was a converted NDPer. Although the NDP brand had become weaker among all other categories of francophone Quebec voters in my analysis, it remained stable among converted NDPers at a relatively positive rating of approximately 3.30 out of 5 in both waves of the survey. Similarly, though Mulcair's dislike-like thermometer dropped among all other categories of francophone Quebec voters in my analysis between the two waves of the survey, his rating among converted NDPers actually rose from 6.69 out of 10 to 6.95 out of 10. In contrast, the assessments of Duceppe and Harper among converted NDPers worsened from Wave 1 to Wave 2.

Finally, specific issues, sociodemographics, and voter contact were not overly important in determining whether a voter was a converted NDPer in francophone Quebec. Whereas solid NDPers were urban, converted NDPers were suburban and rural. Compared with voters living in the urban cores of Quebec's cities, those who lived in suburban areas were 10.6 percent more likely to be converted NDPers, and those who lived in rural areas were 14.5 percent more likely to be converted NDPers. This sociodemographic profile might help to explain the finding that converted NDPers in francophone Quebec were also more likely to have low levels of postmaterialism.[4] On specific issues, agreement with the NDP's promise of fifteen-dollar-a-day child care increased the probability of being a converted NDPer. However, converted NDPers comprised the category of voters in my analysis who found it the most difficult to connect the NDP with a short description of its platform (only 53 percent could do so). In any case, these voters in francophone Quebec were not particularly happy with the NDP platform, giving it a rating of 6.71 out of 10, noticeably lower than the 7.37 out of 10 among solid NDPers in francophone Quebec. There is also little evidence that a strong ground game in francophone Quebec pushed the party over the top with converted NDPers. In fact, being contacted by the NDP reduced the probability that a voter became a converted NDPer, a counterintuitive finding since one goal of contacting swing voters is to persuade them to support the party on election day.

Importantly, the NDP campaign in Quebec in 2015 was not a complete failure among francophone voters. After all, the SOM survey illustrates that converted NDPers made up roughly 20 percent of the francophone electorate. Indeed, the Liberal triumph in taking half of Quebec's seats was aided by the vulgarities of the first-past-the post system and the party's strength among allophone and anglophone voters.[5] The SOM survey shows that New Democrats actually beat Liberals among francophone voters, with just over one-quarter voting LPC and just under one-third voting NDP.

Overall, the campaign designed by NDP operatives did work with these converted NDPers in francophone Quebec. These voters, many of whom appeared to be flirting with the BQ, were attracted to the NDP through accepting strategic voting arguments, trusting the party on their top-of-mind issues, and liking the NDP-Mulcair brand. Getting these voters on side was a success of political operatives in 2015. Indeed, without these converted NDPers in francophone Quebec, the party's results in that province would have been much worse.

FIGURE 7.9

Significant average marginal effects on the probability of being an anti-NDPer in the ROC, 2015 federal election

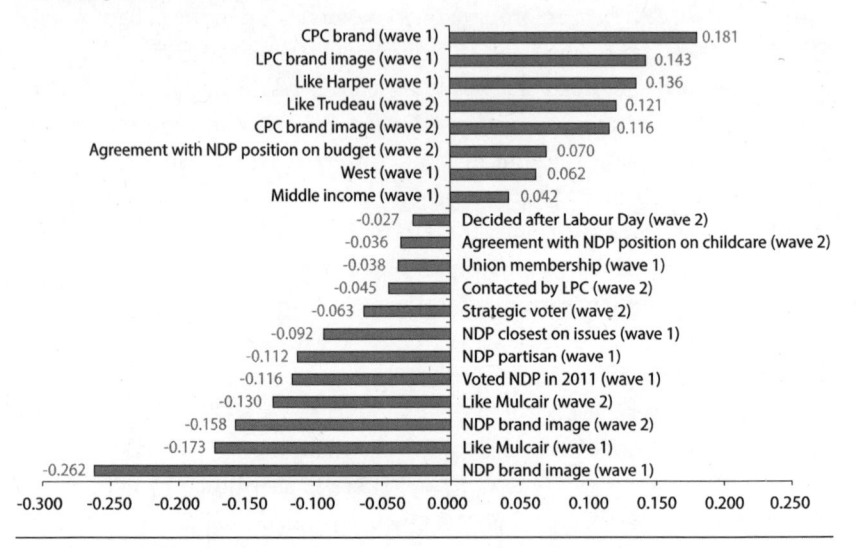

CPC brand (wave 1)	0.181
LPC brand image (wave 1)	0.143
Like Harper (wave 1)	0.136
Like Trudeau (wave 2)	0.121
CPC brand image (wave 2)	0.116
Agreement with NDP position on budget (wave 2)	0.070
West (wave 1)	0.062
Middle income (wave 1)	0.042
Decided after Labour Day (wave 2)	-0.027
Agreement with NDP position on childcare (wave 2)	-0.036
Union membership (wave 1)	-0.038
Contacted by LPC (wave 2)	-0.045
Strategic voter (wave 2)	-0.063
NDP closest on issues (wave 1)	-0.092
NDP partisan (wave 1)	-0.112
Voted NDP in 2011 (wave 1)	-0.116
Like Mulcair (wave 2)	-0.130
NDP brand image (wave 2)	-0.158
Like Mulcair (wave 1)	-0.173
NDP brand image (wave 1)	-0.262

NOTE: Effects are significant at $p \leq .05$; number of wave in brackets behind name of variable, 1 = first wave and 2 = second wave.
SOURCE: 2015 Canadian Federal Election Panel Survey on Social Democracy.

Anti-NDPers: The Party's Roadblock

Anti-NDPers made up roughly 40 percent of the English Canadian electorate, and about two-thirds voted for the Conservatives and one-third for the Liberals. These voters comprised a formidable obstacle to electoral success for the NDP. Overall, Figure 7.9 shows that disdain for the party among anti-NDPers was deep seated and well established, and the campaign devised by NDP operatives in 2015 did little to change their opinions.

In terms of sociodemographic characteristics, anti-NDPers were slightly more likely to be middle-income earners as opposed to high-income earners, live in Western Canada, and not be members of unions. These findings might reflect the Conservatives' traditional strength across the western provinces and the New Democrats' traditional weakness among non-union members (Gidengil et al., 2012, 21–24; Kay and Perrella 2012, 128–30). The finding that anti-NDPers were likely to be middle-income earners is interesting given the prevalent use of the term "middle class" by all parties during the campaign (Basen 2015) and the NDP's deliberate appeals to "middle-class families."

There is little evidence that anti-NDPers in the ROC were waiting until the end of the campaign to decide how to vote in a strategic fashion. A voter who reported having voted strategically was 6.3 percent less likely to be an anti-NDPer, and a voter who decided which party to support after Labour Day was 2.7 percent less likely to be an anti-NDPer. Rather, anti-NDPers in the ROC appeared to be dead set in August against voting for the party. In Wave 1, under 5 percent of ROC anti-NDPers reported having been NDP voters in 2011, having the party closest to them on their most important issues, and being NDP partisans. Also in Wave 1, anti-NDPers living in English Canada had a negative image of the NDP brand (1.85 out of 5) and gave a negative rating to Mulcair on his dislike-like thermometer (4.13 out of 10). Given these bivariate statistics, it is not surprising that all of these variables in Figure 7.9 are significant indicators of being an anti-NDPer.

Moreover, my survey did not find any evidence that the NDP was able to improve its standing among these voters during the 2015 campaign. The NDP's brand and Mulcair's feeling thermometer remained unchanged among ROC anti-NDPers between August and October. The NDP's plan and most of its specific issue positions were not statistically significant in determining whether voters fell into this category. There were two exceptions, though. The proposal for fifteen-dollar-a-day child care was particularly unpopular with these voters, leading to a reduction of the probability of being an anti-NDPer of 3.7 percent if one completely agreed with the plan. The only NDP policy position popular among anti-NDPers was the importance that the party placed on a balanced budget. Whereas 61 percent of anti-NDPers deemed a balanced budget "extremely important" or "quite important," only 13 percent of lost NDPers, 21 percent of converted NDPers, and 10 percent of solid NDPers thought that a balanced budget was "extremely important" or "quite important." Hence, completely agreeing with the NDP's position on the necessity of a balanced budget compared with completely disagreeing with its position increased the probability of being an anti-NDPer by 7 percent. In this sense, NDP operatives' decision to make a balanced budget pledge ended up playing to the base of the Conservatives and, to a lesser extent, that of the Liberals in the ROC, but these voters had already ruled out voting for the NDP long before the campaign even began.

FIGURE 7.10

Significant average marginal effects on the probability of being an anti-NDPer in francophone Quebec, 2015 federal election

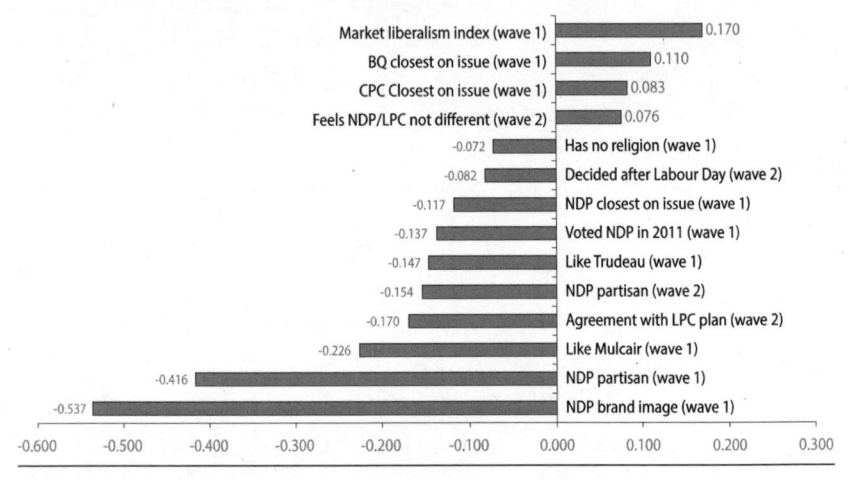

Market liberalism index (wave 1)	0.170
BQ closest on issue (wave 1)	0.110
CPC Closest on issue (wave 1)	0.083
Feels NDP/LPC not different (wave 2)	0.076
Has no religion (wave 1)	-0.072
Decided after Labour Day (wave 2)	-0.082
NDP closest on issue (wave 1)	-0.117
Voted NDP in 2011 (wave 1)	-0.137
Like Trudeau (wave 1)	-0.147
NDP partisan (wave 2)	-0.154
Agreement with LPC plan (wave 2)	-0.170
Like Mulcair (wave 1)	-0.226
NDP partisan (wave 1)	-0.416
NDP brand image (wave 1)	-0.537

NOTE: Effects are significant at $p \leq .05$; number of wave in brackets behind name of variable, 1 = first wave and 2 = second wave.
SOURCE: 2015 Canadian Federal Election Panel Survey on Social Democracy.

Indeed, Figure 7.9 depicts that the fight for the votes of anti-NDPers in the ROC was between the Conservatives and the Liberals. In particular, the brands of these two parties and their leaders were important. The Conservatives had a strong brand among this category of voters at the beginning and the end of the campaign. In fact, their brand among anti-NDPers improved slightly from 2.70 out of 5 in August to 2.86 out of 5 in October. In terms of leadership, Harper's dislike-like thermometer among this category remained almost unchanged from August to October at approximately 6.5 out of 10. Reflecting a strong campaign, the Liberal brand and the Liberal leader rose in popularity from August to October among ROC anti-NDPers. As we can see, the NDP was never really "in the game" when it came to this category of voters. Among them, the campaign in 2015 was more a story of the Conservatives fighting off the surging Liberals as opposed to the New Democrats gaining ground with voters who had been hostile toward it.

Considering the NDP's dominant position in francophone Quebec at the beginning of the 2015 campaign, the anti-NDPer category made up only 24 percent of the electorate. These voters mostly ended up voting for the

Conservative Party and the Bloc Québécois, though one-quarter did vote Liberal. Figure 7.10 illustrates the characteristics and opinions of these voters.

In terms of sociodemographics, anti-NDPers in francophone Quebec were less likely not to have a religion, but no other sociodemographic variable was statistically significant. As in English Canada, anti-NDPers in francophone Quebec were early deciders who displayed a noticeable dislike for the NDP at the beginning of the campaign. A voter who decided which party to support after Labour Day was 8.2 percent less likely to be an anti-NDPer. We can also see that a number of the variables from Wave 1 are significant predictors that a voter will be an anti-NDPer: having a negative image of the NDP brand, not being an NDP partisan, disliking Mulcair, reporting having voted against the NDP in 2011, and not having the party closest on one's most important issue. Given the NDP's social democratic ideology, it is not surprising that these voters also displayed high levels of market liberalism. Moving from 0 out of 5 to 5 out of 5 on the market liberalism index increased the probability that a voter would be an anti-NDPer by 53 percent. There is little evidence in Figure 7.10 that opinions of the NDP among anti-NDPers in francophone Quebec improved during the campaign. The party's issue positions and platform seemed to do little to bring these voters on board. Rather, the competition for these anti-NDPers played out mostly between the CPC and the BQ. These anti-NDPers were likely to be unimpressed with Trudeau in Wave 1 and to disagree with the Liberals' plan in Wave 2. Yet they felt close to the BQ and the CPC on their most important issues in Wave 1, leading to their eventual support for those parties. Such findings indicate the underappreciated effectiveness of the BQ and the CPC campaigns in francophone Quebec and confirm Bélanger and Nadeau's (2016, 127–30) assertion that the "red wave" is an inappropriate way to refer to the 2015 election in Quebec.

Lost NDPers: The Party's Heartbreak

Although NDP operatives would have been happy to gain ground in 2015 among anti-NDPers, these voters were never really targeted by the party. Rather, 36 percent of the English Canadian electorate and 41 percent of the francophone Quebec electorate that I categorize as lost NDPers caused the party's heartbreak on election night. If NDP operatives had found a way to convince more of the voters who were certainly, probably, or considering voting for the party in August actually to do so in October, then the result of the 2015 election would have been the first federal NDP government in

FIGURE 7.11

Significant average marginal effects on the probability of being a lost NDPer in the ROC, 2015 federal election

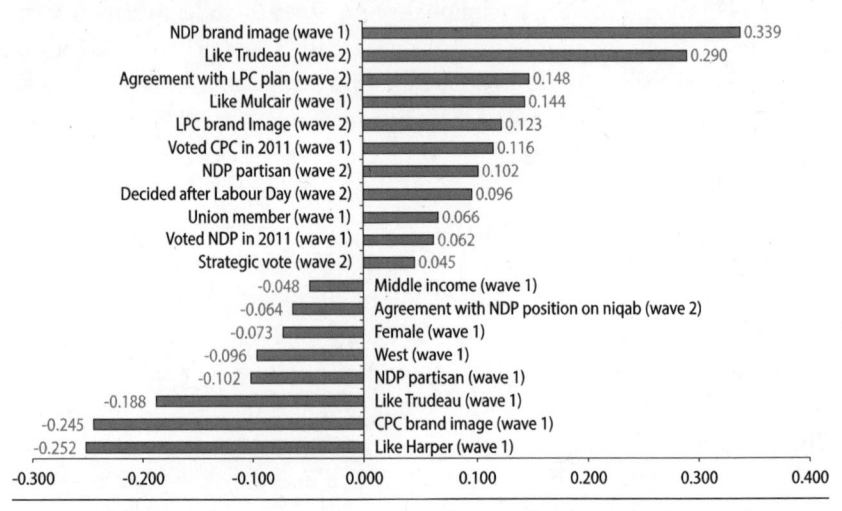

NDP brand image (wave 1)	0.339
Like Trudeau (wave 2)	0.290
Agreement with LPC plan (wave 2)	0.148
Like Mulcair (wave 1)	0.144
LPC brand image (wave 2)	0.123
Voted CPC in 2011 (wave 1)	0.116
NDP partisan (wave 2)	0.102
Decided after Labour Day (wave 2)	0.096
Union member (wave 1)	0.066
Voted NDP in 2011 (wave 1)	0.062
Strategic vote (wave 2)	0.045
Middle income (wave 1)	-0.048
Agreement with NDP position on niqab (wave 2)	-0.064
Female (wave 1)	-0.073
West (wave 1)	-0.096
NDP partisan (wave 1)	-0.102
Like Trudeau (wave 1)	-0.188
CPC brand image (wave 1)	-0.245
Like Harper (wave 1)	-0.252

NOTE: Effects are significant at $p \leq .05$; number of wave in brackets behind name of variable, 1 = first wave and 2 = second wave.
SOURCE: 2015 Canadian Federal Election Panel Survey on Social Democracy.

Canadian history. Instead, these voters turned their backs on the party because of a weak campaign run by the NDP and strong campaigns run by its opponents, particularly the Liberals.

The first notable feature of Figure 7.11 is the disdain of English Canadian lost NDPers for Harper and the CPC brand at the beginning of the campaign. In Wave 1, this category of ROC voters rated Harper 2.03 out of 10 on the dislike-like scale, and the mean of the CPC brand was 1.75 out of 5, even if some of them had voted Conservative four years earlier. A voter who liked Harper at 10 out of 10 compared with a voter who liked Harper at 0 out of 10 in Wave 1 was 25.2 percent less likely to be a lost NDPer. Similarly, a voter who rated the CPC brand at 5 out of 5 compared with a voter who rated the CPC brand at 0 out of 5 in Wave 1 was 24.5 percent more likely to be a lost NDPer. This finding is not surprising considering that the NDP "lost" these English Canadian voters overwhelmingly to the LPC and not the CPC. These lost NDPers clearly thought that it was "time for a change" of the federal government, and the effective campaign run by the Liberals convinced them that such a change could be accomplished by voting LPC.

The sociodemographic groups in English Canada more likely to be lost NDPers are fascinating. Overall, these voters tended to be male, high-income earners, union members, and from Ontario – groups whom NDP operatives had identified as Layton Liberals in the 2011 election. Despite the official affiliation of several Canadian unions with the NDP, union members were 6.6 percent more likely than non-union members to be lost NDPers. My survey illustrates that 50 percent of union members in English Canada were lost NDPers compared with 34 percent of non-union members. Also, 39 percent of men and 34 percent of women in English Canada were lost NDPers. Similarly, 37 percent of high-income earners in English Canada were lost NDPers compared with 33 percent of middle-income earners. Given that the NDP held on to its potential voters better in Western Canada than elsewhere, being from Western Canada as opposed to living in Ontario reduced the probability that a voter was a lost NDPer by 9.6 percent.

There is solid evidence that lost NDPers had some attachment to the party at the beginning of the campaign but were late deciders who generally voted strategically for the Liberals. Almost half of lost NDPers reported having voted for the party in 2011. NDP partisans in 2015 comprised about 18 percent of the ROC electorate in both the pre-election survey and the post-election survey. The problem for the party was that some of them decided not to vote for it. Indeed, 15 percent of lost NDPers actually identified themselves as NDP partisans at the end of the campaign. So in Figure 7.11 we can see that both NDP voters in 2011 and NDP partisans in Wave 2 in 2015 were likely lost NDPers.

The probability of being a lost NDPer increased by almost 10 percent if one was a late decider and by 4.5 percent if one was a strategic voter. The sample was small for strategic voters in this category ($n = 343$). The NDP was the preferred party of approximately 65 percent of lost NDPers who were strategic voters, whereas only 25 percent cited the Greens, 6 percent cited the Liberals, and 3 percent cited the Conservatives as their preferred party. Again I was hampered by a small sample size ($n = 218$). However, if we look at English Canadian strategic voters who fell into the lost NDPer category who actually preferred the NDP as opposed to the party that they voted for, 92 percent voted Liberal. Clearly, strategic voting hurt the NDP in this important category of ROC voters as the Liberal campaign persuaded strategic voters to support the LPC as the campaign progressed.

What is interesting about these strategic voters, and all strategic voters in my survey, is that they did not vote solely based on an evaluation of which party was best situated to win in their local riding. In Wave 2, strategic voters in English Canada were asked if they did not vote for their preferred party because they thought that it "could not win the election nationally, because you felt they could not win in your own local riding, both, or for another reason?" Only 30 percent of strategic voters in English Canada responded that they did not support their preferred party because they thought that it could not win in their own riding. Another 40 percent stated that it was both national and local considerations, 10 percent stated that it was only national considerations, and 20 percent stated that it was "another reason." So clearly the reporting of horse-race national polls and feelings about how the national race was shaping up influenced strategic voters in English Canada. This finding confirms that NDP operatives were logical in their goal of setting up the media narrative of a two-way race between Conservatives and New Democrats at the end of the campaign in 2015. My survey also confirms that the Liberal campaign was effective in capitalizing on its growing momentum as reported in national public domain polls as the campaign closed to attract strategic voters to abandon the New Democrats as a way of ousting the Harper Conservatives.

Leadership and brand had a larger impact on being a lost NDPer in the ROC than variables related to ideology, issues, and platforms. Variables related to a voter's underlying values or spending and taxing preferences were not statistically significant. Still, issues and platforms were not completely unimportant. The NDP's position on the niqab slightly hurt the party among ROC lost NDPers. Figure 7.11 shows that a voter who completely disagreed with the party on the niqab issue was 6 percent more likely to be a lost NDPer. Also, a voter who completely agreed with the Liberal platform was approximately 15 percent more likely to be a lost NDPer than a voter who completely disagreed with it – evidence that the platform resonated with this key group of swing voters in English Canada. Agreement with the NDP platform had no statistically significant effect on being a lost NDPer. In fact, the NDP platform as constructed by political operatives was not as popular as the LPC platform among lost NDPers. The LPC platform had an agreement rating among ROC lost NDPers of 7.42 out of 10 compared with 6.07 out of 10 for the NDP platform. Also, none of the wedge issues on which NDP operatives chose to focus the campaign had a statistically significant impact on being a lost NDPer in English Canada, nor did having the NDP as the party closest to one on their most important issue. The issues that party operatives decided to put at the forefront of the campaign simply did not resonate with voters in English Canada who hesitated between the New Democrats and the Liberals.

As mentioned, the larger problem for NDP operatives, beyond the party's platform and the wedge issues that they chose to emphasize, ended up being leadership and brand. Figure 7.11 illustrates that ROC lost NDPers were excited about the New Democrats and Mulcair in August but were excited about the Liberals and Trudeau in October after witnessing the effective LPC campaign. Both bivariate and multivariate statistics bear out this conclusion. Rating Trudeau at 10 out of 10 on the dislike-like feeling thermometer in August decreased the probability of being a lost NDPer by 18.8 percent, whereas rating him at 10 out of 10 in October increased the probability by 29 percent. Put into bivariate statistics, the mean of lost NDPers' rating of Trudeau rose from 7.18 out of 10 at the beginning of the campaign to 8.30 out of 10 at the end. In contrast, Mulcair's dislike-like thermometer sank among lost NDPers in English Canada from 7.52 out of 10 in August to 6.99 out of 10 in October. The brand variables tell a similar story. Between the start and the end of the campaign, the NDP brand weakened from 3.01 out of 5 to 2.90 out of 5 among lost NDPers in the ROC, whereas the LPC brand strengthened from 2.85 out of 5 to 3.28 out of 5 among these voters.

Reflecting the LPC's strong campaign focused on Trudeau's youth and energy (Clarke et al., 2017; Jeffrey 2016, 72–77), the party brand strengthened the most in terms of being "exciting" and "charming," whereas the NDP brand weakened the most in terms of being "exciting," "charming," and "tough." So we can see in Figure 7.11 that moving from 0 out of 5 to 5 out of 5 on the NDP's brand index in August increased the probability of being a lost NDPer by 33.9 percent but that the NDP's brand index in October was not found to be a statistically significant indicator of being a lost NDPer in English Canada. Maintaining momentum and excitement were definitely problems for NDP operatives as the 2015 campaign headed into the home stretch.

To win the government in 2015, the NDP needed francophone Quebec voters to maintain their tradition of bloc voting for one party that stretches back to the first federal elections following Confederation (see Gagnon and Boucher 2017). A repetition of the NDP's results in Quebec in the 2011 election was the critical foundation on which any NDP government would have to be built. The party had the ability to construct such a bloc of francophone Quebec voters at the beginning of the campaign if it could convince a lion's share of its potential supporters to vote NDP on election day. As it turned

FIGURE 7.12

Significant average marginal effects on the probability of being a lost NDPer in francophone Quebec, 2015 federal election

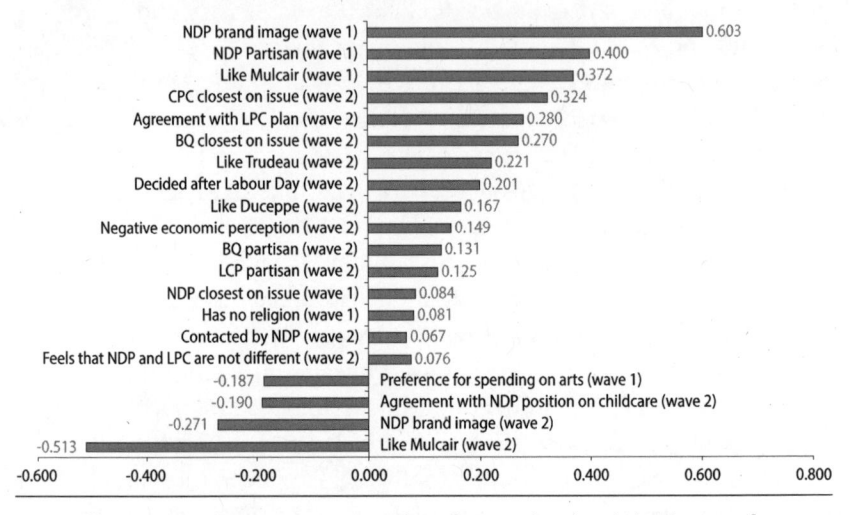

NDP brand image (wave 1)	0.603
NDP Partisan (wave 1)	0.400
Like Mulcair (wave 1)	0.372
CPC closest on issue (wave 2)	0.324
Agreement with LPC plan (wave 2)	0.280
BQ closest on issue (wave 2)	0.270
Like Trudeau (wave 2)	0.221
Decided after Labour Day (wave 2)	0.201
Like Duceppe (wave 2)	0.167
Negative economic perception (wave 2)	0.149
BQ partisan (wave 2)	0.131
LCP partisan (wave 2)	0.125
NDP closest on issue (wave 1)	0.084
Has no religion (wave 1)	0.081
Contacted by NDP (wave 2)	0.067
Feels that NDP and LPC are not different (wave 2)	0.076
Preference for spending on arts (wave 1)	-0.187
Agreement with NDP position on childcare (wave 2)	-0.190
NDP brand image (wave 2)	-0.271
Like Mulcair (wave 2)	-0.513

NOTE: Effects are significant at $p \leq .05$; number of wave in brackets behind name of variable, 1 = first wave and 2 = second wave.
SOURCE: 2015 Canadian Federal Election Panel Survey on Social Democracy.

out, 41 percent of the francophone Quebec electorate ended up being lost NDPers – they were certainly, probably, or considering voting NDP at the start of the campaign but eventually voted for another party. Unlike in English Canada, where lost NDPers went largely to the Liberals, lost NDPers in francophone Quebec voted LPC or BQ and to a lesser extent CPC. This finding reinforces the view of a "rainbow coloured Quebec" in the 2015 election characterized by the fragmentation of voters' support among four parties as opposed to following the tradition of voting for a single party (Bélanger and Nadeau 2016; Gagnon and Boucher 2017). Figure 7.12 illustrates which characteristics and opinions of francophone Quebec voters ultimately pulled them in three directions and away from voting as a bloc for the New Democrats.

Sociodemographic characteristics, contact by the NDP, values, and spending and taxing preferences do not appear to have been important determinants of being a lost NDPer in francophone Quebec. One exception is that having no religion, normally a characteristic that would attract voters to the NDP, increased the probability of being a lost NDPer in francophone

Quebec by 8.1 percent. Another exception is that a preference for more spending on arts and culture was not prevalent among lost NDPers – they preferred less spending or the same amount of spending in this area. They did report being contacted more by the NDP than by the CPC, BQ, or LPC. However, reflecting the lack of impact that voter contact can have on vote choice, contact by the NDP actually made these voters more likely to support its opponents.

In francophone Quebec, lost NDPers split off in three directions partly because the NDP had lost momentum by the end of the campaign. Indeed, deciding after Labour Day which party to support increased the probability of a francophone voter in Quebec becoming a lost NDPer by 20 percent. Rating Mulcair at 10 out of 10 on the dislike-like feeling thermometer compared with 0 out of 10 meant that the probability of a voter at the start of the campaign being a lost NDPer increased by 37.2 percent. Rating Mulcair at 10 out of 10 compared with 0 out of 10 meant that the probability of a voter at the end of the campaign being a lost NDPer decreased by 37 percent. Bivariate statistics clarify this finding. Among lost NDPers in francophone Quebec, Mulcair's likeability decreased from a positive 6.48 out of 10 in August to a neutral 5.18 out of 10 in October. Reflective of the effective campaigns run by the LPC and the BQ, both Trudeau's and Duceppe's ratings on the dislike-like thermometer increased among this group of voters in Wave 1 compared with Wave 2. Trudeau's rating shot up from 4.41 out of 10 to 6.01 out of 10, and Duceppe's rating rose from 5.12 out of 10 to 5.56 out of 10. So the likelihood of being a lost NDPer in Quebec increased with a voter's ratings of Trudeau and Duceppe in the postelection survey. Confirming the popularity of the Liberal platform noted by Jeffrey (2016, 77–79), lost NDPers in francophone Quebec were also impressed with the Liberal platform. A voter who rated agreement with the Liberal plan at 10 out of 10 was 28 percent more likely to be a lost NDPer than a voter who rated agreement at 0 out of 10. Indeed, bivariate statistics confirm that lost NDPers agreed with the Liberal platform at 6.93 out of 10 compared with the NDP platform at 6.65 out of 10.

A similar situation emerges with the variables measuring the party that voters held to be closest to them on their most important issue and the variables concerning party identification. Having the NDP as the party closest to a voter on their most important issue in August increased the probability of being a lost NDPer in francophone Quebec by 8.4 percent. However, my survey does uncover some evidence of the effectiveness of both the BQ and the CPC campaigns in Quebec. Having the CPC or the BQ as the party closest to the voter in October increased the probability of being a lost NDPer by 32 percent and 13 percent, respectively. Using bivariate statistics, we can see that 25 percent of lost NDPers reported having the NDP closest to them on their most important issue in August compared with just 3 percent in October. On the other hand, the percentage of lost NDPers who reported that either the CPC or the BQ was closest to them on their most important issue was higher in October than in August. On top-of-mind issues, the CPC and the BQ had gained considerable ground on the NDP. These concerns for lost NDPers in both Wave 1 and Wave 2 were the economy and, to a much lesser extent, the environment and sovereignty. Losing the confidence of these voters on the economy (a key issue for the CPC in the 2015 campaign) was critical for the NDP considering that lost NDPers in francophone Quebec were likely to think that the economy was getting worse.

In terms of party identification, the percentage of the francophone Quebec electorate identifying as New Democrats dropped only slightly from 17 percent to 16 percent from Wave 1 to Wave 2. However, the decrease of voters who identified as New Democrats was acute in the lost NDPer category. Whereas 15 percent of them identified as New Democrats in Wave 1, only 7 percent of them did so in Wave 2. Conversely, the LPC and the BQ increased their percentages of partisans in this category of voters. These parties gained partisans in this crucial slice of francophone Quebec during the 2015 campaign, whereas the NDP lost partisans.

As in English Canada, there was a decline in the NDP brand in francophone Quebec during the campaign that appeared to have an impact on whether voters became lost NDPers. Voters who rated the NDP at 5 out of 5 on the brand index in Wave 1 were 60 percent more likely to be lost NDPers, whereas voters who gave the same rating in Wave 2 were 27 percent less likely to be lost NDPers. This finding reflects the bivariate statistics that the NDP brand among lost NDPers in francophone Quebec weakened from 3.20 out of 5 to 2.92 out of 5 between August and October. In particular, lost NDPers saw the NDP brand as less exciting, charming, and tough than at the beginning of the campaign. Simultaneously, the brands of three of the parties competing with the NDP in francophone Quebec strengthened, reflecting the effectiveness of their campaigns.

Finally, as in English Canada, NDP operatives were unable to construct wedge issues in francophone Quebec between the New Democrats and the Liberals that could push voters away from supporting one of the NDP's closest ideological competitors. An interesting finding in Figure 7.12 stems from the following question posed to respondents: "During the recent federal election campaign, did you find that there were major differences, minor differences, or no differences at all between the Liberals and the NDP?" In francophone Quebec, voters who believed that there were minor or no differences between the New Democrats and the Liberals as opposed to major differences at the end of the campaign were 7.6 percent more likely to be lost NDPers. Since 77 percent of these voters in francophone Quebec thought that there were minor or no differences between the New Democrats and the Liberals, it is evident that NDP operatives had not done a good job of putting up barriers to prevent voters from migrating to the Liberals as the campaign progressed. Francophone Quebecers appeared to discern little difference between the Liberals and the New Democrats and therefore were susceptible to moving toward the Liberals as their momentum grew.

Losing Momentum in the NDP's Campaign in 2015

The data from my two surveys analyzed above allow for an evaluation of the campaign strategy devised by NDP operatives for the 2015 election. The disappointing results for the NDP in English Canada can be explained by the party's inability to generate excitement and momentum among lost NDPers – the roughly 36 percent of English Canadian voters who were certainly, probably, or considering voting for the NDP in August who ultimately decided to support the LPC. For the most part, these voters had an intense dislike of Stephen Harper and a very negative view of the Conservative Party of Canada in general when the campaign started. Some of these voters even had attachments to the NDP in the sense that they had voted for the party in the previous election and considered themselves to be New Democrats. Male voters, high-income earners, union members, and Ontario residents – groups prominent among "Layton Liberals" in 2011 – were well represented in the ranks of lost NDPers. Interestingly, the party did not seem to be offside with the underlying values or general policy preferences of lost NDPers in English Canada. The market liberalism and postmaterialism indices as well as spending and taxing preferences were not statistically significant predictors of being a lost NDPer. The party's ground game did not seem to play a large role either. In fact, lost NDPers in English Canada reported very similar levels of contact by the NDP and the LPC.

What happened was that agents within the NDP failed to find wedge issues that excited this important segment of the English Canadian electorate. It is telling that none of the wedge issues was statistically significant in explaining whether an English Canadian voter was a lost NDPer. Lost NDPers were indifferent to party strategists' wedge issues when making their voting decisions. Bivariate statistics reinforce this point. On three of the wedge issues (cap and trade, pharmacare, and Bill C-51), English Canadian lost NDPers mostly agreed with the party, but that agreement did not stop them from voting Liberal.[6] On child care and the Trans-Pacific Partnership, the NDP's positions were not overwhelmingly popular with lost NDPers. Roughly 50 percent of these voters were either very or somewhat favourable to the NDP's fifteen-dollar-a-day child-care plan announced a year before the election took place. The plan was neither popular enough nor fresh enough in voters' minds to swing lost NDPers to the party in the dying days of its campaign. The NDP's opposition to the TPP at the end of the campaign was not helpful with lost NDPers in English Canada because only 37 percent of them thought that the TPP was a "very bad thing" or a "bad thing." Similarly, the NDP's commitment to balanced budgets was not popular with lost NDPers, and only 38 percent of them agreed that balanced budgets were either "extremely" or "quite" important. As noted above, the stance on balanced budgets was only popular with English Canadian voters who would never consider voting for the party, whereas the stances on the TPP and Bill C-51 resonated more with loyal NDP voters in English Canada as opposed to swing voters.

While the New Democrats' wedge issues were failing to capture the imaginations of lost NDPers, the Liberals were generating excitement around their leader, party, and policies. The Liberal platform of middle-class tax cuts and short-term deficits to fund infrastructure spending was more memorable and agreeable to lost NDPers in English Canada than the New Democrat platform. Lost NDPers agreed more with the LPC platform than the NDP platform, and doing so increased the probability of being a lost NDPer. Part of the NDP's troubles with its platform might have stemmed from poor communication. Whereas 94 percent of lost NDPers in English Canada could correctly identify the Liberal platform, only 80 percent could correctly identify the NDP platform. The Liberals appeared to have a more popular platform that was communicated better.

In addition, among this segment of English Canadian voters, the popularity of Trudeau grew while the popularity of Mulcair dropped. Indeed, liking Trudeau at the end of the campaign was an important variable that increased the likelihood of being a lost NDPer. To examine Mulcair's leadership further, respondents were asked how well six positive adjectives described Mulcair in both the pre-election survey and the postelection survey. Within the crucial 36 percent of the ROC electorate that I labelled lost NDPers, Mulcair was seen as less intelligent, trustworthy, sensible, and strong in terms of his leadership at the end of the campaign than at the start. In particular, he was seen as less inspiring. That was his weakness at the start of the campaign, and it got worse by the end. Given political operatives' decision in paid advertising and earned media to insist on his experience and that he would be a safe choice for prime minister, this finding is not surprising. Mulcair's cautious branding was not meant to inspire voters. Conversely, the findings in my survey reflect the effective branding of Trudeau among NDP/LPC switchers. Lost NDPers' opinions of Trudeau had improved across all six adjectives. His weaknesses at the beginning of the campaign were not being seen as sensible, inspiring, and strong as a leader. However, his scores among lost NDPers on all of these adjectives had improved dramatically by the end of the campaign. In particular, Trudeau was seen as substantially more inspiring than Mulcair when the campaign ended.[7]

With the Liberal leader gaining popularity and the Liberal platform being well received by lost NDPers, the strength of the LPC brand surpassed the strength of the NDP brand in this segment of the English Canadian electorate by the end of the 2015 campaign. As shown above, the LPC brand strengthened the most, and the NDP brand weakened the most, in terms of being exciting and charming. The brand of the Liberals and the likeability of Trudeau even improved among solid NDPers, illustrating that not even the NDP's base was excited about the party's campaign.

NDP/LPC switchers, in particular union members and residents of Ontario, waited until the second part of the campaign to choose the party best positioned to displace the Harper government, and these voters sensed the Liberals' momentum. With Trudeau and the Liberal campaign generating excitement, strategic voters and late deciders within the lost NDPer category started to think that the Liberals were the most credible alternative to the Conservatives. The NDP campaign was like a balloon slowly losing air. Among lost NDPers, Mulcair and his party were obviously becoming less seen as the best bet to oust Harper and his party, for which they harboured considerable hostility.

Francophone Quebec was a slightly different story for the NDP compared with English Canada. First, though the NDP garnered 25 percent of the popular vote in Quebec as a whole according to Elections Canada, my survey estimates that its popular vote in francophone Quebec was just over 30 percent. So almost one in three francophone Quebecers did vote NDP. This finding points to the success of the NDP campaign in convincing voters in the converted NDPer category, who tended to live in rural and suburban areas, to vote for the party. These converted NDPers were drawn to the BQ but convinced to vote NDP through a combination of voting strategically, being impressed with Mulcair, and having a positive image of the party's brand.

However, the NDP's hope of sweeping francophone Quebec was crushed by the 41 percent of the francophone Quebec electorate whom I categorized as lost NDPers who ended up voting for the BQ, the CPC, or the LPC. In short, the NDP lost a multifront war for these voters with its three opponents in francophone Quebec during the 2015 election. The wedge issues that NDP operatives had set up did not resonate with lost NDPers there. They generally agreed with the NDP's position on cap and trade and pharmacare, but they still voted for other parties.[8] On balanced budgets and Bill C-51, roughly 60 percent of lost NDPers in francophone Quebec were against the party's positions on these issues. Despite the damage that the NDP claimed the TPP would cause to Quebec's dairy industry, only 23 percent of lost NDPers thought that the TPP was a "very bad thing" or a "bad thing." According to my multivariate model, one of the wedge issues supposed to push swing voters to support the NDP actually did the opposite – disagreeing with the NDP's child-care promise made francophone voters in Quebec more likely to be lost NDPers. The party platform did not appear to give the NDP a significant boost either. Only 60 percent of lost NDPers in francophone Quebec could correctly identify a description of the NDP platform. Poor communication of the platform and lack of resonance of the NDP's wedge issues appeared to leave impressions that the New Democrats were not very different from the Liberals. Believing that there were minor or no differences between the New Democrats and the Liberals increased the likelihood of being a lost NDPer in francophone Quebec.

With the NDP's wedge issues and platform not functioning as planned in francophone Quebec, the party's campaign appeared to suffer from a loss of momentum among lost NDPers as election day approached. Within this crucial segment of the electorate, Mulcair's personal popularity sagged, the NDP's brand was seen as less exciting and charming, and the party was no longer seen as being the closest to many of these voters on their most important issues (usually the economy). The party's opponents appeared to gain momentum in francophone Quebec because of their effective campaigns. Among lost NDPers, the likeability scores of Duceppe and Trudeau rose, the Liberal platform became popular, the BQ and the LPC gained partisans, and the percentage of voters who reported the BQ or the CPC as the closest to them on their most important issues increased. In short, the lacklustre campaign of the NDP opened the door for all three of its opponents to create momentum in their campaigns in order to convince voters who had been potential NDP supporters in August to turn toward them in October.

The NDP's loss of momentum was particularly damaging among roughly half of the francophone Quebec electorate who were late deciders. This loss of momentum allowed the party's opponents to get back in the game. Strategic voting was not a significant independent variable that increased the probability that francophone Quebec voters would be lost NDPers. Some of these voters did jump on board with the Liberals, and strategic voting might have played a role. Approximately 30 percent of Liberal voters in francophone Quebec reported that the LPC was not actually their preferred party – 54 percent preferred the NDP, and 30 percent preferred the BQ.[9] However, not all of the lost NDPers went to the LPC, for many went to the CPC and the BQ. It made little sense to vote strategically for the BQ or the CPC because strategic voting in Canada since 2000 had always been about preventing the Conservatives from getting into power and because voting NDP or LPC was a better way of blocking a Conservative majority in 2015 than voting BQ. Indeed, only about 10 percent of BQ and CPC supporters in francophone Quebec were strategic voters. In this sense, the NDP's disappointing results in Quebec had less to do with strategic voting than they did English Canada. Rather, it appears that the declining momentum of the NDP provided francophone Quebec voters with a chance to re-evaluate their options, and some decided to move strategically to the Liberals, whereas others moved to the Bloc Québécois or the Conservatives.

Interestingly, the ground game of the NDP in francophone Quebec was superior to those of its opponents. According to my survey, roughly half of francophone Quebecers were contacted by the New Democrats compared with 28 percent contacted by the Conservatives. Only 7 percent were contacted by the Liberals and only 4 percent by the Bloc Québécois. However, the NDP's effective voter contact was apparently overpowered by difficulties with its leader, the national campaign, and the generation of excitement.

With momentum such an important factor in both anglophone and francophone Canada, what accounted for the NDP's loss of momentum? Particularly the loss after Labour Day? NDP operatives interviewed for this book pointed to two specific issues in the second part of the campaign that sapped momentum: questions about how the party would pay for expanded social programs while keeping its commitment to balanced budgets and the controversy over the niqab. NDP operatives claimed that these issues made the party's publicly reported polling numbers drop and allowed the Liberals to remain as a viable party to displace the Conservatives, thus preventing a two-way NDP-CPC race from developing. Operatives thought that the NDP campaign was not adequately prepared for the niqab issue and that pushing fiscal responsibility too hard gave the Liberals the opportunity to paint themselves as more progressive than the New Democrats.

My analysis is generally congruent with the gut feelings of these operatives. My surveys indicate that the NDP platform was not well communicated and that its promise of balanced budgets was attractive only to anti-NDPers who do not vote for the party in any event. In my models related to English Canada, the stance on the niqab helped the NDP among converted NDPers and hurt it among lost NDPers. Since the latter voters were more numerous than the former voters, the niqab controversy contributed to the party's disappointing results in English Canada. However, in my models related to francophone Quebec, the variable concerning to the niqab was not significant because only 3 percent of francophone Quebecers were strongly or somewhat favourable to the NDP's position on permitting the niqab at citizenship ceremonies. So voters in all four of the categories that I analyzed were equally opposed to the NDP's stance on the niqab, and therefore it was not an independent variable that explained why respondents fell into one category versus another. Still, it is undeniable that the NDP was hurt terribly by the niqab controversy in Quebec. Public domain polls showed that the party's support in Quebec dropped precipitously following the emergence of the controversy, whereas support for all three of its opponents rose. The drop in NDP support in Quebec was quickly followed by a drop in NDP support in other parts of the country as English Canadian strategic voters deserted the party in favour of the Liberals (Coletto 2016, 321). The niqab controversy and doubts about the NDP platform (particularly balanced budgets) were the most likely catalysts of the waning momentum in late September and early October.

However, focusing too much on these two issues can prevent reflection on a broader point. The NDP experienced such heartbreak on election night in 2015 mainly because its operatives had failed to build a campaign to generate momentum and excitement as election day approached. There were several examples of this problem. NDP operatives decided to brand Mulcair as an experienced and steady leader and the party as representing cautious, as opposed to risky, change. Not surprisingly, lost NDPers found Mulcair uninspiring and the NDP brand unexciting and not very charming. As opposed to arousing enthusiasm for the party, the wedge issues constructed by NDP operatives were ineffective in influencing the voting decisions of lost NDPers. I found no evidence that the NDP platform and the wedge issues raised in advertising pushing significant numbers of swing voters toward the party. At best, swing voters were indifferent to or unaware of the NDP's plans. At worst, they disagreed with them. The political operatives' decision to base their campaign on the emergence of a two-way NDP-CPC race was ill fated as well. The party's focus late in the campaign on strategic voting seemed to be somewhat ludicrous given the Liberals' lead in public domain polling at the beginning of October. So, though controversies over the NDP's position on the niqab at citizenship ceremonies and on balanced budgets were unhelpful, the NDP campaign suffered from some deeper-seated problems.

Conclusion

Ultimately, the NDP campaign failed to generate the excitement and momentum needed to attract late deciders after Labour Day. At the same time, the Liberals ran a very effective campaign in English Canada, and the LPC, BQ, and CPC ran decent campaigns in francophone Quebec. Whether it was the strategic consideration of getting rid of the Harper Conservatives or simply being impressed with the Liberal platform and brand and Trudeau as a leader, English Canadian NDP/LPC switchers ended up voting Liberal. In francophone Quebec, all three of the NDP's opponents benefited as the party's campaign faltered, and these competitors found ways to draw potential NDP supporters to themselves.

During the period between the NDP's darkest days following the 2000 election and the eve of the 2015 election, a generation of activists, politicians, and operatives had found ways to rebuild the party and turn it into a contender to form the government. The party had re-invented itself as the "new NDP." However, despite the best efforts of agents within the NDP, the party was unable to prevent large segments of the electoral market that it had stolen from the Liberal Party and the Bloc Québécois in previous elections from migrating back to them. Ultimately, postmodern campaign techniques, a political market orientation toward voters and competitors, and sophisticated electoral market segmentation did not result in the party forming the government. Therefore, the big question is whether moderation and modernization of the NDP were really the way to go after all.

8
Which Way Now?

The promise of the political marketing of the federal NDP encompassed in moderation and modernization can be summed up in one word: *power*. From my interviews with NDP operatives and politicians from the Jack Layton and Tom Mulcair eras, it was apparent that the ultimate purpose of moderation and modernization of the party was to end its status as a spectator in Canadian politics. Being the "conscience of Parliament," articulating biting left-wing critiques of government policy, pushing the governing Liberals to the left, or creating a space in which democratic socialists could debate were not the principal tasks of the "new NDP." Only by gaining access to the levers of power could the "new NDP" put its social democratic ideology into action and make actual improvements in Canadians' lives. And, of course, ascending to power meant winning elections.

In some ways, an unspoken bargain had been struck between Layton's team of operatives and the party faithful that allowed for the creation of the "new NDP." As long as the NDP kept winning, party members were content to allow the professionals at party headquarters to craft election platforms and campaign strategies. They were happy to be seen primarily as donors and foot canvassers, and they accepted that speaking of profound societal change could scare potential supporters away from the party. They recognized that the NDP needed to be more independent from labour and could not formally affiliate with social movements. They realized that fiercely independent MPs such as Svend Robinson were not congenial to the overall brand that the party was slowly building. They trusted that the professionals at party headquarters knew what was best. The reward of moderation and modernization for party members would be the elation of seeing NDP cabinet ministers and possibly even an NDP prime minister. After Layton's untimely death, this bargain persisted between Mulcair's team, many of whom had been part of Layton's entourage, and party members. Going into the

2015 election, the expectations of the party were astronomical. The NDP appeared to be destined to make history. But the euphoria of victory and the exhilaration of power never came. The bargain was broken.

The result was that the NDP had come full circle and found itself in a position surprisingly similar to that of election night in 2000. As the Liberals were preparing to take office and Trudeau was picking his new cabinet, the New Democrats were facing leadership questions and organizational upheavals. The party also found itself at a familiar ideological crossroads. Should it continue on with the moderate version of social democracy espoused by Layton and Mulcair, or should it take a chance and leap to the left? The British Labour Party had faced a similar situation following the Tony Blair years (Cramme and Diamond 2012) and during the leadership race that replaced Ed Miliband with Jeremy Corbyn (Manwaring and Beech 2018).

After some initial hesitation, Mulcair decided to stay on as leader of the NDP. He organized a debriefing of the election campaign that would report back to party members on what had gone wrong, and he embarked on a tour around Canada to meet with New Democrats to talk about the upcoming Liberal budget. No member of the caucus publicly questioned Mulcair's leadership, and a number of MPs, particularly from Quebec, publicly urged Mulcair to stay on as leader (Boutilier 2016). At the NDP convention in Edmonton in April 2016, he made a passionate plea to delegates to unite behind his leadership because "millions of Canadians are looking to us. They are counting on us to fight for them and stand up to well-connected and powerful interests. We can't let them down. We can't get distracted. We have to push forward. If you keep standing with me, then together, we will never stop fighting."[1] After a standing ovation for Mulcair, the 1,800 delegates proceeded immediately to vote to have a new leadership race by a margin of 52 percent to 48 percent and to postpone holding a vote on a new leader until the fall of 2017.

Besides the vote on Mulcair's leadership, the national media focused on the debate on the Leap Manifesto at the convention. In many ways, the Leap Manifesto was a complete repudiation of the moderation and modernization of the NDP both in its ideas and the process by which it was created. The debate on the document represented an identity crisis for the party. The tone of the text and the controversial ideas that it endorsed were much different from any NDP document released during the Layton and Mulcair eras. The document made bold statements about ending the use of fossil fuels in thirty years, banning the construction of new pipelines, eliminating free-trade agreements, cutting military spending, and imposing an international financial transaction tax. Both the ideas and the phrases lacked moderation, warning Canadians that "small steps will no longer get us where we need to go. So, we need to leap."[2]

Modernization of the NDP had entailed that ideas released to the public as "NDP policy" were crafted and market-tested by political operatives at party headquarters. In this way, party policy would respond to the needs and desires of key voters within certain segments of the electoral markets whose preferences were discovered by using formal market intelligence such as polls and focus groups. Similar to how the NPI had been created fifteen years earlier, the Leap Manifesto was created at a two-day meeting of activists from various social movements and citizens' groups in downtown Toronto in the spring of 2015. The intention of the meeting was to create a statement of principles based on the values of the people gathered in the room and then to go out and educate Canadians about the merits of the manifesto's ideas. Leap activists held educational events in the lead-up to the 2015 election and a press conference with many prominent Leap supporters with one month to go in the campaign. At that time, Mulcair was decidedly cool toward the manifesto and said only that he welcomed debate, and no NDP candidate or sitting NDP MP publicly supported it (Hopper 2015).

Although the leadership of the party never endorsed the document, grassroots NDP activists from a number of riding associations decided to devise a resolution prior to the Edmonton convention stating that the federal NDP recognize the Leap Manifesto as a "high-level statement of principles" and that the manifesto be debated by NDP riding associations across Canada. Passing the resolution came to be touted by high-profile left-wing activists such as filmmaker Avi Lewis and author Naomi Klein as well as former Ontario NDP leader Stephen Lewis and former MPs Libby Davies and Craig Scott. Conversely, Alberta NDP cabinet ministers called the text "unacceptable" and "short-sighted," and NDP Premier of Alberta Rachel Notley used her speech to convention delegates to plead with them not to pass the resolution because implementation of the ideas in the manifesto would endanger the livelihoods of Alberta workers and their families (Kirkup 2016). Ignoring the warnings of Canada's only sitting NDP premier, delegates passed the resolution regarding the Leap Manifesto and then proceeded the next day to vote in favour of a leadership race.

Against this backdrop of questions about leadership and party identity, the NDP was also in organizational upheaval. Several of the political operatives who had been at the forefront of moderation and modernization of the party left to pursue other opportunities following the 2015 campaign. With the loss of fifty seats, hundreds of NDP staff on Parliament Hill and in constituency offices across the country lost their jobs. Party donors voiced their disappointment with the outcome of the election, and the party's fundraising numbers hit lows not seen in many years. To make matters worse, with the elimination of the per-vote subsidy, there were no quarterly allowances from Elections Canada to make up for the shortfall. The staff at party headquarters had to be cut drastically, and the party eventually decided to hire Robert Fox as its national director, an outsider whose previous experience was as the executive director of the human rights NGO Oxfam. Although less high profile than the Leap Manifesto, the task force on the shortcomings of the 2015 campaign publicly released a report containing criticisms of the growing centralization of the party. The report noted that NDP members thought that they had "no effect on the strategic decision making happening in the central campaign," wanted more opportunities for "engagement on issues and feedback on the work of the leader and caucus," and desired to "increase transparency in nomination and vetting procedures." Some of the report's recommendations were intended to reduce the centralization of power in the party, such as empowering the federal executive and Federal Council to provide consistent feedback to party headquarters, ensuring that a draft platform and campaign strategy are provided to the Election Planning Committee six months before the next election for consultation, and creating a committee appointed by the federal executive to vet candidates for nominations in a more transparent manner. Conversely, other recommendations of the report advised continuation of modernization of the party in terms of improving its voter contact database, investing in professional organizers in areas where no NDP MPs were present, and supporting ongoing activist training to build up local campaign skills. The report was referred to the party's national director, federal executive, and Federal Council, charged with looking into which of the recommendations would be implemented.

The Paradox of Moderation and Modernization
The 2015 election left the NDP's leadership dazed and confused like a prizefighter who has just been unexpectedly knocked out and the party's membership like a crew of mutinous sailors distrustful of their captain. The

bewilderment among the NDP's leaders and the rebelliousness among the party's rank and file members comprise what could be called the "paradox of moderation and modernization." Simply put, moderation and modernization brought the federal NDP closer to power than it had ever been in its eighty-year history, but this revolution in its political marketing did not take it all the way to forming the government or at least having NDP cabinet ministers in a minority government led by another party.

At the heart of this paradox is the firm belief of a generation of NDP leaders, politicians, and operatives that, if the party moderated its language, ideas, and image and implemented the most up-to-date and sophisticated campaign techniques, it would win power. Such a belief was particularly strong immediately following the 2011 federal election. In my interviews with NDP operatives at that time, they argued that moderation and modernization meant that the party was on track to replace the Liberals eventually as the credible, pan-Canadian, left-of-centre alternative to the governing Conservatives (McGrane 2011). With the New Democrats as the official opposition, they would continue to eat away at the Liberals' popular vote in English Canada and maintain their Quebec base. They thought that the Liberals were a spent force and that, like the United Kingdom, Canada would move to a two-party system, with the CPC as the dominant party of the centre-right and the NDP as the dominant party of the centre-left.

Although Trudeau's coronation as Liberal leader had temporarily inflated the Liberals in 2014, the NDP was flying high in the polls going into the 2015 election. In my conversations with party operatives at the start of the campaign, they were confident that, if they kept on doing what they had been doing since Layton had become leader, the party would be successful. The tenets of moderation and modernization dictated that the party should do two things as it prepared for the 2015 election. First, it should build a highly professionalized and sophisticated ground game based on the latest campaign technologies and voter contact tactics. Second, it should inoculate itself against brand weaknesses (e.g., being seen as too radical to be trusted with the government) and build on its brand strengths (e.g., Mulcair's experience). So party operatives devised an air game based on experienced leadership and safe change that would keep the NDP in front of the LPC and ensure a two-way NDP-CPC race in the final weeks of the campaign. Then strategic voting could be turned against the Liberals as voting for the New Democrats would emerge as the only way to get rid of Harper. If the political operatives could build a strong ground game and effectively implement their strategy in the air game, then the NDP would be successful.

However, the paradox is that NDP operatives appeared to do everything that they were supposed to do in the campaign in 2015. Moderation and modernization of the political marketing of the party had reached their zenith, and the party was ready to form the government (either minority or majority) after years of transforming how it was organized and how it acted both inside and outside the House of Commons. Of course, things did not work out, and despite all of the changes the NDP was relegated to its perennial position as a third party that appeared to have little chance of holding political power.

There were two different reactions within the NDP to the paradox that I am describing. The first reaction was to continue on with moderation and modernization. The second reaction was to turn away from moderation and modernization and move in radical new direction.

The first reaction, mostly from operatives themselves and relayed to me in interviews following the 2015 campaign (see McGrane 2016), was an optimistic view of the state of the party following the disappointing results of the 2015 election. These NDPers started by pointing out that the glass should be seen as "half full." One needs only to look at the 2000 election to see how far the party had come in the past fifteen years. In terms of both seats and popular votes, the NDP was at a historic high compared with all previous elections excluding the 2011 election. Also, the party had sixteen seats in Quebec, and one in four Quebecers had voted for it in 2015. The NDP was better organized in Quebec, more bilingual, and more attune to Quebec issues than at any previous time in its history.

For these political operatives, the moderation and modernization of the party that had brought electoral success during the 2000s would be its greatest strength going forward. The key to success would be continued ideological moderation to allow the NDP to be perceived as a governing party. Indeed, public domain polling early in the 2015 campaign indicated that enough Canadians had come to trust the party to be a responsible and stable alternative to the Harper Conservatives for the NDP to form at least a minority government. Although many of these Canadians eventually voted for the Liberals, the accomplishment of the NDP as the frontrunner to form the government at the beginning of a federal election should not be underestimated, and this accomplishment had come by presenting a moderate form of social democracy, as outlined in Chapter 5. The ideological template for the federal NDP moving forward should be the Notley government in Alberta or past NDP governments in Manitoba and Saskatchewan. The party should offer a progressive form of politics with language that reassures voters and offers practical and achievable solutions to their problems, especially as the Liberals begin to disappoint Canadians as they face the tough job of governing and making difficult choices as opposed to just campaigning. The policy ideas and issue framings that could form the foundation of this type of progressive left-of-centre politics should be sought through the continued use of formal market intelligence such as focus groups and polls.

This point of view sees that the legacy of the changes in the political marketing of the NDP over the past fifteen years is its organizational strength. The party has been thoroughly professionalized, and its ground game performed well throughout the 2015 campaign. The party also gained considerable experience using sophisticated techniques in terms of digital campaigning, volunteer mobilization, fundraising, microtargeting, and voter contact that will serve it well in the future. The new database system will be continually improved, for provincial NDP parties will use it in various upcoming elections. The NDP and labour have become much less dependent on each other over the past two decades, and both are now comfortable in their new relationship, and the party will likely continue to have the strong support of partisan unions in the form of parallel campaigns on the ground and advertising campaigns that indirectly support the NDP. The local infrastructure of the party was built up by professional organizers in the four years leading up to the 2015 election, and the party now has active electoral district associations in many more areas of the country compared with the early 2000s. Future success will come if the party continues to adopt cutting-edge campaign technologies, fundraising techniques, and ways of volunteer mobilization and recruitment implemented by professional organizers.

Overall, this reaction to the moderation and modernization paradox attributes the disappointing results in the 2015 election to a combination of strategic errors made during the campaign and events out of the party's control as opposed to weaknesses related to the party's ideological direction or the professionalized and technologically sophisticated ground game that the NDP had developed. The party might have done better had it aggressively attacked the Liberals sooner, had it put forth a more nuanced position on deficit spending, or had it created a set of policy offerings unique to Quebec. Similarly, the NDP was put in a difficult position when the niqab ruling came down in the middle of the campaign, and the long campaign period allowed Trudeau to prove himself to voters and eventually steal the NDP's momentum as the campaign came to a close.

The fact that the NDP fell from first to third over the two months of the campaign in 2015 illustrates just how fickle voters can be. They now have little loyalty to any party and are willing to change their voting intentions quickly. NDP/LPC switchers who went Liberal on election day in 2015 might be convinced to switch back to the NDP in the next election. The key is to push onward with the agenda of moderation and modernization of the political marketing that got the party to this point in the first place. Going back to the party of the early 2000s is a sure way to fall back into irrelevance.

The second reaction, from activists on the party's left who coalesced around the Leap Manifesto, is a starker view of the NDP's situation after the 2015 election. After a decade of Harper as prime minister, Canadians wanted a dramatic change from the governing Conservatives. Part of the NDP's problem was its reliance on political marketing. By concentrating too much on polling, marketing, and branding, the professionals of the central campaign devised an overly cautious strategy. In fact, in presenting the NDP as safe and cautious change, party operatives allowed the Liberals to outflank the New Democrats on their left. In particular, the New Democrats' pledge to ensure balanced budgets allowed the Liberals to represent the urgent and drastic change that many voters desired. In many ways, the NDP's embrace of branding and marketing was the culprit. If staff at party headquarters had been more active in soliciting advice and feedback from grassroots NDP members, instead of listening to focus groups and marketing agencies, then the party's campaign could have avoided these pitfalls. If political operatives had listened more to party members and stayed closer to left-wing policies passed at conventions, then they would have run a bolder campaign representing the profound change that Canadians were actually craving.

For this group, the appropriate response to the disappointing results of the 2015 election is to turn away from the moderation and modernization of the party over the past fifteen years. In terms of ideology, New Democrats should not be afraid to be genuine social democrats and propose large-scale societal change inspired by the Leap Manifesto – pushing for the rapid transition to a carbon-free economy, promoting true reconciliation between Indigenous and non-Indigenous Canadians, and expanding the welfare state through a guaranteed annual income. Instead of cautiously referring to how the NDP embodies pragmatism, the party should try to excite Canadians by using audacious language that reflects the urgency of the problems facing society – racism, sexism, global warming, and poverty. With the Trudeau government styling itself as "progressive," a move to the left is needed now more than ever to differentiate New Democrats from Liberals. The NDP is bound to lose even more seats and votes in the next election if it merely depicts itself as a slightly left-wing version of the Liberal Party of Canada. The ideological model for the NDP is Bernie Sanders in the United States. He was not scared to declare himself a democratic socialist, condemn wealth inequality, and propose radical policies such as free college tuition. His campaign was able to generate considerable excitement during the primaries, and Sanders might even have fared better against Trump than Clinton did.

When it comes to the modernization of the NDP, those who take this view argue that power has become much too centralized within party headquarters. Instead of using polls and focus groups, policy and platform development should be undertaken in consultation with party members to ensure that what the NDP talks about during elections reflects true social democratic values. Educating Canadians about the problems facing society and the need for drastic action to solve those problems should be prioritized. For this type of education of the public to succeed, the NDP must connect with citizens' groups and unions to build a movement for social change. Politics should not be just about telling voters what they want to hear but also about educating citizens on what needs to be done. There is also a need to wrestle control of strategy away from party headquarters in Ottawa. Local activists should be given the resources to devise and carry out their own strategies tailored to what is taking place in their ridings. In particular, the vetting process must not be used as an excuse to disqualify candidates based on their ideology, and party headquarters should respect the choices of local party members when it comes to choosing candidates. Avoiding a bad headline is not a good reason to thwart internal party democracy.

These two reactions to the paradox of moderation and modernization represent the two extremes of the debate within the NDP. In reality, most party activists probably fall somewhere between these two extremes. They are a mix of the sentiments of right-wing marketing enthusiasts and left-wing marketing skeptics outlined in Chapter 5. Nonetheless, the party will have to decide if it wants to continue the transformation of its political marketing initiated by Layton at the beginning of the 2000s or if it wants to dial back that transformation.

Lessons Learned

Although it is tempting, I will not finish this book by attempting to solve the problem of whether the NDP should push forward with, or turn backward from, its moderation and modernization. That is a debate that the activists and leaders of the party should have. Rather, I will outline seven lessons that come out of this study. On an academic level, these lessons could be useful for future research on political marketing in Canada and future research on the NDP. On a practical level, these lessons might be useful for the NDP's debates on what direction the party should take heading into the future. In addition, the following discussion could be applicable to European debates as several social democratic parties whose success defined postwar European politics are now struggling to remain relevant (Manwaring and Kennedy 2018). It is hoped these lessons contain some tips for left-wing parties around the world who are trying to win elections in the early twenty-first century.

The First Lesson: Change the Rules, Change the Game

Changes to party financing rules in 2004 led to both a quarterly infusion of per-vote subsidies and an organizational distance between federal NDP headquarters and provincial NDP offices as well as between the federal NDP and its affiliated unions. The resulting organizational upheaval and the newfound financial resources opened up an opportunity for Layton and his team to transform the political marketing of the party. The lesson for political marketing scholars is that institutional rules governing political parties, particularly if those rules shift suddenly, can have drastic implications for the political marketing strategies of parties. For NDP activists, it is important to realize that changes to the external rules governing the party contained in the Elections Act and regulations created by Elections Canada, and even internal changes to the party's constitution, do affect daily party life. Rule changes force organizational changes, thereby shifting how power is distributed in the party, altering the allocation of scarce resources, and engendering innovation in decades-old practices. The effects of rule changes are not always apparent when the changes take place, but it is wise for activists and scholars alike to pay attention when new rules are implemented.

The Second Lesson: Money Matters

The moderation and modernization of the NDP required vast amounts of money. The human resource costs involved in professionalizing party headquarters were significant, and the party's parliamentary operations received a boost of human resources when the NDP became the official opposition. Also, the infrastructure required for the adoption of postmodern campaign techniques – such as creating a national database, implementing sophisticated fundraising techniques, expanding the party's digital presence, and microtargeting specific segments of voters – was expensive. The extent to which the growth of local NDP organizations was initiated and directed by professional organizers should not be underappreciated. Particularly in places such as Quebec, professional organizers in the 2000s did the hard work of recruiting volunteers, moving them up the ladder of engagement, and ensuring succession planning to maintain functioning EDAs over time. Party headquarters also provided local volunteers with training and digital infrastructure to build up their organizations. Ironically, professionals drove the building up of the party's grassroots in the 2000s, and EDAs became dependent on professionals to provide resources and guidance and to ensure that the EDAs continued to function as volunteers drifted away and were replaced by new recruits. Moderation, as described in this book, also requires substantial financial resources. Moderation of the NDP from 2000 to 2015 was intimately connected to the gathering of market intelligence, such as polls and focus groups, an ongoing expense for the party. Professionals to interpret and use this market intelligence once it was gathered were also needed. So both moderating the language that the NDP used to communicate its messages, and moderating the ideas that the party presented to reflect better the needs and desires of targeted voter segments, required significant outlays of capital.

For political marketing scholars, the case of the NDP brings up the interesting question of the role that money plays in the adoption of postmodern campaign techniques and the embrace of a political market orientation toward voters and competitors. How much does willingness to adopt postmodern campaign techniques matter compared with simply having the money to do so? Political parties might remain in the modern era of campaigning and remain member-oriented because they do not have the money to do otherwise. For New Democrats, the challenge is that per-vote subsidies have now ended, and the party does not have the drama of minority Parliaments and imminent elections to spur on fundraising. It might also prove to be harder for the NDP to use the actions of the Trudeau government as fundraising tools compared with the more blatantly right-wing agenda of the Harper government. The extent to which the NDP *wants to continue on* with moderation and modernization of its political marketing is one question. The extent to which the NDP *will have the financial resources to continue on* with moderation and modernization of its political marketing is another question.

To use Flanagan's (2012) terminology, remaining competitive with the Liberals and the Conservatives in the "political arms race" as the 2019 federal election approaches will be expensive. The NDP could turn back from its trajectory of moderation and modernization because it does not have the money to continue it. With less money, there are fewer professionals, the biggest advocates of moderation and modernization in the first place, to now push for a continuation of the political marketing implemented by Layton and his team. Some of the tasks previously done by professionals in the NDP will now have to be transferred back to volunteers. Even if volunteers are keen on continuing on with moderation and modernization of the party, they might simply not have the time or the expertise to do so. In short, it is possible that the NDP might simply not have the money to continue along the trajectory, especially if the per-vote subsidy does not return.

The Third Lesson: Strategic Voting Is a Reality of the First-Past-the-Post System

As Chapter 4 illustrates, strategic voting was an obsession of NDP operatives from 2000 to 2015. These operatives were rational in their obsession with it. Chapters 6 and 7 show that the electoral success of the NDP in the later 2000s was attributable to its ability to steal market share from the Liberals among strategic voters and those looking for specific outcomes such as a minority government or ensuring that Harper was no longer prime minister. In 2015, lost NDPers in English Canada were disproportionately strategic voters who went over to the Liberals at the last minute to avoid another Harper majority government.

As long as Canada has a first-past-the-post electoral system, strategic voting will be the bane of the federal NDP, especially since Liberals appear to be masters of the strategic voting game. In Johnston's (2017) analysis of Canadian elections since Confederation, the chapter on the CCF-NDP argues that one reason for the party's lack of electoral success is that voters who might be predisposed to support the party always hesitate because its weakness in certain regions makes it an unlikely contender to form the government. For instance, whether voters support the NDP in Western Canada or Atlantic Canada might be affected by their evaluations of the party's chances in Quebec and the fear that they might be wasting their votes (Ibid.,180–81). Since the Liberals generally benefit when this happens, strategic voting is like a coin – it accounts for LPC success on one side and NDP failure on the other in federal elections since the 1930s.

My study generally confirms Johnston's (2017) findings. With the exception of the 2011 election, in the six elections since 2000, the Liberals have been very successful among strategic voters whether they started the campaign in the government, as the official opposition, or as the third party in the House of Commons. Only in 2011 did the NDP really find an answer to the question of strategic voting. For political marketing scholars, the case of the NDP illustrates the important role that electoral systems play in structuring a party's tactics and strategies. As a third party and as a social democratic party, the NDP would market itself much differently in a proportional representation system as opposed to a first-past-the-post system. For NDP activists, strategic voting simply cannot be ignored. The polling for this book estimated that about 25 percent of voters in 2015 could be classified as strategic voters. If that estimate is correct then approximately 4.19 million voters in 2015 were strategic voters (i.e., they did not vote for their preferred party). Often these voters look to national polls for clues on how to vote strategically. Although using national polling to figure out how to vote strategically at the riding level represents flawed logic and a misunderstanding of how Canadian elections work, it does appear to be taking place. Nationally reported opinion polls and perceived momentum going into election day end up having disproportionate impacts on this crucial segment of voters. In future elections, it seems to be essential that the NDP construct its tactics with strategic voting as an important consideration and that the party realize that strategic voting is affected by national "horse-race" polling numbers heavily reported in the media.

The Fourth Lesson: Symbols, Emotions, and Momentum Are More Important than Policies

It is a mistake to think about elections as policy debates and policy dialogues. Policy matters in elections but not in the way that we think it does. Policy needs to be connected to feeling. It needs to cut through the white noise of politics. The 2015 election provided an important example in this regard – the Liberals' deficit promise. New Democrats responded to this pledge with facts and figures and a history lesson about how Tommy Douglas had balanced budgets in the 1940s and 1950s in Saskatchewan. However, the deficit promise became a symbol of the LPC, as opposed to the NDP, being the party that represented "#realchange." It was a well-calculated risk by the Liberals to generate excitement about Trudeau's leadership. On an emotional level, the promise spoke to the urgency of the situation and the dire need to remove Harper from office. The Liberals became the party of change and were given a crucial boost of momentum at the end of the campaign. The pledge was also very memorable, and voters were much more likely to assign the Liberals correctly to a description of their platform than they were to assign the New Democrats correctly to a description of their platform. Although the NDP in 2015 might have had reasonable policy offerings that fit well within the tradition of social democracy, its policies were not memorable, not communicated well, and did little to generate emotion and excitement.

The niqab debate during the 2015 election illustrated that policies can become symbols that create negative emotions and stall momentum. The NDP stated unequivocally that it supported the wearing of niqabs during citizenship ceremonies. In Quebec, this policy position appeared to become a symbol of how the NDP, and Mulcair in particular, did not understand the values of Quebecers. The party that was supposed to represent Quebec in Ottawa was at odds with almost all Quebecers on an issue that touched the province's identity politics and was heavily mediatized. The NDP's rational arguments that Canadians should follow the courts' directions on issues of religious freedom and that the issue was a distraction from more pressing matters fell flat. The timing of the niqab controversy at the end of September as the campaign was heading into its final stretch was very damaging to the NDP. The party lost momentum heading toward election day, and voters in Quebec who had leaned toward the NDP began to look at other options. And, as I illustrated in Chapter 7, the NDP fared particularly poorly among late deciders in francophone Quebec to the benefit of the BQ and the LPC and, to a lesser extent, the CPC.

Both political marketing scholars and NDP activists must pay more attention to the emotional impacts of policies. When evaluating policy ideas for inclusion in election platforms, the question should not be just "will this work?" but "how will this policy make voters feel?" If a policy is intended to generate momentum, then the timing of its release should be considered carefully. NDP operatives thought that their policy for a fifteen-dollar-a-day national child-care program gave them a boost of momentum, but this policy was announced over a year before election day, so momentum had dissipated by the time voters were marking their ballots.

The Fifth Lesson: The Leader's Brand Is the Party's Brand

The move to the one-member-one-vote selection process appears to give leaders a high degree of legitimacy as the sole spokespersons for their parties and encourages the party to mould itself to the new leader's image. The success of Jack Layton and Justin Trudeau, as party leaders, provides good evidence of this presidentialization of Canadian politics. Through the expenditure of millions of dollars in advertising and a considerable amount of money on the salaries of media relations staff in the Leader's Office, Layton's brand was built up over consecutive elections and minority Parliaments from 2004 to 2011. As shown in Chapter 4, there was a consistent and continuous effort over these eight years to brand Layton as the fighter for Canadian families, the honest broker, the politician with practical solutions, and the potential prime minister. During this period, the NDP brand began to take on the traits of Layton himself. The NDP became the party of pragmatic and moderate social democracy that wanted to play a role in governing to get results for Canadians. When I examine voter behaviour in Chapter 6, it became apparent that the Layton brand juxtaposed well with the Ignatieff and Dion brands. These Liberal leaders were seen as stuffy, aloof, intellectual, and lacking understanding of the issues facing so-called average Canadians. Conversely, Layton was seen as having strong character traits such as being empathetic and trustworthy. The Layton/NDP brand ended up being the main driver of the NDP's success in 2011.

In 2015, the tables were turned. The Liberals had made considerable investments in building up Trudeau's brand as inspiring, exciting, and representing positive change. The entire party was modelled on his image of putting forth real change after ten years of the Harper Conservatives. For its part, the NDP touted the experienced leadership of Mulcair. He was a serious politician who was reassuring and capable (i.e., safe change) compared with Trudeau, a political neophyte (i.e., risky change). The NDP brand as a whole took on the mantle of cautious change that Mulcair represented. As it ended up, Trudeau was speaking to people's hearts, whereas Mulcair was speaking to people's minds. When the NDP campaign began to lose momentum after Labour Day, this message of cautious change modelled on the personality of Mulcair was unable to generate the excitement needed for the party to recover (see Chapter 7).

For scholars of political marketing, the extent to which a party's brand exists independent of a leader's brand is an interesting question. Contemporary political parties appear automatically to mould themselves to the image of a new leader to such an extent that the whole notion of a "leader brand" separate from a "party brand" might be superfluous. NDP members and operatives should remember that a leader's style can be as important as a leader's policies. The recent electoral battles between the two main centre-left parties in Canada were defined in terms of leader brands. As the cases of Layton and Trudeau illustrate, left-of-centre voters in Canada appeared to be more attracted to leaders branded as dynamic, inspiring, and optimistic as opposed to leaders branded as experienced and competent. NDPers must remember that elections are battles for *both the heads and the hearts* of voters – good policy ideas coupled with sharp critiques of right-wing opponents are not enough.

The Sixth Lesson: The Ground Game Can Take You Only So Far

Part of the modernization of the federal NDP from 2000 to 2015 was an increased emphasis on using the latest voter contact methods and building up an army of both volunteer and paid foot/phone canvassers. In particular, large sums of money were spent on hiring organizers and recruiting volunteers to ensure that local NDP campaigns in Quebec resembled those of Vancouver or Winnipeg, where the party traditionally had solid local organizations. As illustrated in Chapter 7, the ground game that the NDP developed in francophone Quebec was superior to those of its opponents. The polling done for this book indicated that roughly half of francophone Quebecers were contacted by the NDP compared with 28 percent contacted by the Conservatives, 7 percent by the Liberals, and 4 percent by the Bloc Québécois. Yet, my statistical models showed that there was little correlation between voting for the NDP in francophone Quebec and being contacted by the party. Indeed, SOM data show that over half of francophone Quebecers voted for the BQ and the LPC even though those parties appeared to have abysmal ground games in francophone Quebec. Ultimately, an effective ground game cannot overpower difficulties in the air game. The NDP's strong voter contact effort in francophone Quebec appeared to be unable to offset the difficulties that the party was having with the popularity of its leader, the niqab issue, and the lack of excitement that its national campaign was generating.

For political marketing scholars, this finding is interesting when studying the effectiveness of "field" operations compared with political advertising and media relations. The appropriate ratio of spending on voter contact versus paid and earned media requires more research. Also, the findings on the minimal positive effects of the NDP's ground game confirm recent research that voter contact is really about motivating a party's supporters to get out and vote as opposed to persuading potential supporters to vote for one's party (Kalla and Broockman 2018). Possibly, direct voter contact by political parties is simply an ineffective way of persuading voters.

For NDP activists, this leaves a conundrum. One way to look at the party's 2015 results is to point out that the NDP would have done even worse in Quebec if it had not had an effective ground game. Perhaps the push to modernize the party's ground game there during the Layton and Mulcair years prevented further seat losses in 2015. Yet one must ask whether the NDP paid too much attention to its ground game in Quebec and not enough attention to its air game there. As noted in Chapter 4, several NDP operatives regretted not developing Quebec-specific messages and policy offerings during the 2015 campaign. Like political marketing scholars, NDPers have to ask themselves hard questions about the appropriate balance between resources dedicated to voter contact and resources dedicated to earned/paid media. With less money coming into party coffers in the future, such a discussion is even more pressing.

The Seventh Lesson: Meeting Voters Where They Are Comes with a Risk

Layton and his team of operatives made a conscious decision to meet Canadians where they were. They did not try to mobilize nonvoters. They did not focus on educating Canadians on why they should support particularly left-wing policies or try to shape their policy preferences. Rather, they sought to accommodate the pre-existing ideas of voters. For example, when voters reacted negatively to an inheritance tax as a mechanism for raising revenues to pay for social programs in the NDP's 2004 platform, the tax was replaced with increasing corporate taxes in subsequent platforms. The mission of Layton and his team was never really to push Canadians to become more left wing. It was to emphasize ideas that fit within the broad framework of the NDP's social democratic ideology and that were popular with left-of-centre Canadians currently voting LPC or BQ. At the same time, the NDP under Layton appealed to these soft LPC and BQ voters with strategic voting arguments. As such, the NDP message was not "vote for us because we are socialists" but "vote for us because the Liberals need a time out" or "vote for us because the BQ will never be able to get into power" or "vote for us because Jack Layton would make a great prime minister (or deputy prime minister in a coalition government)." Using an approach that accommodated voters' preferences and appealed to the broader strategic context of Canadian federal politics, the NDP was able to steal market share from the Liberal Party and the Bloc Québécois in various segments of the electoral market during the Layton years.

However, the approach devised by Layton's team and carried forward by Mulcair's team never really sought to create solid NDP partisans dedicated to social democratic values and policies. So NDP voters in 2011 were susceptible to being swayed away from the party in 2015 once circumstances had changed. The Liberal campaign in 2015, based on strategic appeals and an exciting, charming leader, was not all that different from the NDP campaign in 2011. And the Liberals were able to steal that market share right back from the NDP as Layton Liberals turned into Trudeau New Democrats. The New Democrats won in 2011 because they were better than the Liberals at the politics of leadership and strategic voting, and they lost in 2015 because the Liberals were better at this type of politics.

This final lesson brings us back to the title of this concluding chapter, which way now? NDP members are facing up to the perennial question are we a political party or a political movement? Certainly, the direction in which Leap Manifesto proponents are heading is for the party to focus on educating Canadians about the dangers of climate change, persistent wealth inequality, and the historical injustices committed against Indigenous people. Reminiscent of the ideas of the Waffle in the early 1970s and the NPI in the late 1990s, the NDP would be more than just an electoral machine. It would reaffirm its commitment to its radical left-wing principles and build a large movement for social change that includes unions and other civil society groups. Its tactics would be protesting, coalition building, raising awareness, and mobilizing nonvoters.

The other way to look at the NDP is as a political party that exists solely for the purpose of winning elections. As Chapter 2 revealed, social movements have been relatively uninterested in affiliating formally with a political party, and the Canadian labour movement is enjoying its independence and has no longing for the NDP to become once again its political arm. The party should continue to be relatively independent from unions and use social movements only as third-party validators at election time. Public education should be outsourced to left-wing think tanks such as the Broadbent Institute and the Canadian Centre for Policy Alternatives. The main rebuilding tasks for the party would follow the trajectory of moderation and modernization: adopting better fundraising strategies and donor relations, training more activists on Populous, hiring more regional organizers, and improving microtargeting abilities. The leader's image is the blueprint for the party's brand. The development of policies and messages should remain with the professionals at party headquarters and in the Leader's Office on Parliament Hill. Moderation and modernization got the NDP close to power, and next time they will take the party all the way if it just stays on this course.

From 2000 to 2015, the "new NDP" emerged as the party reinvented itself and revolutionized its political marketing. Given the disappointing results of the last election and the election of Jagmeet Singh as leader, it will be fascinating to see where the NDP heads in the future. Indeed, as political marketing literature continues to develop in Canada, the case of the NDP will be illuminating in terms of understanding how political marketing works and how it affects the lives of voters, politicians, and activists on Canada's left.

Appendix A
List of Semi-Structured Interviews

This appendix contains a list of semi-structured interviews performed for this book arranged alphabetically by last name. Most of these participants were interviewed only once, but some were interviewed two or three times. Many of the interviewees changed titles multiple times during their time with the NDP. The titles given are those most pertinent to the topics of their interviews. The date of the interview is in year-month-day format.

Anderson, Drew, director of fundraising and membership (2005–10) and director of communications (2010–11) at NDP Party Headquarters, interview dates: 2011-04-17 and 2014-10-30.

Ashton, Niki, MP for Churchill from 2008 to 2015, interview date: 2014-11-16.

Audet, Nicolas-Dominic, party organizer in Quebec from 2006 to 2008 and executive director of the NDP Quebec Section from 2008 to 2010, interview date: 2014-10-25.

Bélanger, Karl, various positions in the NDP Leader's Office from 1997 to 2016, interview dates: 2011-04-20, 2014-10-25, and 2015-11-03.

Bhattacharya, Chanchal, member of the NDP Policy Committee from 1999 to 2005, interview date: 2015-04-08.

Blaikie, Bill, MP for Winnipeg Transcona from 1979 to 2008, leadership candidate in 2002–03, interview date: 2015-03-03.

Blaikie, Rebecca, executive director of the NDP Quebec Section from 2006 to 2008 and president of the NDP from 2011 to 2016, interview dates: 2014-10-24 and 2015-12-01.

Blakeney, Hugh, chief of staff for Alexa McDonough from December 2000 to February 2003, interview date: 2015-03-19.

Broadbent, Ed, leader of the NDP from 1975 to 1989 and MP for Ottawa Centre from 2004 to 2006, interview date: 2015-03-23.

Bussières, Charles, organizer for the NDP Quebec Section from 2003 to 2015, interview date: 2015-04-07.

Capstick, Ian, NDP caucus press secretary (2003-10) and English media relations for the NDP leader (2004, 2006, and 2008 elections), interview date: 2015-04-01.

Cardy, Dominic, NDProgress organizer, interview date: 2015-03-10.

Comartin, Joe, MP for Windsor-Tecumseh from 2000 to 2015, leadership candidate in 2002-03, interview date: 2014-10-28.

Cox, Bruce, campaign manager for Layton leadership campaign (2002-03), national NDP campaign director for 2004 election, interview dates: 2015-03-03 and 2015-03-11.

Cullen, Nathan, MP for Skeena-Bulkley Valley from 2004 to 2015, interview date: 2014-10-28.

Davies, Libby, MP for Vancouver East from 1997 to 2015, interview date: 2014-10-27.

Dewar, Paul, MP for Ottawa Centre from 2006 to 2015, interview date: 2014-10-30.

Dorse, Kevin, researcher for NDP caucus from 1998 to 2010, interview date: 2015-04-08.

Ducasse, Pierre, leadership candidate (2002-03) and special adviser on Quebec issues to Layton and the NDP caucus (2005-09), interview dates: 2014-11-18 and 2014-11-25.

Fortin, Karine, NDP deputy national director from 2014 to 2016 and director of communications for the NDP Leader's Office from 2012 to 2014, interview dates: 2015-04-02 and 2015-11-13.

Fraser, Heather, director of organization for the NDP from 2000 to 2008, interview date: 2014-10-27.

Gébert, Raoul, member of the executive of the NDP Quebec Section from 2004 to 2007 and 2010 to 2012, president of the Outremont NDP Riding Association from 2008 to 2009, and chief of staff for Mulcair from 2012 to 2015, interview dates: 2014-10-26, 2015-03-24, and 2015-11-03.

Giambrone, Adam, president of the NDP from 2001 to 2006, interview date: 2014-12-16.

Gillespie, Ian, database and direct mail coordinator in the NDP Leader's Office from 2004 to 2011 and special adviser to the NDP leader from 2012 to 2015, interview date: 2014-10-31.

Godin, Yvon, MP for Acadie-Bathurst from 1997 to 2015, interview date: 2014-10-30.

Hare, David, director of party operations for the NDP from 2013 to 2015, interview dates: 2015-03-23 and 2015-11-12.

Harris, Dan, MP for Scarborough Southwest from 2011 to 2015, interview date: 2016-11-13.

Hartmann, Franz, social movement outreach coordinator in the NDP Leader's Office from 2004 to 2006, interview date: 2015-03-20.

Heath, Jamey, director of communications and research in the NDP Leader's Office from 2003 to 2006, interview date: 2015-05-25.

Hébert-Daly, Éric, assistant federal secretary of the NDP from 2002 to 2004 and federal secretary of the NDP from 2004 to 2008, interview date: 2014-10-30.

Kerwin, Pat, CLC political action director from 1977 to 2003 and CLC representative in the NDP caucus from 1977 to 2003, interview date: 2015-03-25.

Lagace-Dowson, Anne, NDP candidate in Westmont–Ville-Marie in 2008, interview date: 2015-04-14.

Lavigne, Brad, national director of the NDP from 2008 to 2011 and senior campaign adviser for the 2015 campaign, interview dates: 2011-05-18, 2014-10-31, and 2015-11-13.

Linner, Thomas, war-room researcher for the 2015 NDP campaign, interview date: 2015-11-02.

Mallett, Danny, political action and campaign director for the CLC from 2003 to 2011 and the CLC representative in the NDP caucus from 2003 to 2011, interview dates: 2011-05-17, 2014-11-10, and 2015-11-05.

Martin, Pat, MP for Winnipeg Centre from 1997 to 2015, interview date: 14-10-29.

Masse, Brian, MP for Windsor West from 1997 to 2015, interview date: 2014-11-19.

McDonough, Alexa, leader of the NDP from 1995 to 2003 and MP for Halifax from 1997 to 2008, interview date: 2015-04-02.

McGrath, Anne, President of the NDP from 2006 to 2008, chief of staff for the NDP leader from 2008 to 2011, national director of the NDP from 2014 to 2015, interview dates: 2014-10-27 and 2015-12-01.

Milling, Sue, assistant campaign chair for the 2004 NDP campaign and co-chair of the NDP Election Planning Committee and deputy campaign director in the 2006 and 2008 federal elections, interview date: 2015-03-30.

Monk, Kathleen, deputy director of communication and outreach in the NDP Leader's Office (2006–10) and director of strategic communications (2010–11) in the NDP Leader's Office, interview dates: 2011-05-18 and 2015-03-25.

Moran, Steve, president of the NDP Quebec Section (2004–06), deputy director of policy for the NDP leader (2008–11), chief of staff for the NDP house leader (2011–12), deputy chief of staff for the NDP leader (2012–15), interview dates: 2014-10-31 and 2015-11-24.

Nash, Peggy, president of the NDP from 2008 to 2011 and MP for Parkdale–High Park from 2006 to 2008 and 2011 to 2015, interview date: 2014-10-29.

Newman, Julien, communications officer responsible for Quebec in the NDP caucus office from 2008 to 2011, interview date: 2014-10-21.

Nystrom, Lorne, MP from 1968 to 1993 for Yorkton-Melville and from 1997 to 2004 for Regina-Qu'Appelle, leadership candidate in 2002–03, interview date: 2015-03-06.

Peel, Tara, candidate search coordinator from 2004 to 2008 for the NDP, interview date: 2015-03-24.

Penner, Bob, organizer of Layton leadership campaign and pollster for 2004 NDP campaign, interview date: 2015-03-23.

Pratt, James, director of field organization for the NDP from 2014 to 2015 and director of outreach for the NDP Leader's Office from 2011 to 2013, interview date: 2015-03-25.

Proctor, Dick, MP for Palliser from 1997 to 2004 and chief of staff for the NDP leader in 2004, interview date: 2015-03-02.

Proctor, Merran, member of the NPI Steering Committee, interview date: 2015-03-03.

Rebick, Judy, organizer of the NPI, interview date: 2015-03-12.

Rotman, Nathan, director of organization for the NDP from 2008 to 2011, director of outreach and operations at the NDP Leader's Office from 2011 to 2012, national director of the NDP from 2012 to 2014, interview dates: 2011-05-18 and 2015-03-24.

Roy, Michael, digital director of the NDP from 2014 to 2015, interview date: 2015-03-23.

Sampson, Danielle, deputy director of organization and associate director of training and development for the NDP from 2013 to 2015, interview date: 2015-03-26.

Smallman, Vicky, co-chair of the Policy Committee of the NDP Federal Council from 2000 to 2006, interview date: 2014-10-29.

Smith, Rick, voter contact coordinator on the Layton leadership campaign (2002-03), interview date: 2014-11-03.

Soule, George, media relations in the NDP Leader's Office from 2009 to 2014 and media relations for the NDP from 2014 to 2015, interview dates: 2015-03-23 and 2015-11-10.

Stanford, Jim, organizer of the NPI, interview date: 2015-03-17.

Stoffer, Peter, MP for Sackville–Eastern Shore from 1997 to 2015, interview date: 2014-10-28.

Topp, Brian, war-room director for the NDP campaign in 2004, national campaign director for the NDP campaigns in 2006 and 2008, platform and debate coordinator for the NDP campaign in 2011, president of the NDP from 2011 to 2012, interview date: 2015-03-26.

Watkins, Emily, director of leader's affairs for the NDP from 2011 to 2013, director of outreach and stakeholder relations in the NDP Leader's Office from 2014 to 2015, policy officer in the NDP caucus office from 2003 to 2011, interview dates: 2015-04-13 and 2015-11-04.

Watson, Chris, federal secretary of the NDP from 2002 to 2004, interview date: 2015-03-20.

Watson, Lucy, election readiness coordinator from 2014 to 2015, interview dates: 2015-03-25 and 2015-11-09.

Appendix B
Canadian Election Studies, 2000–11; and Ipsos-Reid Exit Polls, 2006–11

The wording and coding of the questions on the surveys that produced the analysis in Chapter 6 are contained below. Although the questionnaires were translated and available in both French and English, only the English wording of the question is included here.

Sociodemographic Variables (Canadian Election Study for the ROC)
For all sociodemographic variables, respondents who answered "I don't know" were coded as missing and excluded from the analysis.

Atlantic: 1 = lives in Atlantic Canada; 0 = does not live in Atlantic Canada

West: 1 = lives in Western Canada; 0 = does not live in Western Canada

Female: 1 = female; 0 = male

Under 35: 1 = age 35 or younger; 0 = age 36 or older

Over 54: 1 = age 55 or older; 0 = age 54 or younger

Catholic: 1 = Catholic; 0 = not Catholic

No religion: 1 = has no religion; 0 = has a religion

Did not finish high school: 1 = did not complete high school; 0 = completed high school

University graduate: 1 = completed university; 0 = did not complete university

Union member: 1 = belongs to a union; 0 = does not belong to a union

Underlying Values Variables (Canadian Election Study for the ROC)

Accommodation of Quebec: This variable combined the respondent's answers to two questions in an index recoded to range from 0 to 1. The two questions were "how much do you think should be done for Quebec?" and "how do you feel about Quebec?" 1 = much more and really like, 0 = much less and really dislike, and "I don't know" was assigned the midpoint of 0.5. Alphas ranged from 0.60 to 0.61.

Continentalism: This variable combined the respondent's answers to two questions in an index recoded to range from 0 to 1. The two questions were "do you think Canada's ties with the United States should be much closer, somewhat closer, somewhat more distant, or much more distant?" and "how do you feel about the United States?" 1 = much closer and really like, 0 = much more distant and really dislike, and "I don't know" was assigned the midpoint of 0.5. Alphas ranged from 0.43 to 0.47.

Market liberalism: This variable combined the respondent's answers to five questions in an index recoded to range from 0 to 1. Four of the questions asked about the levels of agreement with the following statements: "The government should leave it entirely to the private sector to create jobs," "people who don't get ahead should blame themselves, not the system," "when businesses make a lot of money, everyone benefits, including the poor," and "if people can't find work in the region where they live, they should move to where the jobs are." Also included was the question "how much should be done to reduce the gap between the rich and the poor in Canada: much more, somewhat more, somewhat less, or much less?" 1 = strongly agree to first four questions and do much less, 0 = strongly disagree to first four questions and do much more, and "I don't know" was assigned the midpoint of 0.5. Alphas ranged from 0.54 to 0.55.

Moral traditionalism: This variable combined the respondent's answers to four questions in an index recoded to range from 0 to 1. The first question asked about the level of agreement with the following statement: "Society would be better off if fewer women worked outside the home." The second question was "how much do you think should be done for women: much more, somewhat more, somewhat less, or much less?" The third question was "how do you feel about feminists?" The fourth question was "how do you feel about gays and lesbians?" 1 = strongly agree, much less, and really dislike, 0 = strongly disagree, much more, and really like, and "I don't know" was assigned the midpoint of 0.5. Alphas ranged from 0.53 to 0.56. In 2000, "how do you feel about gays and lesbians?" was not asked, so the level of agreement with the statement "gays and lesbians should be allowed to get married" was used as a substitute.

Political cynicism: This variable combined the respondent's answers to five questions in an index recoded to range from 0 to 1. The first question was "on the whole, are you very satisfied, fairly satisfied, not very satisfied, or not satisfied at all with the way democracy works in Canada?" The second question was "do political parties keep their election promises: most of the time, some of the time, or hardly ever?" The third question was "and on the same scale, how do you feel about politicians in general?" The fourth and fifth questions asked about the levels of agreement with the statements "the government does not care much about what people like you think" and "politicians are ready to lie to get elected." 1 = not satisfied at all, hardly ever, really dislike, and strongly agree, 0 = very satisfied, most of the time, really like, and strongly disagree, and "I don't know" was assigned the midpoint of 0.5. Alphas ranged from 0.67 to 0.68. In 2000, "politicians are ready to lie to get elected" was not asked, and no other question was used as a substitute.

Regional alienation: "In general, does the federal government treat your province better, worse, or about the same as other provinces?" 1 = worse, 0.5 = about the same, 0 = better, and "I don't know" was assigned the midpoint of 0.5.

Party Identification Variables (Canadian Election Study for the ROC)

In each Canadian Election Study from 2004 to 2011, respondents were asked "in federal politics, do you usually think of yourself as a: Liberal, Conservative, N.D.P., Bloc Québécois, Green Party, or none of these?" In 2000, "Progressive Conservative" and "Canadian Alliance" were used instead of "Conservative."

NDP ID: 1 = identifies as NDP, 0 = does not identify as NDP, and "I don't know" was assigned 0.

LPC ID: 1 = identifies as Liberal, 0 = does not identify as Liberal, and "I don't know" was assigned 0.

CPC ID: 1 = identifies as Conservative, 0 = does not identify as Conservative, and "I don't know" was assigned 0. For the 2000 election, the "CPC ID" is the combined number of Canadian Alliance identifiers with Progressive Conservative identifiers.

Economic Perspective Variables (Canadian Election Study for the ROC)

National economy: "Over the past year, has Canada's economy gotten better, gotten worse, or stayed about the same?" 1 = better, 0.5 = stayed about the same, 0 = worse, and "I don't know" was assigned the midpoint of 0.5.

Personal finances: "Over the past year, has your financial situation gotten better, gotten worse, or stayed about the same?" 1 = better, 0.5 = about the same, 0 = worse, and "I don't know" was assigned the midpoint of 0.5.

Issue Position Variables (Canadian Election Study for the ROC)

Personal taxes: "Should personal income taxes be increased, decreased, or kept about the same as now?" 1 = increase, 0.5 = about the same, 0 = decrease, and "I don't know" was assigned the midpoint of 0.5.

Corporate taxes: "Should corporate taxes be increased, decreased, or kept about the same as now?" 1 = increase, 0.5 = about the same, 0 = decrease, and "I don't know" was assigned the midpoint of 0.5. This question was not asked in the 2000 Canadian Election Study.

Defence spending: "Should the federal government spend more, less, or about the same as now on defence?" 1 = more, 0.5 = about the same, 0 = less, and "I don't know" was assigned the midpoint of 0.5.

Education spending: "Should the federal government spend more, less, or about the same as now on education?" 1 = more, 0.5 = about the same, 0 = less, and "I don't know" was assigned the midpoint of 0.5.

Health care spending: "Should the federal government spend more, less, or about the same as now on health?" 1 = more, 0.5 = about the same, 0 = less, and "I don't know" was assigned the midpoint of 0.5.

Welfare spending: "Should the federal government spend more, less, or about the same as now on welfare?" 1 = more, 0.5 = about the same, 0 = less, and "I don't know" was assigned the midpoint of 0.5.

Environment spending: "Should the federal government spend more, less, or about the same as now on the environment?" 1 = more, 0.5 = about the same, 0 = less, and "I don't know" was assigned the midpoint of 0.5.

More immigration: "Do you think Canada should admit more immigrants, fewer immigrants, or about the same as now?" 1 = more, 0.5 = about the same, 0 = fewer, and "I don't know" was assigned the midpoint of 0.5.

Leadership Evaluation Variables (Canadian Election Study for the ROC)

In each Canadian Election Study from 2000 to 2011, respondents were asked the following question about the leaders of the major federal political parties: "On a scale of one to one-hundred where one is *really dislike* and one-hundred is *really like,* how do you feel about ... ?" (emphasis in original). The responses for the NDP, LPC, and CPC leaders for each election were recoded on a scale of 0 to 1. For the 2000 election, "CPC leader" is the respondent's highest score given to either Stockwell Day or Joe Clark.

Sociodemographic Variables (Ipsos-Reid Exit Polls for Quebec)

For all sociodemographic variables, respondents who answered "I don't know" were coded as missing and excluded from the analysis.

Montreal: 1 = lives in Montreal; 0 = does not live in Montreal

Female: 1 = female; 0 = male

Under 35: 1 = age 35 or younger; 0 = age 36 or older

Over 54: 1 = age 55 or older; 0 = age 54 or younger

No religion: 1 = has no religion; 0 = has a religion

High school: 1 = high school graduate or did not complete high school; 0 = has education beyond high school

University graduate: 1 = completed university; 0 = did not complete university

Union household: 1 = belongs to a union household; 0 = does not belong to a union household

Low income: 1 = has a household income under $39,000; 0 = does not have a household income under $39,000

High income: 1 = has a household income over $80,000; 0 = does not have a household income over $80,000

Immigrant: 1 = not born in Canada; 0 = born in Canada

Gay: 1 = self-identifies as gay, lesbian, or transgendered; 0 = does not self-identify as gay, lesbian, or transgendered

Renter: 1 = rents their dwelling; 0 = does not rent their dwelling

Rural: 1 = lives in a city with a population under 100,000 residents; 0 = does not live in a city with a population under 100,000 residents

Anglophone: 1 = speaks English as their mother tongue; 0 = does not speak English as their mother tongue

General Orientation Variables (Ipsos-Reid Exit Polls for Quebec)

Government intervention: In all three exit polls, the following question was asked: "Which comes closer to your view? 1 = Government should do more to solve problems, 0 = Government is doing too many things that should be left to businesses and individuals." "I don't know" was assigned the midpoint of 0.5.

Same-sex marriage: In 2006, respondents were asked "which comes closest to your views about gay and lesbian couples, do you think: 1 = They should be allowed to legally marry, 0.5 = They should be allowed to legally form civil unions, but not marry, 0 = There should be no legal recognition of their relationships." In 2011, respondents were asked "what is your view on same-sex marriage? 1 = Favour same-sex marriage, 0.5 = Oppose same-sex marriage, but would accept same-sex civil union for gay and lesbian couples, 0 = Oppose entirely same-sex marriage." "I don't know" was assigned the midpoint of 0.5.

Antiparty sentiment: In all three exit polls, respondents were asked their level of agreement with the statement "I don't really like any of the parties in this election." 1 = strongly agree, 0.75 = somewhat agree, 0.25 = somewhat disagree, 0 = strongly disagree. "I don't know" was assigned the midpoint of 0.5.

Hard sovereignist and soft nationalist: In the 2006 and 2008 exit polls, respondents were asked their level of agreement with the statement "it would be better in the long run if Quebec were to separate from the rest of Canada." In 2011, respondents were asked their level of agreement with the statement "I want Quebec to become sovereign, that is, no longer part of the Canadian federation." The hard sovereignist variable was coded as follows: 1 = strongly agree, 0 = somewhat agree, somewhat disagree, strongly disagree, and "I don't know." The soft nationalist variable was coded as follows: 1 = somewhat agree, somewhat disagree, and "I don't know," 0 = strongly agree and strongly disagree.

Economic Perception Variables (Ipsos-Reid Exit Polls for Quebec)

Canada headed in wrong direction: In all three exit polls, respondents were asked "overall, would you say that Canada is on the right track these days, or headed in the wrong direction?" 1 = wrong direction, 0 = right track. "I don't know" was assigned the midpoint of 0.5.

Personal finances getting worse: In 2008 and 2011, respondents were asked "how do you expect your personal financial or economic situation to be one year from now compared to what it is like today? Do you expect that your personal financial or economic situation will be in better shape than it is now, worse shape than it is now, or no different from now?" 1 = worse shape, 0.5 = no difference, 1 = better shape. "I don't know" was assigned the midpoint of 0.5.

Most Important Issue Variables (Ipsos-Reid Exit Polls for Quebec)

In 2006 and 2008, respondents were asked "which one of the following issues mattered most in deciding which party's candidate you voted for today?" In 2011, respondents were asked "what was the most important issue in determining your vote?" The list of issues given to respondents varied slightly for each election. In 2006, the list was as follows:

- fixing our healthcare system
- cleaning up corruption
- managing the economy
- protecting the environment
- reducing taxes
- social programs like childcare
- pensions
- moral issues like abortion and same sex marriage employment/jobs
- keeping Canada together/National unity

- fixing our relationship with the US
- criminal justice and public safety issues
- immigration policies
- preserving the Atlantic Accord.

In 2008, the list was as follows:

- fixing our healthcare system
- cleaning up corruption
- managing the economy
- protecting the environment
- reducing taxes
- social programs like childcare
- pensions
- moral issues like abortion and same sex marriage employment/jobs
- keeping Canada together/National unity
- fixing our relationship with the US
- criminal justice and public safety issues
- immigration policies
- preserving the Atlantic Accord.

In 2011, the list was as follows:

- unemployment/jobs
- deficit/budget
- taxes
- economy in general
- healthcare/medicare
- the environment
- global warming
- energy
- gas prices
- fighting poverty
- social programs like childcare, pensions
- education
- agriculture
- crime

- law and order
- immigration
- international issues/war in Afghanistan
- aboriginal issues
- national unity/Quebec sovereignty
- federal/provincial issues
- regional inequality
- arts and culture
- abortion
- same-sex marriage
- corruption
- government accountability/transparency
- the Census
- national unity.

Health voter: 1 = "fixing our healthcare system" in 2006 and 2008 and "healthcare/medicare" in 2011, 0 = not "fixing our healthcare system" in 2006 and 2008 and not "healthcare/medicare" in 2011. "I don't know" was assigned 0.5.

Corruption voter: 1 = "cleaning up corruption" in 2006 and 2008 and "corruption" in 2011, 0 = not "cleaning up corruption" in 2006 and 2008 and not "corruption" in 2011. "I don't know" was assigned 0.

Economy voter: 1 = "managing the economy" or "employment/jobs" in 2006 and 2008 and "economy in general" or "employment/jobs" in 2011, 0 = not "managing the economy" or "employment/jobs" in 2006 and 2008 and not "economy in general" or "employment/jobs" in 2011. "I don't know" was assigned 0.

Environment voter: 1 = "protecting the environment" in 2006 and 2008 and "the environment" or "global warming" in 2011, 0 = not "protecting the environment" in 2006 and 2008 and not "the environment" or "global warming" in 2011. "I don't know" was assigned 0.

Social program voter: 1 = "social programs like childcare, pensions," 0 = not "social programs like childcare, pensions." "I don't know" was assigned 0.

Leader Evaluation Variables (Ipsos-Reid Exit Polls for Quebec)

In 2006 and 2008, respondents were asked "now, forgetting for a minute about the federal parties and what they stand for, and forgetting about which party you might be supporting, which of the federal party leaders do you think would make the best Prime Minister of Canada?" In 2011, respondents were asked "which of the federal party leaders do you think would make the best Prime Minister of Canada?" As noted in the text, Gilles Duceppe and Elizabeth May were not included as possible choices in 2006. Only Paul Martin, Stephen Harper, and Jack Layton were given as possible choices in that election poll. In 2008 and 2011, the leaders of the five major parties were included as possible choices.

Layton as best PM: 1 = Layton chosen as best PM, 0 = Layton not chosen as best PM, and "I don't know" was assigned 0.

Harper as best PM: 1 = Harper chosen as best PM, 0 = Harper not chosen as best PM, and "I don't know" was assigned 0.

Martin/Dion/Ignatieff as best PM: 1 = Martin/Dion/Ignatieff chosen as best PM, 0 = Martin/Dion/Ignatieff not chosen as best PM, and "I don't know" was assigned 0.

Leader voter: In all three exit polls, respondents were asked "and, would you say that your vote today was mostly for your local candidate, mostly for their party leader, or mostly for their party's stand on the issues?" 1 = mostly for the leader, 0 = mostly for the local candidate and mostly for the party's stand on the issues. "I don't know" was assigned 0.

Strategic Consideration Variables (Ipsos-Reid Exit Polls for Quebec)

Governing party/PM deserves to be re-elected: In 2006, respondents were asked "which of the two opinions below is closest to your own? 1 = The federal Liberal Party deserves to be re-elected under the leadership of Paul Martin, because all things considered, they've been doing a good job of running the country, 0 = The Liberals don't deserve to be re-elected and it is now time to give one of the other parties a chance to run the country." In 2008, respondents were asked "which of the two opinions below is closest to your own? 1 = The Conservative Party deserves to be re-elected under the leadership of Stephen Harper, because all things considered, they've been doing a good job of running the country, 0 = The Conservatives don't deserve to be re-elected and it is now time to give one of the other parties a chance to run the country." In 2011, respondents were asked "which of these statements is closest to your point of view? 1 = Stephen Harper deserves re-election, 0 = Stephen Harper does not deserve to be re-elected." In all three exit polls, "I don't know" was assigned 0.

Strategic voter: In 2006 and 2008, respondents were asked "now, would you say that you voted for this party today because you thought they would offer the best government for Canada, or because you were trying to stop another party from winning and forming the government? 1 = Trying to stop another party from winning and forming the government, 0 = Thought they would offer the best government for Canada." In 2011, respondents were asked "what was your main reason or reasons for voting for this party today? 1 = I wanted to make sure another party did not win, 0 = I like this party the best, I wanted to express my disgust with all of the other parties, and I wanted to prevent a coalition government." In all three exit polls, "I don't know" was assigned 0.

Wants the local MP in government: In 2006 and 2008, respondents were asked their level of agreement with the statement "it's important that my MP be from the party that wins this election." In 2011, the wording of the question was changed slightly to "it's important to me that my MP be a member of the party that forms the government after this election." In all three exit polls, the coding was 1 = strongly agree, 0.75 = somewhat agree, 0.25 = somewhat disagree, 0 = strongly disagree, and "I don't know" was assigned the midpoint of 0.5.

Wants a minority government: In all three exit polls, respondents were asked "and, in your opinion what would you say would be the best outcome for Canada from this election – a minority government, or, a majority government?" 1 = minority government, 0 = majority government, and "I don't know" was assigned the midpoint of 0.5.

Decided after the leaders' debates: In all three exit polls, respondents were asked "when did you finally decide who you were going to vote for today?" In 2006, the choices were thus: "Before the campaign started, Before Christmas, After Christmas but before the January debates, Shortly after the January debates, In the last week of the campaign, and In the voting booth today." In 2008 and 2011, the choices were thus: "Before the campaign started, Before the debates, Shortly after the debates, In the last week of the campaign, In the voting booth today." 1 = decided after leaders' debates, 0 = decided before leaders' debates, and "I don't know" was assigned 0.

Appendix C
2015 Canadian Federal Election Panel Survey on Social Democracy

The wording and coding of the questions for the 2015 Canadian Federal Election Panel Survey on Social Democracy are contained below. Only the English wording of the questions is included. The questionnaire was translated and available in both French and English in Quebec. Also, questions pertaining to the Bloc Québécois and Gilles Duceppe were asked only in Quebec. All of the five-point and ten-point scales pertaining to answers to these questions were recoded to range from 0 to 1.

Sociodemographic Variables (Asked in Wave 1 Only)

For all of the sociodemographic variables, respondents who answered "I don't know" or "clicked through" the screen so as not to answer the question were coded as missing and excluded from the analysis.

West: 1 = lives in British Columbia, Alberta, Saskatchewan, Manitoba, Yukon, Northwest Territories, or Nunavut; 0 = does not live in British Columbia, Alberta, Saskatchewan, Manitoba, Yukon, Northwest Territories, or Nunavut

Atlantic: 1 = lives in New Brunswick, Nova Scotia, Prince Edward Island, or Newfoundland and Labrador; 0 = does not live in New Brunswick, Nova Scotia, Prince Edward Island, or Newfoundland and Labrador

Quebec City: 1 = lives in Quebec City Census Metropolitan Area; 0 = does not live in Quebec City Census Metropolitan Area

Rest of Quebec: 1 = lives neither in Quebec City Census Metropolitan Area nor in Montreal Census Metropolitan Area; 0 = lives in Quebec City Census Metropolitan Area or Montreal Census Metropolitan Area

Senior: 1 = older than 65; 0 = younger than 65

Ages 45 to 64: 1 = between the ages of 45 and 64; 0 = not between the ages of 45 and 64

Female: 1 = female; 0 = male

Education: 1 = completed university; 0 = did not complete university

Union member: 1 = a member of a union; 0 = not a member of a union

Has no religion: 1 = has no religion; 0 = has a religion

Religiosity: "How important is religion to you?" 1 = very important or somewhat important, 0 = somewhat or very unimportant

Visible minority: 1 = identifies as a visible minority; 0 = does not identify as a visible minority. This variable was excluded from the analysis of francophone Quebec because of the small number of respondents who identified themselves as visible minorities.

Immigrant: 1 = not born in Canada; 0 = born in Canada. This variable was excluded from the analysis of francophone Quebec because of the small number of respondents who reported not being born in Canada.

Low income: 1 = under $60,000 total annual household income; 0 = over $60,000 total annual household income

Middle income: 1 = between $60,000 and $99,000 total annual household income; 0 = between $60,000 and $99,000 total annual household income (the reference category is high income [$100,000 and over])

Rural: 1 = lives in a community of under 100,000 residents; 0 = lives in a community of over 100,000 residents

Suburban: Using geomapping techniques based on self-reported postal codes, inner-city residents are defined as respondents living within a ten-kilometre radius of city hall for a large Census Metropolitan Area (population over 500,000) or within a five-kilometre radius of city hall for a small Census Metropolitan Area (population under 500,000). A suburban resident is defined as a respondent living outside a ten-kilometre radius of city hall for a large Census Metropolitan Area (population over 500,000) or outside a five-kilometre radius of city hall for a small Census Metropolitan Area (population under 500,000). 1 = a suburban resident; 0 = not a suburban resident. More information on this approach to defining suburban and inner-city residents can be found in McGrane, Berdahl, and Bell (2017).

Partisanship (Asked in Both Wave 1 and Wave 2)

NDP partisan/LPC partisan/CPC partisan/BQ partisan: "In federal politics, do you usually think of yourself as a: Liberal, Conservative, New Democrat, or Bloquiste?" Dummy variables were created for each party. "I don't know" and "clicking through" the screen were coded as 0.

Party Voted for in the 2011 Election (Asked in Wave 1 Only)

Voted NDP in 2011/voted LPC in 2011/voted CPC in 2011/voted BQ in 2011: "In the last FEDERAL election held on Monday May 2nd 2011 ... what party did you vote for? Liberal Party of Canada (Michael Ignatieff), Conservative Party of Canada (Stephen Harper), New Democratic Party (Jack Layton), Bloc Québécois (Gilles Duceppe), Green Party (Elizabeth May), Other, I did not vote in the last federal election, or I don't remember." Dummy variables were created for each party. "I did not vote in the last federal election," "I don't remember," and "clicking through" the screen were coded as 0.

Underlying Values (Asked in Wave 1 Only)

Market liberalism index: This index combined the respondent's answers to four questions in an additive five-point scale then recoded to range from 0 to 1. "For each of the following statements, please indicate if you 1 = strongly disagree, 2 = somewhat disagree, 3 = neither agree nor disagree, 4 = somewhat agree, or 5 = strongly agree: 1.) Government should leave it to the private sector to create jobs; 2.) Government regulation stifles personal drive; 3.) People who don't get ahead should blame themselves, not the system; and 4.) When businesses make a lot of money, everyone benefits, including the poor." Agreeing with all of these statements meant that the respondent had a higher level of market liberalism. "I don't know" and "clicking through" the screen were coded as the midpoint of 0.5. Cronbach's alpha in the ROC = 0.77; Cronbach's alpha in francophone Quebec = 0.66.

Postmaterialism index: This index combined the respondent's answers to four questions in an additive five-point scale then recoded to range from 0 to 1. "For each of the following statements, please indicate if you 1 = strongly disagree, 2 = somewhat disagree, 3 = neither agree nor disagree, 4 = somewhat agree, or 5 = strongly agree: 1.) It is more difficult for non-whites to be successful in Canadian society than it is for whites; 2.) Society still has a long way to go to reach the point where women and men have equal opportunities for achievement; 3.) The world is always changing and we should adapt our view of moral behaviour to these changes; 4.) Protecting the environment is more important than creating jobs." Agreeing with all of these statements meant that the respondent had a higher level of postmaterialist values. "I don't know" and "clicking through" the screen were coded as the midpoint of 0.5. Cronbach's alpha in the ROC = 0.66; Cronbach's alpha in francophone Quebec = 0.51.

Taxing and Spending Preferences (Asked in Wave 1 Only)

Personal tax preference: "Should personal income taxes be ... 1 = decreased a lot, 2 = decreased some, 3 = neither decreased nor increased, 4 = increased some, or 5 = increased a lot?" "I don't know" and "clicking through" the screen were coded as the midpoint of 3.

Corporate tax preference: "And what about corporate taxes? Should they be ... 1 = decreased a lot, 2 = decreased some, 3 = neither decreased nor increased, 4 = increased some, or 5 = increased a lot?" "I don't know" and "clicking through" the screen were coded as the midpoint of 3.

Health spending preference/poverty spending preference/terrorism spending preference/arts and culture spending preference/Aboriginal spending preference: "Should the FEDERAL government spend 1 = a lot less, 2 = a little less, 3 = about the same as now, 4 = a little more, and 5 = a lot more on health care, reducing poverty, fighting terrorism, arts and culture, and Aboriginals?" "I don't know" and "clicking through" the screen were coded as the midpoint of 3.

Sovereignty (Asked in Wave 1 and Wave 2 in Quebec Only)

Sovereignty: "Are you 1 = very opposed, 2 = somewhat opposed, 3 = neither favourable nor opposed, 4 = somewhat favourable, 5 = very favourable to the sovereignty of Québec, that is Québec is no longer part of Canada?" "I don't know" and "clicking through" the screen were coded as the midpoint of 0.5.

Party Closest to Voters on Their Most Important Issues (Asked in Both Wave 1 and Wave 2)

NDP closest on issue/LPC closest on issue/CPC closest on issue/BQ closest on issue: There were two parts to these variables. First, the respondent was asked "what is the SINGLE most important issue to you personally in FEDERAL Canadian politics?" and given a blank text box in which to respond. Second, the respondent was asked "in your view, which party is closest to your position on this issue? Conservative Party, Liberal Party, NDP, Bloc Québécois, Green, None of these." Dummy variables were created for each party. "None of these," "I don't know," and "clicking through" the screen were coded as 0.

Evaluations of Party Leaders (Asked in Both Wave 1 and Wave 2)

Harper like/Mulcair like/Trudeau like/Duceppe like: "On a scale of 0 to 10, where 0 means that you really dislike Harper/Mulcair/Trudeau/Duceppe and 10 means that you really like Harper/Mulcair/Trudeau/Duceppe, how much do you like Harper/Mulcair/Trudeau/Duceppe?" "I don't know" and "clicking through" the screen were coded as the midpoint of 5.

Timing of Vote Decision and Strategic Voting (Asked Only in Wave 2)

Decided after Labour Day: There were two parts to this variable. First, the respondent was asked "if you voted in the recent federal election, which party did you vote for?" Second, the respondent was asked "when did you decide you were going to vote for [the party given in the answer to the first question]? Before the election campaign officially started on August 2, 2015, during the first five weeks of the campaign from August 3 to Labour Day (August 7), 2015, during the month following Labour Day (August 7 to October 4, 2015), during the last two weeks of the campaign (October 5 to October 18, 2015), on election day (October 19, 2015), or I don't remember." Respondents who answered after Labour Day were coded as 1, and respondents who responded before Labour Day were coded as 0. "I don't remember" and "clicking through" the screen were coded as missing values and excluded from the analysis.

Strategic voter: "When you were making up your mind how to vote, did you *very much* or *somewhat* prefer another party but decided against it because you thought that the party had little chance of winning? Yes, I *very much* preferred another party but thought they had little chance of winning; Yes, I *somewhat* preferred another party but thought they had little chance of winning; No, I did not prefer another party than the one that I voted for" (emphasis in original). Respondents who answered that they "very much" or "somewhat" preferred another party were coded as 1, and respondents who answered that they did not prefer another party were coded as 0.

Economic Perceptions (Asked Only in Wave 2)

Negative economic perception: "Over the *past year*, has *Canada's* economy: 1 = improved a lot, 2 = improved a little, 3 = stayed about the same, 4 = worsened a little, 5 = worsened a lot?" (emphasis in original). "I don't know" and "clicking through" the screen were coded as the midpoint of 3.

Campaign Issues (Asked Only in Wave 2)

Feels NDP/LPC not different: "During the recent federal election campaign, did you find that there were major differences, minor differences, or no differences at all between the Liberals and the NDP?" Respondents who answered "major differences" were coded as 1, and respondents who answered "minor differences" or "no differences" at all were coded as 0. "I don't remember" and "clicking through" the screen were coded as missing values and excluded from the analysis.

Agreement with NDP position on TPP: "Based on what you have seen, read, or heard, do you think that the Trans-Pacific Partnership (TPP) is: 1 = a very good thing, 2 = a good thing, 3 = neither a good thing nor a bad thing, 4 = a bad thing, 5 = a very bad thing, or 6 = I have never heard of the Trans-Pacific Partnership?" "I don't know," "I have never heard of the Trans-Pacific Partnership," and "clicking through" the screen were coded as the midpoint of 3.

Agreement with NDP position on Bill C-51: "How do you feel about Bill C-51, the Conservative government's anti-terrorism legislation? Do you: 1 = strongly approve, 2 = somewhat approve, 3 = neither approve nor disapprove, 4 = somewhat disapprove, 5 = strongly disapprove, or 6 = I have never heard of Bill C-51?" "I don't know," "I have never heard of Bill C-51," and "clicking through" the screen were coded as the midpoint of 3.

Agreement with NDP position on child care: "What do you think of a national childcare program that creates new daycare spaces at no more than $15 a day? Are you: 1 = very opposed, 2 = somewhat opposed, 3 = neither favourable nor opposed, 4 = somewhat favourable, or 5 = very favourable?" "I don't know" and "clicking through" the screen were coded as the midpoint of 3.

Agreement with NDP position on budget: "How important is having a balanced federal government budget to you? Is it: 1 = not important at all, 2 = not very important, 3 = neither important nor unimportant, 4 = somewhat important, 5 = very important?" "I don't know" and "clicking through" the screen were coded as the midpoint of 3.

Agreement with NDP position on pharmacare: "What do you think about expanding Canada's health care system to include access to prescription drugs for all Canadians at little or no cost? Are you: 1 = very opposed, 2 = somewhat opposed, 3 = neither favourable nor opposed, 4 = somewhat favourable, or 5 = very favourable?" "I don't know" and "clicking through" the screen were coded as the midpoint of 3.

Agreement with NDP position on cap and trade: "What do you think about a cap-and-trade system that creates specific greenhouse gas emissions limits for Canadian businesses? Are you: 1 = very opposed, 2 = somewhat opposed, 3 = neither favourable nor opposed, 4 = somewhat favourable, or 5 = very favourable?" "I don't know" and "clicking through" the screen were coded as the midpoint of 3.

Agreement with NDP position on niqab: "What are your feelings on Muslim women being permitted to wear a Niqab (a religious facial covering that only allows for their eyes to be seen) during Canadian citizenship ceremonies? Are you: 1 = very opposed, 2 = somewhat opposed, 3 = neither favourable nor opposed, 4 = somewhat favourable, or 5 = very favourable?" "I don't know" and "clicking through" the screen were coded as the midpoint of 3.

Agreement with NDP position on coalitions: "In your view, are coalition governments (where two or more parties are given cabinet ministers): 1 =

a very bad thing, 2 = a bad thing, 3 = neither a good thing nor a bad thing, 4 = a good thing, 5 = a very good thing?" "I don't know" and "clicking through" the screen were coded as the midpoint of 3.

Contact of Voter by Parties (Asked Only in Wave 2)

Contact by NDP/LPC/CPC/BQ: "During the recent federal election campaign, which parties or candidates do you remember personally contacting you? By contacting you personally, we mean visiting your home, phoning you with a live person, phoning you with a recorded message, texting you, or e-mailing you. Please check all that apply: Conservative Party of Canada, New Democratic Party of Canada (NDP), Liberal Party of Canada, Bloc Québécois, Green Party of Canada, parties and candidates contacted me but I do not remember which ones, and no parties or candidates contacted me." Dummy variables were created for each party. "Parties and candidates contacted me but I do not remember which ones," "no parties or candidates contacted me," "I don't remember," and "clicking through" the screen were coded as 0.

Awareness of and Agreement with Parties' Platforms (Asked Only in Wave 2)

Correctly identified CPC plan: "In the recent election, which political party laid out a plan to fight Jihadist terrorists at home and abroad while protecting Canada's economy through balanced budgets and low taxes? Was it: the Conservative Party of Canada, the Liberal Party of Canada, the New Democratic Party of Canada (NDP), the Bloc Québécois, or the Green Party of Canada?" 1 = Conservative Party of Canada, 0 = all other responses were coded as 0, including "I don't know" and "clicking through" the screen.

Correctly identified NDP plan: "In the recent election, which political party laid out a plan to raise the corporate tax rate to pay for increased investment in social programs, like health care and childcare, while balancing the budget? Was it: the Conservative Party of Canada, the Liberal Party of Canada, the New Democratic Party of Canada (NDP), the Bloc Québécois, or the Green Party of Canada?" 1 = New Democratic Party, 0 = all other responses were coded as 0, including "I don't know" and "clicking through" the screen.

Correctly identified LPC plan: "In the recent election, which political party laid out a plan to raise income taxes on the wealthy to cut taxes for middle class families and promised to run short-term deficits to grow the economy through doubling federal funding on infrastructure? Was it: the Conservative Party of Canada, the Liberal Party of Canada, the New Democratic Party of Canada (NDP), the Bloc Québécois, or the Green Party of Canada?" 1 = Liberal Party of Canada, 0 = all other responses were coded as 0, including "I don't know" and "clicking through" the screen.

Correctly identified BQ plan: "In the recent election, which political party laid out a plan to promote the sovereignty of Quebec and to defend Quebec's interests in Ottawa through opposing pipelines crossing Quebec's territory and opposing the wearing of Muslim face coverings at Canadian citizenship ceremonies? Was it: the Conservative Party of Canada, the Liberal Party of Canada, the New Democratic Party of Canada (NDP), the Bloc Québécois, or the Green Party of Canada?" 1 = Bloc Québécois, 0 = all other responses were coded as 0, including "I don't know" and "clicking through" the screen.

Agreement with CPC plan/agreement with NDP plan/agreement with LPC plan/ agreement with BQ plan: Immediately after respondents were asked to identify which party had proposed the plan, they were asked "on a scale of 0 to 10, where 0 means that you STRONGLY DISAGREE with all parts of this plan and 10 means that you STRONGLY AGREE with all parts of this plan, how much do you agree with this plan?" "I don't know" and "clicking through" the screen were coded as the midpoint of 5.

Party Brands (Asked in Both Wave 1 and Wave 2)

First, the respondent was asked "how well would you say each of the following terms describes the Conservative Party of Canada/the Liberal Party of Canada/the New Democratic Party of Canada (NDP)/the Bloc Québécois? 1 = Not well at all, 2 = Slightly well, 3 = Moderately well, 4 = Very well, 5 = Extremely well." The respondent was given the following terms: "honest," "exciting," "competent," "charming," and "tough." Responding that all of these terms described a party "extremely well" meant that the respondent had a very strong image of the party brand. Responding that all of these terms described a party "not well at all" meant that the respondent had a very weak image of the party brand. "I don't know" and "clicking through" the screen were coded as the midpoint of 3. An index was created that combined the respondent's responses on these five adjectives in an additive five-point scale then recoded to range from 0 to 1. So each respondent was accorded an image score on party brand for each of the major parties in the election measured at both the start and the end of the campaign.

Cronbach's alpha CPC Brand Image Index in ROC (Wave 1) = 0.84; Cronbach's alpha CPC Brand Image Index in ROC (Wave 2) = 0.84; Cronbach's alpha CPC Brand Image Index in francophone Quebec (Wave 1) = 0.84; Cronbach's alpha CPC Brand Image Index in francophone Quebec (Wave 2) = 0.84; Cronbach's alpha NDP Brand Image Index in ROC (Wave 1) = 0.91; Cronbach's alpha NDP Brand Image Index in ROC (Wave 2) = 0.88; Cronbach's alpha NDP Brand Image Index in francophone Quebec (Wave 1) = 0.88; Cronbach's alpha NDP Brand Image Index in francophone Quebec (Wave 2) = 0.87; Cronbach's alpha LPC Brand Image Index in ROC (Wave 1) = 0.92; Cronbach's alpha LPC Brand Image Index in ROC (Wave 2) = 0.91; Cronbach's alpha LPC Brand Image Index in francophone Quebec (Wave 1) = 0.87; Cronbach's alpha LPC Brand Image Index in francophone Quebec (Wave 2) = 0.87; Cronbach's alpha BQ Brand Image Index in francophone Quebec (Wave 1) = 0.90; and Cronbach's alpha BQ Brand Image Index in francophone Quebec (Wave 2) = 0.89.

Notes

INTRODUCTION
1 Theories of political market orientation that compete with Ormrod's model are those of Jennifer Lees-Marshment (2001) and Aron O'Cass and Ranjit Voola (2010).
2 For instance, when presenting his platform ten days before the election, Tom Mulcair stated that "only the NDP is in a position to defeat Stephen Harper and form a more progressive government in Ottawa" (NDP 2015).

CHAPTER 1: FERMENT IN THE PARTY
1 A description of the role that each interviewee played in the NDP is contained in Appendix A.
2 According to media reports, some MPs, such as Pat Martin, John Solomon, and Chris Axworthy, were against the resolution condemning the third way, whereas MPs such as Libby Davies and Svend Robinson supported it. Similarly, the new CLC president, Ken Georgetti, found the debate at the convention a unifying experience for the party, whereas the CAW president, Buzz Hargrove, threatened to withdraw the support of his union because the NDP was not left wing enough, and Sid Ryan from the Canadian Union of Public Employees (CUPE) strongly opposed personal tax reductions as party policy.
3 There were 58,202 votes cast, and the breakdown was as follows: Layton (53.5 percent), Blaikie (24.7 percent), Nystrom (9.3 percent), Comartin (7.7 percent), Ducasse (3.7 percent), and Meslo (1.1 percent).

CHAPTER 2: THE RISE OF PARTY HEADQUARTERS
1 For a description of the index, see Gibson and Römmele (2009).
2 These transgressions included a video of one candidate smoking marijuana while driving and a reported instance of another candidate swimming naked in front of adolescents. See Erickson and Laycock (2009, 120).
3 During the English-language leaders' debate, Layton turned to Ignatieff and asked "why do you have the worst attendance record in the House of Commons of any member of Parliament? You know, most Canadians, if they don't show up for work, they don't get a promotion." See Wherry (2015).

4 The highest-profile case of this nature was Paul Manly, the son of former NDP MP Jim Manly, who had been detained recently by Israeli authorities when they boarded a ship of peace activists headed to the Gaza Strip. Even though the executive of the local EDA approved of his candidacy, the party would not let him run as a candidate. The younger Manly publicly claimed that the NDP had vetted him out because of "what I said and did when my father was in Israel. There was also concern that I was running to make Israel and Palestine an election issue." Quoted in Mas (2014).

5 From July 1 to September 30, 2015, New Democrats raised $9 million compared with $7.3 million for Liberals and $10 million for Conservatives (Canadian Press 2015).

6 I worked with NDP headquarters to administer this online survey to party members. A link to the survey was sent out to the party's email list of members, and that approach generated a significant number of respondents. To address some of the underrepresentation of certain regions in the sample, I ran Facebook and Twitter ads targeted at those who liked or followed NDP politicians, riding associations, or provincial parties. These ads specified that the survey was intended for NDP members only, and a screening question made respondents self-identify as members before continuing. The party provided its current membership numbers, which allowed me to weight the data set by region (Atlantic, Quebec, Ontario, Prairies and the North, and British Columbia). The party does not keep track of other sociodemographic characteristics of its members, so further weighting was not possible.

7 The scales for the statements "I trust the professionals at party headquarters to make campaign strategies," "party policy should be made by experts and professionals," and "unions should have less influence on the NDP" were reversed so that "strongly disagree" is coded as 1.0, "somewhat disagree" is coded as 0.75, "somewhat agree" is coded as 0.25, and "strongly agree" is coded as 0.0. To preserve cases, all indices were constructed using mean scores, with missing values assigned the midpoint of 0.5.

8 The scales for the statements "the NDP has moved too far to the centre and should move back to the left," "the federal NDP should focus less on winning elections and more on member education and building our movement," and "the NDP should clearly state that it is a 'socialist' party" were reversed so that "strongly disagree" is coded as 2.0, "somewhat disagree" is coded as 0.75, "somewhat agree" is coded as 0.35, and "strongly agree" is coded as 0.0. To preserve cases, all indexes were constructed using mean scores, with missing values assigned the midpoint of 0.5.

9 The eleven activities ranged from attending NDP events to volunteering for the party to donating to the party.

10 Sociodemographic variables are dummy variables for Atlantic Canada, Quebec, the Prairies, and British Columbia, with Ontario as the reference category; sex (female = 1, male = 0); age in years; education (0 = some elementary or high school, 8 = professional degree/doctorate); income (0 = less than $20,000, 20 = over $200,000); religiosity (1 = religion very unimportant, 2 = somewhat unimportant, 3 = somewhat important, 4 = very important); visible minority (1 = visible minority, 0 = not visible minority); immigrant (1 = born outside Canada, 0 = born in Canada); union membership (1 = union member, 0 = non-union member); rural (1 = rural resident, 0 = urban/suburban resident); francophone (1 = francophone, 2 = nonfrancophone).

CHAPTER 3: IMPOSING DISCIPLINE AND ORDER

1 For a description of the lottery system for private members' bills adopted in 2005, see Blidook (2012, 29–35).
2 From 2011 to 2015, Bruce Hyer, Claude Patry, Sana Hassainia, and Jean-François Larose left the NDP caucus, citing dissatisfaction with having to support common policy positions with which they personally disagreed. Respectively, they left over the following issues: the long gun registry, the Clarity Bill, the Israel-Palestine conflict, and regional economic development.
3 Both John Rafferty and Bruce Hyer voted against the caucus on abolition of the long gun registry in 2012. It was a whipped vote. Whereas Hyer left to join the Green Party, Rafferty remained in the caucus and was a candidate for the NDP in the 2015 election.
4 I would like to thank Alex Steffen for his excellent research assistance in constructing this data set.
5 Arar was a dual Syrian-Canadian citizen detained by the American government while travelling through JFK Airport in New York on the suspicion that he was a terrorist. He was held by the Americans for two weeks and then sent to Syria, where he was tortured for a year in prison and subsequently returned to Canada. The case brought up a number of questions about the civil rights of Canadians suspected as terrorists and the cooperation of the Canadian government with American intelligence agencies.
6 The Airbus affair involved former Progressive Conservative Prime Minister Brian Mulroney, accused of accepting kickbacks from German businessman Karlheinz Schreiber from the sale of Airbus planes to Air Canada (then owned by the federal government).
7 Nigel Wright, chief of staff to the prime minister, personally paid for fraudulent expense claims made by Senator Mike Duffy. Questions swirled around the extent to which Wright was paying for Duffy's silence and how much the prime minister himself knew about the scandal.
8 At the time of the interviews, the NDP caucus comprised 56 percent Quebec MPs, 36 percent female MPs, 15 percent visible minority MPs, and 23 percent MPs under the age of thirty-five. The interview sample comprised 57 percent Quebec MPs, 34 percent female MPs, 17 percent visible minority MPs, and 28 percent MPs under the age of thirty-five.

CHAPTER 4: DARE TO DREAM

1 For instance, the passage of text in a November 22, 2000, NDP news release read "New Democrat Leader Alexa McDonough today condemned the Chrétien government for abandoning its responsibility to fund social housing." This passage was coded under the themes "housing" and "attack Chrétien government."
2 Found in the Whitehorn Archives.
3 In the last week of the campaign, after a member of Trudeau's campaign team had to resign after advising an oil company on how to fast-track a pipeline through a new Liberal government, the NDP released hard-hitting television commercials in French and English that invoked the sponsorship scandal from the Chrétien years.

CHAPTER 5: CONTINUITY AND CHANGE

1 In the ROC sample, 11 percent of respondents indicated that they would certainly vote for the NDP compared with 19 percent who would probably vote for the party and 28 percent who would consider voting for the party. In the Quebec sample, 14 percent of respondents indicated that they would certainly vote for the NDP compared with 21 percent who would probably vote for the party and 29 percent who would consider voting for the party.

CHAPTER 6: STEALING MARKET SHARE

1 Basic outlines of the difficulties of the Liberal Party campaigns and the unpopularity of their leaders in the later 2000s can be found in Fournier et al., (2013); Gidengil et al., (2012); and Jeffrey (2009, 2011).
2 In terms of partisanship, on each CES respondents were asked "in federal politics, do you usually think of yourself as a: Liberal, Conservative, N.D.P., Bloc Québécois, Green Party, or none of these?"
3 According to CES data, 15 percent of English Canadian women and 9 percent of English Canadian men voted NDP in 2000. In the subsequent elections, the ratio was 24 percent women and 20 percent men in 2004; 25 percent women and 19 percent men in 2006; 25 percent women and 18 percent men in 2008; and 28 percent women and 26 percent men in 2011.
4 According to CES data, NDP partisans in the English Canadian electorate increased from 8 percent in 2004 to 10 percent in 2011.
5 The percentage of English Canadian NDP identifiers who voted for the party increased from 80 percent in 2004 to 90 percent in 2011.
6 On a scale of 0 to 1, where 0 = the economy had become worse, 0.5 = the economy stayed the same, and 1 = the economy had become better, the mean for the 2008 election was 0.34. The mean was 0.65 in 2006, 0.48 in 2004, and 0.62 in 2000. The mean for the 2011 election was 0.58.
7 On a scale of 0 to 1, where 0 = spend less on defence, 0.5 = spend the same on defence, and 1 = spend more on defence, the mean for the 2000 election was 0.60. The mean for 2004 and 2006 was 0.70, for 2008 it was 0.56, and for 2011 it was 0.50.
8 Within the English Canadian electorate as a whole, Chrétien scored 52 out of 100 on the likeability scale in 2000, and Martin scored 50 out of 100 in 2004 and 47 out of 100 in 2006. Dion scored 40 out of 100 in 2008, and Ignatieff scored 36 out of 100 in 2011.
9 In 2006, the CES contained 630 Quebec voters for the four major parties, and only 60 of them were NDP voters. Similarly, in the 2008 CES, there were only 78 NDP voters of the 624 voters for the four major parties in Quebec. Even in the 2011 CES, there were 729 voters for the four major parties in Quebec, and 309 of them were NDP voters. In contrast, the Ipsos-Reid sample sizes in Quebec were huge (844 NDP voters of 7,442 voters in 2006; 1,371 NDP voters of 7,376 voters in 2008; 2,243 NDP voters of 8,780 voters in 2011).
10 Differences in question wording and the categories provided for respondents hamper direct comparisons. Nonetheless, the Ipsos-Reid data illustrate that the split was

as follows: 34 percent hard sovereignist, 30 percent soft nationalist, and 34 percent hard federalist in 2006; 23 percent hard sovereignist, 36 percent soft nationalist, and 41 percent hard federalist in 2008; and 22 percent hard sovereignist, 38 percent soft nationalist, and 40 percent hard federalist in 2011.

11 It is important to keep in mind that hard federalist is the reference category in Table 6.10. The table indicates that in 2008 hard federalists were thirty-three points more likely than hard sovereignists to vote LPC and that hard federalists were twenty-five points more likely than soft nationalists to vote LPC. The numbers are similar for the CPC: hard federalists were twenty-eight points more likely than hard sovereignists to vote CPC, and hard federalists were twenty-one points more likely than soft nationalists to vote CPC. Conversely, hard federalists were thirteen points more likely than hard sovereignists to vote NDP and only five points more likely than soft nationalists to vote NDP in 2008. By 2011, on the one hand, the probability of hard federalists voting CPC or LPC compared with the other two categories had dropped significantly. On the other hand, the probability of hard federalists voting NDP compared with the other two categories had increased noticeably.

12 Harper was chosen as best prime minister by 20 percent, Dion by 16 percent, and Duceppe by 15 percent. May was chosen by 2 percent, and "I don't know" was selected by 12 percent.

13 In 2006, 40 percent of BQ voters found a "Liberal-led minority government supported by the Bloc Québécois" very or somewhat acceptable, and 30 percent of BQ voters found a "Liberal-led minority government supported by the NDP" very or somewhat acceptable.

14 In 2011, 45 percent of NDP voters desired a majority government compared with 44 percent who wanted a minority government and 11 percent who responded "I don't know."

CHAPTER 7: HEARTBREAK

1 My definition of Quebec "francophone" does include the seventy-seven respondents or 3.9 percent of the SOM sample who reported having French and another language as their mother tongues.

2 The weights were created using the ipfraking package in Stata that uses a procedure known as iterative proportional fitting or raking. See Kolenikov (2014).

3 In this category, I also included the tiny number of respondents who said that they would probably not or never vote for the NDP in August and then voted for the party in October.

4 A recent study of ten provincial election surveys in Canada revealed that a primary difference between inner-city residents and Canadians living in suburbs and rural areas was the level of postmaterialism. See McGrane, Berdahl, and Bell (2017).

5 Despite receiving 35 percent of the popular vote in Quebec, the Liberals received 53 percent of the seats there. Within the larger SOM survey, which included respondents who filled out only Wave 2 as well as respondents who filled out both Wave 1 and Wave 2, the sample size for anglophones is 567 and for allophones 301. In this survey, Liberal support among anglophones was 50 percent and among allophones 51 percent.

6 In English Canada, 71 percent of lost NDPers were very favourable or somewhat favourable to cap and trade, 84 percent were very favourable or somewhat favourable to pharmacare, and 82 percent somewhat or strongly disapproved of Bill C-51.
7 In August, 75 percent of lost NDPers in English Canada stated that "inspiring" described Trudeau "extremely well," "quite well," or "moderately well" compared with 70 percent who stated that "inspiring" described Mulcair "extremely well," "quite well," or "moderately well." In October, 91 percent of lost NDPers in English Canada stated that "inspiring" described Trudeau "extremely well," "quite well," or "moderately well" compared with 60 percent who stated that "inspiring" described Mulcair "extremely well," "quite well," or "moderately well."
8 In francophone Quebec, 81 percent of lost NDPers were very or somewhat favourable to cap and trade, and 70 percent were very or somewhat favourable to pharmacare.
9 To increase the sample size, these percentages were taken from the second wave of the SOM survey with respondents who did not fill out the first wave included. In total, 7,067 respondents were francophone voters, and 1,562 reported being strategic voters.

CHAPTER 8: WHICH WAY NOW?

1 The full text of Mulcair's speech to delegates is available at http://nationalpost.com/news/the-full-text-of-tom-mulcairs-speech-at-the-ndp-convention.
2 The full text of the Leap Manifesto is available at http://leapmanifesto.org/en/the-leap-manifesto/.

References

Adams, Paul. 1999. "NDP's Path Still Veers to the Left." *Globe and Mail*, August 30, A1.
Alberts, Sheldon. 1999. "NDP MP's Blair-Like Ideas Given a Cool Reception: Party at a Crossroads." *National Post*, April 28, A7.
Anderson, Cameron. 2010. "Economic Voting in Canada: Assessing the Effects of Subjective Perceptions and Electoral Context." In *Voting Behaviour in Canada*, edited by Cameron Anderson and Laura Stephenson, 139–62. Vancouver: UBC Press.
Anderson, Cameron, and Laura Stephenson. 2010. "The Puzzle of Elections and Voting in Canada." In *Voting Behaviour in Canada*, edited by Cameron Anderson and Laura Stephenson, 1–42. Vancouver: UBC Press.
Archer, Keith. 1985. "The Failure of the New Democratic Party: Unions, Unionists, and Politics in Canada." *Canadian Journal of Political Science* 18 (2): 353–66.
–. 1987. "Canadian Unions, The New Democratic Party, and the Problems of Collective Action." *Labour/Le Travail* 20 (Fall): 173–84.
–. 1990. *Political Choices and Electoral Consqeuences: A Study of Organized Labour and the New Democratic Party*. Montreal: McGill-Queen's University Press.
Archer, Keith, and Alan Whitehorn. 1997. *Political Activists: NDP in Convention*. Toronto: Oxford University Press.
Avakumovic, Ivan. 1978. *Socialism in Canada: A Study of the CCF-NDP in Federal and Provincial Politics*. Toronto: McClelland and Stewart.
Baines, Paul. 1999. "Voter Segmentation and Candidate Positioning." In *Handbook of Political Marketing*, edited by Brian Newman, 403–20. London: Sage Publications.
Basen, Ira. 2015. "On the Campaign Trail, Everyone's Singing the Middle-Class Blues." September 13. http://www.cbc.ca/news/politics/on-the-campaign-trail-everyone-s-singing-the-middle-class-blues-1.3224398.
Beer, Samuel. 1969. *Modern British Politics: A Study of Parties and Pressure Groups*. London: Faber and Faber.
Bélanger, Éric, and Richard Nadeau. 2009. "The Bloc Québécois: Victory by Default." In *The Canadian Federal Election of 2008*, edited by Jon H. Pammett and Christopher Dornan, 136–61. Toronto: Dundurn.
–. 2011. "The Bloc Québécois: Capsized by the Orange Wave." In *The Canadian Federal Election of 2011*, edited by Jon H. Pammett and Christopher Dornan, 111–37. Toronto: Dundurn.

–. 2016. "The Bloc Québécois in Rainbow-Coloured Quebec." In *The Canadian Federal Election of 2015*, edited by Jon H. Pammett and Christopher Dornan, 117–40. Toronto: Dundurn.

Bellavance, Joel-Denis, and Sheldon Alberts. 1999. "CAW Leader Brands Motion to Accept Business Donations 'Betrayal.'" *National Post*, August 28, A7.

Blaikie, Bill. 2003. "NDP Must Speak from the Heart Again." *Toronto Star*, January 15, A18.

–. 2011. *The Blaikie Report: An Insider's Look at Faith and Politics*. Toronto: United Church Publishing House.

Blais, André, Elisabeth Gidengil, Richard Nadeau, and Neil Nevitte. 2002. *Anatomy of a Liberal Victory: Making Sense of the Vote in the 2000 Canadian Election*. Peterborough, ON: Broadview Press.

Blatchford, Andy. 2015. "Did Trudeaumania 2.0 Make a Difference in This Election?" *Toronto Star*, October 19, A16.

Blidook, Kelly. 2012. *Constituency Influence in Parliament: Countering the Centre*. Vancouver: UBC Press.

Boutilier, Alex. 2016. "Thomas Mulcair Gets Boost from Quebec Caucus." *Toronto Star*, March 21, A1.

Breton, Charles, Fred Cutler, Sarah Lachance, and Alex Mierke-Zatwarnicki. 2017. "Telephone versus Online Survey Modes for Election Studies: Comparing Canadian Public Opinion and Vote Choice in the 2015 Federal Election." *Canadian Journal of Political Science* 50 (4): 1005–36. https://doi.org/10.1017/S0008423917000610.

Brodie, Janine. 1985. "From Waffles to Grits: A decade in the life of the New Democratic Party." In *Party Politics in Canada*, edited by Hugh Thorburn, 245-60. Scarborough: Prentice-Hall.

Bryden, Joan. 2015. "Liberals Spent Way Less than the Maximum – and the Tories – to Win." *Toronto Star*, October 23, A9.

Bryman, Alan. 2007. "Barriers to Integrating Quantitative and Qualitative Research." *Journal of Mixed Methods Research* 1 (1): 8–22. https://doi.org/10.1177/2345678 906290531.

Budge, Ian, David Robertson, and Derek Hearl, eds. 1987. *Ideology, Strategy, and Party Change: Spatial Analysis of Post-War Elections Programmes in Nineteen Democracies*. Cambridge, UK: Cambridge University Press. https://doi.org/10.1017/CBO 9780511558771.

Budge, Ian, and Dennis Farlie. 1983. "Party Competition: Selective Emphasis or Direct Confrontation? An Alternative View with Data." In *Western European Party Systems*, edited by Peter Mair, 267–305. London: Sage Publications.

Budge, Ian, Hans-Dieter Klingemann, Andrea Volkens, Judith Bara, and Eric Tanenbaum. 2001. *Mapping Policy Preferences: Estimates for Parties, Electors, and Governments*. Oxford: Oxford University Press.

Butler, Patrick, and Neil Collins. 1996. "Strategic Analysis in Political Markets." *European Journal of Marketing* 30 (10–11): 25–36. https://doi.org/10.1108/03090569610 149773.

Camfield, David. 2011. *Canadian Labour in Crisis: Reinventing the Workers' Movement*. Halifax: Fernwood.

Cameron, Duncan. 2005. "The NDP and the Making of a Citizens' Party." In *Challenges and Perils: Social Democracy in Neoliberal Times*, edited by William Carroll and Robert Ratner, 137–51. Halifax: Fernwood.

Campbell, Colin, and William Christian. 1996. *Parties, Leaders, and Ideologies in Canada*. Toronto: McGraw-Hill Ryerson.

Canadian Labour Congress. 2005. *Capacity Building for Change*. Ottawa: Canadian Labour Congress.

Canadian Manufacturers and Exporters. 2015. "NDP Policy Announcement Sends Mixed Signals to Manufacturing: CME." January 27.

Canadian Press. 2015. "Election 2015 Fundraising Results: Liberals Raised Less Money than Tories, NDP." October 30. https://www.huffingtonpost.ca/2015/10/30/liberals-first-at-ballot-box-but-third-in-fundraising-sweepstakes_n_8434614.html.

Carey, John. 2009. *Legislative Voting and Accountability*. Cambridge, UK: Cambridge University Press.

Carroll, William. 2005. "Social Democracy in Neoliberal Times." In *Challenges and Perils: Social Democracy in Neoliberal Times*, edited by William Carroll and Robert Ratner, 7–24. Halifax: Fernwood.

CBC. 2014. "Andrea Horwath Campaign Leaves Prominent NDP Supporters 'Deeply Distressed.'" May 23. http://www.cbc.ca/news/canada/toronto/ontario-votes-2014/andrea-horwath-campaign-leaves-prominent-ndp-supporters-deeply-distressed-1.2652766.

Chow, Olivia. 2014. *My Journey*. Toronto: HarperCollins.

Clarke, Harold, Allan Kornberg, and Thomas Scotto. 2009a. *Making Political Choices: Canada and the United States*. Toronto: University of Toronto Press.

–. 2009b. "None of the Above: Voters in the 2008 Federal Election." In *The Canadian General Election of 2008*, edited by Jon H. Pammett and Christopher Dornan, 257–89. Toronto: Dundurn.

Clarke, Harold, Jason Reifler, Thomas Scotto, and Marianne Stewart. 2016. "It's Spring Again! Voting in the 2015 Federal Election." In *The Canadian General Election of 2015*, edited by Jon H. Pammett and Christopher Dornan, 327–56. Toronto: Dundurn.

Clarke, Harold, Thomas Scotto, Jason Reifler, and Allan Kornberg. 2011. "Winners and Losers: Voters in the 2011 Federal Election." In *The Canadian General Election of 2011*, edited by Jon H. Pammett and Christopher Dornan, 271–302. Toronto: Dundurn.

Clarke, Harold, Timothy Gravelle, Thomas Scotto, Marianne Stewart, and Jason Reifler. 2017. "Like Father, Like Son: Justin Trudeau and Valence Voting in Canada's 2015 Federal Election." *PS: Political Science and Politics* 50 (3): 701–7. https://doi.org/10.1017/S1049096517000452.

Clarkson, Stephen. 2001. "Liberal Threepeat: The Multi-System Party in the Multi-Party System." In *The Canadian General Election of 2000*, edited by Jon H. Pammett and Christopher Dornan, 13–88. Toronto: Dundurn.

–. 2004. "Disaster and Recovery: Paul Martin as Political Lazarus." In *The Canadian General Election of 2004*, edited by Jon H. Pammett and Christopher Dornan, 28–65. Toronto: Dundurn.

–. 2006. "How the Big Red Machine Became the Little Red Machine." In *The Canadian General Election of 2006*, edited by Jon H. Pammett and Christopher Dornan, 24–58. Toronto: Dundurn.

Cochrane, Christopher. 2015. *Left and Right: The Small World of Political Ideas*. Montreal: McGill-Queen's University Press.

Coletto, David. 2016. "Polling and the 2015 Federal Election." In *The Canadian Federal Election of 2015*, edited by Jon H. Pammett and Christopher Dornan, 305–26. Toronto: Dundurn.

Coletto, David, and Munroe Eagles. 2011. "The Impact of Election Finance Reforms on Local Party Organization." In *Money, Politics, and Democracy: Canada's Party Finance Reforms*, edited by Lisa Young and Harold Jansen, 104–29. Vancouver: UBC Press.

Comartin, Joe. 2002. "Winning ... for a Change." Alan Whitehorn Collection.

Conway, J.F. 2016. "Federal NDP's Pact with Satan Implodes." *Canadian Dimension*, May, 26. https://canadiandimension.com/articles/view/federal-ndps-pact-with-satan-implodes.

Cramme, Olaf, and Patrick Diamond. 2012. *After the Third Way: The Future of Social Democracy in Europe*. London: Policy Network.

Creswell, John. 2003. *Research Design: Qualitative, Quantitative, and Mixed Methods Approaches*. Thousand Oaks, CA: Sage.

Cross, Michael. 1974. *The Decline and Fall of A Good Idea: CCF-NDP Manifestoes, 1932–1969*. Toronto: New Hogtown.

Cross, William. 2004. *Political Parties*. Vancouver: UBC Press.

Cross, William, Jonathan Malloy, Tamara A. Small, and Laura B. Stephenson. 2015. *Fighting for Votes: Parties, the Media, and Voters in an Ontario Election*. Vancouver: UBC Press.

Curry, Bill, and Stuart Thompson. 2013. "Conservative MPs Break Ranks More Often than Opposition." *Globe and Mail*, February 3, A1.

Docherty, David. 1997. *Mr. Smith Goes to Ottawa*. Vancouver: UBC Press.

Duverger, Maurice. 1963. *Political Parties, Their Organization and Activity in the Modern State*. London, UK: Wiley.

Ducasse, Pierre. 2003. "Pragmatic Radicalism: A Vision of Hope on the Left." *Policy Options*, March, 9–11.

Elections Canada. 2015. *Analysis of Financial Trends of Regulated Federal Political Entities, 2000–2014*. Ottawa: Elections Canada.

Ellis, Faron. 2016. "Stephen Harper and the 2015 Conservative Campaign: Defeated but Not Devastated." In *The Canadian General Election of 2015*, edited by Jon H. Pammett and Christopher Dornan, 23–56. Toronto: Dundurn.

Ellis, Faron, and Peter Woolstencroft. 2006. "A Change of Government, Not a Change of Country: The Conservatives and the 2006 Election." In *The Canadian General Election of 2006*, edited by Jon H. Pammett and Christopher Dornan, 93–121. Toronto: Dundurn.

–. 2009. "Stephen Harper and the Conservatives Campaign on Their Record." In *The Canadian General Election of 2008*, edited by Jon H. Pammett and Christopher Dornan, 16–62. Toronto: Dundurn.

–. 2011. "The Conservative Campaign: Becoming the New Natural Governing Party." In *The Canadian General Election of 2011*, edited by Jon H. Pammett and Christopher Dornan, 15–44. Toronto: Dundurn.

Engelmann, F. 1956. "Membership Participation in Policy-Making in the C.C.F." *Canadian Journal of Economics and Political Science* 22: 161–73.

Erickson, Lynda, and David Laycock. 2002. "Post-Materialism versus the Welfare State?" *Party Politics* 8 (3): 301–25. https://doi.org/10.1177/1354068802008003003.

–. 2009. "Modernization, Incremental Progress, and the Challenge of Relevance: The NDP's 2008 Campaign." In *The Canadian General Election of 2008*, edited by Jon H. Pammett and Christopher Dornan, 98–134. Toronto: Dundurn.

Erickson, Lynda, and Maria Zakharova. 2015. "Members, Activists, and Party Opinion." In *Reviving Social Democracy: The Near Death and Surprising Rise of the Federal NDP*, edited by David Laycock and Lynda Erickson, 165–96. Vancouver: UBC Press.

Eulau, Heinz, and John Wahlke. 1978. *The Politics of Representation: Continuities in Theory and Research*. Beverly Hills, CA: Sage.

Evans, Bryan. 2012. "From Protest Movement to Neoliberal Management: Canada's New Democratic Party in the Era of Permanent Austerity." In *Social Democracy after the Cold War*, edited by Bryan Evans and Ingo Schmidt, 45–98. Edmonton: Athabasca University Press.

Farrell, David, and Paul Webb. 2000. "Political Parties as Campaign Organisations." In *Parties without Partisans: Political Change in Advanced Industrial Democracies*, edited by Russell Dalton and Marting Wattenberg, 124–46. Oxford: Oxford University Press.

Fekete, Jason. 2013. "Tories Slam NDP Leader Mulcair on Taxes." *Ottawa Citizen*, September 17, A3.

Fife, Robert. 1998. "NDP's McDonough Hopes to Be Like Blair." *National Post*, December 21, A1.

Flanagan, Tom. 2009. *Harper's Team: Behind the Scenes of the Conservative Rise to Power*. 2nd ed. Montreal: McGill-Queen's University Press.

–. 2012. "Political Communication and the Permanent Campaign." In *How Canadians Communicate IV: Media and Politics*, edited by David Taras and Christopher Waddell, 129–48. Edmonton: Athabasca University Press.

–. 2013. "Something Blue: The Harper Conservatives as Garrison Party." In *Conservatism in Canada*, edited by James Farney and David Rayside, 79–94. Toronto: University of Toronto Press.

–. 2014. *Winning Power: Canadian Campaigning in the 21st Century*. Montreal: McGill-Queen's University Press.

Forum Research. 2015. "NDP Leads in First Post-Writ Poll." August 3. http://poll.forumresearch.com/post/334/new-democrats-headed-for-solid-minority.

Fournier, Patrick, Fred Cutler, Stuart Soroka, Dietlind Stolle, and Éric Bélanger. 2013. "Riding the Orange Wave: Leadership, Values, Issues, and the 2011 Canadian Election." *Canadian Journal of Political Science* 46 (4): 863–97. https://doi.org/10.1017/S0008423913000875.

Gagnon, Alain, and François Boucher. 2017. "Party Politics in a Distinct Society: Two Eras of Block Voting in Quebec." In *Canadian Parties in Transition*, 4th ed., edited by Alain-G. Gagnon and A. Brian Tanguay, 65–89. Toronto: University of Toronto Press.

Gatehouse, Jonathan. 1998. "Move to Right Will Kill NDP: Hargrove." *National Post*, December 22, A1.

Gauvin, Jean-Philippe, Chris Chhim, and Mike Medeiros. 2016. "Did They Mind the Gap? Voter/Party Ideological Proximity between the BQ, the NDP, and Quebec Voters, 2006–2011." *Canadian Journal of Political Science* 49 (2): 289–310. https://doi.org/10.1017/S000842391600038X.

Gibson, Rachel, and Andrea Römmele. 2001. "Changing Campaign Communications: A Party-Centered Theory of Professionalized Campaigning." *Harvard International Journal of Press/Politics* 6 (4): 31–43. https://doi.org/10.1177/108118001129172323.

–. 2009. "Measuring the Professionalization of Political Campaigning." *Party Politics* 15 (3): 265–93. https://doi.org/10.1177/1354068809102245.

Giddens, Anthony. 1998. *The Third Way: The Renewal of Social Democracy*. Cambridge, UK: Polity Press.

–. 2007. *Over to You, Mr. Brown: How Labour Can Win Again*. Cambridge, UK: Polity Press.

Gidengil, Elisabeth, Neil Nevitte, André Blais, Joanna Everitt, and Patrick Fournier. 2012. *Dominance and Decline: Making Sense of Recent Canadian Elections*. Toronto: University of Toronto Press.

Gidluck, Lynn. 2012. *Visionaries, Crusaders, and Firebrands: The Idealistic Canadians Who Built the NDP*. Toronto: James Lorimer.

Glaser, Barney. 2004. "Remodeling Grounded Theory." *Forum Qualitative Social Research* 5 (2): 1–22.

Greene, Jennifer, and Valerie Caracelli. 1997. "Defining and Describing the Paradigm Issue in Mixed-Method Evaluation." *New Directions for Evaluation* 74: 5–17. https://doi.org/10.1002/ev.1068.

Greenspon, Edward. 2001. "Covering Campaign 2000." In *The Canadian General Election of 2000*, edited by Jon H. Pammett and Christopher Dornan, 165–90. Toronto: Dundurn.

Hannay, Chris. 2013. "The Politics of Website Design: The NDP MPs Advertise Party, Conservatives Don't." *Globe and Mail*, December 23, A7.

Happy, J.R. 1986. "Voter Sensitivity to Economic Conditions: A Canadian-American Comparison." *Comparative Politics* 19 (1): 45–56. https://doi.org/10.2307/421780.

Harrell, Margaret, and Melissa Bradley. 2009. *Data Collection Methods: Semi-Structured Interviews and Focus Groups*. Santa Monica, CA: RAND Corporation.

Heath, Jamey. 2007. *Dead Centre: Hope, Possibility, and Unity for Canadian Progressives*. Mississauga, ON: John Wiley and Sons.

Hopper, Tristin. 2015. "Leap Manifesto Plan to Overthrow Capitalism Puts Spanner in NDP Plans to Convince Centrist Voters." *National Post*, September 16, A8.

Horowitz, Gad. 1968. *Canadian Labour in Politics*. Toronto: University of Toronto Press.

Jansen, Harold, and Lisa Young. 2009. "Solidarity Forever? The NDP, Organized Labour, and the Changing Face of Party Finance in Canada." *Canadian Journal of Political Science* 42 (3): 657–78. https://doi.org/10.1017/S0008423909990412.

–. 2011. "Cartels, Syndicates, and Coalitions: Canada's Political Parties after the 2004 Reforms." In *Money, Politics, and Democracy: Canada's Party Finance Reforms*, edited by Lisa Young and Harold Jansen, 82–103. Vancouver: UBC Press.

Jeffrey, Brooke. 2009. "Missed Opportunity: The Invisible Liberals." In *The Canadian General Election of 2008*, edited by Jon H. Pammett and Christopher Dornan, 63–97. Toronto: Dundurn.

–. 2011. "The Disappearing Liberals: Caught in the Crossfire." In *The Canadian General Election of 2011*, edited by Jon H. Pammett and Christopher Dornan, 45–74. Toronto: Dundurn.

–. 2016. "Back to the Future: The Resurgent Liberals." In *The Canadian General Election of 2015*, edited by Jon H. Pammett and Christopher Dornan, 57–84. Toronto: Dundurn.

–. 2017. "The Liberal Party of Canada: Rebuilding, Resurgence, and Return to Power." In *Canadian Parties in Transition*, 4th ed., edited by Alain-G. Gagnon and A. Brian Tanguay, 65–89. Toronto: University of Toronto Press.

Jenson, Jane, and Denis Saint-Martin. 2003. "Routes to Social Cohesion? Citizenship and the Social Investment State." *Canadian Journal of Sociology* 28 (1): 77–99. https://doi.org/10.2307/3341876.

Johnston, Richard. 2017. *The Canadian Party System: An Analytic History*. Vancouver: UBC Press.

Jonasson, Stefan. 2015. "Winnipeg NDP Candidate Quits over Social Media Posts Linking Jewish Sect to Taliban." September 24. http://www.cbc.ca/news/canada/manitoba/winnipeg-ndp-candidate-quits-over-social-media-posts-linking-jewish-sect-to-taliban-1.3243053.

Kalla, Joshua, and David Broockman. 2018. "The Minimal Persuasive Effects of Campaign Contact in General Elections: Evidence from 49 Field Experiments." *American Political Science Review* 112 (1): 148–66.

Kam, Christopher. 2009. *Party Discipline and Parliamentary Government*. Cambridge, UK: Cambridge University Press. https://doi.org/10.1017/CBO9780511576614.

Kanji, Mebs, Antoine Bilodeau, and Thomas Scotto, eds. 2012. *The Canadian Election Studies: Assessing Four Decades of Influence*. Vancouver: UBC Press.

Katz, Richard, and Peter Mair. 1995. "Changing Models of Party Organization and Party Democracy: The Emergence of the Cartel Party." *Party Politics* 1 (1): 5–28. https://doi.org/10.1177/1354068895001001001.

–. 2009. "The Cartel Party Thesis: A Restatement." *Perspectives on Politics* 7 (4): 753–66. https://doi.org/10.1017/S1537592709991782.

Kavanagh, Dennis. 1995. *Election Campaigning: The New Marketing of Politics*. Hoboken, NJ: Blackwell.

Kay, Barry, and Andrea Perrella. 2012. "Eclipse of Class: A Review of Demographic Variables, 1974–2006." In *The Canadian Election Studies: Assessing Four Decades of Influence*, edited by Mebs Kanji, Antoine Bilodeau, and Thomas Scotto, 121–36. Vancouver: UBC Press.

Kennedy, Mark. 2015. "NDP Policy Manual Removed from Party's Website Because It 'Is Not the Platform': NDP Adviser." *Ottawa Citizen*, August 26, A8.

Kirkup, Kristy. 2016. "Alberta NDP Take Aim at Tom Mulcair over 'Leap Manifesto.'" *Canadian Press*, April 9.

Kohut, Tania. 2015. "Trudeau Skirts Suggestion that Liberals Leaning Further to Left than NDP." August 27. https://globalnews.ca/news/2189566/trudeau-skirts-suggestion-liberals-leaning-further-left-than-ndp.

Kolenikov, Stanislav. 2014. "Calibrating Survey Data Using Iterative Proportional Fitting (Raking)." *Stata Journal* 14 (1): 22–59.

Koop, Royce, and Amanda Bittner. 2013. "Parties and Elections after 2011: The Fifth Canadian Party System?" In *Parties, Elections, and the Future of Canadian Politics*, edited by Royce Koop and Amanda Bittner, 308–31. Vancouver: UBC Press.

Kvale, Stienar, and Svend Brinkmann. 2009. *Interviews: Learning the Craft of Qualitative Research Interviewing*. London: Sage.

Lavigne, Brad. 2013. *Building the Orange Wave: The Inside Story behind the Historic Rise of Jack Layton and the NDP*. Madeira Park, BC: Douglas and McIntyre.

Lawton, Valerie. 2001a. "Robinson Calls for New Left-Wing Party." *Toronto Star*, June 7, A6.

–. 2001b. "NDP Moves to the Left but Pulls Up Too Short for Some." *Toronto Star*, November 24, A30.

Laycock, David. 2015. "Conceptual Foundations of Continuity and Change in NDP Ideology." In *Reviving Social Democracy: The Near Death and Surprising Rise of the Federal NDP*, edited by David Laycock and Lynda Erickson, 109–39. Vancouver: UBC Press.

Layton, Jack. 2003a. "Before You Vote, Ask Yourself: *Who Can Re-Engergize Our Party and Elect More NDP MPs?*" Alan Whitehorn Collection.

–. 2003b. "Jack Layton Knows that This Has to Change: When We Lose MPs ... Canadians Lose Hope." Alan Whitehorn Collection.

Lees-Marshment, Jennifer. 2001. "The Marriage of Politics and Marketing." *Political Studies* 49 (4): 692–713. https://doi.org/10.1111/1467-9248.00337.

Levitz, Stephanie. 2011. "Jack Layton Named 2011's Newsmaker of the Year." *Globe and Mail*, December 22, A1.

Liberal Party of Canada. 2015. "More Economists Blast Flawed NDP Costing." News release, September 21. https://www.liberal.ca/more-economists-blast-flawed-ndp-costing/.

MacKinnon, Mark. 2001a. "New Democrat MP Urges Massive Overhaul of Party." *Globe and Mail*, January 9, A4.

–. 2001b. "No Clear Path as NDP Tries to Find Its Way." *Globe and Mail*, June 11, A4.

Manwaring, Rob, and Matt Beech. 2018. "The Case of the British Labour Party: Back into the Wilderness." In *Why the Left Loses: The Decline of the Centre-Left in Comparative Perspective*, edited by Rob Manwaring and Paul Kennedy, 25–38. Bristol: Policy Press.

Manwaring, Rob, and Paul Kennedy. 2018. *Why the Left Loses: The Decline of the Centre-Left in Comparative Perspective*. Bristol: Policy Press.

Marland, Alex. 2012. "Amateurs versus Professionals: The 1993 and 2006 Canadian Federal Elections." In *Political Marketing in Canada*, edited by Alex Marland, Thierry Giasson, and Jennifer Lees-Marshment, 44–61. Vancouver: UBC Press.

–. 2016. *Brand Command: Canadian Politics and Democracy in the Age of Message Control*. Vancouver: UBC Press.
Marland, Alex, Thierry Giasson, and Anna Lennox Esselment. 2017. *Permanent Campaigning in Canada*. Vancouver: UBC Press.
Marland, Alex, Thierry Giasson, and Jennifer Lees-Marshment. 2012. *Political Marketing in Canada*. Vancouver: UBC Press.
Marland, Alex, Thierry Giasson, and Tamara Small. 2014. *Political Communication in Canada: Meet the Press and Tweet the Rest*. Vancouver: UBC Press.
Marzolini, Michael. 2004. "Public Opinion Polling and the 2004 Election." In *The Canadian General Election of 2004*, edited by Jon H. Pammett and Christopher Dornan, 290–313. Toronto: Dundurn Press.
Mas, Susan. 2014. "NDP Blocks Paul Manly, Son of Former MP, from Seeking 2015 Bid in B.C." July 2. http://www.cbc.ca/news/politics/ndp-blocks-paul-manly-son-of-former-mp-from-seeking-2015-bid-in-b-c-1.2694452.
McDonough, Alexa. 1998. "The New Left." *National Post*, December 28, A15.
McGrane, David. 2011. "Political Marketing and the NDP's Historic Breakthrough." In *The Canadian Federal Election of 2011*, edited by Jon H. Pammett and Christopher Dornan, 77–110. Toronto: Dundurn.
–. 2014. *Remaining Loyal: Social Democracy in Quebec and Saskatchewan*. Montreal: McGill-Queen's University Press.
–. 2016. "From Third to First and Back to Third: The 2015 NDP Campaign." In *The Canadian Federal Election of 2015*, edited by Jon H. Pammett and Christopher Dornan, 85–116. Toronto: Dundurn.
–. 2017. "Election Preparation in the Federal NDP: The Next Campaign Starts the Day after the Last One Ends." In *Permanent Campaigning in Canada*, edited by Alex Marland, Thierry Giasson, and Anna Lennox Esselment, 145–83, Vancouver: UBC Press.
–. 2019. "What Does 'Progressive' Mean? The Political Theory of Social Democracy and Reform Liberalism in Canada." In *Applied Political Theory and Canadian Politics*, edited by David McGrane and Neil Hibbert. Toronto: University of Toronto Press.
McGrane, David, Loleen Berdahl, and Kirk Clavelle. 2015. "Priming the Voter: Assessing the Implications of Economic Perceptions on Evaluations of Leaders and Parties." *Canadian Political Science Review* 9 (1): 92–111.
McGrane, David, Loleen Berdahl, and Scott Bell. 2017. "Moving Beyond the Urban/Rural Cleavage: Measuring Values and Policy Preferences across Residential Zones in Canada." *Journal of Urban Affairs* 39 (1): 17–39.
McLeod, Ian. 1994. *Under Siege: The Federal NDP in the Nineties*. Toronto: James Lorimer.
McNeney, Denver. 2015. "Letting the Press Decide? Party Coverage, Media Tone, and Issue Salience in the 2015 Canadian Federal Election Newsprint." In *Canadian Election Analysis 2015: Communication, Strategy, and Democracy*, edited by Alex Marland and Thierry Giasson, 74–75. Vancouver: UBC Press.
Meslo, Bev. 2002a. "Bev for Leader: For a Socialist and Feminist New Democratic Party." Alan Whitehorn Collection.

–. 2002b. "Socialist Caucus Candidate Bev Meslo Shakes Up NDP Establishment." Alan Whitehorn Collection.
Miles, Matthew, and Michael Huberman. 1994. *Qualitative Data Analysis: A Sourcebook.* Thousand Oaks, CA: Sage.
Morton, Desmond. 1986. *The New Democrats, 1961–1986: The Politics of Change.* Toronto: Copp Clark Pitman.
Nadeau, Richard, and Frédérick Bastien. 2017. "Political Campaigning." In *Canadian Parties in Transition*, 4th ed., edited by Alain-G. Gagnon and A. Brian Tanguay, 364–87. Toronto: University of Toronto Press.
NDP. 2004. *Platform 2004: New Energy, a Positive Choice.* Ottawa: NDP.
–. 2015. *Building the Country of our Dreams.* Ottawa: NDP.
–. 2016. *Campaign 2015 Review: Working Group Report.* Ottawa: NDP.
NDProgress. 2001. "NDProgress Conference Report and Executive Summary. April 28–29, 2001." Ottawa: NDP.
New Politics Initiative. 2001a. *The New Politics Initiative: Open, Sustainable, Democratic.* Toronto: New Politics Initiative.
–. 2001b. "New Politics Initiative Newsletter #4: November 7, 2001 – Convention Update and Other News." Toronto: New Politics Initiative.
–. 2001c. "Press Release, November 26, 2001: New Politics Initiative Will Continue." Toronto: New Politics Initiative.
Newman, Isadore, and Carolyn Benz. 1998. *Qualitative-Quantitative Research Methodology: Exploring the Interactive Continuum.* Carbondale: University of Illinois Press.
Norris, Pippa. 2000. *The Virtuous Circle: Political Communication in Post-Industrial Societies.* Cambridge, UK: Cambridge University Press. https://doi.org/10.1017/CBO9780511609343.
Nystrom, Lorne. 2002. "Leading Change!" Alan Whitehorn Collection.
–. 2003. "NDP Must Ditch Mythic Past." *Toronto Star,* January 14, A19.
O'Cass, Aron, and Ranjit Voola. 2010. "Explications of Political Marketing Orientation and Political Brand Orientation Using the Resource-Based View of the Political." *Journal of Marketing Management* 27 (5–6): 627–45.
Ormrod, Robert. 2005. "A Conceptual Model of Political Market Orientation." *Journal of Nonprofit and Public Sector Marketing* 14 (1–2): 47–64. https://doi.org/10.1300/J054v14n01_04.
–. 2006. "A Critique of the Lees-Marshment Market-Oriented Party Model." *Politics* 26 (2): 110–18. https://doi.org/10.1111/j.1467-9256.2006.00257.x.
–. 2007. "Political Market Orientation and Its Commercial Cousin: Close Family or Distant Relatives?" *Journal of Political Marketing* 6 (2–3): 69–90.
Palmer, Bryan. 2016. "Snatching Defeat from the Jaws of Victory: The New Democratic Party and the Canadian Elections." *New Labor Forum* 25 (1): 86–94. https://doi.org/10.1177/1095796015620147.
Pammett, Jon H. 2001. "The People's Verdict." In *The Canadian General Election of 2000*, edited by Jon H. Pammett and Christopher Dornan, 293–318. Toronto: Dundurn.
Panebianco, Angelo. 1988. *Political Parties: Organization and Power.* Cambridge, UK: Cambridge University Press.

Panitch, Leo. 1961. *The Canadian State: Poltical Economy and Political Power.* Toronto: University of Toronto Press.

Panitch, Leo, and Colin Leys. 2003. *The End of Parliamentary Socialism: From New Left to New Labour.* London: Verso.

Patten, Steve. 2017. "Databases, Microtargetting, and the Permanent Campaign." In *Permanent Campaigning in Canada,* edited by Alex Marland, Thierry Giasson, and Anna Lennox Esselment, 47–66. Vancouver: UBC Press.

Penner, Erin, Kelly Blidook, and Stuart Soroka. 2006. "Legislative Priorities and Public Opinion: The Representation of Partisan Agendas in the Canadian House of Commons." *Journal of European Public Policy* 13 (7): 1006–20. https://doi.org/10.1080/1350176060023979.

Penner, Norman. 1992. *From Protest to Power: Social Democracy in Canada 1900-Present.* Toronto: James Lorimer.

Pétry, François. 2015. "Ideological Evolution of the Federal NDP, as Seen through Its Election Campaign Manifestos." In *Reviving Social Democracy: The Near Death and Surprising Rise of the Federal NDP,* edited by David Laycock and Lynda Erickson, 140–62. Vancouver: UBC Press.

Pilon, Dennis, Stephanie Ross, and Larry Savage. 2011. "Solidarity Revisited: Organized Labour and the New Democratic Party." *Canadian Political Science Review* 5 (1): 20–37.

Plasser, Fritz, and Gunda Plasser. 2002. *Global Political Campaigning: A Worldwide Analysis of Campaign Professionals and Their Practices.* Westport, CT: Praeger.

Raj, Althia. 2013. "Tom Mulcair Says NDP Won't Tax Super-Rich, but Toronto Candidate Linda McQuaig Favours Idea." *Huffington Post,* September 17, https://www.huffingtonpost.ca/2013/09/17/tom-mulcair-linda-mcquaig-tax-rich_n_3941946.html.

–. 2015. "Morgan Wheeldon Speaks Out about Being Forced to Resign as NDP Candidate." *Huffington Post,* August 11. https://www.huffingtonpost.ca/2015/08/11/morgan-wheeldon-ndp-candidates-israel_n_7973876.html.

Robertson, David. 1976. *A Theory of Party Competition.* London, UK: Wiley.

Roy, Jason, and David McGrane. 2015. "Explaining Canadian Provincial Voting Behaviour: Nuance or Parsimony?" *Canadian Political Science Review* 9 (1): 75–91.

Saldana, Johnny. 2009. *The Coding Manual for Qualitative Researchers.* London: Sage.

Savage, Larry. 2012. "Organized Labour and the Politics of Strategic Voting." In *Rethinking the Politics of Labour in Canada,* edited by Stephanie Ross and Larry Savage, 75–87. Halifax: Fernwood.

Sayers, Anthony. 1999. *Parties, Candidates, and Constituency Campaigns in Canadian Elections.* Vancouver: UBC Press.

Scammell, Margaret. 2007. "Political Brands and Consumer Citizens: The Rebranding of Tony Blair." *Annals of the American Academy of Political and Social Science* 611 (1): 176–92. https://doi.org/10.1177/0002716206299149.

Small, Tamara. 2017. "Two Decades of Digital Party Politics in Canada." In *Canadian Parties in Transition,* 4th ed., edited by Alain-G. Gagnon and A. Brian Tanguay, 388–408. Toronto: University of Toronto Press.

Smith, Gareth. 2009. "Conceptualizing and Testing Brand Personality in British Politics." *Journal of Political Marketing* 8 (3): 209–32. https://doi.org/10.1080/15377 850903044858.

Smith, Gareth, and Andy Hirst. 2001. "Strategic Political Segmentation: A New Approach for a New Era of Political Marketing." *European Journal of Marketing* 35 (9–10): 1058–73. https://doi.org/10.1108/EUM0000000005958.

Smith, Joanna. 2013. "NDP Convention in Montreal about Preparing for 2015 Federal Election." *Toronto Star,* April 11, https://www.thestar.com/news/canada/2013/04/11/ndp_convention_in_montreal_about_preparing_for_2015_federal_election.html.

Soroka, Stuart, Erin Penner, and Kelly Blidook. 2009. "Constituency Influence in Parliament." *Canadian Journal of Political Science* 42 (3): 563–91. https://doi.org/10.1017/S0008423909990059.

Stanford, Jim. 2006. "There Are Good Reasons for the CAW and the NDP to Split Up." *Globe and Mail,* March 27, A13.

Stoffer, Peter. 2001. "A New Beginning: An Open Letter to NDPers." December.

Strömbäck, Jesper. 2007. "Political Marketing and Professionalized Campaigning." *Journal of Political Marketing* 6 (2–3): 49–67.

Tashakkori, Abbas, and John Creswell. 2007. "The New Era of Mixed Methods." *Journal of Mixed Methods Research* 1 (1): 3–7. https://doi.org/10.1177/2345678906293042.

Tashakkori, Abbas M., and Charles B. Teddlie. 1998. *Mixed Methodology: Combining Qualitative and Quantitative Approaches.* Thousand Oaks, CA: Sage.

–. 2003. *Handbook of Mixed Methods in Social and Behavioral Research.* Thousand Oaks, CA: Sage.

Topp, Brian. 2010. *How We Almost Gave the Tories the Boot: The Inside Story behind the Coalition.* Toronto: James Lorimer.

Truelove, Graeme. 2013. *Svend Robinson: A Life in Politics.* Vancouver: New Star Books.

Turcotte, André. 2011. "Polls: Seeing through the Glass Darkly." In *The Canadian Federal Election of 2011,* edited by Jon H. Pammett and Christopher Dornan, 195–218. Toronto: Dundurn.

–. 2012. "Under New Management: Market Intelligence and the Conservative Party's Resurrection." In *Political Marketing in Canada,* edited by Alex Marland, Thierry Giasson, and Jennifer Lees-Marshment, 76–90. Vancouver: UBC Press.

–. 2016. "A Debate about the Debates." In *The Canadian Federal Election of 2015,* edited by Jon H. Pammett and Christopher Dornan, 253–74. Toronto: Dundurn Press.

Turk, James, and Charis Wahl. 2012. *Love, Hope, Optimism: An Informal Portrait of Jack Layton by Those Who Knew Him.* Toronto: James Lorimer.

Van Aelst, Peter, and Stefaan Walgrave. 2002. "New Media, New Movements? The Role of the Internet in Shaping the 'Anti-Globalization Movement.'" *Information Communication and Society* 5 (4): 465–93. https://doi.org/10.1080/13691180208538801.

Waddell, Christopher. 2009. "The Campaign in the Media 2008." In *The Canadian General Election of 2008,* edited by Jon H. Pammett and Christopher Dornan, 217–56. Toronto: Dundurn.

Wesley, Jared, and Mike Moyes. 2014. "Selling Social Democracy: Branding and the Political Left in Canada." In *Political Communication in Canada: Meet the Press and*

Tweet the Rest, edited by Alex Marland, Thierry Giasson, and Tamara Small, 74–91. Vancouver: UBC Press.

Wherry, Aaron. 2015. "Important Moments in Canadian Election Debate History." *Maclean's*, June 29. https://www.macleans.ca/politics/ottawa/a-history-of-debate-moments-that-mattered.

White, Jon, and Leslie De Chernatony. 2002. "New Labour: A Study of the Creation, Development, and Demise of a Political Brand." *Journal of Political Marketing* 1 (2–3): 45–52. https://doi.org/10.1300/J199v01n02_04.

Whitehorn, Alan. 1992. *Canadian Socialism: Essays on the CCF-NDP*. Toronto: Oxford University Press.

–. 1994. "The NDP's Quest for Survival." In *The Canadian General Election of 1993*, edited by Alan Frizzell, Jon H. Pammett, and Anthony Westell, 122–40. Ottawa: Carleton University Press.

–. 1997. "Alexa McDonough and Atlantic Breakthrough for the New Democratic Party." In *The Canadian General Election of 1997*, edited by Alan Frizzell and Jon H. Pammett, 91–103. Toronto: Dundurn.

–. 2001. "The 2000 NDP Campaign: Social Democracy at the Crossroads." In *The Canadian General Election of 2000*, edited by Jon H. Pammett and Christopher Dornan, 113–38. Toronto: Dundurn.

–. 2004. "Jack Layton and the NDP: Gains but No Breakthrough." In *The Canadian General Election of 2004*, edited by Jon H. Pammett and Christopher Dornan, 106–38. Toronto: Dundurn.

–. 2006. "The NDP and Strategic Voting." In *The Canadian General Election of 2006*, edited by Jon H. Pammett and Christopher Dornan, 93–121. Toronto: Dundurn.

Wilkins-Laflamme, Sarah. 2016. "The Changing Religious Cleavage in Canadians' Voting Behaviour." *Canadian Journal of Political Science* 49 (3): 499–518. https://doi.org/10.1017/S0008423916000834.

Williamson, John. 1999. "She Did It Their Way." *National Post*, August 30, A19.

Wiseman, Nelson, and Benjamin Isitt. 2007. "Social Democracy in Twentieth Century Canada: An Interpretive Framework." *Canadian Journal of Political Science* 40: 567–89.

Wring, Dominic. 2005. *The Politics of Marketing the Labour Party*. London, UK: Macmillan. https://doi.org/10.1057/9780230597617.

Young, Walter. 1969. *The Anatomy of a Party: The National CCF, 1932–1961*. Toronto: University of Toronto Press.

Zakuta, Leo. 1964. *A Protest Movement Becalmed: A Study of Change in the CCF*. Toronto: University of Toronto Press.

Index

10 percenters, 96. *See also* postmodern campaigning
270 Strategies, 75
2015 Canadian Federal Election Panel on Social Democracy, 20, 21, 23, 201–11, 275–77

Aboriginal peoples: and affirmative action, 59; and Leap Manifesto, 326, 336; and NDP platforms, 184, 186, 192–93; and the NDP in Question Period, 105–6; and voting NDP, 285
advertising: analysis of NDP's, 129–74. *See also* air game; email lists; ground game; media relations; political marketing; social media; voter contact
air game: definition of, 77, 124–25. *See also* ground game
anti-NDPers, 284, 300–3, 316
Arar, Maher, 33
Archer, Keith, 178
asymmetrical federalism, 35, 65, 250
Audet, Nicolas-Dominic, 64

Bélanger, Eric, 303
Better Balanced Budget, 138
Bill C-13 (*Keeping Canada's Economy and Jobs Growing Act*), 77
Bill C-51 (*Anti-Terrorism Act*), 167, 297, 312
Blair, Tony, 15–16, 26–30, 35–36, 176, 320

Blaikie, Bill, 25, 31–32, 36–37, 64, 72, 137
Blaikie, Rebecca, 64
Blakeney, Allan, 196
Bloc Québécois (BQ), 36, 66, 69, 97, 99, 117, 135, 138, 143–44; in 2008 election, 144–51; in 2011 election, 151–60; in 2015 election, 161–74; and voter behaviour, 236–73, 279–83, 292–94, 297–99, 302–3, 308–11
Bloc recursive model, 219–20
Blue State Digital strategies, 75
Butler, Patrick, 8, 123, 125
Boivin, Françoise, 66
Boucher, Françoise, 243
branding: of Layton, 99–100, 120, 133–34, 160; of Mulcair, 120, 163; of NDP, 12, 31, 35, 50, 67, 73, 85–86, 90–94, 99–100, 119–21, 133–34, 163–64, 169, 177, 185–88, 207–10, 255, 276, 286; of Trudeau, 313, 317, 333–34. *See also* political marketing
Breton, Charles, 276

cadre party, 17, 19
Calvert, Lorne, 147
Campaign Central, 75
campaign strategies: definition of, 123–28. *See also* market, positioning
Canadian Alliance, 131–32
Canadian Auto Workers (CAW) union, 27, 49, 52, 53, 69, 144
Canadian Election Studies, 20, 214–36

Canadian Federation of Independent Business, 69
Canadian Labour Congress (CLC), 43, 49, 51–52, 68–69, 92, 101, 103
Canadian Manufacturers and Exporters, 70
Canadian Union of Postal Workers, 29
Canadian Union of Public Employees (CUPE), 29, 68
candidates (NDP): B tour of, 163, 167–68; in commercials and news releases, 131, 136, 154, 166; donation to, 40, 48; expenditures of, 65; nomination of, 12, 40, 56, 59–60, 65–69, 71–72; "paper," 26, 43, 46; vetting of, 12, 42, 59–60, 72, 80, 322, 327
centralization of power: in the NDP, 18, 47, 80, 87, 322
Chhim, Chris, 238
Clarity Bill, 26, 64, 137
Clark, Joe, 233
Clarke, Harold, 214
Chrétien, Jean, 129, 132, 223, 233–35
coalition government, 99, 159, 265–67, 286, 336
Collins, Neil, 8, 123, 125
Comartin, Joe, 31, 35
commercials. *See* advertising
Communications, Energy, and Paperworkers of Canada (CEP), 29, 69
Conservative Party of Canada (CPC), 48, 56, 63, 70–72, 74–76, 79, 110–11, 119, 124, 291; in 2004 election, 132–38; in 2006 election, 138–44; in 2008 election, 144–51; in 2011 election, 151–60; in 2015 election, 161–74; and party financing reform, 49; and voter behaviour, 212–318
conversion rates, 275, 277–83
converted NDPers, 283, 294–99, 301, 314, 316
Corbyn, Jeremy, 320
Creba, Jane, 144

databases, 41, 63, 75–76, 322, 325, 329

Davies, Libby, 26, 31, 321
Day, Stockwell, 233
Desjarlais, Bev, 93
Dion, Stéphane, 145–50, 162, 192, 235, 257–59, 261–62, 266, 291, 333
Doer, Gary, 147
Douglas, Tommy, 131, 171, 196, 332
Ducasse, Pierre, 35, 63, 65, 97, 136
Duceppe, Gilles, 25, 109, 129, 155–59, 257–58, 275–80, 309, 315
Duncan, John, 94
Duncan, Linda, 94
Duverger, Maurice, 17, 19

economic perceptions: and voting behaviour, 229–30, 255, 290–310
economic voting theory, 229
Election Planning Committee, 12
electoral market segmentation: definition of, 13–14; and NDP, 6, 16, 22, 100, 123, 127, 130, 133, 136, 140, 150, 152, 175, 210, 212–74, 318
Erickson, Lynda, 20, 178
email lists, 9–10, 75, 79, 118
Emery, Marc, 98
environmental policy: and activity of NDP MPs, 116–18; and NDP in the House of Commons, 108–14; and NDP member attitudes, 199–205; and NDP MPs attitudes, 206; and NDP news releases, 130, 135–36, 140, 148–50, 164; and NDP platforms, 108–96; and Quebec values, 158; and voter behaviour, 231–33, 253–55, 288–315
ethnic communities, 61
ethnic media, 94, 104

Fabian Society, 196
Federal Steering Committee on the Future of the New Democratic Party, 32–33
Federation of Canadian Municipalities, 37, 38
Fédération des travailleurs et travailleuses du Québec (FTQ), 69

First Nations peoples. *See* Aboriginal peoples
Flanagan, Tom, 48, 94, 330
flexible partisans, 227–28. *See also* partisanship
foreign policy, 35, 110, 135–36, 167, 183, 189
Fournier, Patrick, 222, 238
Fox, Robert, 322
freelancing: of NDP MPs, 90–93, 101, 120
free trade policy, 32–33, 83, 108, 130, 169, 176, 203–6
fundraising, 42–44, 54–58, 77–79, 152–53, 329–30

Gagnon, Alain, 243
Gauvin, Jean-Philippe, 238
gays and lesbians: and affirmative action, 59; rights, 135, 150, 138, 189, 208, 224; and voting NDP, 243–45, 270–71
general orientations: and voter behaviour in Quebec, 245–47
Georgetti, Ken, 49
Giambrone, Adam, 32, 57
Green Party of Canada, 145, 215
Greenpeace, 53
ground game: definition of, 125. *See also* air game

Hargrove, Buzz, 27, 49, 52, 142
Harper, Stephen, 109, 234–36, 257–62, 290–93, 302–6, 332; in 2004 election, 132–38; in 2006 election, 138–44; in 2008 election, 144–51; in 2011 election, 151–60; in 2015 election, 161–74
Hartmann, Franz, 52–54
Hatch, Marcel, 26
Heath, Jamey, 97, 99
Horwath, Andrea, 74

Ignatieff, Michael, 61, 147, 15–57, 162, 167, 235–36, 258–62, 291, 306, 333
Indigenous peoples. *See* Aboriginal peoples

intergovernmental affairs, 103–5, 183–85, 190–91
internal party democracy: and the NDP, 29, 85–86, 327
internet panel surveys, 197, 276
interviews: semi-structured, 20–22, 80, 90, 123, 128; structured, 21
Ipsos-Reid, 20, 236–68
issue positions: and voter behaviour, 231–33, 288–311
issue ownership theory, 105, 182, 184

Jansen, Harold, 18, 58
Johnston, Richard, 330–31
journalism: interpretive, 72. *See also* scandal

Kerwin, Pat, 49, 92, 101
Keynesianism, 196, 205, 208
Klein, Naomi, 28, 321

labour movement (Canada): and relationship to the NDP, 18–19, 30–31, 45–46, 48–52, 80–81, 86, 92, 100–1, 140
Labour Party (Great Britain), 15, 30, 176
labour policy, 182–83, 187, 189–90, 194–95
late deciders, 266–67, 270, 272, 276, 287, 305, 317, 332. *See also* strategic voting
Lavigne, Brad, 53, 146
Laycock, David, 20, 178
Layton, Jack, 3, 5, 24, 30, 54–59, 87–93, 96–99, 184–87; in 2004 election, 132–38; in 2006 election, 138–44; in 2008 election, 144–51; in 2011 election, 151–60; brand, 99–100, 120, 133–34, 160; leadership campaign, 36–39, 47; and New Politics Initiative, 37; and political market orientation of the NDP, 7–8, 47; and Quebec, 36, 38, 64–66; in Question Period, 109–12; and voter behaviour, 233–36, 255–62
Layton Liberals, 152–54, 176, 304, 311, 336
leaders' tour, 12, 47, 65–66, 71–74, 152, 162, 164, 320

leadership evaluations: and voter behaviour, 231–36, 255–59, 288–311
leadership races (NDP), 34–38, 320
leadership traits, 259–62, 306–7
Leap Manifesto, 320–22, 326–27, 336
Lees-Marshment, Jennifer, 6–7
Lewis, Avi, 321
Lewis, Stephen, 321
Liberal Party of Canada (LPC): 70–74, 76, 79, 99, 110, 124; in 2000 election, 129–32; in 2004 election, 132–38; in 2006 election, 138–44; in 2008 election, 144–51; in 2011 election, 151–60; in 2015 election, 161–74; ideology of, 16; and party-financing reform, 49; platforms, 188–96; and unions, 68; and voter behaviour, 212–318
Lost NDPers, 284, 303–17, 330. *See also* strategic voting

Mallett, Danny, 49, 101
market: challenger, 125; follower, 125–26; intelligence, 6–7, 60–61; leader, 125; liberalism: 223–26, 269, 285–86, 296, 303, 311; positioning, 125–27
market share: in 2000 to 2011 federal elections in Quebec, 239–41; in 2000 to 2011 federal elections in rest of Canada, 213–71; in 2015 federal election, 280–83
Marland, Alex, 15, 94
Martin, Paul, 52, 64, 98, 132, 137, 150–51, 138–43, 192, 257
mass party, 17, 19
McDonough, Alexa, 24–27, 32–34, 46, 90–93, 103–5, 137, 184, 233–36; in 2000 election, 129–32
McGrath, Anne, 71
McLaughlin, Audrey, 99
Medeiros, Mike, 238
media relations: and NDP Parliament Hill staff, 54, 100, 104, 333–35; and NDP party headquarters, 43, 73; and Quebec, 213, 257, 273
Meslo, Bev, 34

message control, 60, 62, 72, 94, 110, 125, 140
microtargeting, 9, 15, 325, 329,
Miliband, Ed, 320
military policy, 37, 112, 130, 135, 156, 186–87, 194, 321
minority governments, 54, 99–100, 110–11, 136–40, 161–62, 213, 242, 265–67
mixed-methods research, 19–20
moderation: definition of, 5–14;
modern campaigning: definition of, 9–13; and mass party/cadre party conceptual framework, 17–18
modernization: definition of, 5–14;
most important issue: and voter behaviour, 251–55, 288–311
Moyes, Mike, 15
Mulcair, Tom, 65–69, 74, 93, 97, 101–6, 158, 186–87, 206–7, 320; in 2015 election, 161–74; brand, 120, 163; in Question Period, 112–13; and voter behaviour, 288–311

Nadeau, Richard, 303
narrowcasting, 61, 96, 118
National Unity, 105, 142, 224
nationalism: Québécois, 65, 250
NDP/CPC Switchers, 281
NDP/LPC Switchers, 100, 163–66, 173, 278–80, 313, 317, 326
NDProgress, 30–34, 49
NDPVote, 63, 76
New Democratic Party of Canada (NDP): 2002–03 leadership race, 34–38; affirmative action policy, 59; B tour, 163, 167, 168; brand, 12, 31, 35, 50, 67, 73, 85–86, 90–94, 99–100, 119–21, 133–34, 163–64, 169, 177, 185–88, 207–10, 255, 276, 286, 307; campaign strategies, 129–74; conventions, 26–27, 29–34, 44–46, 60–65, 72, 86, 93, 120, 320–22; Election Planning Committee, 12, 44–46, 60, 73, 322; and electoral market segmentation, 6, 16, 22, 100, 123, 127, 130–36,

140, 150–52, 175, 210, 212–74, 318; Federal Council, 12, 26, 32, 42–46, 53, 60–63, 73, 86, 92, 103, 322; federal electoral district associations (EDAs), 42, 48, 54–59, 65–66, 71–72, 74, 77; Federal Executive, 34, 43, 45, 61, 72–73, 322; federalized structure of, 41–43, 54–56, 70–71; finances of, 26, 45, 57–60, 77–78; in the House of Commons, 90–122; ideology of, 16–17, 177–211; ideology of members, 176–81, 196–202; ideology of MPs, 196–210; ideology of voters, 196–202, internal left-right spectrum, 196–210; internal party organization, 17–18, 40–79; Leader's Office, 91–121; member views on political market orientation, 80–87; MPs' activities, 115–19; MPs' views on democratic representation, 119–21; news releases and television commercials, 129–74; platforms, 181–96; and Quebec, 26, 43, 63–66, 77–78, 96–97, 135–36, 143–74; relationship to the labour movement, 18–19, 30–31, 45–46, 48–52, 80–81, 86, 92, 100–1, 140; reliance on volunteers and staff on short-term contracts, 43–45, 58, 71; and voter behaviour, 212–318

New Politics Initiative (NPI), 28–34, 37, 49, 52, 54, 85, 321, 336

news releases: analysis of NDP's, 129–74

niche marketer: definition of, 126

Niqab court ruling, 171–73, 276, 282, 286–87, 296, 306, 316–17, 325, 332–35

North American Free Trade Agreement (NAFTA), 28, 34

Notley, Rachel, 321

Nystrom, Lorne, 25, 31–32, 35, 53

Obama, Barack, 37

Office of the Leader of the Official Opposition (OLO), 69–70, 73–74, 103–4, 119–20

open coding, 115, 120, 128, 203

opposition research, 59, 61, 98, 103, 159

Ormrod, Robert, 6, 39

partisanship, 13, 219, 227–29, 285–92, 297–305, 315, 336. *See also* flexible partisans

party financing reform, 47–50, 56–58, 63

party political personality, 287–88

party system (Canada), 23, 323

per-vote subsidy: and higher finances for NDP, 4, 6–7, 57–60, 63, 132, 137–40; and permanent campaign, 48; and polling, 14, 322, 328–30, 148, 151, 236; and professionalization, 40–41, 77–78, 87–89, 273–75; and Quebec, 66–67

Pilon, Dennis, 18

pipelines, 206, 282, 321; Energy East, 172,

platforms: of Liberals, 190–96; of NDP, 181–96; and voter behaviour in 2015 federal election, 288–311

polling: internal NDP, 6–7, 43, 66–67, 129–31, 146–54, 158; public domain, 145–46, 157–60, 161–73

political market orientation: competitor oriented, 8; definition of, 5–9; externally oriented, 8–9; internally oriented, 8–9; and research on the NDP, 18–19; views of NDP members about, 80–87; voter oriented, 7–8

political marketing: application to research on the NDP, 15–19; definition of, 5. *See also* media relations

political operatives: definition of, 13

pool of accessible voters, 278–80

Populus, 75–76

Pot TV, 98

premodern campaigning: definition of, 9–13. *See also* modern campaigning

presidentialization of politics: definition of, 12; in NDP, 62, 120, 163, 333

postmaterialism, 285–86, 294, 299, 311

postmodern campaigning: definition of, 9–13

professionalization: definition of, 12; of the NDP, 56–61, 63–66, 71–75

Proportional Representation, 35, 109, 186, 290, 331

quarterly allowances. *See* per-vote subsidy
Quebec: and 2004 election, 135–36; and 2006 election, 143; and 2008 election, 144–51; and 2011 election, 151–60; and 2015 election, 161–74; NDP organization in, 63–66; and Pierre Ducasse, 35, 97; sovereignty, 247–50; traditional NDP weakness in, 26, 43; unions, 66, 69; voter behaviour, 236–73, 279–83, 291–94, 297–99, 302–3, 308–11
Question Period, 91, 94–114
Question Period Team, 94–95, 105

RCMP, 144
Rebick, Judy, 28
registered sympathizers, 78
research: by Canadian Labour Congress, 68; by NDP caucus and NDP party headquarters, 43–46, 59–61, 71–74, 86–91, 98–100
RILE method, 181–82, 184
Robinson, Svend, 25, 28, 31, 91, 93, 120, 319
Romanow, Roy, 196
Ross, Stephanie, 18

Saganash, Romeo, 66
Sanders, Bernie, 327
Savage, Larry, 18
scandal, 90, 108–10, 114, 132, 237, 253–55
Scott, Craig, 321
Schröder, Gerhard, 16
Sherbrooke Declaration, 65
Smith, Gareth, 287
social democracy, 8, 15–17, 72, 86, 177–210
Social Democratic Forum on Canada's Future, 45
social investment, 208
social media, 9, 72, 75–79, 118
social movements: definition of, 8–9; relationship to the NDP, 37, 52–54, 80–81, 85–86, 96–97, 140; and research on NDP, 18–19
sociodemographic characteristics: and NDP members, 83–85; and voters, 76, 218–22, 243–45, 288–311
solid NDPers, 283, 288–94, 295–99, 301, 313
stakeholder relations, 9, 54, 69–70, 103
Stanford, Jim, 28
strategic voting: in 2000 election, 49; in 2004 election, 137, 139; in 2006 election, 140, 142, 144; in 2008 election, 147; in 2011 election, 152–55, 157, 159; in 2015 election, 76, 164–65, 173, 175; and Canadian Autoworkers, 52, 69; definition of, 14; and First-Past-the-Post System, 330–31; and voting behaviour, 242, 262–68, 287, 298–99, 306, 315–17. *See also* late deciders; NDP/CPC switchers; NDP/LPC switchers
Stoffer, Peter, 30
steelworkers, 29, 52
Stronach, Belinda, 138

Think Twice coalition, 144
third-party validators, 19, 70
third way social democracy, 15, 27, 34, 35
Transpacific Partnership (TPP), 169, 286, 291, 312, 314
Topp, Brian, 72, 99, 139
Trudeau, Justin, 74; in 2015 election, 161–74; 276, 289–96, 303–09, 312–15, 320–26, 332–36
Turmel, Nycole, 66, 103, 105

Unifor, 69
unions. *See specific unions*
United Food and Commercial Workers (UFCW), 29, 52, 68
universe of voters: definition of, 125; of NDP in 2015 election, 197, 210

veterans, 112–13, 118, 140, 156, 168, 176, 187, 194

voter contact, 44, 48, 63–69, 74–77, 299, 308, 334–35. *See also* air game; email lists; ground game; social media
values: of NDP members, 181; and voter behaviour, 223–27, 228–311

Walmart, 110
war room, 47, 71, 171
Wasylycia-Leis, Judy, 144
Weir, Elizabeth, 32
Wesley, Jared, 15
White, Bob, 49
Whitehorn, Alan, 14, 21, 178

women: and affirmative action, 59, 180; and NDP platforms, 181–95; and NDP's women's commission, 73; and voting NDP, 222–24, 305; and women's issues debate in 2015 federal election, 170
women's groups, 117–18
World Trade Organization (WTO), 28–29
Wynne, Kathleen, 74

Young, Lisa, 18, 58
Young, Walter, 14

Zakharova, Maria, 178